MAINSTREAM of AMERICA

Mainstream of America Series ★

EDITED BY LEWIS GANNETT

_____

DREAMERS OF
THE AMERICAN DREAM

Books by STEWART H. HOLBROOK

DREAMERS OF THE AMERICAN DREAM

THE AGE OF THE MOGULS

IRON BREW
A Century of American Ore and Steel

THE YANKEE EXODUS
An Account of Migration from New England

ETHAN ALLEN
A Biography

THE STORY OF AMERICAN RAILROADS

HOLY OLD MACKINAW
A Natural History of the American Lumberjack

LOST MEN OF AMERICAN HISTORY

BURNING AN EMPIRE
America's Great Forest Fires

THE ROCKY MOUNTAIN REVOLUTION

FAR CORNER
A Personal View of the Pacific Northwest

Dreamers of
The American Dream

STEWART H. HOLBROOK

Doubleday & Company, Inc., Garden City, New York

To Sibyl

ACKNOWLEDGMENTS

THERE is an immense amount of published material dealing with most but not quite all of the people and events of this book. Selection was the problem, and selection often turned out to be an empirical process. Not a half of the works I happened to read first were the best ones for my purpose; and I owe a great deal to the superior bibliographical knowledge, both general and special, of friends who put me on the right track.

Controversy almost automatically plays about the efforts of dreamers and prophets. The books about them, as well as their own books, are likely to be partisan. The dice are loaded, one way or the other. All one can do is to read accordingly — that is, with "an open mind." I do not think there is any such thing as an open mind. The best one can hope to achieve is a measure of tolerance for ideas one actually believes are wrongheaded, perhaps even downright idiotic; and to temper enthusiasms for other propositions one finds appealing.

But I can and do cheer the writers listed in my bibliography. Whether they were for or against, they were commonly dedicated characters who, in their enthusiasms or their loathings, often revealed more than they had planned to say.

And I must express my appreciation to the living persons and the learned institutions who and which gave me counsel in locating the right books, or in some other manner helped me to find my way among the babel of long-dead prophets and the many confusing guideposts to a more perfect union and society. My thanks go to Samuel Hopkins Adams, Mrs. John Angell, John Ankcorn, Mrs. Claire A. Argow, Paul Bailey, Reginald C. Brummer, Miss Jean Crawford, Miss Audrey A. Davis, Miss Margaret Duniway, Lewis Gannett, Otto Hartwig, Miss Elizabeth Johnson, Miss Jean McFarland, Pierrepont Noyes, Miss Louise Prichard, Mrs. Constance Noyes Robertson, Leslie Scott, George T. Springer, Glenn Stanton, Mrs. Helen Beal Woodward; and Miss Esther Watson, who prepared the manuscript for the printer. I am deeply indebted to the able and courteous staffs of the American Antiquarian Society, Worcester; the Minnesota Historical Society, the New York Public Library, the Oregon Historical Society, the Portland (Oregon) Public Library, the Reed College Library, the Vermont Historical Society, and the Wisconsin Historical Society.

Contents

Contents   ix

Part One

THE PERFECT SOCIETY

1.

THE FLIGHT OF A GENIUS

THE bouldered hills and moody valleys of the Green Mountains have produced an uncommon number of dreamers and prophets. Why this is true is so far from clear that generations of social historians and philosophers have failed to come up with anything approaching agreement. What is clear, however, is that a majority of Vermonters have been chary of their native oracles, so inhospitable, indeed, that the old adage about honor anywhere save in their own country might have been the observation of some Green Mountain cynic.

Such melancholy reflections may have crossed the mind of John Humphrey Noyes on October 26, 1847, an otherwise handsome day of late Indian summer, when autumn blazed through the sugarplaces and lighted the beech ridges, and blue haze hung over the river meadows. On this day John Noyes was put under arrest in his native town of Brattleboro for violation of the 99th Chapter of the Revised Statutes of the State of Vermont, which had to do with adultery. Though he cheerfully waived examination, and provided the necessary bail of two thousand dollars, Noyes was in no manner admitting the charge. It were far better, said he, that the Revised Statutes were revised again to fit the common-sense tenets of his Perfectionist group in the nearby hillside village of Putney.

"In a holy community," Noyes had written in a recent issue of the Perfectionist paper, "there is no more reason why sexual intercourse should be restrained by law, than why eating and drinking should be— and there is as little reason for shame in the one case as in the other."

This is fairly strong meat, then or now, but it was the fare propounded by one of the most devoutly religious men in the United States whose vision, for forty years, was of a universal society wholly free from contention and crime and sin, and yes, of death. Here was no man for small dreams. John Noyes's dream stemmed from first principles. It dissipated the Chaos and Old Night of Man's futile gropings. It lighted the way to heaven on earth here and now. But not, apparently, in Vermont.

At the time of his arrest John Noyes was thirty-six years old. His was a tall figure, slim as a rail. He wore a blue coat which seemed to accentuate the disordered halo of his russet hair. His face, so his followers declared, shone like an angel's with some strange light from within. He had been a brilliant student at Dartmouth college from which he had been graduated at nineteen with the highest honors, and began the study of law. This he soon quit for theology at Andover, then at Yale Divinity School, and founded in New Haven what he called a "free church." It was altogether too free, filled with heresies. The high command of divinity dismissed him from Yale and took away his license to preach.

Heresy in that time and place was a serious business. To be outlawed by one's church was often worse than being outlawed by one's state. Young Noyes met it head-on. "I have taken away their license to sin," he remarked, "but they keep on sinning. So, though they have taken away my license to preach, I shall keep on preaching." So he did, and here he was, ten years later, charged with violation of Number 7 in the Decalogue and Chapter 99 of the Vermont laws.

It was a shocking thing, not merely the nature of the charge, but worse in that it involved three of Vermont's first families: The Honorable John Noyes, Sr., the well-to-do merchant and former Congressman who had once been headmaster of Chesterfield Academy; and his wife Polly, daughter of Rutherford Hayes, a successful and respected farmer whose grandson, Rutherford B., was to be elected the nineteenth President of the United States. The third Brattleboro family involved was that of the Honorable Larkin Mead and his wife, who had been Mary Noyes, among whose children were Larkin G. Mead, soon to be a famous sculptor; William Rutherford Mead, the even more famous architect; and Elinor Mead, who was to become Mrs. William Dean Howells. It is thus obvious that John Humphrey Noyes possessed neither the background of poverty nor that of the ignorance from which had sprung so many of the founders of America's odd sects and strange religions.

Eighteen titillated and possibly profoundly shocked grand jurors had returned a true bill against him, charging that "on June 10, 1847, he with force of arms did carnally know one Fanny M. Leonard, the wife of one Stephen R. Leonard, and with her did commit adultery," the which, it appeared, was "against the peace and dignity of the State of Vermont." There was more of it, too, for the same jury proceeded to indict Noyes again because on the twentieth day of August, he "with Achsah Campbell did have intercourse and connection which in the case the said Achsah Campbell had been a married woman (instead of a widow) would have constituted the crime of adultery."

As soon as he was released on bond posted by his group, the Putney Corporation of Perfectionists, John Noyes went calmly about preparing the November issue of their magazine. But a deluge of troubles now began to break in waves over these non-conformists. Attorney Larkin Mead, Noyes's brother-in-law, sent private word that warrants for George and Mary Cragin of the Putney group were in the sheriff's hands. (Adultery again.) And the Perfectionist leader's own brother, Horatio Noyes, hastened to Putney with the idea of removing his sisters, Harriet and Charlotte, from "the web of immorality," their own and his own brother had woven. Horatio was dumfounded when his sisters told him they were quite content to remain where they were, and that they "and the whole membership of the group" were as involved as John. Horatio Noyes drove back to Brattleboro, both furious and panicky.

Next attorney Mead called John Noyes to his office to warn him that he feared mob action against the group by the non-Perfectionists of Putney. He advised in most emphatic terms that John himself, and the two Cragins whose arrests were impending, leave the embattled village without delay and get out of Vermont. He advised, too, that all others of the group who were not natives or long residents of Putney leave the state. Otherwise, said Mead—intimating that mass violation of the Seventh Commandment was no laughing matter—Putney would rise and smite them. He made it clear that haste was called for. Noyes himself was not even to return to Putney on any account; he was to leave *now,* secretly, for Massachusetts or New Hampshire. As for the Cragins, they too should be beyond Vermont's borders come daylight.

All right, then, said John Noyes, if it were as bad as all that, he would go. Not to escape the law, he explained, "but to prevent an outbreak of lynch law among the barbarians of Putney." Within the hour he left Brattleboro on foot, heading south. Somewhere along the way a stage caught up with him and he slept that night in Leverett, Massachusetts.

Back in seething Putney, George and Mary Cragin hurriedly packed and made arrangements for departure. Shortly after midnight William Hinds, the fourteen-year-old lad who worked in the Perfectionist store, drove up with horse and carriage. The Cragins, with their sleeping son Victor, got in, and young Willie Hinds drove as quietly as possible through the frosty sleeping village that was as dark as if Moses had stretched out his hand toward heaven. The flight out of Egypt had begun.

The Cragins and young Hinds knew well enough they might be stopped by the sheriff's men. About one mile north of Brattleboro a man on foot suddenly appeared in the road ahead. He held up one arm to stop the carriage. Young Hinds obeyed. But the stranger merely wanted to know the way to Dummerston. He thanked them and went on. The four refugees passed through Brattleboro just at daybreak.

Two hours more they were safely in Massachusetts where they stopped briefly beside the road to give thanks to God for deliverance.

The Cragins left Putney none too soon. Daylight found the sheriff there, looking vainly for them. No other warrants were issued, but the Perfectionist exodus went ahead anyway. The Gould family left for New York State. Louisa Tuttle started for her former home in Connecticut. The Burnhams took off for northern Vermont. During the next few days other "foreigners" departed. But John Miller and John Skinner stayed to face the storm. So did John Noyes's wife, Harriet, his younger brother, George, and his sisters Charlotte and Harriet. A number of recent converts, all of whom had been born or reared in Putney, also remained.

Facing the storm in Putney could not have been overly pleasant. Attorney Mead had been right. Townsmen had already organized a sort of vigilante group headed by Preston W. Taft, of a Vermont family later to become famous in national politics. The vigilantes passed resolutions pointing out, in no mealymouthed manner, that "certain practices" of the Perfectionists were not only illegal but "vile." They sent copies to Vermont newspapers. The press was quick to respond to the spiciest story in years. The Brattleboro *Phoenix,* for example, spoke with editorial loathing of "the monstrous doctrines" of the Putney Corporation of Perfectionists and claimed it had indubitable evidence "of systematic seduction and licentiousness practiced under the badge of religion."

Trouble was piling up. Deputy Sheriff Gates Perry came to Putney to attach the real estate owned by the group. There were rumors that one prominent local citizen was going to prosecute for the attempted seduction of his daughter. Dr. John Campbell also told an audience that if there were no law to break up the Perfectionists, then the decent people of Putney would "make the law and act upon it." Campbell also made a violent physical attack on Perfectionist John Miller. Miller, who was acting for Noyes in the emergency, received several threatening letters that mentioned tar and feathers.

But no further violence occurred. The sheriff's attachments put lock and key on the Perfectionist press and office. And the bitterness continued. The remnants of John Noyes's group, mostly women and children, had to carry on as best they might in the face of open hostility. Even the more kindhearted of their townsmen feared to be seen talking with them. All they could do was to wait in the hope that their prophet with the russet halo and shining face, now fled for cause into the wilderness, would soon call them to join him. In Noyes they had every faith. He would not fail them.

The scattered disciples and those who remained in Putney were right.

Noyes was not to fail them. He was even then making every effort to find in the outer darkness a place where Perfectionism could flower and shine so brightly that the great mass of heathens who thought themselves Christians would be forced by example to see their errors. Only then was the perfect society possible.

The fact that his Perfectionists had been driven from Vermont in no manner discouraged Noyes. He knew well enough how inhospitable the state had been to other native prophets. Back in the 1790s Vermonters had urged a small band of fanatics called Dorrilites to leave; and had broken up another group led by Nathaniel Wood, an unfrocked Congregational minister, who claimed divine inspiration. Still later they had treated harshly a sect of religious primates, followers of Isaac Bullard and who called themselves Pilgrims.

John Noyes might reflect, too, that though Joseph Smith and Brigham Young were born in the Green Mountains, when the Mormon leaders returned to their native state in the 1830s, seeking converts, the response had been discouraging, while elsewhere the converts were numbered by the thousands. No, Vermont would not do. It bred radicals but refused to harbor them. William Miller, late of Poultney, Vermont, had only recently discovered as much. He had been unable to attract many natives to prepare for the Second Coming he had been preaching. Not until he was invited to Boston, where swarming disciples built a huge temple for him, did Miller's Adventist faith make much progress.

John Humphrey Noyes's many heresies rejected the idea of an imminent Second Coming. It had, he said, already taken place, probably about A.D. 70. He rejected the teaching of both Catholic and Protestant churches, which were "based on misinterpretation of the Bible." Man, he held, may have been born sinful, but Man could also achieve absolute perfection, not in heaven, but here on earth. Vermont, perhaps, excepted.

It is probable that neither Putney nor Vermont would have objected to the abstraction of Perfectionism. It was merely one of the many new products that had appeared in the United States since the early nineteenth century, an era of ferments unparalleled before or since. It had first been called "Oberlin Perfectionism" because it seemed to emanate from the new college in Ohio founded by two Congregational missionaries from Pawlet, Vermont. The Oberlin brand of Perfectionism was wholly spiritual, not unlike that of the Shakers, whom Noyes had visited in Connecticut and New Hampshire. It sought, among other things, to make believers immune to the temptations of sex. What caused the trouble at Putney was the attempt to activate its teachings, to bring Perfectionism out of the vague mists of the intellect and make it a guide for rational living.

John Noyes had been brooding over it ever since he had startled the clergy at Yale by announcing that his heart was clean, that "the Father and the Son had come and made it their abode" and that he was henceforth without sin. He had it all figured out. And now he saw what Perfectionism could and must do. This was to break the four-linked chain of evil which held humanity in thrall: First, a breach with God; second, a disruption of the sexes involving a special curse on women; third, oppressive labor, bearing especially on men; fourth, death. "The chain of redemption," he explained, "brings reconciliation with God, proceeds to a restoration of the true relations between the sexes, then to a reformation of the industrial system, and ends with victory over death." If this sounds like considerable of an order, it seemed reasonable enough to John Humphrey Noyes, who was to initiate experiments in every phase of life. He was either a genius or one of nature's divine madmen. Perhaps he was both.

When, as related, young Noyes was dismissed from Yale Divinity School, he wandered through Massachusetts, then into New York State, meeting the "forward thinkers" who had begun calling themselves Perfectionists. For William Lloyd Garrison's *Liberator* he wrote a letter renouncing allegiance to a government that permitted slavery, and from it Garrison developed the idea of a revolt of the North against "the reprobate slaveholding Government at Washington" which the fiery editor used in his subsequent agitating.

Yet Noyes was not diverted, by these fringe or piecemeal reforms, from his overwhelming dream of a perfect society. He continued on his rounds of the Perfectionist circuit, to discover at last that the scattered groups and individuals were each too sure of their own rightness to accept the ideas of others. Worse, all of them struck Noyes as so many dilettantes, theorists, prima donnas. All right, let them theorize. He would return to Vermont, where his father, mother, brothers, and sisters were living in Putney, and there found a colony that would show Perfectionism could be brought out of the fogs of the abstract and become a living, breathing way of life.

There lived in nearby Westminster, scene of the celebrated "Massacre" of Revolutionary times, Miss Harriet Holton, granddaughter of the Honorable Mark Richards, a former lieutenant governor of Vermont, by local standards a wealthy man, who doted on his grandchild. Miss Holton was of a cool, independent mind and of a great deal of determination. She went to hear Noyes speak, and came away more than a little impressed both by the man and his message. She also sent him eighty dollars as a contribution to a Perfectionist periodical he hoped to start in Putney.

One thing led to another, and Noyes soon proposed marriage—that is, a kind of marriage. He informed Harriet Holton that he desired his partner in what might be matrimony but surely was not to be considered *wedlock* to "love all who love God, whether man or woman, and as freely as if she stood in no particular connection" to Noyes. This privilege, he specified, was to be reciprocal. He was not to monopolize his wife, nor she him. None of this shocked Miss Holton, as emancipated a Yankee maid as one could wish. They were married in the bright smiling June of 1838, and the bride's well-fixed grandfather provided a dowry sufficient to support the young couple for six years. More immediately, the generous dowry permitted purchase of something Noyes greatly desired, a printing press. Almost as soon as it arrived in Putney, there issued forth the first number of *The Witness,* which a little later was to become *The Perfectionist.* Aiding Mr. and Mrs. Noyes, in setting type and folding papers, were the groom's sisters, Charlotte and Harriet Noyes.

Now to prove the practicality of Perfectionist living. Noyes organized the Putney Corporation of Perfectionists. The group included only Noyes, his wife, his two sisters, his younger brother George, and a few local sympathizers. They met on Sundays to discuss the world and its pigheaded and irrational ways. Now came John Miller, a Quaker teacher from New Hampshire, who soon married Harriet Noyes, the tall, red-haired, and impulsive sister of the prophet. The more beautiful Charlotte, at the behest of Brother John, married John L. Skinner, another convert. The hand of fellowship was offered to Mr. and Mrs. William Sherwood, who had become interested in the group from reading *The Perfectionist.* Now came a tramp printer, Harvey Bowles, who was welcomed both for his belief and his occupation.

The group's paper was being read. It was effective. Within a short time five more converts came, but only three remained. The others were a John B. Lyvere, who was expelled because it was only too apparent he had small interest in transforming society but lusted after the female Perfectionists, and one Almira Edson, who was asked to leave for unspecified reasons. By early 1843 the Putney group numbered twenty-eight adults and nine children. All were living in three houses. A Perfectionist store had been opened on the village green. So had a chapel. Among the new converts received at this time were the Cragins, already mentioned.

Steps toward achieving the goals outlined by John Noyes were in evidence. A sign on the community pantry called attention to the need of "Health, Economy & Woman's Rights," and went on to explain that two of the usual meals, namely dinner and supper, were omitted from Perfectionist domestic arrangements. Instead, "We shall keep in this pantry a supply and variety of eatables, which we invite you to partake of at such times and in such manner as appetite and fancy may suggest." Thus was woman freed of much needless labor which convention had heaped upon her. Nor was this all by any means. Perfectionist women were offered a means of satisfying the mating urge without the onerous burden of bearing unwanted children. Here, said Noyes, was "the universal trap, the tyranny of child bearing." He was not like the Shakers, opposed to all human procreation. He was opposed to excessive procreation, which he said was almost universal, and opposed to random procreation, which he said was unavoidable "in the marriage system."

In six years of marriage his wife Harriet had given birth to five children. Only one had survived. Though this was not unusual in that day of high infant mortality, and was accepted without question as God's will, it was not so accepted by John Noyes. Neither his wife nor himself meant to remain a mere slave to nature if they could prevent it.

Up to this time the Perfectionists seem to have stirred only a casual interest among Putney townspeople. They were tolerated, much as Baptists and Catholics were tolerated, and accepted as harmless heretical eccentrics. Now, however, John Noyes began to impart to his disciples two ideas that were indeed daring. He called them "complex marriage" and "male continence." They complemented each other. In effect, complex marriage held that all members of the group loved one another equally well; that the curse of conventional marriage, or "wedlock," was in its stressing of exclusiveness, of "fidelity"; and that this curse should be done away with. Members of the group ought to cohabit with whom they pleased. Yet it was expressly forbidden that children should be conceived of any such union.

Because he objected to the use of contraceptives, advocated by Robert Dale Owen, at his short-lived colony at New Harmony, Indiana, which seemed "a sinfully easy solution," Noyes, who was Puritan enough to cherish discipline for its own sake, offered instead the self-control he called "male continence." (Physicians were to call it *coitus reservatus* and either praised or deplored it.) Male continence would prevent "random procreation" while permitting cohabitation. The propagation of Perfectionist children was naturally a part of Noyes's master plan for the new society, but it must wait until the group had proved the "rightness" of complex marriage.

After months of serious discussion the Putney group adopted the principle of complex marriage. The first to take advantage of it were the Cragins and the Noyeses. John Noyes and Mary Cragin "entered upon a second honeymoon," wrote Robert A. Parker, the biographer of Noyes, while "George Cragin and Mrs. Noyes followed in their footsteps with the docility of true believers." Other members were not long in adopting the practice.

Though Noyes was not yet ready to announce publicly the principle and the methods of Perfectionist marriage, and knowledge of its practice in Putney was to be kept from the Philistines, unorthodoxy in such matters has some of the qualities of quicksilver, and within a short time the village had a rich and scandalous subject for gossip. The gossip was in no way withered when the young Campbell sisters, Helen and Emma, were "converted to the principles of Perfectionism." That their mother, Achsah, was already privy to certain of these principles was to be made clear a little later by the true bill returned against John Noyes by the Windham County Grand Jury.

The scandal about the Campbell daughters was presently all but forgotten when Lucinda Lamb, fifteen years old, told friends she had accepted Perfectionist teachings. She might as well have stood on Putney Common and shouted that henceforth her name was Messalina. Talk of the "seduction" of this fair young flower of the village sent townsmen and townswomen in haste to explain to Lucinda's father exactly what was meant by "Perfectionist teachings." Mr. Lamb, who, to tell the truth, could not have been keeping up with local affairs, was struck speechless. He snatched Lucinda from the clutches of "those seducers" and sent her away into the care of relatives in Massachusetts.

Within the month George Noyes, younger brother of the prophet, was married to Helen Campbell, and sister Emma Campbell took William Woolworth, a recent convert, as husband. But this double conventional wedding, even though legalized by the proper licenses and a civil ceremony, did not lay the gathering storm. "The church and the village are astir," wrote Harriet Noyes to George Cragin, then on a speaking tour, "people are taking sides, gossips are lively, suspicious conjunctions are observed."

All unheeding, John Noyes, the universal reformer, now invaded a field new to him but a field within the stated goals of Perfectionism. This was to conquer death. "Christ," he announced, "is the only physician in our Perfectionist community." To prove as much, Noyes prayed with and for Mrs. Daniel Hall, bedridden and blind, and she was marvelously restored to complete health. Even some of the Philistines, who were suffering from various ills which had failed to respond to a variety of patent medicines, were given pause. But shortly thereafter they returned to their elixirs and opodeldoc and cordials when Noyes failed to save Mary Knight, who died from consumption.

The enemies of Perfectionism in Putney now combined forces to drive Noyes out of Vermont. The spearhead of attack was unexpected. He was Daniel Hall, husband of the woman Noyes and the unseen power of God had caused to take up her bed and walk. Mr. Hall appreciated these offices, but Noyes was no man to leave well enough alone; he proceeded to give Mr. Hall a treatise on the doctrine of complex marriage. Mr. Hall was profoundly shocked. He silently hitched up his horse and buggy, drove to Brattleboro, the county seat, and there placed the whole hideous business of John Noyes in the hands of the state's attorney, who in good time presented the matter to the grand jury. The Diaspora of the Putney Perfectionists followed.

2.

ONEIDA: A LIGHT FOR THE WORLD

IT was through the medium of God's Press, as he often referred to the Perfectionist paper, that the exile John Noyes soon came upon a new home for the faithful. He found it on Oneida Creek in the tall-timbered country of the old Oneida Indian Reservation, Madison County, New York, where Jonathan Burt, a devout disciple of Noyes through reading *The Perfectionist,* had attempted to found a colony along the lines of the Putney Corporation. Burt had bought a sawmill there and with a few other families was moving steadily toward financial bankruptcy at the time Noyes fled Vermont. Burt invited him to visit Oneida. Noyes did so late in 1847, and in spite of his own troubles was able to put new heart into Burt's group, to fire them with some of his own enthusiasm. With a fine casual gesture Noyes also tossed to Burt, as though it were so much buckwheat, a bag containing five hundred dollars in gold pieces, to meet a long-overdue payment on Oneida colony land. This money doubtless came from the estate of the grandfather of Noyes's wife, the late and Honorable Mark Richards, who by then must have been resting fitfully, if at all, in his grave near Putney. In any case, it not only saved the Oneida land from foreclosure, but permitted purchase of a parlor stove to heat one of the three miserable cabins that comprised Burt's colony.

The Oneida group tacitly accepted Noyes as a welcome leader, God-given in a time of trouble, and urged him to bring his scattered Putney followers to Oneida. After two or three days given to discussion Noyes agreed. True, the Oneida colony could offer little more than a safe harbor from the Philistines. It was a primitive place, and now snow-bound in February. There was a dearth of cabins. The sawmill could not operate until the leaky dam was overhauled and completely rebuilt.

Jonathan Burt put as good a face on conditions as possible. They could sell all the lumber they could make, come spring, to a railroad project. The land itself was good. Noyes knew what a devoted band of men and women could accomplish in a short time. He was as anxious to be convinced as Burt, and he presently sent word to his followers. They began to respond almost immediately.

The first contingent received a warm welcome from Noyes and Burt and the other Oneidans. But Mrs. Burt was as cool as the weather. It seems she had not yet been wholly converted to the idea of complex marriage. The new arrivals turned to with a will, and during the next few weeks they, with Burt's revivified original group, performed wonders. The dam was repaired. Logging got under way. The sawmill began to make boards and timbers. The making of furniture was started. Mary Cragin opened a school in a corner of one of the cabins, with twelve girls and boys as pupils.

Now came the faithful from Putney, grateful to escape the open hostility in Vermont, to find the pioneers had whacked up a board cabin to receive them. Then came more of the scattered members. One should not get the idea that these pilgrims were either poor or disgruntled people. In large part they came from substantial families, intelligent and naturally "progressive." They sold their houses back home, or their excellent farms, and they arrived well fed, well clothed, bringing furniture, heirloom portraits, musical instruments, books, and enthusiasm. All was now bustle and work at Oneida colony. These were young people inspired by the strong personality and magnetism of John Humphrey Noyes, who gradually came to be known as Father Noyes, though he was still in his thirties. Only Jonathan Burt and George Cragin were older.

The sawmill turned out prodigious amounts of lumber. The group was rich in artisans—a stonemason, several carpenters, a part-time architect; a pail maker, a lead-pipe maker, a blacksmith or two, a shoemaker, printers, millwrights, and one who even in that day called himself a landscape architect. As for the women, many of them had been reared in Vermont, a place where girls were early trained in common domestic pursuits, and to be competent at the retting of flax, the carding of wool, and both weaving and spinning. Most of them could make hats and baskets. The policy of one formal meal a day, breakfast, and the ever-ready and open pantry, which had been instituted at Putney, was continued at Oneida.

By midsummer the colony numbered only fifty-one, yet Noyes, as certain as ever of success, said it was time to erect a community building which he liked to call the Mansion House, a sort of headquarters that would represent the very source, the fountainhead, of a new and rational way of life, namely Perfectionism. So one night the prophet, using the North Star as guide, staked out the ground, 188 by 70· feet, on a rise of ground that commanded an impressive view. It was to be three stories and to contain communal dining room, parlor, reception room, school, and printing office. The second story was to be made into sleeping quarters for married pairs and for single females. Over all was the garret dormitory for unmarried men and for boys. The structure, Noyes vowed, would be heated by steam, which at that time was a radical new thing in up-state New York. The big building was not finished when winter came, but in moved the colonists to spend Christmas Eve and make something of a celebration of it.

The spring of '49 found the Perfectionists' hearts filled with gladness, their eyes steady on their goal. Not even the gold rush to California caused a ripple of interest at Oneida. The Mansion House was completed, and a Children's House, in keeping with the doctrines of Father Noyes, under construction. In this was to be reared all Perfectionist progeny, not by their parents but by suitable members trained and appointed for the purpose. This, said Noyes with a wave of his hand, would "prevent the idolatrous love of mother and child."

One is not to think for a moment that a dreamer of Noyes's stature had no other reforms in store for the community. Woman's dress, he announced, was both inappropriate and immodest. In a state of nature, he observed, the difference between the sexes could hardly be distinguished "at five hundred yards," yet when dressed conventionally, their clothing "telegraphed their sex" as far as they could be seen. Thus did "the false principle of shame and sexual isolation betray the world." To defy that five-hundred-yard giveaway, Oneida Community must forthwith have a rational dress for women that would become "the uniform of a vital society."

Noyes well knew that tampering with women's dress was possibly more fraught with danger than even complex marriage.* Yet he was a wise man. He turned the job of design over to the community women. For days on end they fashioned, then cut cloth into this or that pattern, and finally arrived at a garb which henceforth was to mark all females of Oneida. The skirt was cut to knee length; tailored pantalettes reached down to the ankle. Three bold and popular members were chosen to display the new dress. Many of the sisters were shocked and distressed, yet within a short time the garb ceased to seem odd, at least in the community. A little later Noyes suggested short hair for women. This was a step so serious as to call for biblical

---

*In 1850 James Jesse Strang, the apostate Mormon, was defied when he decreed bloomers for the women of his colony on Big Beaver Island, in Lake Michigan, and thereby suffered considerable loss of influence.

reference. In the Book, Paul seemed to favor *long* hair for women; but Noyes was ready to dissolve objection by what appears to have been a rather fine interpretation. Paul, he said, really favored long hair "not for adornment but for a covering." Somehow or other this took away any lingering doubt. Oneida women cut their hair short and came to like it thus.

In later years Pierrepont Noyes, a son of the prophet, remarked that both the official garb and the short hair were mainly for the purpose of discouraging vanity. He recalled, too, that the community provided "going-away clothes." Any man or woman preparing for a trip outside on business, visited Mr. Aiken or Mrs. Van Velzer, keepers of the wardrobes, and was fitted out in one of the conventional suits or dresses kept for that purpose. It isn't clear that Oneida men had any special community garb, but Mr. Noyes, who ought to know, says both men and women used going-away clothes.

Prospective members were constantly coming to Oneida and asking to join. After an examination shrewdly calculated to plumb their characters, they either were politely rejected, or accepted conditionally. At the end of three years there were two hundred and five adults in the community. Communal sharing of everything was so effective that even the children's toys were held in common. Pierrepont Noyes, who was born and reared in the community, recalls that, though this or that sled might be a favorite with a certain boy, the idea of personal ownership never entered the youngsters' heads.

The idealism of Oneida was not without practicality. This was in striking contrast to the "fuzzy thinking" Noyes had observed in the Brook Farm group near Boston, the Hopedale community, also in Massachusetts, both of which soon failed, as did at least thirty-odd more American experiments suggested by the theories of Charles Fourier, a French dreamer with truly grandiose plans for a new world. The division of labor at Oneida was wonderfully well organized; and all physically able Oneidans *worked*. Their gardens did famously. So did their orchards. Wheat, oats, flax, and barley grew in the newly cleared fields. In the pastures were fine cattle and a host of sheep. The community raised or made virtually everything needed, and their first business with the outside was the sale of their preserves.

In all the excitement of the expanding community Noyes did not forget complex marriage. "Religion," he said again and again, "is the first subject of interest, and sexual morality the second, in this our great enterprise of establishing the Kingdom of God on earth." He comprehended what a heroic task it was to be, to eradicate the ages-old Christian idea of exclusiveness in marriage. And he may have underestimated the savagery with which non-Perfectionists were to meet the attempt. Yet, none save a dedicated dreamer would dare to expound such a notion.

Noyes would permit no applicants to join the community until they had been thoroughly briefed. He explained that the practice was to introduce male continence "under skilled guidance." It would never do, he said, for two inexperienced persons to hurry into intimate relationship. Young men were to be taught the mysteries by older women; young girls by the older men. It would be interesting to know how many applicants for membership in Oneida Community, together with their sex and age, objected to the skilled-guidance feature of Perfectionism; but unfortunately no records were kept in regard to this item.

The community pledged itself to protect members from social approaches that might be deemed unattractive. No woman could be approached in this matter except through a third party. Exclusive bonds between two members were most positively forbidden. It was amusingly typical of Noyes as a reformer that he hotly resented the charge of "free love" which was to plague Oneida throughout its three decades of community Perfectionism. Complex marriage, said Noyes, was *not* free love; it merely meant that each was married to all. This rather fine distinction was ignored by the press, which was soon to devote enormous attention to Oneida Community. It was also ignored by all outsiders.

The cohabitation of adult members was a matter of simple agreement between the parties concerned, though arrangements for what was delicately called a "transaction" must, as already mentioned, be made through a third party. The conceiving of children was strictly forbidden these pairings, which, said Noyes, were for the gratification of "ordinary amative instincts." Propagation was to be reserved for "its legitimate occasions" when conception was intended. It speaks well for community discipline that during Oneida's first two decades, the group of some forty families increased its population by less than two births a year. Noyes explained this policy as dictated by temporary expediency. Only when the community had proved itself would it be ready for the daring venture which Noyes was planning for it. This was to be "planned, scientific procreation," of which more in its place.

Meanwhile, as a corrective to "wrong" thinking about love, or any other matter of community interest, Noyes instituted "mutual criticism." This was done at meetings regularly called for the purpose. Everyone was expected to give voice to opinion on the faults of others; there was to be no whispering behind doors; it was to be a matter for open discussion. Noyes himself often used these meetings to break down the respect which these men and women of conventional and usually Puritan Yankee homes held the holy bonds of matrimony. "Love," he liked to tell them over and over, "is something to give, not to claim." He hoped that "mutual criticism" would in time wholly dissipate the "romantic notions" about idolatrous love.

The more immediate effect of the critical discussions was a sort of cleansing process akin to what many decades later was to be given the name of psychoanalysis. "It may seem," Noyes explained, "a somewhat heroic method of treatment when a person is suffering in body, to apply a castigation to the character through the spiritual or moral part; but this is precisely the thing needed to cleanse and purify the system of disease." He claimed for it the healing of many ills ranging from sore throats and headaches to "advanced stages of serious chronic diseases." Unquestionably mutual criticism often threw the subject—the patient— into a violent sweat that had therapeutic value. Noyes declared he had seen the treatment "raise up a person apparently from death's door." Was this not progress toward achievement of one of Perfectionism's goals, the "Victory over Death"?

It will be recalled that another goal of John Noyes's Perfectionism was a reformation of the industrial system. It seems improbable that he devoted much effort to anything of an industrial nature until, in 1854, he was forced by circumstances to recognize the need for a greater income for the community. Canned fruits, a modest manufacture of traveling bags, and the sale of a few game traps, which up to this point had comprised Oneida's commerce with the outside, were not enough to meet the increasing needs of the group. New storehouses, barns, and sheds must be built. The older structures needed repairs. And the Perfectionist periodical, now called *The Oneida Circular,* had become a heavy burden of expense. On its masthead this organ stated it was worth "at least two dollars a year but is sent to all applicants, whether they pay or not." A majority of "subscribers" did not pay; but if they read the paper, they got a good stout dose of Perfectionism in every issue. Noyes was determined to keep the *Circular* going; it was the only way to report the progress of Oneida Community.

In this his moment of great need Father Noyes suddenly reflected on the art and craft of Sewell Newhouse, an odd character who had joined the community. As his contribution to the general welfare, Newhouse had been making, wholly by hand, some two thousand game traps a year, which were sold for community benefit. The fame of these traps had spread to the Rocky Mountains and beyond. No one man, nor a dozen men, could begin to meet the demands for them that came by mail and messenger.

Like Noyes, Newhouse was a native of Brattleboro, a gigantic man who had migrated to the back country of New York in 1820 and set up as a trapper. He was as dignified as an Iroquois chief and "had the measured tread of a stag." Some thought his countenance reminded them of a sullen eagle. He found the commercial traps of the time to be faulty. He made his own, and by experience had discovered a method of tempering steel which made the springs and jaws of Newhouse traps hold fast to everything they clamped upon. In time he gave up trapping for making traps. He was thus engaged when he and his wife joined Oneida Community.

So, now when added income was needed, Noyes suggested to the finest trapmaker in North America that he teach his secrets of tempering to a selected group of young men of the community, and Oneida go into manufacture on a large scale. But here Noyes ran up against the innate pride and secrecy of the expert craftsman. For twenty years Newhouse had performed all his wonders behind the locked doors of his shop, as secretive as any necromancer. Father Noyes, however, was a match for the stubbornness of the convert, and after a vast amount of "communizing and the democratic power of inspiration" he prevailed on Newhouse to initiate a dozen or so of young Perfectionists into his methods.

Newhouse traps proved to be the turning point in the financial status of Oneida Community. By a miracle of dedicated effort a large brick factory was erected; and Noyes and Newhouse worked out power methods to perform what had been done by hand. A virtual assembly line was inaugurated. Newhouse insisted that nothing be done to lower the quality of the product. Noyes agreed. The traps were stamped with both the Newhouse and the Oneida names and from that day on, those names meant superior goods. In fur-bearing country across the continent, in Canada and the United States, full-time trappers could not get enough of the Oneida-Newhouse brand. Orders came from the most remote regions; and one day there appeared at the Mansion House doors an agent-buyer from the hoary old Hudson's Bay Company, come to purchase the entire output if he could get it.

The trap business grew so rapidly that outsiders had to be employed, and came to number more than two hundred and fifty. They complemented a hundred or more community men and many community boys. The boys worked in the basement of the Mansion House where the chains for the smaller traps were put together by the youngsters, who sat on high stools around a big table, operating simple machines. Pierrepont Noyes remembers that each boy had a daily stint of one hundred chains, whether it took him an hour or two hours. It wasn't long before Oneida Community was making and selling 275,000 traps a year. Oneida-Newhouse, indeed, had done for the steel trap what Winchester and Remington were to do for the rifle, and Samuel Colt was already doing for the revolver. Never again, in Noyes's time, was the community to be in financial straits.

Silk manufacture was next. Three young people of Oneida were sent to work in a Connecticut silk factory and learn methods of processing. They returned to install a modest industry which produced five thousand pounds of finished products annually. The canning of fruits was continued and expanded.

At about the same time Oneida went into the trap business a branch community of Perfectionists was taking form at rustic Wallingford, on the old turnpike between Hartford and New Haven in Connecticut. In Wallingford farmer Henry Allen had become convinced that the doctrines expounded by Noyes were both right and rational. He adopted them for his own family, and invited others who believed likewise to join in founding a Perfectionist colony on the Allen farm. Some forty persons accepted. More land was bought. Several buildings for communal living were erected. Everything was on a smaller scale than at Oneida, but the doctrines, even unto complex marriage, were the same. The community was successful from the first, and it was Noyes's practice to spend a few days there each month. He even moved *The Oneida Circular* printing office to Wallingford.

Another use to which the Wallingford branch was put was to help in breaking up the "special" or "idolatrous" attachments which resisted Oneida's mutual criticism. For instance, when it became apparent that George Cragin had a most special attachment for Edith Walters, eighteen, he was hustled off to Wallingford. It was here Cragin got the idea of making silverware. Working with Dr. Theodore Noyes, eldest son of the prophet, who was acting as a sort of lieutenant at Wallingford, they set up the machinery and presently the first tinned iron spoon was cut and finished. Millions of spoons, though of a much finer quality, along with millions of knives, forks, and other tableware, were to follow. Not for some years, however, would silverware become the Perfectionists' first industry.

During the sixties and seventies, when many young men were sent from Oneida to attend Yale University, Wallingford, only half an hour from New Haven, became a sort of headquarters for them. Several of these young Oneidans were to be graduated from Yale Medical School and contribute their knowledge to Father Noyes's master plan for "rational procreation," to which he gave the uneuphonic name of stirpiculture long before Sir Francis Galton invented the much better word *eugenics* to describe the same thing.

"How long," dreamer Noyes asked the question, "how long must we be born and grow up fools, to become wise only by suffering as our fathers suffered before us?" He answered the question: "Our tribulations," he cried, "will end when special and persistent attention is turned to the business of breeding human beings."

Such was the monumental task John Noyes now set for Perfectionism. Oneida Community must light the world, even if in the process it shocked the world, too.

3.

THE COMPLEX FAMILY PORTRAIT

JOHN HUMPHREY NOYES was so much a product of his time that he liked to think up euphemisms for words and phrases which had come to be considered indelicate. That he understood the actual need to cloak some of his radical doctrines in language acceptable to the unenlighted public is clear from his use of "complex marriage" and "male continence." What Noyes meant by stirpiculture was nothing less than the "scientific breeding" of human beings.

"The race cannot be raised from ruin," he cried, "till propagation is made a matter of science." Early in 1869 he told his followers the time had come to inaugurate the experiment at Oneida. Though this was a decade after Charles Darwin's *Origin of Species* appeared, the concept of his master plan had not reached him by way of Darwin's theory of selection and evolution. It had come to him independently as early as 1847, when he began at Putney to expound it in a pamphlet which he was obliged to finish in exile at Oneida and which was published as *Bible Communism* a year later.

The implications of Darwin's work were such as to horrify all conventional thinkers. Even Francis Galton, who drew heavily on Darwin to discuss the problem of racial improvement, stopped short of Noyes's stirpiculture. "When Galton comes to the point," Noyes complained, "where it is necessary to look beyond his theory to the duties it suggests, he subsides into the meekest conservatism."

Not so the father of Oneida Community. "Let us," said Noyes, "march right up to this terrible analogy which has been so long troubling the world and find out exactly what it is, and how far the obligation which it suggests is legitimate." Whereupon he told his Perfectionists they had already cleared the way for the experiment. Had they not already abolished conventional matrimony, which was an absolute bar to scientific propagation? He went on to say that even common licentiousness was often not without compensations in the light of the propagative law. "Who can say," he demanded of his followers, "who can say how much the present race of men in Connecticut owe to the numberless fornications and adulteries of Pierpont Edwards? Corrupt as he was, he must have distributed a good deal of the good blood of his noble father, Jonathan Edwards . . . Such are the compensations of nature and providence." But better to let science lend a hand to the propagation of men of superior health and intellect. He announced that a committee on stirpiculture would be chosen to select the parents of Oneida Community children.

All was ready for complex marriage to reach its goal in the complex family. Fifty-three young women of the community signed a resolution which said they would put aside all envy and, if need be, become martyrs to science and cheerfully resign all desire to be mothers if for any reason "Mr. Noyes deem us unfit material for propagation." Thirty-eight young men of the community signed a statement "offering ourselves to be used in forming any combinations that may seem to Mr. Noyes to be desirable . . . We desire to be servants of the truth."

This is perhaps the place for an aside, to note that at least nine of the fifty-eight children born of the stirpicultural regime in the decade after 1869 were sired by John Noyes, who was fifty-nine years old when the experiment began. A total of one hundred men and women participated in the "transactions." Nine applications of would-be parents were vetoed on the grounds of unfitness. Forty-two applications were approved. The seeming discrepancy is accounted for by the fact that more than one child was born of several matings. And let us not forget the activity of Father Noyes himself.

Until they could walk, infants remained in the care of their mothers. They were then admitted to the day nursery in the Children's House, but returned nightly to their mothers. Finally, they were put wholly in charge of the children's department. From infancy to adolescence the stirps received care such as few private families could afford. Sickness and disease were incomparably less common to these children than elsewhere in the United States. Of the fifty-eight children born of selected parents, only six had died by 1921, when the ages of the stirps ranged from forty-two to fifty-two years. The norm of the country at that time indicated forty-five deaths for a comparable number. If physical health and longevity, along with what appears to have been high intelligence, are accepted as worthy goals, then the Oneida experiment in stirpiculture and communal child care were markedly successful.

These records were of course not available when there began what one sociologist declared to have been "one of the greatest pressure campaigns against any religious group in history." It probably would

not have mattered much, anyway, for Perfectionist doctrines were
anathema to the clergy who were still powerful in secular as well as
spiritual matters. And the clergy simply had to get rid of so dangerous
a man as Noyes.

Getting rid of Noyes was going to take time and a great deal of effort.
The practice of stirpiculture began just when Oneida Community entered
its era of greatest prosperity. The Newhouse traps were in enormous
demand. They were most profitable. Orders for Oneida silk and Oneida
canned goods were increasing. Material success brought a new respect.
If these Perfectionists were daft, as a majority of Americans believed,
they were at least honest as well as up-and-coming businessmen. This
was a fact not to be laughed at. For a time, indeed, the scandalous matter
of "sexual irregularities" seemed to be forgotten.

Oneida Community was still riding high, though had not yet reached
its zenith, when the Midland railroad extended its line through the
property and set up a depot called Community a short distance from
the Mansion House. Now began a trek of curious visitors from all parts
of New York and many other states. They came by the hundred, and at
last by the thousand (on a Sunday), to wander over the trim acres and
well-managed woodlands, to see the trap factory, the canning factory,
and the minor industries. And also to inspect the showpiece of the
community, which was the magnificient new Mansion House. But
above all, perhaps, they came to gaze at the short-haired and pantaletted
maidens of the strange sect who more often than not were engaged in a
hat-braiding bee, or a sewing bee, under the big elms on the spacious
lawns around the Mansion House.

Father Noyes rose equal to the opportunity. Guides were furnished
to all who came. They replied in straightforward manner to all questions
of the visitors, even those regarding the complexities of complex marriage and stirpiculture. Noyes got out a *Handbook of Oneida Community,* which told visitors and prospective visitors what they would
find. It called attention to the larger buildings. It proudly mentioned
that they were heated by steam. The community library contained
3581 volumes and subscribed to one hundred and forty periodicals.
Plays and light operas were given by local talent. There was also a
printing office, a store, the academy, a laundry, the barns, forges, and
machine shop, to say nothing of the trap works and silk department.
The Children's House, swarming with young Perfectionists, and wonderfully furnished and equipped, never failed to "bring cries of admiration"
from visitors.

The *Handbook* went on to boast a little, pointing out that community members "represented fourteen states of the Union, Canada, England, and the Island of Ceylon." In the back of the *Handbook* were listed the several Oneida publications for sale, among them *The Trapper's Guide, by Sewell Newhouse,* price $2.00; and a number entitled *Male Continence, or Self Control in Sexual Intercourse.* This work was what might have been called a "loss-leader." It could be had at the modest price of one dozen copies for fifty cents. When the community guides were pressed, rather haltingly, for details about "how do you manage the—the matter of, of conception?" they pointed to the male-continence pamphlet. One may guess that thousands of this work were bought by visitors. That it "spread the good word" into wide fields is certain. That it stimulated the all-out attack on Noyes and Oneida can hardly be doubted.

What was it like, being born and reared at Oneida? Pierrepont Noyes, one of its outstanding products, told the story in a charming book,* and elaborated on it to this writer as recently as 1954. Mr. Noyes was born in the community in 1870, on a day when a full thousand visitors inspected Oneida while the colony band played in the quadrangle of the Mansion House. His father was the prophet, his mother Harriet Worden. He had several half brothers, among them George and Dr. Theodore Noyes. He early became conscious of the distinction between "us" and "outsiders." He came almost as soon to realize that the outsiders looked down on community children as the results of irregularities in marital relations. But, he recalls, the Oneida youngsters were too well indoctrinated from birth to feel anything but (secretly) superior to outside children—in education, in manners, and in health. Now and then they might envy the "worldly ways" of outside kids, but merely in the same childish way they wanted to be pirates, train robbers, circus performers, or Indians. Pierrepont liked and respected his father, though he seemed remote, like a power, rather than a man and a father. He was but nine when Father Noyes left Oneida for good, and "a black cloud of fear descended upon the Mansion House and threw its shadow over the Children's House." These things heralded the beginning of the end for complex marriage, though not the end of Oneida Community.

The black cloud of fear so well remembered by Pierrepont Noyes was the climax of a storm that had been gathering within the community itself. Disgruntled members, expulsions, attempts at blackmail, and finally a fatal schism were involved. One problem was by name William Mills, who, with his wife and daughters, joined Oneida colony, and who proceeded almost at once to make advances to community women. The goatish Mills could not have been overly attractive, for his every advance

* *My Father's House,* New York, 1937.

was rejected. He then told Noyes that a much better method than that in practice would be the drawing of lots from a hat. Noyes curtly rejected the idea. He castigated Mills severely. The cunning Mills then sought by indirection to put himself in a position to be much in company of the younger girls. He invented nothing less than a dishwashing machine, which, he said, was too delicate to be operated by anyone except himself, and forthwith resumed his unwelcome advances to the maidens detailed for kitchen duty. When he tried to get youngsters of twelve and thirteen to drink what he said was homemade wine, the community elders took a hand. For the first and last time a member was thrown bodily out the Mansion House door and told not to return. He brought suit for an immense sum, but finally settled for $2500.

Another problem was an unstable youth, Charles Guiteau, who had been admitted to the community on the plea of his father, a devout reader of *The Oneida Circular.* The young man was an unreliable worker, a conceited exhibitionist, and unamenable to "mutual criticism." He was asked to leave, and did so, only to bring suit charging he had been "exposed to gross immorality in the colony" and that Oneida owed him some $9000 "in wages." The case was dropped by Guiteau's lawyer when he discovered that his client was insane. A bit later Guiteau proved it by shooting James A. Garfield, President of the United States.

The Mills and the Guiteau suits were aired in the unfriendly press and made fine fodder for the really dedicated enemies of Noyes and Oneida. These were legion. They were headed for years by Dr. Tayler Lewis, a professor at Union College; and the redoubtable Rev. John William Mears, professor of moral philosophy at Hamilton College. The former had the ear of *The Independent,* a national weekly much read by the clergy and other influential people. Mears was making a career as an enemy of sin, which, as Mears saw it, was based largely on two items, they being rum and complex marriage. He ran for Congress on the Prohibition, or temperance, ticket, and devoted even more effort during six years to putting Oneida out of business.

The attack got under way with lectures and articles dealing with the "impure and shocking practices" of the Oneida group. It proceeded to meetings largely attended by Presbyterian and Methodist clergymen and lay members of those churches, who passed resolutions denouncing "this hideous thing that hides from the light of day, and in mid-night dens revels in debauchery." That "this hideous thing" was explained and described in a pamphlet openly for sale, and doing remarkably well at fifty cents a dozen copies, at Oneida Community, in no way deterred the Christian laity and their shepherds.

The meetings and resolutions continued throughout 1873–74. Various committees were appointed "to investigate and report." The Baptists, then the Congregationalists at last joined the hue and cry to lay the Beast of Oneida. Reporters and sketch artists came to Oneida from *Harper's Weekly, Frank Leslie's Illustrated Newspaper,* and from the daily press of Chicago, New York, and Boston. *The National Police Gazette,* which also recognized good material and whose wildly imaginative artists could readily illustrate exposés of Oneida without troubling to go there, devoted whole sections of its pink pages to what it alleged was going on in the community. A typical page in the *Gazette* depicted "obscene orgies" by showing a bewhiskered and lascivious-looking male, nude from the waist up, standing in a pool surrounded by bewitching young females displaying generous portions of their beautiful nude bodies. Another page had a bearded male, patently a slavering old debauchee, embracing a maiden in preparation to explaining to her the mysteries of complex marriage. The *Gazette's* writers were no more trammeled by fact than were its artists. Their leering prose pretended that the editors of this popular magazine for pimps were shocked at such goings-on.

Yet it seems possible that Oneida might have survived all that the reverend professors and all their cohorts, including the *Police Gazette,* could muster in the way of smearing propaganda. District Attorney Barnett of Utica stood as firm as a rock. "It is easy to reason," he said publicly, "that the social habits of the Perfectionists are wrong simply because they do not conform to our own—that is, with what we *say* they are, but if indictments could be procured on the ground of immorality, then who wouldn't be liable?" The magazine *Puck* defended Oneida in prose and colored cartoons, and attacked Mears and the clergy, remarking that the Oneida people "dwell in peace and harmony," adding that "they have no church scandals," a reference to the current difficulties in which America's best-known preacher of the time found himself. *The Nation* remarked with obvious joy that, if the clergy were to prove adultery, they first had to prove marriage, "and at Oneida they have no marriage."

But what the assembled clergy perhaps could not have done from the outside could be and was accomplished from within. To begin with, Dr. Theodore Noyes, who came out of Yale with a medical degree, told his father he did not believe that any radical experiment like Oneida could accomplish anything lasting; all advance, he said, had to be made slowly by an evolutionary process. Though this shook old Noyes not at all, it doubtless weakened the faith of the younger men in the community. It seems more than possible, too, that several of the young women of Oneida had come to resent the part they played in complex marriage;

they did not like the idea of the communal family. And then came James William Towner, a born schismatic.

Towner had joined Oneida in 1874, bringing with him a group of twelve people, survivors of a "free love" colony that had gone on the rocks at Berlin Heights, Ohio. Towner was an ambitious man who would have liked to take charge of Oneida. Around him in good time he gathered various rebels who wanted to do away with this or that doctrine of Perfectionism. Towner gradually drew them to agree with what he said was his "well considered opinion." Father Noyes must go.

Increasing deafness had by now made the prophet virtually unapproachable, yet the elder members would not listen to talk of unseating him. There were, however, other ways of getting him to give up the reins. If, for instance, some member of the community should lodge a complaint with the district attorney, charging, say, any one of a number of sexual delinquencies that are commonly described as "a statutory offense," Noyes's arrest would surely follow; and disaffected members could give evidence to convict him.

Warned by loyal members of this plan, Noyes refused to leave until the same members expressed fear that arrest of the prophet on a charge of sexual irregularities would result in an open scandal and wreck the community. After all, the clergy were hoping, if not actually praying, for something like this. Noyes recognized the danger. On a night in June 1879 he left Oneida secretly for Canada.

The prophet had fled, and the angels, observed Mr. Parker, Noyes's incomparable biographer, must have wept—wept at the bitterly contrasting destinies of the two grandsons of the late Rutherford Hayes of Brattleboro, Vermont—mediocrity in the White House, these two years past, and now genius on its way to exile.*

On August 20 the big bell in the Mansion House tower was tolled, and the adult members of Oneida Community gathered to hear a message from the prophet read. He was in Ontario. He advised "certain modifications" in community affairs. Complex marriage was to be abandoned, though Noyes made it clear that abandonment did not mean renunciation of its rightness, even its perfection. Members should continue to hold the property and business of Oneida in common. They should continue to live in a common household and eat at a common table. The only important change was that in regard to complex marriage.

Members of the local, state, and national press were soon pounding at the big doors of the Mansion House. Was it true? Did Noyes mean that

---

* Rutherford Birchard Hayes (1822–93) nineteenth President of the United States, a first cousin to John Humphrey Noyes.

complex marriage was abandoned? The answer was yes and yes. The newspaper boys hastened to interview the Rev. Mr. Mears, to ask if he were now content. Yes, said Mears, he was content—if and when the reformed colonists would announce in the public press the names of the parties who "hereafter propose to live together in the sacred relation of husband and wife." Mears also made the gratuitous suggestion that the columns of the Utica *Herald* would be a proper place for the marriage notices.

Straightening out the relative marital status of some three hundred persons who had lived many years under the system of complex marriage might well have appalled Solomon himself. It was done, however, and the marriages for the most part were made by contract as stipulated by the laws of the state of New York, though a few couples also celebrated their entry into conventional respectability with elaborate weddings.

The marriages and all other community affairs were now in the hands of a council of elders. But Noyes was still the actual head. Nothing important was done except with his advice. It was he, still mentally alert in spite of years and deafness, who proposed the Plan of Division, by which, on January 1, 1881, community property came to an end, and more than one hundred adults and many minors were each assigned shares in a joint-stock company incorporated as Oneida Community, Ltd. It would appear, from a lack of suits against the new concern, that the transition to stock ownership was made with great common sense and fairness.

At this period the schismatic Towner, who had failed to be made head of Oneida, pulled up stakes and took off for Southern California, which even then was something of a promised land for cultists. The prophet went into residence at Niagara Falls, Ontario. In a little while the new Oneida company leased a factory on the American side of the falls and into it moved the silverware business from Wallingford; and along with the business went men and women who had been born or reared either at Wallingford or Oneida. All of them were now stock-holders as well as employees of Oneida Community, Ltd. The chain part of the steel-trap business was also moved to the falls, though on the Canadian side.

Prophet Noyes lived on in what was called the Stone Cottage on the bluff overlooking the falls where now stands Hotel Brock and where also stands the busy factory of Oneida Community's Canadian branch. Noyes became a sort of biblical elder, still giving counsel when asked, somewhat mellowed, but still positive as to the rightness and common sense of the many experiments he had advocated. His crime was that he had put them into practice. He died in the Stone Cottage April 13, 1886, age seventy-five years.

4.

RETREAT AND TRANSITION

WHEN John Noyes died, Oneida Community, Ltd., had a working capital of more than half a million dollars and had been paying an annual dividend of 6 per cent. Direction of the concern was in the hands of a board of nine men, seven of whom had been among the prophet's oldest and most trusted associates. Among them all, however, was none with anything of the force of his strong character.

Having lost their shepherd of so many years, as Walter D. Edmonds has pointed out, they "felt the need for guidance." It was possibly foreordained that the older followers of Noyes should still seek guidance from their dead leader in the mystic valley of the shadows. Younger members of the community had no faith whatever in the possibility of communication with the dead. The result of this conflict of beliefs was a struggle for control of stock shares that must be unique in the corporate history of American business. Three years after the prophet's death, spiritualism had split Oneida Community, Ltd., into two rival factions. In 1889 the spiritualist group voted sufficient shares to elect five of the nine board members, and took control of the company.

Whatever guidance the Spiritualists may have received from beyond the grave, it was not good; the majority of Oneida directors failed to recognize the fast-changing character of the business world. They either ignored or never knew of the advances being made in the technology of manufacture and distribution, and the new tempo of selling methods. They believed that Industry and Thrift, which they liked to spell with capital letters, were enough. That these two qualities, fine as they were and of which Oneida possessed a great store, were *not* enough gradually became apparent; and the Panic of 1893 brought convincing evidence to all save the most hidebound that Oneida was being carried rapidly toward financial wreck.

During much of the next year a battle of proxies so bitterly shook Oneida Community, Ltd., that many shareholders believed the whole great venture of John Humphrey Noyes had become a thing of the past. By year's end, however, what with a lot of pleadings, warnings, and threats, the non-Spiritualist party won control by a slim 16 shares of the

24,000 voted, and Dr. Theodore Noyes, eldest son of the prophet, went in as president; and Pierrepont Noyes was appointed superintendent of the company's factories at Niagara Falls.

The entry of Pierrepont Noyes—"a mere boy of twenty-four," the dead-end Spiritualists protested—into the management of the company was to be the turning point. He had been born, as said, and grown up in the Community. After schooling at Colgate he had gone to work in the company's Niagara Falls plant, where he was unhappy and discouraged with what he considered the outmoded machinery and the all-around antique attitude of the executives. He quit. He married a Community girl and went to New York City to establish a silverware business of his own. It was doing so well that only his elder brother's pleading moved him to sell his own prosperous business and return to the Community. Years later he told a visitor that the compelling impulse to return had been in terms of what failure of the concern would have meant to the older members.

From the day he took over the Niagara Falls operation, the career of Pierrepont Noyes and Oneida is a heart-warming story in which brilliant executive ability and idealism can scarcely be separated the one from the other. The young man was soon put in charge of the company which he, and others he selected for important posts, proceeded to build into the immensely successful makers of "Community Plate" and meanwhile show other industrialists how men and management could work together for the benefit of all.

One of Pierrepont Noyes's many happy innovations was engaging a young artist named Coles Phillips to paint illustrations for Community Plate advertisements. These were a spectacular success. The Coles Phillips Girl was as distinctive and popular as the "Girls" drawn by Charles Dana Gibson and Harrison Fisher; and she put Community Plate into the homes of several generations of American young people. It was also by Noyes's urging that Oneida hired talent to design tableware patterns of real beauty. One after the other, too, he sold or discontinued the company's silk, canned goods, and even the steel-trap businesses, to concentrate on Community Plate.

In 1955 the great main and modern plant of what is now Oneida, Ltd., ranged over many acres in Sherrill, New York, a "factory town" that belies most conceptions of an industrial community. Nearby the old Mansion House still stands on the original site of the Oneida colony. Ivy-grown and serene, amid great old elms, wide green lawns, and curving drives and paths, its mansard roof and bell-tower cupola compose a perfect period piece of nostalgic beauty. Inside, and much as they were in Father Noyes's day, are the galleried sitting rooms, the dining hall, the library and theater, and vast closets in which still hang some of the short-skirted and pantaletted gowns and the "going-away" clothes of the men and women who took part in the great experiment of Perfectionism, by all odds the most thoroughgoing attempt to found a new society since, perhaps, New Testament times.

In an apartment of the Mansion House still lived Pierrepont Noyes and his wife, a daughter of one of the prophet's most able associates. At eighty-five Mr. Noyes stood as tall and straight as a pine. His dark eyes lighted and glowed as he responded candidly to a visitor's questions with all the animation of a man half his age. The visitor came away in the belief he had met a keen intelligence marked by no little of the idealism that had moved the founder of Oneida Community to his heroic dream.

Was John Humphrey Noyes a genius? Many unconventional thinkers have believed so. Havelock Ellis called him "one of the noblest pioneers America has produced." George Bernard Shaw paid him eloquent tribute as an unquestioned genius. H. G. Wells made a pilgrimage to Oneida in an effort to make up his mind. By then Noyes was dead. Mr. Wells talked long with the charming old ladies and gentlemen he found in rocking chairs on the Mansion House veranda or strolling about the grounds they had known since childhood. They answered his questions. They showed him the daguerreotypes and photographs of Oneida's past. The English socialist and writer stared at the stuffy-appearing young men in frock coats, at the "decorous gentility" of the short-haired young women. They seemed to stare back at him, as if in challenge to solve the enigma they presented even to a radical Briton to whom no ideas were shocking. But at last he gave it up as "some quality of the New England mind" he could not fathom. It seemed to him a "secret gone forever."

Many another seeker of truth has been as baffled as Wells at the enigma of John Noyes and his Perfectionists. The secret is perhaps not to be divulged any more than that the fragrance could return to a pressed lilac fluttering out of the pages of some old book in the Mansion House library, perhaps a work of Emanuel Swedenborg or, nearer home, of Jonathan Edwards, both of whom had looked straight into hell and, like Noyes, had come away with a new vision.

Whether or not Noyes was a genius is a matter of opinion, but surely the effort to activate his enormous dream was the work of one of the company of divine madmen. Others might conceive an abstraction about correcting the mistakes of God, in the matter of Adam and Eve, by re-forming and changing humanity all the way back to Genesis. But only as an abstract idea. None save Noyes dared to translate such criticism of Deity into reality.

Part Two

THE SHAKERS OF TREES

1.

VISIONS OF THE NIGHT

JOHN HUMPHREY NOYES did not appear suddenly in a void. He was a man of his time, and Perfectionism was only one of the many strange flowers that bloomed so riotously in the bright morning sun of the young republic. Most of these dream flowerings, including the republic itself, were the work of home-grown visionaries.

Dreamers and visionaries have always been a little suspect. This is probably just as well, for a goodly number of dreamers became prophets and of these only too many turned out to be false prophets. And, anyway, prophets of all sorts, whether true or false, have been responsible for an infinite amount of trouble. Time out of mind it has been charged against them, by the solid, down-to-earth and respectable members of society, that dreamers can find their way only by moonlight, which is a notoriously dangerous beacon filled with distortions, given to aberrant fancies, turning grossly imperfect things into beautiful images.

The charge is doubtless true. Yet dreamers pay it no heed. They find the big and thoughtful night stimulating. They hear trumpets blowing at dawn. They see the morning before the rest of us and find satisfaction in being first, though one wonders if this may not often be their punishment, too, for the clear morning light can be harsh treatment for visions seen in the night.

It was the good, solid, down-to-earth king's men, the respectable Tories of late colonial days, who denounced the Liberty Boys as visionaries and predicted that their dawn should find them hanging by the neck. Yet, somewhere between the signing of the Declaration and the guns at Yorktown the visionaries were transformed into true prophets. We honor them as the Founding Fathers. If we still honor them by name as heroic individuals, it is largely because of their comparative antiquity. Time has the power to preserve and embellish, and it is sometimes stronger than man's tendency to forget. Even so, the Founding Fathers lived and died hardly a moment too soon. Only a little later their dreams and their efforts might well have been strained through the screen of history and declared by learned men to have been nothing more than grains of sand blown about on the surging winds of economics.

By now most of us are privy to the proposition, widely held by modern writers, that conditions chiefly of an economic nature are the dynamic forces that make history move. They tend to dismiss entirely the individual as an agent of change, or movement, and to credit all to what they are pleased to call trends, or influences, or forces. The individual is ignored as airily as if he were a protoplasm operating in a void. To my mind this theory is tenable only in part, good only to a certain point beyond which volition takes over. I happen to believe that man, even one man or one woman, often has had an immense effect in slowing or hastening these forces that make history.

As I understand his attitude, the true no-nonsense interpreter of human effort seems to say with assurance that here is a so-called hero who in fact did nothing but to shake the tree when the fruit was ripe. Does he, then, think it was a small thing to shake the tree? Many a shaker of trees has wound up hanging from one, or nailed to it.

This book is about certain shakers of trees in the United States of America. None of my crew was quite hanged or nailed. Hanging and nailing were going out of fashion as therapy for visions seen. Yet some of them just barely escaped the total remedy, while many more went to prison, and a multitude were subjected to all manner of violence, to ostracism, boycott, and every sort of cruel, petty abuse. This was not so because they were common disturbers of the peace, but rather because they were uncommon disturbers of the peace of mind of a majority of their fellow Americans.

Years ago I came to know and admire an old anarchist who operated a monthly periodical of decided opinions and who tacked to the masthead of his little journal a legend: "Discontent; Mother of Progress," it said. He contended that most if not all social progress stemmed from a person or a group of persons who for one reason or another were discontented, either with their own lot or with that of their fellows. He had it all worked out this way: Discontent mothered the American Revolution; and that event, together with similar upheavals before and after, freed minds that had grown sterile or timid from the dogmas and superstitions of the ages. It was gradually seen that man and his world *could* become perfect through man's own efforts. True, the Almighty had not been wholly dismissed from service, but His style had changed somewhat. He was now less a savage Old Testament worthy than a commonly well-disposed if erratic arranger of events to the end that heaven should help those who helped themselves. Many came to believe it possible to build a heaven here below—that is, if the "conjunctions of Providence" favored it. Deity was often referred to as Providence.

When at last the ancient barriers to thought gave way, great winds were released to fan embers of discontent. They swept over seventeenth-century Europe and England to cross the ocean and to mingle here with later winds which, one day soon or late, were to rise and blow back to Europe to some purpose.

In America these surging drafts set in motion an astonishing number of old men who dreamed dreams and young men who saw visions, even as predicted by Joel, a warranted prophet since biblical times. What was more, these latter-day prophets acted. Their efforts were as numerous as the goals they sought. Taken all together, they comprised what has been described variously as the age of reform, the rise of liberalism, the era of ferment, and the search for Utopia. Such was the anarchist editor's interpretation of matters. So far as I am concerned it is sound enough. It jibes pretty well with the more elaborate explanations of academic philosophers, though it may lack the gentility and verbosity of their prose.

The first American dreams of record were dreamed on little ships which crossed the stormy Atlantic, bearing passengers who could have been hardly aware that one day they would be remembered as pioneers; and the Mayflower Compact, though it was soon defied and rejected, is often regarded as the birth certificate of democracy.

The greatest American dream is outlined in the majestic periods of the Declaration of Independence and given substance by the Constitution. The ink was little more than dry when the latter document was seen to be imperfect, and it was promptly amended by ten articles called the Bill of Rights. It was then agreed that this was the proper working plan of the several states to form a more perfect union. Note the qualification of "more perfect." The glorious morning of Independence was revealing still more imperfections. Two additional amendments were needed by 1804; but sixty years were to pass before Article XIII was adopted. It abolished slavery.

Abolition was for five decades the first goal of the agitators of the age of reform. All other crusades operated on sufferance, though there were times when a visitor from abroad, or even a casual native observer, must have wondered whether the still more perfect union awaited the abolition of Negro slavery or merely destruction of the liquor trade. And on a still evening one might hear voices, female voices but far from plaintive, declaring that the *first* order of business, in the sight of God, was to bring to an end the "prolonged slavery of one-half of the human race," namely women.

The chattel slavery of the Negro, the "slavery" of woman, and the Viper in the Glass, here were the three menaces to be attacked in the era of fermentations. The first was to disappear only after a shooting war. (For arbitrary reasons this book will not deal with abolition.) The other two curses managed to last out the century and another two decades before, almost simultaneously, woman was "emancipated" and prohibition triumphed, technically.

These three major crusades by no means exhausted the ideas of our native dreamers, nor their restless energies. One and the same man could be an active abolitionist, his wife a woman's-rightser, and both carry the white banner of temperance, even while they had the tender heart and found the time to call attention to the plight of the deaf and dumb, the blind, the insane, and even the plight of convicted criminals. If so, they might be sneered at by tax-conscious citizens and called moony humanitarians, yet they would not be put in the category of the really dangerous fellows, who were those radicals that spoke up like churls for the non-existent rights of the workingman, or who proposed to monkey with the methods of public-land distribution. Such anarchists as questioned God's will in the matter of a workday from sunrise to sunset, or who would "interfere with property," were agents of Antichrist. Hanging was too mild a correction for them. These and other so-called lesser crusades were carried on simultaneously with the trio of major reforms, but were usually led by what one may consider specialists.

Then there was also a continuous seeking for perfection by a multitude of visionaries who are well if rather brutally described as cranks, crackpots, fanatics, and outright loons, all wanting the role of prophet and sometimes achieving it. These are the fringe characters. They are not in the main canon. A few of their dreams had the fatal quality of being starkly rational. More were obviously delirium. All of them added notably to the antic flavor of the time, and by their very noise and number tended to obscure the needed and substantial reform movements just getting under way. Let us sample briefly a few of these prophets of the fringe before getting on to the outstanding movers and shakers.

Ralph Waldo Emerson attended a fairly representative congress of dreamers in 1840, and heard their plans for the millennium. This was the well-publicized Chardon Street Convention, in Boston, called by the Friends of Universal Reform. Though it seems to have carried a heavy load of religious sectaries, the very title of this meeting is a measure of its infinite ambitions. The unofficial master of ceremonies was Amos Bronson Alcott, a lovable person given to mooning, either wholly incapable or merely uninterested in supporting his numerous family, which included a daughter, Louisa May, then eight years old; but he was the perfect man to chair a meeting like this on Chardon Street. Mr. Emerson thought the convention was as picturesque as it was disorderly. Among those present, he observed, were:

Madmen, mad-women, men with beards*, Dunkers, Muggletonians, Groaners, Agrarians, Seventh-Day Baptists, Quakers, Abolitionists, Calvinists, Unitarians, and Philosophers—all came successively to the top, and seized their moment, if not their hour, wherein to chide, or pray, or protest.

Emerson remarked on the great variety of garb and speech in the assembly, which was matched only by the general confusion and eccentricity of many of those taking part. But what struck him most of all was the "prophetic dignity" of speakers amid opposition and ridicule. These were the simon-pure dreamers whose minds were made up to obey only "the great inward Commander." The assembly was typical of the eagerness and fanaticism of the New England reformers of 1840, but Mr. Emerson by no means listed all or even half of the visions seen or the things desired. At that period such a gathering could have included many more. Perhaps the Sage of Concord included them in his categories of "Madmen and mad-women."

That is exactly what respectable people called John Humphrey Noyes and his Perfectionists, whom we have met, and Frances Wright and her Free-Enquirers, whom we shall come to meet. But where were the spokesmen of the Mormons and other new sects? Surely they were busy somewhere in the United States. So, on a lesser abstract level, were the disciples of Sylvester Graham, the whole-wheat man and vegetarian, who held meat eaters unfit to be members of society and unfit to enter the Kingdom of Heaven. It was only three years since Graham publicly damned the bakers of Boston for "adulterating" their product and called on housewives to make their own bread at home. For this he was set upon in the streets and beaten by the commercial bakers, and thus became a martyr to attract converts all over the country, Horace Greeley among them. The cultists who called themselves Grahamites have disappeared, and the founder's name survives chiefly in the cracker he devised as "the perfect diet."

Not even the name of the founder of Thomsonianism survives a century after his death. He was Samuel Thomson, the enemy of Epsom salts and calomel and bleeding, and for decades he harassed the conventional schools of medicine by "exposing" them as black magic and quackery. Calling himself the Botanic Man, he prescribed an herb,

---

* Though the original settlers and their immediate descendants were handsomely bearded, as later were all self-respecting generals in the Civil War, through the later eighteenth century and the first half of the nineteenth, beards were regarded as heretical, subversive, and eccentric, as, indeed, outside Greenwich Village, they are today. See the edifying chapter, "Chins of the Nation," in a book, *Cream Hill*, by Lewis Gannett, editor of the *Mainstream of American Series*.

lobelia inflata, as the sovereign remedy for virtually all ills, to be followed with a good stout dose of cayenne pepper, and possibly a few vapor baths. He somehow managed to patent this treatment. Thomsonian societies were formed in New England and throughout New York, Pennsylvania, and Midwestern states. These groups were licensed by Thomson, and seem to have been a sort of do-it-yourself plan; with a little instruction and advice from the local Thomsonian agent, the patient administered the therapy.

The conventional physicians, the sound calomel men, became so alarmed at the inroads of Thomson's practice that they fostered many lawsuits against him. Once he was charged with murder, and confined six weeks in jail, then cleared in a trial which served, in the eyes of thousands of his converts, to make him a first-class martyr "to the vile persecutions of the calomel men."

Today we dismiss Graham and Thomson and their followers as mere faddists. In 1840, however, they constituted more than what we think of as a fad. Cult is a better word because it is a stronger one, more fit to describe the almost religious fervor of Grahamites and Thomsonians. In that day Americans were given to whole-hog opinions in religion and all other matters. That their opinions were often subject to sudden change has nothing to do with the vehemence with which they were held, either for a year or a lifetime. In the forties, for instance, one of the most popular numbers of the Singing Hutchinsons, New Hampshire's lyrical gift to the United States, was entitled *Anti-Calomel*:

> *And when I must resign my breath,*
> *Pray let me die a natural death,*
> *And bid the world a long farewell*
> *Without one dose of Cal-o-mel.*

To the Thomsonians it was a war cry, a fighting song against the damnable dispensers of drugs. In that time, too, even the two conventional schools of medicine were as bitterly opposed to one another as were the Whigs and Democrats. Not only the doctors themselves but their patients too. Allopath and homeopath could be libelous terms. The heritage of those opinionated times was to be seen sixty and more years later, at least in many New England villages, where boys got bloody noses in arguments over family physicians, while persecution was sometimes the lot of the children of Christian Scientists.

There are whole libraries of forgotten books dealing with nothing but this period of ferment typified by the Chardon Street congress of freaks, cranks, and visionaries, where the great inward Commander of Emerson's phrase helped to give substance to this or that cherished dream. The dream that failed to achieve substance did not fail for lack of mighty effort. The competition was savage. These were stalwart fellows. The moment a man revealed a vision, he was set upon by a dozen other seers, to beat him down as a false prophet. The survivors were certain to know they had been in a fight, and often bore the scars of sore battle.

Henry Thoreau, himself something of an oddity, professed to abhor reformers. They rubbed him continually "with the greasy cheeks of their kindness." He wanted them "to smooth out the ogling wrinkles of benignity about their eyes," and to say something in a forthright manner. Possibly that is why he excepted John Brown of Osawatamie. Old Brown might be the most lunatic reformer in the country, but he was a *forthright* lunatic.

The Quaker poet Whittier welcomed nearly all men who dreamed dreams. Longfellow, by the very nature of being a poet, must have been a dreamer, yet his dreams never got the least out of hand, as Whittier's did. It is more than possible that Longfellow thought most reformers crazy. He recognized, however, the "divine insanity of noble minds," and wrote that if such a mind could not find what it sought, then it created what it was seeking. That was exactly what several of Longfellow's friends and associates were doing at West Roxbury, a suburb of Boston, where George Ripley and kindred noble minds, including Nathaniel Hawthorne and Charles A. Dana, established the Brook Farm Phalanx, an experiment in plain living and high thinking to prove that the artificialities of conventional family life were ruinous to civilization.

The Brook Farm plan, the way they explained it, involved a practical reconciliation of labor, capital, and culture, by mutual participation in toil and its results. It worked out differently. If Brook Farm proved anything of a practical nature, it was that the milking of cows and the pitching of hay were less favored than the discussion of essays in the Dial, edited by Brook Farmer Margaret Fuller and Mr. Emerson, no Brook Farmer though friendly to all experiments.

Possibly to aid the self-delusion that they *were* farmers, and not just out for a picnic, the Brook Farmer men wore peasant blouses, belted at the waist in the European manner. The women appeared in muslin dresses, complete with flowers and ribbons; or sometimes in gay calico. The division of labor was on the elaborate plan of Charles Fourier, the noted French dreamer, which regimented members into the Farming Series, the Domestic Series, and so forth. These were subdivided and refined into the Cattle Group, the Milking Group, the Plowing Group; the Nursery Group, the Culinary Group. (It seems worth knowing that the Brook Farm dining room had a Graham Table.)

One is prepared to accept the observation of a visitor that this cumbersome machinery of government greatly interferred with Brook Farm's efficiency. Bronson Alcott thought so too, and, further, he said that Brook Farm was not sufficiently ideal. But *he* knew how to operate a community that would fetch the millennium. First, he talked an English immigrant named Charles Lane into buying one hundred acres of farming land and an old house in Harvard town, some thirty miles from Boston. Alcott moved his own family there, and with Lane announced establishment of Fruitlands Community. Fruitlands was to achieve a record: Of all the many communal experiments in living during the period it was to be the shortest-lived. It lasted, after a fashion, six months.

In a way, however, Fruitlands was valuable, in that it showed what could be done when a genuine, thoroughgoing idealist put his hand to it. Alcott set the rules for what he said was the Con-Sociate Family. The place was strictly vegetarian, and more—the eating of not only fish, flesh, and fowl was forbidden, but also butter, eggs, milk, and cheese. So were coffee, tea, and molasses—a product of slavery—and any food at all not grown on community land.

One is not to suppose these Spartan precepts were quite all of old Alcott's plans. Leather could not be used because some poor animal died to produce it. Slavery prohibited cotton products, but right in neighboring Connecticut, Ward Cheney and his brothers were even then raising a variety of mulberry on which silkworms seemed to flourish. By next summer the Con-Sociate Family should dress in silk. Working the silkworms seemed all right to Alcott, but working horses and oxen was somehow wrong. Hence, plowing was to be dispensed with. The men of Fruitlands would return to the spade.

As the men of Fruitlands scratched and dug and prepared to plant their first crops, still another idea occurred to Alcott; they would plant only what he called "aspiring vegetables," meaning those which grow upward, as opposed to the degraded forms which "burrow in the earth." And now, with everything properly planned, the crops of this first and last year of Fruitlands were planted. They were planted too late in the season, and carelessly planted at that.

Well, the crops were in. It was now time to rest from the heat of the day and to cultivate the mind. Alcott babbled on through the hot growing weather, delivering his Orphic Sayings to his half-dozen disciples. Nobody bothered to do any weeding. Then, just before harvest and with the timing of genius, the master led partner Lane and the common hands on a thirty-mile walk to attend a lecture in Boston. It was now September. Those aspiring vegetables and grains were ripening fast at Fruitlands; but it was dandy weather for visiting around, and

Alcott thought it would be a mighty good time to see how Brook Farm was doing. So away they went to West Roxbury, and from there took off a few days later to observe conditions in the Hopedale and the Northampton community experiments. Alcott pronounced all of these places "wholly unideal," then the idealists of Fruitlands at last turned their steps homeward, just possibly noticing the frosts of early morning.

The returning philosophers, still babbling about the lack of idealism at Brook Farm, Hopedale, and Northampton, may have detected a little frost in the greeting of Mrs. Alcott. She had been left in complete charge of the harvest. Her crew of field hands consisted of her daughters Anna, age thirteen, Louisa, twelve, Elizabeth, seven, and infant Abba May. (That all had survived, even though half starved, indicated they were of resistant stock.) After several frosts came a real howler of a storm. The desperate woman led her children into the field, to pick and sickle as best they could, then she harnessed her small helpers to clothes-baskets and linen sheets to haul to cover the crops of Fruitlands.

Even to a woman accustomed to hard work and poverty this harvest alone in the chill downpour and wild winds, driving her under-nourished children like slaves, lest there be nothing to eat at all, was to turn the long-suffering Mrs. Alcott into something of a rebel. It was just about this time she wrote in her journal that "a woman may live a whole life of sacrifice, and at her death meekly say, 'I die a woman.' A man passes a few years in experiments of self-denial and simple life, and he says 'Behold a God!' "

The "harvest" finished Fruitlands. Partner Lane moved in with the Shakers at nearby Shirley. They lived simply enough, though, compared to that of Fruitlands, their fare was Lucullan. The other Fruitlanders had already wandered off. Only the Alcotts remained, living chiefly on the barley which Mrs. Alcott and progeny had rescued from the fury of the autumnal line storm. Friends hearing of their plight came and took them to live briefly in Still River, from which the kindly Emerson moved them to Concord, where they lived, often on Emerson's bounty, until years later Louisa May hit her stride as the author of *Little Women*. Old Bronson chattered on for another twenty years, well fed now and clothed, but pointed out, if at all, not as the Orphic Oracle but as the "grandfather" of *Little Women*. Louisa May remained always what Bronson called her, Duty's Child, and he died in her house on Louisburg Square, in Boston, doubtless without dreaming that generations who never heard his name would make American classics of his daughter's books.

If any scars remained from the dreadful year at Fruitlands, Louisa May got rid of them in *Transcendental Wild Oats*, an essay in the form of fiction, patently based on the Con-Sociate Family and which, for all its broad touches of comedy, contains satiric observations. "At about the time the grain was ready," wrote Louisa, "some call of the oversoul wafted all the men away."

One after the other the many communal-living experiments of the forties bloomed, faded, and disappeared within from three to half a dozen years, though the North American Phalanx of New Jersey survived more than a decade and the Wisconsin Phalanx almost as long. These and many of the others were Fourier-type groups, similar to Brook Farm and Northampton. There were also religious sects like the Rappite-Harmonists, the Separatists of Zoar, the Bethel-Aurora Germans, and of course the Shakers and the Mormons, which were basically not experiments in living but were communities for self-protection against the Gentiles and all other outsiders. Then, at the far pole from these and all other communities, religious or not, was Modern Times, two hundred acres of scrub oak on Long Island, where nothing counted except the individual, who was the Supreme Law Unto Himself.

This resounding declaration of total anarchism was made by Josiah Warren, the first anarchist in the United States, who arrived at that lonely eminence after twenty-five years of watching or taking part in more collapsed "co-operative efforts" than he cared to remember. Modern Times would demonstrate the romantic futilities of such dilettante efforts. Modern Times was the place where each individual was a sovereign, free to differ from every other individual in thought, feeling, word and deed—aye, free to differ from himself, and to change from time to time as it pleased him.

In 1851 when he issued this manifesto, Josiah Warren was fifty-three years old. Boston-born of a family which included General Joseph Warren, who fell at Bunker Hill, Josiah was a short, thickset man with a large forehead and a pair of the most restless bright blue eyes that ever peered reproachfully on the imbecilities of Man. Among his several occupations had been those of printer, inventor, musician, and successful manufacturer of a lard-burning lamp. If he had a weakness it was for the French horn, with which he liked to relax either singly or in company, and only seldom permitted to interfere with his stated mission, which was to make governments, including that of the United States, obsolete, not by the bloody upheavals such as usually accompanied revolutions but by gradual education. Warren was as gentle a person as you'd find. He called himself the "Peaceful Revolutionist." When his good-natured revolution had been accomplished, the governmental apparatus was to rest in what today could be described by a group of experts, a sort of brain trust with technocratic authority.

But the very first thing to be done was to destroy the great obstacle, which was conventional money, and to substitute for this root of evil "the equitable commerce of labor exchange."

Josiah Warren may well have been an original thinker, but he was a dismally poor propagandist. He was far from eloquent on the platform. His writing was clear exposition but of little appeal to a public that thought in terms of gold and silver. His dream of a lifetime was attracting no attention whatever until he made a convert, Stephen Pearl Andrews, who at forty was the reputed master of thirty-two languages, including Hebrew, Sanskrit, and Chinese, and who even then was at work on an international language he called Alwato, a precursor of the much-later Volapuk and Esperanto.

If Alwato alone did not make him a fit spokesman for Warren and Modern Times, it is well to know Andrews was planning, as soon as he had polished up a few details, to announce a major job which he had named universology. This, said he, was a deductive science of the universe. Coupled with Warren's operating ideas, this new world would produce the ideal, the perfect society. Andrews even had a name for it, Pantarchy. He seemed not to mind when the press began referring to him as The Pantarch.

Putting all or even any of these plans into operation might seem to have been a formidable task. They did not appear so to Josiah Warren and Stephen Pearl Andrews. For reasons no longer clear the two prophets chose a wild spot on the Long Island Rail Road to establish world headquarters (Modern Times was near present Brentwood). Here Warren set up what one thinks of as Exhibit A. This was a Time Store to demonstrate his equitable commerce of labor exchange. The shelves and the goods looked like those in any country store. But displayed prominently on a bulletin board were the wholesalers' bills showing what Warren had paid for his merchandise; and, conspicuous on the wall, facing the customer like a presiding deity, was an immense open-face clock, beneath it a dial. It should be mentioned that all goods were marked to show their exact cost to the storekeeper.

A customer enters. As soon as he makes contact with the clerk, the clerk sets the dial under the clock to mark the time, then he waits on the customer. When the business is finished, the customer pays cash equal to the wholesale cost of the article purchased; then the clerk marks on the customer's Labor Note the time the clerk spent in making the sale. The plan was that all customers, all storekeepers, in fact everybody, would eventually have a Labor Note with him. The barter of labor-time would take the place of money. Thus was the fatal profit motive to be eliminated. Simple enough. Or, was it simple? In any case, the Time Store seemed to prove something or other to the small group of incurable idealists who bought, at cost plus a little time on the Labor Notes, the one-acre lots of Modern Times. These real estate transactions were really Single-tax operations thirty years before Henry George, whom we shall come to later.

Even so, there was at first no marked rush to move into the first anarchist community in the United States; and Warren spent many hours blowing away on his beloved French horn, which appears to have been his only vice. But Pantarch Andrews was in far greater haste than Warren to bring on the Peaceful Revolution. He busied himself with the press, and one day the New York *Tribune* ran a story about Modern Times in which Warren was quoted to the effect that life there was a free-and-easy affair, that it had no laws or bylaws, no rules or regulations except such as each individual made for himself, and these were his own business.

The results were sudden, remarkable, and probably inevitable. It was as if a powerful magnet had reached up above the scrub oaks of Modern Times. Foot-loose cranks and fanatics, plus a variety of congenital chasers after swamp fires, arrived by buggy and railroad, ready to trade at the Time Store and just as ready to lend an ear to any other idea that might speed the millennium, or be merely good fun.

Among the practically numberless ideas of Pantarch Andrews was that holy wedlock was somehow an obstacle preventing the general spread of Time Stores and the coming of Pantarchy. It was not very long before a census of Modern Times could have revealed a number of domestic arrangements of an unconventional nature, including one rather boisterous ménage composed of one man and three young women. Warren did not approve of such goings-on, which he thought were irrational and tended to promiscuity, which, in turn, guaranteed diseases resulting to damage to the race. But Andrews was a dedicated antiwedlock man, and so were at least two of his friends who presently arrived in Modern Times.

Thomas Low Nichols and his perfectly legal wife Mary had already made their pitch as reformers in a number of states. They were hydrotherapists, or water-cure physicians. They were aggressive exponents of Sylvester Graham, the vegetarian and unbolted-flour man. They seem also to have been part-time spiritualists and full-time speakers-up for free love. On arrival in Modern Times they announced a campaign for funds to establish a radically new type of educational institution to be called Desarollio, or Unfoldment. Just what was to be unfolded seems not of record, though rumor got around that it had to do with trial marriage. This was sufficient to get the drive for funds off to a good start; and workmen, possibly with Labor Notes in their pockets, were soon at the site laying a concrete wall. And there construction ceased. So, after a little, did the Time Store and with it all activities to bring Pantarchy. The community of Modern Times was gradually obliterated in a real estate development which surives as Brentwood-in-the-Pines.

2.

SCIENCE FAILS IDEALISM

IF the founders of Modern Times, of Brook Farm, Hopedale, and all of the other experiments in communal living had not been so completely wrapped up in their projects, they might have saved themselves much trouble—possibly—by consulting Orson Squire Fowler, called the Prince of Phrenology because of his incomparable eminence in the new and allegedly scientific method of rating the mental faculties and traits of character of human beings. Phrenology was a recent import from Germany, where it was credited to Franz Joseph Gall, a noted physician. Learned men have described it as "an empirical system of psychology." The practitioner examined the cranium for certain protuberances which, according to their location, denoted the subject to be endowed with large or small amounts of thirty-five qualities, such as Idealism, Combativeness, Individuality, Acquisitiveness, even Wit and Wonder, and a good mouth-filling Philoprogenitiveness.

With a science like this at his fingertips, phrenologist Fowler could have performed a screening operation of the greatest value in selecting or rejecting one's associates; and indeed he and his fellow phrenologists were said to have had considerable influence in the appraisal of candidates for political office, for special education, even for careers or occupations. Still, Fowler probably could have done little to dent the armor of case-hardened optimisn which protected the founders of consecrated or patented communities.

There were those who said unkindly of Fowler that he went into the phrenology business to make money. Others were to say unkindly that Fowler's good friend and classmate at Amherst College, who was Henry Ward Beecher, went into the preaching business to make money. Infinitely larger numbers of Americans, however, believed these men to be geniuses, each in his way dedicated to the enlightenment and improvement of the world. Behind Beecher stood the authority of God Almighty, while Fowler was operating in the august name of science, a word only recently endowed with all the qualities of what in earlier times was called magic.

Fowler's exposure to phrenology had come about when as a college youth he attended a lecture in Boston given by an eloquent pupil of Dr. Gall, a sort of period Dr. Freud. He came away fired with this new science and in his possession a chart of the cranium properly staked out in the thirty-five officially recognized divisions. He began at once to operate on the skulls of Amherst undergraduates, reading their bumps at two cents a head. Then, with Beecher, the two young men lectured in nearby towns to excellent audiences. The interest in phrenology was remarkable.

Upon graduation Beecher left to begin his ordained career in the ministry; Fowler took off for New York City, where on Nassau Street he started the professional practice of phrenology. He wrote a book on the science which sold enormously and was to go through sixty-two printings. Other books followed. All of them sold well, including *Fowler on Memory*, seventy years before the pervasive if fictional "Addison Sims of Seattle" began warning people to "train your memory as you would train your muscle."

For much of four decades Fowler wrote, taught, and lectured on phrenology. He issued almanacs and periodicals on the subject. He grew well-to-do. Lest the new science pall on him, he branched out to become an authority on the trait designated on the chart under style of "1. Amativeness," and wrote books about *Love and Parentage* and *Fowler on Matrimony*. As if to prove his special fitness to discuss these matters he married three times.

Then, at the height of his staggering success with phrenology, Fowler paused long enough to set people right in the field of domestic architecture by writing another book, *A Home for All; or, the Gravel Wall, and Octagon Mode of Building*. This was the work, rather than his volumes on phrenology and eugenics, which was to leave fairly permanent monuments to Fowler scattered throughout the Northeastern United States. No man to substitute the word for the deed, Fowler's book was hardly off the press and selling by the thousands of copies before he started construction of a scientific abode which would put the finest mansions in the country in the class of caves and wigwams.

The building material of the millennial house was a mixture of cement, small stones, and sand known as gravel wall, or grout. But the science, which was to say the magic, of the dwelling lay in its form. A sphere, argued Fowler, like many an architect a century later, was the most beautiful form of all. It also enclosed the most space in the least material. Since the octagonal was the practical form nearest to the sphere, it should be adopted. Why? Because the eight sides permitted more receptivity of sunlight. Because the shape also eliminated the dark and useless square corners of conventional houses. And, behold—it decreased the distances between objects in the home because the residents could go directly to them without going around the ugly, non-esthetic angles. Here was science enough to attract the forward thinkers of the day; and once the timid had seen with their own eyes the beauty and convenience of the octagon mode, they could no longer remain content in thrall of antiquated architecture.

Orson Fowler was no halfway man. His own octagonal dwelling was to be no mere mock-up or hurriedly built sample. Erected on an oval knoll near the village of Fishkill on the Hudson River, it was a behemoth of houses, five octagonal stories through which rose a central stair well crowned by a glass-roofed cupola a good eighty feet from the ground. It contained "nearly one hundred rooms," and turned out to be so costly that Fowler was obliged on several occasions to take to the road lecturing to obtain more funds. Long before it was finished, some smart aleck observed in the newspapers that Fowler was no originator, but a copycat, as witness The Octagon in Washington, D.C., designed in 1800 by William Thornton and whose most famous occupant was President Madison, who moved in for a stay after the burning of the White House by the British in 1814. (It was still standing in 1957 and used as headquarters of the American Institute of Architects.)

The ink of this smug sneer was still damp on the paper when Fowler responded as quickly as an offended rattlesnake. Yes, he knew about the structure in Washington that was erroneously referred to by ignorant persons as The Octagon. He suggested that people of clear vision who could count up to six would find it a hexagon; and that if his would-be critics did not know what a hexagon was, they damn well could look it up in the dictionary. Fowler was right enough. Nothing more was said about his lack of originality.

While his own monstrous house was under construction, Fowler's converts were busy erecting family-size octagonals. Carl Carmer, who for many years has lived in a hardy survivor of the Fowler era, has written that the most active years of the fad were from 1850 through 1853, during which "nearly every community in northeastern United States" had at least one ardent follower of the Master who was rearing an eight-sided dwelling with rooms shaped like pieces of pie. It was "scientific." That is what fetched them. Octagonal schoolhouses went up because Fowler said they provided better light, more sociability, and had acoustics superior to those of a square room, where "right angles break the sound and create echoes"; new churches followed the plan, which "facilitated the congregation seeing one another and thereby the interchange of friendly and benevolent feelings." A stagecoach company built an enormous octagonal horse barn. The spiritualist colony at Lily Dale in western New York built an octagonal séance chamber.

That Orson Fowler was honored in his own bailiwick is still clear in the Hudson River Valley, where, so reports Mr. Carmer, in addition to his own dwelling at Fishkill, there are two octagonal homes in Stockport, and octagonal public libraries in Red Hook and Kingston. Other relics still ornament the landscape all the way west to Akron, not far from Buffalo; and in New England they can be found from St. Johnsbury in northern Vermont to Danbury in southwestern Connecticut.

At last, in 1858, the great octagonal of the master builder was finished. So was the fad, for it turned out to be a fad. Some had found octagonals good, more did not. It was much the same with the science of phrenology. Indeed, Orson Fowler's scientific world fell to pieces with shocking speed. Slow-moving men of science finally made up their minds and leaped at phrenology with blunt and pointed weapons and destroyed it, save as a side show for circuses and carnivals. Tragedy visited Fowler's monster at Fishkill when the scientific grout walls allowed seepage from the cesspool to the well. Typhoid did the rest. Fowler sold the house, which was sold again and resold thirty times more within the next few years, during which it became a boys' school, then a boardinghouse, and in 1897 it was ordered to be dynamited as a public danger by town authorities.

Poor old Fowler lived on in a world turned upside down. Discredited as architect, and his once-great audience no longer interested in phrenology, he died forgotten. One is happy to know, however, that long before he died prophet Fowler had the satisfaction of knowing that the magic, or science, of octagonal shape and form had crossed the Mississippi River to establish an outpost in the distant Territory of Kansas.

It seems improbable that a finer example of yeasty optimism could be found than that of an emigrant party incorporated as the Vegetarian Settlement Company, who went to found nothing less than Octagon City. The very style of those titles indicated that here were bold exponents not only of Sylvester Graham but of Orson Squire Fowler to boot. This splendid combination of two nightmares was the work of Henry Stephen Clubb, whose stated ambition was to erect in the center of the United States a permanent home for Vegetarians, a font from which should flow beneficent influences to make all Americans worthy of their great destiny.

Though vegetarianism was his first and greatest love, Mr. Clubb was no monomaniac, and his vegetarian metropolis was to be laid out on the octagon plan, which, said he, was for several reasons the only sensible way "to commence a city." Note that the science of the octagon was here to be applied not merely to construction but, one might say, to geography. It may also be said of Mr. Clubb that he was a man who went to the grass roots of things. It did not matter to him that the townships, sections, and quarter sections of Kansas and of Western United States were being laid out in quadrangles. Mr. Clubb set *his* surveyors to running lines for four Octagon Villages which, in turn, would form Octagon City, a plat of sixteen square miles with an octagonal green of 584 acres, in the middle of which was to be established, so said Mr. Clubb with the assurance of prophecy, an agricultural college and model farm.

If prospective settlers did not immediately grasp the significance of his possibly complicated plan, Mr. Clubb was ready to enlighten them. At this point it might be best to ask readers to accept the plan as explained, if not exactly clarified, by Mr. Clubb himself. One must paraphrase him somewhat, for he was a thorough man, but here in brief is what he told his audience about the advantages of octagons in matters relating to agriculture, civic planning, and moral improvement:

To begin with, every settler would thus live in a village, and at the same time be in the best possible situation on his farm—fair between pasture land in front and arable land in the rear of his dwelling and barn. Consider, please, the social habits of improvement of such proximity; they were evident. And pray reflect that in isolation men become indifferent to the refinements of civilized society. Why, sirs, they may sink into barbarism. But living in these four Octagon Villages, as part of great Octagon City, would cause emulation to excel in the arts of domestic and social life. The outcome could not be otherwise than a vast elevating influence of moral and mental cultivation.

Then, as if it were an afterthought, the thoughtful Mr. Clubb mentioned still another reason for adapting Orson Fowler's floor plan to the scientific arrangement of a city. With an eye to the chance that even vegetarians had speculative faculties, he spoke of "the pecuniary advantages of the Octagonal Plan which arise from the fact that the foundation of a village "always increases the value of the land all around."

No land in all the Octagon City development would be sold except to those who voluntarily signed a pledge to abstain from liquor, tobacco, and the flesh of animals. To such, however, land was offered at $1.25 an acre, or about the same price charged for wild lands elsewhere. One learned as much, and more, from the most attractive literature of the Vegetarian Settlement Company, which early in 1856 reported stock subscriptions to have passed $30,000, while the private capital of members, many of whom appeared to be already on the ground, totaled more than $100,000. It seemed, too, from a reading of the latest bulletin, that the immense and gorgeous Central Octagon Building, doubtless constructed of Fowler's favorite grout, was ready to welcome new arrivals. Vegetarian sawmills and gristmills were reported as "about to commence."

Up in New England, down in New York, west to Indiana, the call was heard, clear and seductive, and out of these meat-eating hells began a trek of vegetarians. (*Hasten you lovers of carrots, you eaters of unbolted grain! The rich land of Kansas awaits the seed. Hasten, flee beyond the fumes of nicotine, beyond the stench of Rum, to where the fine barns will stand back to back and the husbandmen look forth to contemplate the ever widening pie-shaped fields until they are lost on the horizon, not of Jordan but of the Neosho River of southeastern Kansas . . . Hasten now! In autumn ye shall have the fullness of the unbolted wheat . . .*)

Only one member of the Vegetarian Settlement Company seems to have published a memoir. It is a document to shake the most dedicated idealist. The memoirist was Mrs. Miriam Davis Colt of Lyme, New Hampshire; and, though obviously and understandingly numbed by her dreadful experience, she managed to set down a narrative which, if it were widely read, must instantly have halted all emigration to the octtagon-vegetarian region along the Neosho River. The Colts arrived there on May 13, 1856, straining their eyes to catch sight of the majestic Central Octagon House, the receiving station. It turned out to be a modest cabin, hardly a lean-to for the big old houses back in Lyme, New Hampshire. No other structure was in view. There was no sawmill whining away at boards, beams, and two-by-fours. There was no gristmill, thumping out unbolted grain. As far as the eye could reach stretched the prairie—stark, lonely, illimitable, in some way sinister to people used to hills and valleys. But good Mr. Clubb was there, and on the Sabbath he preached an excellent sermon.

How many settlers had already come Mrs. Colt does not say, but of those who came later all went quickly away. The Colts were of sterner stuff. They stayed the summer, plowing and planting during lulls between terrible storms and the hellish heat, which alternated with prairie fires, with clouds of flies and mosquitoes, with searing winds, with winds that froze the blood. In spite of the healthful vegetarian diet, which did not include potatoes because they cost four dollars a bushel, there was much illness. By September the Colts had had enough. A great weariness lay heavy upon their once-stout hearts. The mirage of proper living had been blown away. On their halting way back to non-vegetarian New England, Mrs. Colt's husband and a son were stricken fatally with fever.

I do not believe the Octagon City venture was a mere land-selling scheme. Poor Mrs. Colt charged Mr. Clubb and his associates with nothing morally worse than poor judgment and bad management. Mr. Clubb was no charlatan. The affair has all the ripe stigmata of the mad, earnest, humorless idealism of the period. I have cited it, along with several other efforts that never got anywhere, to show the ebullient assurance, the temper of the times, to indicate the variety of innovations dreamed up in nineteenth-century America.

I am quite prepared to believe that every last one of them, no matter how quaint or loony they appear now, was the dream of an honest man who wanted to make the world a better place for himself, his contemporaries, and those who came after. He was working, even in his maddest moments, to improve and embellish the United States until it should actually become what the Founding Fathers, our greatest of all dreamers, envisioned for it, namely a country as near perfection as anything this side of the veritable Kingdom. . . .

We cannot judge dreamers of this American dream as we judge merchants, or soldiers, or statesmen, or other pragmatic men merely by their success or failure. A splendid failure to achieve what after all may be the impossible is worth notice, even if only because it proved the wrong road was taken. Perhaps there wasn't, and isn't, any right road to the perfections sought. I happen to believe that the most magnificent failure of all our dreamers was that of John Humphrey Noyes, who wanted only to change human nature. . . . Let us now get on the men and women of lesser visions whose prodigious efforts either failed or succeeded, according to how one feels about them, but in some degree had influence on the lives of all of us who came after.

Part Three

THE VIPER IN THE GLASS

1.

THERE WAS A TAVERN IN THE TOWN . . .

A T about the time Oneida Community was being established, a
a major interest of reformers in the United States was that called
temperance. The name was a euphemism. There was really nothing temperate about temperance. It had come to mean total abstinence
from alcohol.

Liquor was never a problem at Oneida, and John Humphrey Noyes
was no abstainer. He seems not to have been more than casually interested in the swiftly rising sentiment against alcohol. It is reasonable
to assume he considered it a minor thing compared to the gigantic task
he had set for himself. Let others talk against the wine cup, against
seegars and tobacco, against calomel and other drugs; let them preach
Armageddon, and the end of time; let them care for orphans and the
poor, let them reform the tariff, the banks, even the currency. All these
things might be good, but they were of secondary importance to organizing the perfect society. When men and women learned to mate properly
in order to produce healthy and intelligent offspring, then these lesser
matters could be considered. That is, if they had not already disappeared.

No, Rum was not the great enemy. Indeed, in the very year when
Vermont voted to prohibit traffic in liquor for beverage purposes, Noyes
wrote in his Perfectionist paper at Putney that there was no reason
whatever why drinking should be restrained by law. He was no more an
anarchist than he was a teetotaler. He simply believed that education
rather than law was the proper way to accomplish reforms.

One of Noyes's distinguished contemporaries, however, had come
to the belief that education alone could not cope with the "all but universal vice of drunkenness." He was the Reverend Lyman Abbott, no
fanatic in liquor or other matters. A Congregational minister so "liberal"
as often to be called a deist, he was also one of the most effective
journalists of the time. His discussions of the abuse of rum were
astonishingly rational for the period. In them one finds no frantic rant-
ings, no hyperbole, but a calm consideration.

As a historian of alcohol as a beverage, Lyman Abbott remarked
that, though the vice of drunkenness had existed even in the time of
Noah, a distinction should be made between the fermented liquors of

that and later eras and "the distilled liquors of our own time." He
thought that the drunkenness of "the worst of the Roman debauchees"
did not produce "the maddening influence" of gin, rum, brandy, whiskey,
and other products of the still. "The epoch of drunkenness as an
epidemic," said he, "dates from the close of the seventeenth century
when the dangerous and deadly art of distillation came into general
use in England." Though at first the strong waters of stills were believed
to be a specific for the plague, they speedily became general as a
medicine, then as a stimulant and beverage. From that time on, said
historian Abbott, hard drinking was a national habit, "the vice of all
classes of society from the highest to the lowest"; and he paused to
reflect how "the medicine orginally prescribed for the plague had proved
worse than the disease." By then a writer in London had already
published a work of which the style was a promise of temperance literature to come, not only in England but in the United States. This pioneer
work was entitled *The Odious, Despicable, and Dreadful Condition of
a Drunkard.*

No matter how odious and dreadful, drunkenness continued for
many years to be considered little more than a mild social vice both
in the British Isles and the United States. Beer and spirits came to New
England with the first arrivals, and so, too, did the ironic term still
used three hundred years later to describe the secret misappropriation
of liquors in storage or transit. In 1630, according to William Bradford,
a consignment of two hogsheads of mead for the colonists was found to
contain no more than six gallons, the remainder, or some one hundred
gallons, "being drunke up under ye name of leackage and so lost."

As the long-time governor at Plymouth, Bradford was no enemy of
strong drink save when it interfered with duty. He was scandalized to
see soldiers "so steeld with drinke as their peeces were too heavie for
them"; and two decades after the colony was founded he complained of
drunkenness on the part of several of his people. Yet, the abuse of
spirits was not his great worry. What floored him, and caused him "to
fear & tremble at the consideration of our corrupte natures," was the
breaking out of "incontinence betweene persons unmarried . . . and some
married persons allso." He reported, too, of sexual aberrations, "things
fearfull to name," and wondered if human nature might not be the
same as waters dammed up, that, when it did find passage, it flowed with
violence. It troubled him that wickedness, being stopped by strict laws,
searches everywhere and "breaks out wher it getts vente."

It is significant that in his *History of Plimmoth Plantation* Bradford
dismisses drunkenness with a few lines and devotes no less than nineteen
pages, much of it set in fine print, to licentiousness. John Humphrey

Noyes would have understood. Let the reform of liquor habits await the transformation of Adam and Eve into rational beings.

One of the first protests against "the flood of Rum" that was inundating New England was made in 1673 by Increase Mather of Massachusetts Bay Colony. He feared it would "drown Christianity" because its use brought a reveling and loose conduct and thus tended to keep people away from the meetinghouse. Mather did not mention anything like abstinence, but merely urged a more rigid enforcement of the laws regulating taverns. Little or no heed was paid to him. Distilleries were in operation throughout the region, and presently comprised the largest and most profitable industry in Massachusetts and Rhode Island, to supply not only the taverns, which multiplied most fearfully, but also the slave trade. Here in this blackhearted business one can see the benefits of mass production in regard to lower costs. The first dealers on the African slave coast were glad to sell a prime Negro for six gallons of rum. Later, as rum became plentiful, the price of a slave rose to more than two hundred gallons. By then the manufacture of rum for the slave trade became unprofitable, and was discontinued.

Yet, the industry was supported by heroic consumers right at home and in other colonies, and it expanded. Drunkenness was regarded as an amiable weakness. The clergy, far from attacking rum, did much to encourage its use. Ordinations, dedications, and other functions of the church were warmed by wine, beer, gin, and rum provided by the parish treasury. In their contracts with laborers farmers agreed to supply them with stipulated measures of strong drink. In Boston, New York, Philadelphia, and Baltimore there soon grew a custom of closing offices and business establishments each workday at eleven o'clock in the morning, so all hands might go out and get a fast one called Leven O'Clock Bitters, a sort of pre-Revolution coffee break.

During this period of the eighteenth century the laws of some of the colonies still mentioned rum as "the good creature of God," but not so in Georgia. Governor James Oglethorpe favored only the use of beer and, to aid establishment of a local brewing industry, he granted each settler forty-four gallons of beer plus sixty-five gallons of molasses to be used for the brewing of more beer. He also warned that the manufacture of ardent spirits was prohibited, and none was to be imported. Whereupon the cranky settlers emphasized the freedom of the New World by turning their molasses into rum. The distillers of Carolina were quick to help out, and within a short time the Georgia colonists were awash with strong drink.

Oglethorpe appealed to the trustees of the colony in London, reporting that the health of his people was being wrecked by the excessive drinking of rum punch. The trustees acted, and in 1734 Parliament passed an act prohibiting the "importation of rum and brandies" into Georgia. At once there developed in the colony a condition not unlike that which faced the United States almost two hundred years later. The settlers felt put-upon to the extent that they neglected their affairs and devoted themselves to showing who was running things down in Georgia. What may well have been the first moonshine stills in North America were soon steaming and bubbling all over the back country of Georgia, making rum for local consumption. Rumrunners started unloading cargoes of rum and brandy from Carolina, and were met by armed and organized gangs who moved the product on foot and on horseback from the lonely coast to points nearer the waiting customers. What were not called speak-easies but performed the same services began operating in cabins on the fringes of settlements and in the back rooms of business houses in the larger towns. The few violators who were caught demanded trial by jury, and were promptly freed. After seven years the trustees were sick of the farce. The importation of ardent spirits was permitted, along with a system of licenses for taverns.

New York City was, of course, safely awash with drink from the earliest times. So, in spite of stiffer regulations, was Philadelphia, where a grand jury whose foreman was Benjamin Franklin, was of the opinion that both the poor and the use of profanity were increasing owing largely to the swarming taverns and plain tippling houses. And Boston was holding its own in the "drinking of drams, flip and toddy, & carousing and swearing." John Adams himself said as much. He also tried to do something about it. Fifty-three years later he recalled that he had been early "fired with a zeal against ardent spirits, and the multiplication of taverns, retailers and dram shops ... and grieved to the heart to see the number of idlers, thieves, sots and consumptive patients ... in those infamous seminaries"; and that he had "forthwith applied to the Court of Sessions to reduce the number of licensed houses." But Adams "only acquired the reputation of a hypocrite and an ambitious demagog." The number of groggeries was not diminished, nor was the taking of drams. "You might as well," said he who by then was a past president of the United States, "you might as well preach to the Indians against rum as to our own people." He washed his hands of the whole business, and in a parting shot remarked that it was in the taverns where "diseases, vicious habits, bastards and legislators are frequently begotten."

Late in the eighteenth century the universal drink of rum met its first serious competitor. This was whiskey distilled in western Pennsylvania. It did not immediately dislodge rum as the favorite in New England and New York, but its sales began to climb and by 1794, when the federal government imposed a tax of nine cents a gallon on all distilled spirits, western Pennsylvania rose almost to a man and staged what went into history as the Whiskey Insurrection. Whiskey was here to stay. The old diehards, the aging men who still wore small clothes and tricorn hats, might stick to rum; the new generations of drinkers took to whiskey.

During the war of the Revolution, the Continental Congress passed a resolution—not an act—that called attention to "the pernicious practice of distilling grain," which meant whiskey, and intimated that perhaps it should be stopped. This may have been a sort of trial ballon, to see if the various states were ready to conserve food sorely needed by the Continental Army. They weren't. No more is heard of the resolution. By the end of the war there were 2579 registered distilleries in the thirteen United States of America.

No hand, lay or clerical, had as yet been raised to strike at the source of ardent spirits, or their outlets. Some few of the laity might and did deplore drunkenness, much as they did poverty and crime, but in a genteel manner that disturbed nobody. As for the clergy, they were in the embarrassing situation of being pretty good customers themselves. Few of them failed to drink at every opportunity, many to excess. And quite a number owned interests in distilleries or taverns, sometimes both. The Rev. Nathan Strong, pastor of the First Church of Hartford, Connecticut, an outstanding revivalist who saved many a soul, operated a distillery "within sixty rods of his church." The Rev. Leonard Woods, a veteran professor at Andover Theological Seminary, remembered when he could "reckon up among my acquaintances forty ministers who were either drunkards, or so far addicted to drinking, that their reputation and usefulness were greatly impaired, if not utterly ruined." Another, unnamed clergyman was quoted in a Boston paper to the effect that "a great many deacons in New England died drunkards." In the Albany region of New York, according to "an aged divine," more than half of the clergy were steady drinkers, and some were downright sots.

The Methodists were having such a time of it with drunken preachers that as soon as Francis Asbury arrived in America, in 1771, as John Wesley's general assistant, the first thing he did was to deliver a sermon on Temperance. He continued to ride herd on his clergy to such effect that by the time he died a bishop, the Methodist General Conference had adopted a motion that no man of their cloth might retail spirits or malt liquors "without forfeiting his ministerial character among us." It seems to have been the first effort of any sect to get the embarrassing mote out of its own eye. It was a bold and honest facing of fact. It also served to clear Methodist decks for action in the coming battles of a hundred-year-war in which most Christian sects were mustered against an enemy as wily as he was strong.

When 1799 turned the corner, however, there was nothing visible or audible to cause the least alarm to the most alert distiller, brewer, or tavern keeper. Perhaps the chief topic in the liquor business was the gradually changing appetite of customers from rum to whiskey. The thought of a cold-water army would probably have been considered too grotesque to be funny.

2.

A MORTAL SIN IS DRAM-TAKING

THE organized campaign against beverage alcohol lasted a full one hundred and twelve years. It began on the evening of April 30, 1808, and climaxed at midnight January 16, 1920, when national prohibition by constitutional amendment became effective.

The first shot was fired by Dr. Billy J. Clark, a young and intrepid physician of Moreau, a hamlet of Saratoga County, New York.

The end of the long struggle was heralded by Billy Sunday, a professional revivalist who at the time was in Norfolk, Virginia, to preach what he said was "the funeral sermon for John Barleycorn," by then a generic term replacing "Rum" to describe all alcoholic liquors. Describing this event, the New York *Times* reported "the deceased" to have arrived at the doors of Mr. Sunday's tabernacle in a twenty-foot coffin hauled by a pair of horses and followed by a most dejected devil. Mr. Sunday was in his best form. "Good-bye, John," he cried. "You were God's worst enemy. You were Hell's best friend." For most Christian men that would have been damnation enough. Not for the Rev. Billy Sunday, no man to shun close association with deity. "I hate you," he shouted at this veritable Cardiff Giant of a corpse. "I hate you with a perfect hatred." Such was the manner John Barleycorn was laid in his grave, at least temporarily.

Dr. Billy Clark must have been something of a dreamer among the thick tall spruces which in 1808 covered the Moreau section of Saratoga County where he practiced. He observed the hard-drinking lumberjacks in the logging camps, and, although hard-drinking was then the custom in all parts of the country, the young doctor came to believe from his many calls to the woods to treat husky loggers in the throes of delirium tremens, and to the groggeries to patch up the victims of payday brawls, that rum was the hard taskmaster of his town, and also of neighboring Northumberland.

Then one night in March he sat down to read a thin pamphlet he had come by. It was *An Inquiry into the Effect of Spirituous Liquors on the Human Body and Mind.* Its author, he noted, was none other than Dr. Benjamin Rush of Philadelphia, former surgeon general of the Continental Army, a signer of the Declaration of Independence, and in 1808 the patriarch professor of the Medical College of the University of Pennsylvania. He was far and away the best-known man of medicine in the United States.

Dr. Rush had written his pamphlet on spirituous liquor back in 1785. It had been reprinted and quoted again and again, and almost ninety years later a writer on temperance declared Dr. Rush to "have laid out nearly all the fundamental lines of argument" along which the campaign against rum had since been pressed. And now, before his fireplace, young Dr. Billy Clark was reading what the great Philadelphia physician and patriot had to say about the effects of liquor. One should note the exactness of Dr. Rush's title. It speaks of spirituous liquors, by which the good doctor meant, and was understood by his readers to mean, only the products of the still. He considered the products of the wine press and the brewery to be healthful rather than otherwise.

Young Dr. Clark read on to learn that his eminent master's experience with alcoholic patients had been much the same as his own, only on a much larger scale, and that his conclusions were these: That there was no food value in ardent spirits; that ardent spirits aggravated all diseases, and were, moreover, the direct cause of many physical and mental ills; and that even moderate use of spirits led inevitably to drunkenness and probable destruction. Dr. Rush added that spirituous liquors should be taken only on the advice of a physician, and more than intimated doubt that they should be taken at all.

Having warmed up, Dr. Rush went on, in a section he called "A Moral and Physical Thermometer of Intemperance," to trace the downward path of the drinker of ardent spirits from the comparatively mild beverage called rum punch to the taking of drams of rum, brandy, and gin. Along this path he was more than likely to become addicted to idleness and gaming, to fall ill and into debt. There was a better-than-even chance, too, that he would, especially if he drank of a morning, look forward to a number of things including "madness and despair," the practice of crime, even to murder, and to die on the gallows.

Young Dr. Clark reflected that he himself had seen these horrible things happen, even among men far removed from city evils and engaged in the healthy outdoor occupation of felling timber.

Before going on to outline his suggestions to cure intemperance Dr. Rush paused a moment to describe graphically the appearance and character of a victim of distilled liquor. "Ardent spirits," he wrote, "causes him in folly to resemble a calf; in stupidity, an ass; in roaring, a mad bull; in quarrelling and fighting, a dog; in cruelty, a tiger; in fetor, a skunk; in filthiness, a hog; and in obscenity, a he-goat."

True enough. Dr. Clark too had observed all these things in the sots of Saratoga County. He read on to know what Dr. Rush recommended as a specific for intemperance. Wine and beer were the prescription. Wine and beer, those were health-giving things. If they should become a habit, then the use of ardent spirits would in time disappear. Getting out onto a limb of prophecy, he stated that by A. D. 1915 the use of spirituous liquors would be "as uncommon as a drink made of a solution of arsenic or a decoction of hemlock." As an afterthought Dr. Rush mentioned that, should there be difficulties during the transition period between universal drunkenness and universal temperance, he believed that a mild dose of laudanum or opium mixed with wine would be of help to the suffering.

Dr. Billy Clark finished the pamphlet in the condition of a man for whom a curtain of ignorance has been pulled suddenly aside, revealing the revision of a healthy, temperate, prosperous, and naturally happy United States, even unto Saratoga County, New York. The way to have such a delightful country was clear. He jumped up, ran to the barn, saddled his horse, and rode three miles through the night and deep mud to rouse his good friend, the Rev. Lebbeus Armstrong of Moreau's First Congregational Church. The hard ride had not dampened his wonderful vision. He entered the pastor's house with the utmost excitement. "Mr. Armstrong," he cried, "we shall become a community of drunkards in this town, lest something be done to arrest the progress of intemperance!" At least that is what history put into his mouth. And possibly he did say it that way, for the prose of the time was given to touches of stuffy elegance, and people unconsciously aped it in diction.

The physician and the clergyman talked half the night, and on parting agreed to meet soon again with others to discuss what might be done to remedy local conditions. Dr. Clark talked up the business while making his rounds, and on the last day of April 1808 forty-three farmers, most of whom also carried on logging operations, met at the Moreau schoolhouse and organized the Union Temperance Society of Moreau and Northumberland. They drew up a formal constitution and bylaws, and elected Colonel Sydney Berry president. As a former county judge he knew a good deal about the part liquor played in matters coming before the court.

The society's bylaws stipulated by name the beverages forbidden to members. They were "rum, gin, whiskey, wine, or any distilled spirits." Yet wine might be drunk "at public dinners"; and its use was not interdicted in a manner "to infringe on any religious ordinance." No mention of beer or other malt beverage was made: it would seem that the society went only halfway with Dr. Bush's favoring of wine and beer. The penalty for violation was twenty-five cents; and if intoxication should result, the penalty was fifty cents. It was understood to be the duty of each member to accuse any other member of a breach of any regulation. The method of accusation and trial was covered by specific bylaws.

There is no record that the Union Temperance Society had any appreciable effect on the use of distilled or other alcoholic liquors in Saratoga County. Possibly the lumberjacks were already immune to temperance appeals. It was their destiny to cut The Big Swath across the continent from Bangor, Maine, to Hoquiam, Washington, a herculean task. They felt they needed unusual sustenance, so in their wake were to be billions of stumps and millions of "dead soldiers" which had contained all of the beverages named by the Union Society, and variants with labels proclaiming Jamaica ginger, lemon extract, Peruna, and Hinckley's Bone Liniment.

The Union Society withered away, and years later the Rev. Lebbeus Armstrong spoke of it as "our little feeble band of Temperance Brethren." Yet it had not been in vain. Historians of the movement have said that the Moreau group was the "first Temperance society in the world to be organized and its meetings conducted according to the rules of parliamentary procedure." In his study of prohibition, *The Great Illusion*, Herbert Asbury cited Dr. Billy Clark's effort as "of great value to the Temperance movement" because it encouraged reform elements elsewhere to emulation.

In his account of the same movement, the Rev. Lyman Abbott said there was never a single source for such things. "Like a mighty river," he wrote, "it rises from half a score of springs, and is augmented in its flow by many more." Only at the close of the first quarter of the nineteenth century, in his opinion, was there anything "worthy of being called a Temperance reformation." One of its springs, said he, was furnished by "Dr. Lyman Beecher's famous Six Sermons on Intemperance," which the father of children among whom were Henry Ward and Harriet—who became Mrs. Stowe—delivered at Litchfield, Connecticut, in 1825.

Lyman Beecher's Six Sermons "aroused intense excitement that was not confined to the neighborhood." They were printed. Other ministers took up the theme. "The conscience of New England was fired. Whiskey and rum were banished, first from the sideboard on ordination occasions, then from ministers' tables altogether," wrote Lyman Abbott. "In fifteen years nineteen twentieths of the clergy of New England were habitual if not total abstainers." Because at that time the clergy of New England were also "the leaders of society," total abstinence became socially respected. . . . "In ten years the consumption of strong drink was decreased more than one-half per capita."

Possibly, yet the statistic cited has the flavor of being snatched from the air, which was to be the custom of both pro- and anti-liquor forces throughout the struggle. But there can be no doubt that temperance was fast becoming "socially respected" by at least a large minority of Americans. This new respectibility did not happen without volition, which was supplied in no small part by the organization in Boston, in 1826, of the American Temperance Society. This group was largely the idea of Justin Edwards, pastor of the South Church in Andover, Massachusetts, a born organizer, a man who seems to have known "all the best people," and who with fifteen of "the most prominent men in Massachusetts" founded the society, and collected the enormous sum of seventy-five hundred dollars with which to put an agent in the field and start publication of the *National Philanthropist*.

Justin Edwards was the right man to make temperance respectable. Tall and erect, with a reserved and stately bearing, he was no orator, or even a back slapper, but of an austerity, homely sincerity, and just enough appealing awkwardness to impress everyone with his uncompromising devotion to the principle not only of temperance but of abstinence. Yet he was something of a realist in that he did not consider it wise, as yet, to call for pledges of teetotalism. "Respectability and Education first." He himself saw to it that the first president of the American Temperance Society was none other than the Hon. Marcus Morton (the First), governor of Massachusetts, long a distinguished ornament of the Bar and, moreover, a descendant of the Pilgrim George Morton, who came on the *Anne* to Plymouth in 1623.

Having thus assured the group of personal and financial respectability, Justin Edwards went into the field. Within months he could report six state and more than two hundred local temperance societies. In less than three years membership had grown to eleven state groups, the local groups numbered more than one thousand, and individual members were a host of one hundred thousand. At the end of the decade Edwards prepared to retire. In his valedictory report, he called attention to the approximately one and one-half million members of the American Temperance Society, a name he suggested changing to the American Temperance Union. He could report that at last the resistant War Department of the United States had seen the error of its ways and had, through Edwards's good friend, Lewis Cass, Secretary of War, abolished the liquor ration in the Army and issued an order prohibiting the sale of ardent spirits at any fort, camp, or garrison. He could report organization of the American Congressional Temperance Society, whose membership consisted of a majority of the Senate and the House of the United

States. He could truthfully say, too, that through the Union's efforts "hundreds of employers of labor" had agreed no longer to furnish liquor to their mechanics, and to do all possible to discourage its use.

Had he thought it wise, Edwards might also have pointed out that the American Temperance Union was now ready to advocate total abstinence not just from spirits but from all intoxicating liquors including wine, beer, and cider. Call it what you would, temperance forthwith meant teetotalism.

We shall meet the American Temperance Union again (along with an even more celebrated temperance union organized by the women), but for the present we may leave the most effective and reverend Justin Edwards in the knowledge that it was he, more than any other one man, who put the drinking of liquor into the category of mortal sin. He was convinced that man's immortal soul was in desperate jeopardy due to rum. He did not believe that any substantial number of people could be made fanatical over the threat of liquor to their physical health or their financial security. These were the things that Dr. Rush had warned of. But Edwards knew that Rush, the rational and scientific, had admitted in a private letter that he believed "that the business must be finally affected by religion alone." This was naturally Edwards's opinion too. The great mass of Christians in the United States must be promised the rewards of heaven, and at the same time be warned of the most dreadful aspects of hell. Religion and only religion could make them into fanatics. It was a glorious dream and it was to remain for nearly a century.

It was not, however, to work without protest. Bishop John Henry Hopkins of the Episcopal Church in Vermont resented the alliance of religion and temperance societies. These groups, said he, attempted to establish virtue by methods not in accord with the word of God. They "gave prominence to one particular vice, contrary to doctrines of the Bible." Abstinence was in no way to be considered a measure of piety. "The outward reformation of a single vice is nothing, when the heart remains unsanctified and the curse of God still hangs upon the soul." In New York City soon appeared a book, *The Humbugs of New York,* the work of David M. Reese, who protested violently against teetotalism, which he said was the reigning humbug; as a moral obligation it was wholly unjustifiable. And in matters of health, he went on, the reformers could in all honesty go no further than to advocate temperance, which meant moderation.

Little or no heed was paid by the reformers to Bishop Hopkins and Mr. Reese, or to a number of more moderate men who deplored the abuses of alcohol as much as anyone but considered the appeals of the Temperance people to be both sacrilegious and non-scientific. The American Temperance Union was in the saddle, God was on their side, and they were prepared to ride rough and terrible over false prophets and all other agents of the Evil One. In addition to the Union's own propaganda, which flowed in reams from its own and subsidized presses, there arose a formidable army of free-lance writers and a few artists who contributed some of the most fearsome art and literature as ever accompanied a campaign.

The Rev. Ebenezer Sparhawk was apparently of the opinion that Dr. Rush had not done justice to the destructive powers of spirituous liquors on the human system. "Alcohol," he cried in most vivid prose, "puts the blood and juices into a most terrible ferment, and disturbs the whole animal economy. It vitiates the humors, relaxes the solids, spoils the constitution, fills the body with diseases, brings on meager looks, a ghastly countenance, and very bad tremblings: yea, when the abuse is persisted in, it quite ruins the health, destroys the strength, introduces decay of nature, and hastens death faster than hard labor."

Here was the sort of effective material on which was based much of the "physiology" contained in school textbooks up to the end of the nineteenth century, and beyond. Many still living got a dose of it in their school days. If Sparhawk didn't scare the daylights out of old topers and tender youth, then they were as ready as ever they would be to face the horrors prepared for them by Dr. Thomas Sewell of Columbian College (later George Washington University), a man of imagination and talent. It was Dr. Sewell who invented the Stomach School of Temperance Art. In six detailed drawings, often published in what was rightly called "full color," he displayed the progressive hell through which the digestive apparatus of dramtakers went their dreadful way from light pink ("Healthful") through an arresting cerise which one thought of as American Beauty ("After a Long Debauch") to a deep purple streaked with ominous brown and black. This last was the terminal stage. "Death by Delirium Tremens," said the caption.

These handsomely executed plates of Dr. Sewell were basically the material used to illustrate most school physiologies for decades. They were enough to give pause to all who might contemplate a beer. Youngsters blenched at sight of them, then tossed in their dreams and cried aloud to wake at midnight, trembling from the experience.* Whether or not these plates had a lasting effect is unknown, but either they or plagarisms were used continuously for some eighty years.

There were tremendous liars in prose to match the artists of the Stomach School. In small Lyme, New Hampshire, a Jonathan Kittredge perpetrated a magnificent piece of folklore which he published in a pamphlet entitled *Address on the Effects of Ardent Spirits*. This may

* Dr. Sewell's art so frightened the author, in grammar-school days, that he was not to touch alcohol in any form until he was nearly seventeen years of age. S. H. H.

have been the first, though by no means the last, account of the Drunkard Who Went Up in Flames. Mr. Kittredge lost no time in beating
about the bush. "Some drunkards," he wrote, "are killed instantly;
some die a lingering, gradual death; some commit suicide in fits of
intoxication; and some are actually burnt up." He let readers contemplate only briefly these hideous ends of sots, then he documented specific
instances. One was an intemperate man who, "a few years since," was
wholly consumed when "his breath came in contact with a lighted
candle." Kittredge either got around a good deal, or the neighborhood
of Lyme was soggy with alcohol, for he goes on to cite another case, a
female old soak who "had drunk nothing but ardent spirits for several
years." One day when rocking in her elbow chair, she let go a belch near
a candle and instantly started to illuminate. "Water was brought and
thrown on the body in abundance," Kittredge continued with relish,
"yet the flame appeared more violent, and was not extinguished until
the whole body was consumed."

Another writer, who roguishly signed himself Dr. Springwater, published a pamphlet whose title indicated the only specific against self-
arson—*The Cold-Water Man; or, A Pocket Companion for the Temperate.* The need for absolute abstinence, however, was not preached by
America's best-selling author of the period, who was Mason Locke
Weems, commonly called Parson Weems and whose *Life and Memorable
Actions of George Washington,* for which he invented the cherry-tree
story, was to pass through some seventy editions. In a later charming
book, *The Drunkard's Looking Glass,* Parson Weems spoke in favor of
control of one's appetite for liquor. He counseled using a *little* wine for
the stomach's sake, and also "cyder, beer, ale, etc." He thought hot
coffee in the morning was an excellent cure for dram-taking.

As the campaign of the American Temperance Union warmed up,
however, the advocates of genuine temperance were drowned by the
army of cold-water men. Even the learned and eminent Dr. Eliphalet
Nott, president of Union College, saw no reason to disbelieve in Mr.
Kittredge's warning beacons of flaming drunkards. In one of a series of
lectures to his students Dr. Nott explained that the fatal internal fires
which were consuming so many sots were "kindled spontaneously in the
fumes of alcohol that escape through the pores of the skin." Dr. Nott
remarked on the prevalence of these cases, and said he presumed "no
person of information will now be found to call the reality of their
existence in question." Dr. Nott was right; Jonathan Kittredge of Lyme,
New Hampshire, had supplied a most durable contribution. (As late as
1867, a George McCandlish, of Jackson, Michigan, a responsible man,
signed the pledge promptly after he had served on a coroner's jury while
a Dr. Harding and a Dr. Seys performed a post-mortem on a local

character who had died "in a fit of intoxication." When the physicians had removed the top of the skull, said McCandlish, "they tested it for alcohol, by holding a lighted match near it. The brain immediately took fire, and burned with a blue flame, like an alcohol lamp.")

During the eighteen thirties, when inebriates were apparently most prone to ignition, there was hardly a man who dared propose the elimination of all spirituous liquors by state law. But there was one such, and he made himself heard in both Massachusetts, where he was born, and in Maine, where he lived for many years. He was General James Appleton, who in the War of 1812 had commanded a brigade of the Massachusetts line, later became a successful man of affairs, but withal was a "fanatic for popular education, and against Slavery and Rum." General Appleton possessed "a high forehead, keen but kindly eyes with the suggestion of a dreamer in them, and a mouth and jaw indicative of grim determination."

As a member of the Massachusetts General Court he had, as early as 1832, attempted to have that legislative body pass a law to prohibit sales of liquor in quantities of less than thirty gallons. It failed of passage. Going to live in Portland, he was elected to the Maine legislature, and soon presented a bill to make Maine, where logging and selling rum were leading industries, as dry as the Sahara. It was tabled. But the idea of a law against ardent spirits did not die in Maine. Within two years Mississippi passed an act, a one-gallon law, which made selling by the drink illegal. Tennessee repealed statutes licensing tippling houses; if you wanted a drink there you must buy one quart or more. Illinois soon had a law providing for suppression of tippling houses by petition of the counties. This was a sort of local option. Rhode Island and New Hampshire passed town local-option laws in 1839. Connecticut followed with an act providing that only by a majority vote at town meetings could a liquor license be granted.

By 1840 the attempt to do something about ardent spirits was trending away from emotional appeal and toward some sort of control by law. This same year just happened to be the time when the classic figure of the Reformed Drunkard appeared. Probably one or even a score of Reformed Drunkards would not have affected things. But the Reformed Drunkards of 1840 appeared suddenly, and without warning, en masse. By the end of the year they numbered at least three thousand, and were organized into shouting bands. Half a million more were soon to sign what was called the Washington Temperance Society pledge. It was an epidemic and it brought the utmost confusion to the ranks of the American Temperance Union. The great unwashed, the "men of the gutter," had taken control of the crusade that had been started by their betters. Worst of all, from the viewpoint of the clergy, religion played almost no part in this new movement. The Reformed Drunkards did not open and close their meetings with prayer. They did not turn their meetings into religious revivals. The pious came to consider them atheists. But for about four years the massed Reformed Drunkards of the United States carried the banner against drunkenness.

3.

THE REFORMED DRUNKARD APPEARS

THE uproar and tumults occasioned by five hundred thousand pseudo-reformed drunks went into history under style of the Washingtonian Movement, the originators of which were six admitted old soaks of Baltimore. It was characteristic of the befuddled inspiration of drunks that in their great yearning for dignity these half-dozen topers should have chosen the revered name of Washington to describe an organization whose stated ideal was as foreign to the Father of his Country as its membership would have appalled him. George Washington was neither drunkard nor abstainer, nor was he the type to enjoy the company of tavern tosspots.

The tosspots who thought up the Washington Temperance Society were two blacksmiths, George Steers and David Anderson; W. K. Mitchell, a tailor; J. F. Hoss, a carpenter; James McCurley, a coachmaker; and Archibald Campbell, a silversmith. All were stout drinkers of spirits and malt liquors who met almost every evening in Chase's Tavern, in Baltimore, to stay there until the clock in the steeple struck one, or even two. Although women and song are more often associated with tippling, it is also true that the bottle is occasionally the source of unusual and even astonishing notions. On the night of April 6, 1840, to one of the jovial company in Chase's Tavern came the notion to appoint a committee of two to attend a lecture on temperance that evening in a nearby church. The ribald suggestion was greeted with cheers. Straws were drawn, and the two losers, fairly reeking with spirits, made their uncertain way to the church, and there underwent the ordeal of a talk by the Rev. Matthew Hale Smith, described as a notable cold-water man of the period.

The Rev. Mr. Smith was not only in top form that night; he spoke with such power as to send the two drunks back to Chase's Tavern uneasy in conscience and half convinced there was something to be said for abstinence. After a couple of reviving draughts this committee of two told their comrades of the horrendous indictment of alcohol delivered by the speaker. Debate ensued, and grew hot. The tavern keeper, a loudmouth who loathed reformers, took it upon himself to abuse the Rev. Mr. Smith, and this interference so angered the debating drunks that they vowed they should organize a total abstinence club to be called the Washington Temperance Society. The clock in the steeple struck one, or two, whichever it was, and six of the best customers Chase's Tavern ever had went home.

Next evening they met again, not in the tavern but in the carpenter shop of J. F. Hoss, where they proceeded to organize their society and to elect W. K. Mitchell, the tailor, president. They drew up and signed a pledge, set the initiatory fee at twenty-five cents, the dues at twelve and one-half cents a month, and each agreed to bring a friend to the next meeting. "A drinking tavern," as Lyman Abbott remarked, "was a strange manger for such a child to be cradled in." Then he reflected that life was filled with such dramatic episodes. "Life," he said, "is never spontaneous. The flower that seems to spring uncaused from the soil has been brought to birth by wing or wind. . . . The axiom is as true in morals as in physics." The Washingtonian Movement, he thought, did not spring spontaneously from a drinking tavern. Temperance sentiment was in the very air. The seed was carried by some invisible minister of grace and goodness and dropped in the unpromising soil. "The growth was marvellous, miraculous."

Marvelous indeed, perhaps miraculous. It was almost as if the six reformed drunks of Baltimore had cried fire in the night and had been heard all over the United States. Two months after they signed their own pledge, they had to rent a large hall for their meetings. From every dive in the city and from every "respectable" hotel came staggering or weaving an astonishing number of drinking men to sign the pledge. By the end of 1840 the Washington Temperance Society had developed dozens of speakers to carry the word to Philadelphia, New York, and Boston.

Among these speakers was a truly gifted man, John H. W. Hawkins, a hatter by trade, long sunk in intemperance, who one night had wandered, stupid with drink, into the Washingtonian hall and there signed the pledge which freed him ever more from what he said was the Viper in the Glass. Here was a man to palsy the hand of him who reached for the cup that cheers and destroys. For nigh fifteen years he had been, according to his own account, almost continuously in some stage of intoxication. But having signed the Washingtonian pledge he "became as firm in his abstinence as before he had been persistent in the taking of drams."

John Hawkins appears to have been a natural leader and a speaker of tremendous horsepower. Now that he had crawled up from the gutter, he was prepared to free thousands of victims from what he termed the slavery of drink. His abilities were quickly apparent to the Washingtonian command, who sent him and four other Reformed Drunkards off to see what if anything could be done with the depraved city of New York. Working singly and in pairs, they held nightly meetings, and even matineés, in New York churches, and soon had a good part of the town in turmoil. Their approach to the subject of liquor was soon standardized: The speaker appeared as a Horrible Example who had passed the nadir of experience and was again on the way up to civilized society. He told of the First Step, the swift downward path, pausing now and then to elaborate on the fauna of alcohol, and the arrival at Guttersburg, Delirium Falls, or Paupersville, where the very gates of Hell yawned. When done properly this was a most effective act. It was followed immediately by an appeal to the audience to "come up and sign the Pledge," and the assembled tipplers, shaken by the horrors they already knew or seemed soon to face, were responsive. They might backslide, as a majority of them did, but for the moment they signed and added to the swarming thousands of the reformed.

Washingtonian John Hawkins and his four comrades were encouraged by the attendance at their meetings during three weeks in New York, and also happy at results. Five hundred new pledges. To close the current campaign, Hawkins staged a mass meeting in City Hall Park which attracted more than four thousand people. Hawkins posted himself and companions atop of rum kegs from where each was to describe the worst incidents he could dredge up from his sottish past. Hawkins by now had come to know his own power. He was the last speaker. He wound up and let them have the heart-rending story of Hannah Hawkins, his little daughter, and her immortal plea: "Papa, please don't send me for whiskey today."

Little Hannah Hawkins, the archetype of Drunkard's Daughters beyond knowing, fetched the City Hall Park's congress of inebriates to the number of some fifteen hundred pledges even while the echoes of John Hawkins's appeal were bouncing off the brick walls of neighborhood tippling houses. He and his troop returned to Baltimore with more than twenty-five hundred pledges in their carpetbags. They were just in time to help celebrate the first anniversary of the historic first meeting of the Six Washingtonians. One thousand Reformed Drunkards led a monster parade through the city. They were followed by two thousand children who were members of the Cold-Water Army. The youngsters wore bright blue and white uniforms and carried banners inscribed with temperance slogans.

The Hawkins troop did not rest. Augmented by a dozen more speakers they took off for Boston and another triumph. They moved to Philadelphia, then into Ohio, into Kentucky. Hundreds of local Washingtonian societies were formed. It was their duty to round up local prospects, of which there seemed to be no end, and to send them in turn to bring more teetotalers into the fold. During the next three years the Washingtonian Movement continued to sweep all before it. The conventional and respectable American Temperance Union seemed drowned in the disorderly shoutings which shook the windows and left the stench of the alcoholic unwashed in Washingtonian meeting halls. The clergy was offended because religion was ignored; and the professionals of the Temperance Union had little faith in the epidemic of reformations.

The Washingtonians began to recede in 1844, but not before they reached and marked their high tide with a glorious event on May 30 in Boston. Banks and many businesses closed for the day. Twelve thousand of the reformed paraded in sections, each headed by a brass band. In line, too, were the little ones of the Cold-Water Army. The event closed with a mass meeting on the Boston Common, where twenty thousand people heard an address by Governor Briggs of Massachusetts and a powerful appeal by Washingtonian John Hawkins. They also were moved by the singing of The Hutchinson Family, already mentioned, a group of brothers and sisters from rustic New Hampshire who were just starting a remarkable career of half a century devoted to "good causes."

The Hutchinsons are worth knowing. They were thirteen of the sixteen children of Jesse and Polly Hutchinson of Milford, in the old Granite State. All were natural singers, and to call the roll was to name Noah, Andrew, John, Zephaniah, Caleb, Joshua, Asa, Abby, Judson, Rhoda, Adroniam, Benjamin, and Jesse, Jr. (Three more died while infants.) John, Asa, and Jesse had attended a lecture by Washingtonian John Hawkins in 1841, had signed the pledge, and though most of the early professional appearances of the Family were at abolition meetings, nine of them were on the platform when Hawkins spoke to the immense crowd on the Common. When Hawkins had finished with Hannah's "Papa, please don't send me for whiskey today," the Hutchinsons raised their voices in praise of "cold water" while volunteers passed through the crowd handing out pledges. The day's bag of drunkards ran "to several thousand names."

The Hutchinsons doubtless could have spent the rest of their long career singing only for temperance, but they didn't. They were too filled and running over with various isms to play favorites. They began with abolition and temperance and, soon or late, took up Grahamism (diet), Thomsonism (or botanic doctoring), anti-calomel, hydrotherapy, phrenology, woman suffrage, Amelia Bloomer's dress reform, and spiritualism. They were to go to England, where they were entertained by both Queen Victoria and Charles Dickens, who found them fresh and quaint. By 1870 the Hutchinsons were, save for the South, a national institution something like Niagara Falls. We shall meet them again.

As for the Washingtonians, they began to fade in 1844, and their boasted half-million reformed drunkards either returned to the saloons or joined the American Temperance Union or one or another of the new anti-liquor groups such as the Sons of Temperance, the Good Templars, the Knights of Jericho, the Order of Rechabites, and even the Female Abstinence Society of Boston. Nobody seems to have attempted to check either the rise or decline of the Washingtonians, although one historian guessed the movement might have resulted in "a clear gain of one hundred thousand permanently reformed victims of liquor." Lyman Abbott wrote that among the fatal weaknesses of the Washingtonians was their false assumption that a pledge of abstinence meant an abstainer. "They proclaimed Boston reformed because four fifths of all Boston drunkards had signed the pledge." Their call was only "to men swept by on the current to swim for their lives, and they counted every man saved who attempted to swim." But too many could swim only a little while, and many more could not swim at all. The kindly Mr. Abbott chided his brother clergymen who could see nothing good about the Washingtonians. "It is not for us now to go back to their methods," he admitted, "but we owe them an incalculable debt for sounding the alarm." He also added that if the Washingtonian movement had done the world no other service than to give it John B. Gough, then the world owed the Washingtonians an enormous debt.

John Bartholomew Gough was "the finest pearl dragged from the cesspool of Rum by the Washingtonians." This event happened in 1842 in Worcester, Massachusetts, when he was twenty-five years old and despondent. He was drunk when he signed the pledge, but when asked to explain why he had done so, he steadied himself against the table on the platform, "his face a ghastly gray, his eyes glassy," and delivered such a hideous picture of drunkenness as to mark him for a splendid future in temperance work: "Come hither and sit beside me and tell your name," Satan shouted, "and as he mounts to the throne he cries 'My name is Alcohol' . . . And Hell resounds with acclaim!" It was gorgeous stuff. Within the week John Gough was on the road as a lecturer, a success from the first. Yet, the devil lay in wait for him in Boston. He broke his pledge and returned to Worcester in what he thought was disgrace.

Yet Dr. Lyman Beecher had heard him speak, and now the great man sent for him. "Mr. Gough," he demanded in a voice that shook the rafters"—the way Gough remembered it—"Mr. Gough, why do you remain in the hands of atheism? Your gift is from God. Why not serve Him with it?" Whereupon John Gough resolved to serve God, and he tore through Massachusetts like a cyclone, not for the irreligious Washingtonians, but for the American Temperance Union. He soon "lifted the Temperance movement from mere reform to a religious plane." In his first year as a speaker he gave nearly four hundred talks, received 2218 pledges, collected $1059 out of which he paid his own expenses. By 1845 he had left all other temperance lecturers, even John Hawkins, in shadow.

Then, in September, he left Temperance Union headquarters for a series of highly publicized lectures in New York City, and disappeared. Friends announced that he had doubtless been done away with by liquor interests who feared his eloquence. The police were ordered to find him alive or dead. Seven days later, when they found him, he was alive but most terribly hung over in a house of prostitution on Walker Street in New York. It would have wrecked the career of any but a remarkable man, which John Gough was. He told the press, and seems to have made it stick, that he "had been drugged and abducted for a triple purpose—partly robbery, partly blackmail, partly his over-throw as a Temperance lecturer." The robbery, he said, was effected, but he had refused to pay blackmail. He left his "overthrow" to the opinion of his public. His public rallied. Shortly before his death, forty-one years later, he had given nine thousand six hundred talks to nine million people. He died in harness, while on a speaking tour, at Frankford, Pennsylvania.

John B. Gough may have been what so many of his contemporaries said he was, namely, the greatest temperance speaker of the age. His voice has now been stilled seventy years, and we cannot judge his eloquence and magnetism on the platform. But he left a book from which it is possible to know something of the content of his nine thousand and six hundred lectures. This is a good fat work, bound in the favorite brown and gold of the period, entitled *Sunlight and Shadow*. It purports to be a chatty miscellany of travel and reminiscences, but it is well laced with some of the most heart-rending "anecdotes" imaginable, often illustrated by pen-and-ink artists who were equal to picturing the visions offered by Gough's text. Consider the graphic possibilities when John Gough told the one about the drunkard's daughter and her little Testament:

... clasping it in her hands she fell asleep on the wretched rags called a bed ... The father went to her bedside. He was mad for drink. He looked around the room, but there was nothing left he could dispose of. Yet he *must* have drink. The little creature lay on the bed, the Testament clasped in her hand. He stretched out his shaking hand, seized the Testament, and sneaked out like a guilty thing to a grogshop. All he could get for the poor little book was a half pint of whiskey. He drank the Devil's drink almost at a draught.

The sot now returned to the bedside of his dying daughter. He hadn't fooled *her*. She had waked to see him leaving with the Testament. Now she spoke:

Papa, I am going to die. I shall go to Heaven because He said little children were of the Kingdom. But suppose, Papa, that Jesus should ask me what you did with my Testament. Oh, Papa! what shall I tell him?

The good work of John Bartholomew Gough was thus carried on posthumously by his book. One who has read it is prepared to believe that Gough's influence was felt so long as temperance remained a matter of religious emotion and his *Sunlight and Shadow* was considered entertaining and instructive literature.

As the decade of the forties was drawing to a close, the vast emotionalism stirred in the American people by the Washingtonians was turned away from temperance and was soon to disappear largely in the rising agitation for abolition. Many a stout temperance advocate had room also for abolition; and in many parts of the North the two movements came to be considered synonymous. So much so that the South believed temperance to be nothing more than another Yankee plot, and dropped it.

These were the conditions which in 1849 faced one of the most appealing figures of the period, the Rev. Father Theobald Mathew, who arrived in New York from Ireland where for ten years past his labors for total abstinence had met with phenomenal success. Catholic immigrants to America during the mid-forties, many of whom had signed Father Mathew's pledge in the old country, were instrumental in encouraging priests and bishops in the United States to found temperance groups. This had already resulted in church-organized Father Mathew Societies in Boston, Providence, New York, Albany, and Philadelphia.

New York City gave Father Mathew an ovation on his arrival at Castle Garden. Frail and ill, and obviously aged beyond his years, which were sixty, the gentle priest immediately took the hearts of Catholics and Protestants alike. After three weeks in the city and vicinity during which he "administered his pledge to thousands of Irish-Americans," he moved to Boston. Here he was embarrassed by the aggressive Massachusetts Anti-slavery Society with an invitation to address a mass meeting celebrating the anniversary of the abolition of slavery in the British West Indies. Father Mathew replied that he had come to America as a Catholic priest and as an advocate of temperance; and that because he planned to visit the slave-holding states, he had best decline the honor of addressing the meeting. William Lloyd Garrison, the abolitionist who took pride in being adamant to the extent and even beyond of boorishness, hastened to write in the *Liberator* that Father Mathew was a man without honor, one who sacrificed his principles to expediency. Sentiment, however, was on the side of the priest, and much of the lay press of the North defended his course as the best way out of a trying situation. When Father Mathew left for his Southern tour, the *South Carolina Temperance Advocate* stated the conviction that the priest was not a fanatic on the slavery issue, and cordially invited him to come there. Georgia also welcomed this "Irish apostle of Temperance." President Taylor entertained him at the White House.

Father Mathew's tour of the South was climaxed in New Orleans, where some twelve thousand signed the pledge. He appears to have done well also in Richmond, Charleston, Augusta, and Mobile. In those and many smaller towns Father Mathew Societies were soon flourishing. Late in 1851, when about to return to Ireland, he published a "Farewell Address to the Citizens of the United States." In it he thanked heaven that he had been instrumental "in adding to the ranks of Temperance over 60,000 disciples in America." Even the New York *Herald,* which seemed to delight in attacking temperance reformers, was impressed by the Irish priest's labors. In him, said James Gordon Bennett's paper, there was "no hypercritical cant or pretentions to pharisaical sanctity." He stuck to his task of "reclaiming his fallen brother, welcoming the prodigal son back into the bosom of society, uttering the joyful tidings that no man is past the hour of amendment."

"In the opinion of many Temperance workers," wrote John Allen Krout, "there was one important defect in Father Mathew's theory and practice." * He did not stress adequately "the moral culpability of the liquor dealer" and thus reach the conclusion "that legal restriction was necessary to combat the evil of intemperance." Neither did the Washingtonians; and though, as we have seen, the American Temperance Union had made several efforts to have the sale of intoxicating liquor restricted by law, they failed. Yet, in the same year Father Mathew left for home, the state of Maine passed the first recognizable prohibition law in the United States.

* See *The Origins of Prohibition,* 1925.

4.

THE ERA OF NEAL DOW AND
TIMOTHY SHAY ARTHUR

THE man who added law to moral suasion and made Maine either in-famous or blessed, as the first state to abjure temperance for downright prohibition, was neither a reformed drunkard nor a clergyman. Neal Dow was born in 1804, in Portland, the son of Quaker parents, entered the tanning business of his father, speculated with success in the timberlands, and by early manhood was one of the rising young businessmen of his native city.

Though trained in the discipline of the Society of Friends, it tells something of Dow's character that he was later dismissed from the Society because he came to advocate the use of "carnal weapons" and went away to war in 1861 as colonel of a Maine Volunteer Regiment. His war on intemperance began long before when as an employer of labor he was impressed by the inefficiency of drunken hands in his tanning works. His first efforts were to plead with local grogshop keepers, who ignored him. Then, with an astuteness beyond his years, he started to labor with the really great heroes of Portland, who were the members of local fire-engine companies. If he could get *them* on his side, then ordinary men might listen. Being himself a member of Deluge Engine Company, and knowing the value of example, Dow, with what eloquence one can only guess, persuaded his hard-drinking group to enforce total abstinence at all their meetings. This was good, but it wasn't enough. Portland continued to be the bibulous town where sailors set on shore and loggers down from the woods whooped it up in the classic style of their kind.

Being a civic-minded man, Dow accepted election as overseer of the poor, and was soon in contact with many of the worst victims of rum. He was aghast not only at these horrible examples and their pathetic wives and children, but also to learn how much of the taxpayer's money went to support them. He became convinced of two things: liquor tended to make and fetter poverty; rum was too easily come by. There and then he set out with energy and ability to drive the Viper out of Portland and Maine. Moral suasion would not do. It had been tried and had failed. Let us see what law could achieve.

Bearing down hard on the "enormous burden" saddled on taxpayers by drunkenness, Dow staged a campaign to dry up the city. The first measure he submitted to the voters was defeated. Just then the Washingtonian movement reached Portland, and reformed drunkards swarmed over the town. Unlike most reformers, Dow welcomed the converts, gave them every aid, and before the excitement subsided, the city of Portland had voted 943 to 498 to ban the retail sale of intoxicating liquors within the city limits. This was a triumph for the leadership of Dow, but it did not stop the flow of liquor. Bootleg establishments took the places of licensed taverns and tippling houses.

Dow was not discouraged. He drew up and circulated petitions in every county asking the legislature to enact a law that would make the traffic in rum "an infamous crime." He induced many able men to help, among them the fanatical dry and abolitionist General James Appleton. Noting the rising fervor for abolition, Dow was quick to tie the idea of freeing slaves in the South to the idea of freeing the slaves of liquor in Maine. In talks and articles he made slavery and rum synonymous, and thus many a free-soiler and abolitionist who saw no harm in a snifter or two went over to his side and was ready to vote Maine dry.

While Dow carried on his state-wide campaign, he also did some politicking in his home town, and in 1851 he was elected mayor with a promise to "close every grogshop in Portland." Before he could get around to this task, the state act he had been instrumental in drawing up, was ready to submit to the legislature then in session. Dow went to Augusta in order to lobby the bill through both houses. It passed the lower house by a two-to-one vote, but in the upper house met the strong opposition of Senator Cary, of Cary's Mills, Aroostook County, who spoke at some length and most bitterly about:

... this new manifestation of the spirit of fanaticism under the auspices of that prince of fanatics, the Mayor of Portland. . . . A few years ago this man was at the head of the nigger movement in that city, but even abolitionism was not strong enough for his diseased palate, and he added temperanceism to his former stock of humbugs . . .

And so on, for in that day vitriolic oratory was as common in backwoods Maine as it was on the floor of Congress. But Senator Cary's great effort was in vain, and Maine became the first of the forty-eight states which by 1919 were made dry by national constitutional amendment. The Maine law, says John Allen Krout, was hailed by the prohibitionists as "an unmistakable sign that the temperance movement had been transformed into a campaign for prohibitory legislation." After two generations of combatting intemperance Neal Dow had carried the reform far beyond the feeble early efforts against the use of ardent spirits.

Dow returned to Portland to notify rum sellers there that he would allow them exactly sixty days to get rid of their damnable merchandise. Some of them did not do so, and Mayor Dow in person led raid after raid. With his own hands he laid about him with an ax to wreck bottles and kegs, and on one occasion poured some two thousand dollars' worth of liquor into the cobblestone gutters in front of City Hall.

Passage of the Maine law became the chief topic of discussion when the National Temperance Convention met at Saratoga Springs, New York, late in 1851. Dow explained to three hundred delegates that there was no nonsense about it. It had no loopholes, he said. It banned the sale, the keeping for sale, and the manufacture of all intoxicating liquors. It authorized search and seizure upon complaint of three persons. It provided heavy fines for the first two violations, imprisonment for the third.

The Maine law seemed to be almost as catching as the Washingtonian excitement had been. Even while rum sellers watched, often with arrogance, Minnesota, Rhode Island, Massachusetts, and Vermont, all passed prohibitory laws in 1852. Michigan followed them in 1853, Connecticut in 1854. A year later came glory: Indiana, Delaware, Pennsylvania, New York, New Hampshire, and Iowa went dry, along with the Territory of Nebraska. For many a thoughtful distiller and brewer it must have seemed as though the end of things was in sight; and if temperance workers became a little smug it is scarcely to be wondered at.

It is not to be supposed that the sudden trend of the movement toward prohibitory laws did away with all efforts at moral suasion. In their wake the fading Washingtonians left more than a residue of the identical emotional appeals which had been their contribution to the campaign. The Reformed Drunkard was far from dead. He had merely solidified into the classic figure that was to haunt hung-over Americans for years to come. As a leading character he appeared at the Boston Museum in *The Drunkard, or, The Fallen Saved,* described on the bill as a moral drama in five acts. After a truly sensational run of one hundred and forty consecutive performances the play was moved to New York City and staged most splendidly by no less an impresario than Phineas Taylor Barnum in what he called the Moral Lecture Room in his popular American Museum. Here it broke all house records and was also effective in dissipating the theater curse by attracting to the Moral Lecture Room many people who considered the stage demoralizing. Horace Greeley was quick to give *The Drunkard* a clean bill of health, and wrote in the *Tribune* of his gratification that night after night Mr. Barnum was presenting his "reformatory piece to two or three thousand persons at a time." He thought it would emancipate "the public mind from the shackles of prejudice" and restore to it "a sound and promising condition of moral healthfulness on the subject of Temperance."

Surprisingly enough, in view of the great showman's promotion of humbugs of all kinds, Barnum himself had only recently signed a pledge of abstinence. What is more, he kept it. Never again in his long life did he touch any kind of intoxicating liquor. There was no bar on the museum premises, and when Barnum discovered that men were in the habit of going out for a drink between acts of *The Drunkard,* he refused to give them return checks. And at every performance it was announced from the stage that all who wished to sign the pledge could do so at the box office. He himself often lectured on the evils of drink, and appears to have planted shills in the audience to ask him a question: "Mr. Barnum, how does alcohol affect us, externally or internally?" Then he let them have it. "E-ternally," said Mr. Barnum.

Yet there was nothing phony about his teetotalism. When he dined Jenny Lind on arrival and the famous Swedish Nightingale lifted her wine glass and asked to drink his health, he replied he could not return the compliment. "I must beg," he said, "to be permitted to drink your health and happiness in cold water." Later, when he teamed up with James A. Bailey to produce the immortal circus, each performer, indeed even the roustabouts, had to sign a contract prohibiting the use of intoxicating liquor during the period of employment.* Still later, when Barnum imported Jumbo, who he said was "the only surviving mastadon on earth," and was at the dock to meet the elephant, he protested vigorously when the animal's keeper poured a full quart of whiskey down Jumbo's throat and followed it with a ration of beer. Though there is the flavor of ballyhoo about this incident, there can be little doubt that after he signed the pledge, in 1847, Phineas T. Barnum was a devout, possibly fanatical, teetotal man.

This was not true of one of Barnum's contemporaries who wrote the most celebrated temperance tract of all time. Timothy Shay Arthur, author of *Ten Nights in a Bar Room and What I Saw There,* was a moderate user of spirits, wine, and beer but believed saloons were the great enemy of society. Born in Newburgh, New York, in 1809, he was reared in Baltimore, where he turned to writing for and editing literary magazines which were both genteel and ephemeral. He moved to Philadelphia and began contributing to *Graham's Magazine* and *Godey's Lady's Book,* periodicals of wide circulation. For these he was writing verses, essays, and stories when the Washingtonian mania sud-

* See M. R. Werner's *Barnum,* 1923.

denly erupted in Baltimore. Journalist Arthur knew a good subject when he saw one. Returning to Baltimore, he interviewed the reformed drunkards there, and in 1842 published a small book, *Six Nights with the Washingtonians.* It found a ready market so long as the hubbub lasted, and made Arthur's name known to editors. He followed his first success with a novel *The Maiden,* which proved conclusively that girls pay a fearful price if they do not investigate carefully "the moral antecedents of the men they marry." This went pretty good, and encouraged Arthur to establish a periodical of his own, *Arthur's Home Magazine,* which "achieved a warm public favor" and which he edited to his death.

For his own and other periodicals Arthur wrote novelettes and shorter pieces that dealt with vanity, extravagance, and disregard for the precepts of religion. Then, in 1854, appeared his masterpiece. *Ten Nights in a Bar Room* leaped at once to an enormous sale. During the 1850s its circulation was second only to Mrs. Stowe's *Uncle Tom's Cabin,* and like that book it was dramatized and played everywhere a theater, schoolhouse, or barn could be found or a tent erected. Even the most dedicated enemies of the stage could say nothing but good of *Ten Nights.*

Whether or not the play actually convinced or converted many people who were not already abstainers may be doubted, but few Americans could have escaped seeing it. Up and down and across the United States, for the next six decades, trouped one-show companies playing *Ten Nights,* and repertoire companies who stayed a week in one town and included *Ten Nights* among assorted melodramas like *East Lynne, Lena Rivers,* and *St. Elmo.*

Ten Nights came straight from the fevered minds and brows of trembling Washingtonians. From their hideous accounts author Arthur made a judicious selection of contrasting incidents, strung them like beads on a rosary as frail as it was inconsistent, and brought down the final curtain only after all the villains, who were drunkards or rum sellers, had reformed or died, and a mass meeting of newly teetotal citizens had voted to close the local barroom. Then, said a program note, "The tavern sign is cut down, and thus ends the tavern which led so many to destruction."

Arthur's masterwork called for one song. This was not in the olio between acts but was an integral part of the play. Scene 2 of the first act is the barroom of the Sickle & Sheaf Tavern where Joe Morgan, the leading drunk of the play, has obviously had his fill for the evening, and sits besotted on a chair. Into the room comes his daughter, little, golden-haired Mary. She takes Papa's shaking hand and sings:

> "Father, dear father, come home with me now;
> The Clock in the steeple strikes one;

> You said you were coming right home from the shop
> As soon as your day's work was done.
> Our fire has gone out—our house is all dark—
> And mother's been watching since tea,
> With poor brother Benny so sick in her arms,
> And no one to help her but me."

Father, however, will not listen, thus giving Mary the chance to return again, at about two o'clock, to sing a second verse. Benny is failing rapidly. Father will hear none of it. He pushes her rudely, and out into the night she goes, only to return at three o'clock by steeple-clock time. Benny is now dead. His last words were "I want to kiss Papa goodnight." Nor is Mary long for the world. Within a few months she comes again to the tavern to escort father home, and publican Slade, irritated at customers who have so little control over their families, heaves a glass at drunkard Morgan, misses, and the glass is shattered on the pale brow of little Mary, who is just entering the bar to fetch her old man home again. Mary dies. Morgan vows he shall never touch liquor again.

Both in *Ten Nights* and elsewhere generations of little girls were to sing the song that couldn't move Father from the Sickle & Sheaf but did move Americans to tears and became to temperance people what *John Brown's Body* was to abolitionists. Everybody seemed to overlook or excuse an oddity of the play in which the worst souse of all was the comedy character, Sample Switchel. Switchel *never* stopped drinking yet wound up in the last scene showing no marked deterioration either morally or physically; while Papa Morgan went through attacks of delirium tremens and gave up liquor only after a terrible time of it. Switchel merely stopped drinking with no effort at all whereas, as more than one knowing drinker who saw the play remarked, Switchel should damn well have been shown being lowered into a drunkard's grave. But Timothy Shay Arthur was no man to stop short of violating either the rules of the Greek drama or the poetic license of nineteenth-century authors.*

Ten Nights in a Bar Room was still riding high in its first year as a play when New Hampshire passed a law prohibiting the sale of liquor. Twelve other states and one territory, as already said, had previously passed similar acts. But no other followed New Hampshire into the dry column. Something was happening to the temperance movement. During the next two decades all of the dry states save Maine repealed or

---

* In his *Town Hall Tonight,* Harlowe R. Hoyt remarks of *Ten Nights* that it was last played seriously—not as burlesque—by Robert Dowling, an excellent actor who had "drunk himself into obscurity," turned to cold water and to Arthur's play in his later years, and gave his last performance of it in 1944.

drastically modified their prohibition laws, and even Maine backslid for a time to try a license system. Almost everything that had been won during the reformers' brief success with legislation was lost, and the whole movement seemed to be declining.

Historians of temperance seem to think the decline was due in large part to the deepening shadow cast by slavery. Many if not most of the temperance leaders were also involved with abolition and, as the irrepressible conflict drew nearer, they tended to devote less time to alcohol. In the Northern churches, too, more abolition than temperance was being preached. With increasing numbers of Northerners and Southerners believing the fate of the nation was at stake, people simply lost interest in what comparatively was inconsequential. Should not Kansas be made safe for free-soil before worrying about liquor there? Shootingmen, not lecturers on temperance, were what was needed along the Missouri and the Big Blue.

Once the Civil War got under way, such temperance reformers as were still in the ring devoted their efforts to protecting young soldiers from the intemperance and all-around loose living which have been charged to armies ever since history was written. And at this critical period the once-dry state of Massachusetts turned traitor to the cause of temperance when a legislative committee, headed by wartime Governor John A. Andrew, summarized its conclusions as to alcohol by saying it was neither sinful nor hurtful in every case to use alcohol, and that "it is the right of every citizen to determine for himself what he will eat or drink." These rational and courageous statements were given wide circulation by liquor interests. They were to plague the temperance movement for many years.

Then, in 1862, the United States got into the liquor business itself by passing the first internal-revenue act which provided for a fee on each retail liquor establishment in the country and levied a manufacturing tax of one dollar a barrel a year on beer and ale and twenty cents on a gallon of spirits. The act was intended only as a money-raising measure for the duration of the war, but like many another "war measure" since, it was never done away with.

Looking back many years later, Dr. D. Leigh Colvin, a candidate of the Prohibition party for President in 1936, observed that the Internal Revenue Act of 1862 served "to entrench the liquor traffic in politics" and to make "the government financially interested in the traffic." Dr. Colvin thought it "the most calamitous in its ultimate effect of any action ever taken by Congress." An example of what the good doctor meant was to be seen within three years of the act's passage, when in 1865 the Commissioner of Internal Revenue in his official capacity addressed a meeting of the recently organized United States Brewers Association and pledged himself to "bring about a cordial understanding between the government and the trade."

It was little to wonder that all but the stoutest of heart among temperance men were downcast. The government had "gone into the liquor business." The country was aswarm with new German immigrants who had never heard of either temperance or abstinence and drank beer like water. True enough, they were helping the North to win the war, but they were also responsible for the sudden and alarming rise in the consumption of beer. Massachusetts had not only left the dry column, but had given comfort to the enemy by stating officially there was no reason why eating and drinking should be any business of the law whatever. This heresy was two thirds of what the dangerous radical John Humphrey Noyes had been saying for years.

The war had borne heavily, too, on prohibition's peerless champion, Neal Dow of the state of Maine. After being twice wounded, and captured while recuperating near the lines, the gallant General Dow had spent eight months in fearful Libby Prison before he was exchanged (for General Fitzhugh Lee) and permitted to return home to recover, as well as a man of sixty-one years was able, his health.

In looking back after almost a century 1865 must have seemed to those who were still interested in the matter to mark a return to the darkest days of intemperance.

5.

O PRAYING BANDS OF VISITATION

DURING a period of some fifteen years after 1855 the Army of the Lord (Temperance Division) either stood still or lost ground, mostly the latter. Its legislative triumphs had been brief, and the new partnership of federal government and the liquor traffic had knocked the heart out of most of the dry leaders. When the temperance forces did move again, they were no longer exclusively a male outfit.

The lords of creation had obviously failed. This was no surprise to a small band of discontented amazons who had begun talking far too loudly about womanhood and the rights of women. It was still a man's world. What he unctuously called his "helpmeet" was useful in many ways. She might even be decorative. But she had no place in the affairs of the nation, even in such minor things as temperance.

The astute Justin Edwards had pleaded, back in 1826, to admit women to full membership in the American Temperance Union. He was almost unanimously voted down. Women might well be the greatest sufferers from intemperance, but they must suffer silently, as became the weaker sex. During the Washingtonian excitement a Daughters of Temperance group was organized as a sort of auxiliary of the Sons of Temperance, but the girls were to keep to themselves and had no voice. One of the Daughters happened to be Susan Brownell Anthony, a spinster possessed of an eloquent voice which she meant should be heard. At a mass meeting of the Sons in Albany, New York, she attempted to take the floor. The moderator promptly shushed her, remarking with oleaginous kindness that "the Sisters had not been invited there to speak but to listen and learn." Miss Anthony leaped to her feet and strode from the hall, followed by a few other Daughters.

While the pompous males went on with their deliberations, Miss Anthony led her rebels to the home of an old friend, Lydia Mott, a Quakeress shirtmaker in Maiden Lane. There she organized a meeting for women, secured a basement room in a local church, inserted a notice in the *Evening Journal,* and sent out her friends to pull doorbells—all before supper. The meeting was well attended, and though a heating stove came apart and filled the room with smoke, it was repaired and the women, their eyes running but still fast on their goal, organized the Women's State Temperance Society. The spunk displayed by Miss Anthony attracted a Mr. Townsend, identified significantly if only as a "wealthy manufacturer of sarsaparilla," who offered to pay the expenses of Susan and friends in a state-wide campaign. She teamed up with Amelia Bloomer, among whose activities was dress reform of women, and the Reverend Antoinette Brown, and the three women went ahead to draw crowded audiences both upstate and in New York City.

A year later the Women's State Temperance Society staged a mass meeting in Rochester at which the president, Elizabeth Cady Stanton, not only spoke on Temperance, but demanded that drunkenness be made a legal cause for divorce. Now this was invading a field where women had no business whatever. Laws were made by men, and men went promptly to work on their wives who were members of the group, and even infiltrated its meetings "to free it from any taint of Women's Rights —especially the right to divorce." When Mrs. Stanton failed of re-election as president, Miss Anthony resigned as secretary. She had run her course, says her biographer Katharine Anthony, "as an adjunct of the clergymen's movement for Temperance." The men had had their way, but they were not rid of Miss Anthony. She dropped Temperance work, believing that if women had votes the officials "would no longer fear to enforce the law," and devoted all of her great zeal to turning fainthearted "helpmeets" into *people*—women who one day soon were to cast their votes for governors of states and representatives in Congress.

Susan Anthony's resignation from the group she founded put an end to temperance work by women in New York State. For another twenty years no woman there and few elsewhere made so bold as to invade man's prerogative in the matter of drink. Nor were the males doing much to hold their temperance franchise. They seem not only to have tired, but their enemies grew more powerful. The organized brewers were now in the saddle, riding Congress and the legislatures, demanding removal of this or that restriction, meanwhile telling the people, through their subsidized press, that taxes were sure to go up if the government lost its revenue from the manufacture of malt liquors. Though the distillers were slow to organize, they too grew powerful. But the temperance reformers, as Herbert Asbury remarks, were "stripped of virtually everything save the shining armor of righteousness."

Such was the dismal condition of temperance affairs late in 1873 when what a Miss Willard, a schoolteacher, soon to be famous, described as "a whirlwind of the Lord" roared up out of southern Ohio and blew in every direction. This wind went into history as the Women's Crusade, for it set thousands of angry females to marching against the saloons, and before it was done it had revealed a God-given leader in the person of Miss Willard, arrayed in the white ribbons of a new Pentecost.

The quite improbable agency for this visitation was a pioneer physical culturist who weighed over two hundred pounds, had baby-blue eyes, skin like a peach, an honorary medical degree from Homeopathic Hospital College of Cleveland, and signed himself Dr. Dioclesian Lewis, author of *New Gymnastics* "and many other works." He was perhaps as strange a fanatic as came to the surface during the stew and bubble of the reform era.

In 1873 when he touched off the whirlwind of the lord, Dr. Dio Lewis was fifty years old. He had already tried several things, such as editing a homeopathic magazine in Buffalo. He had founded and operated the Boston Normal Institute for Physical Education; written books entitled *Chastity, or Our Secret Sins* and *Our Digestion,* in addition to his masterpiece on gymnastics, and invented "the first wooden dumbbell" and a game he called beanbag. He had coined a neat slogan, "A Clean Tooth Never Decays," that was to have a long life. He had conducted a sanitarium in Lexington, Massachusetts, a large school for girls in Boston, where he also operated a family hotel, The Bellevue. Between times, in the 1840 decade, he had, though never a victim of drink, gone forth to speak for and with the Reformed Drunkards of the Washingtonian brigades. Later he gave a series of lectures on women's rights. But no matter what he was lecturing about, he seldom failed to get in a few telling blows against corsets for females, and favorable words for shorter skirts and the use of suspenders to take the strain off the pelvic regions, thus to save them "for more worthy purposes."

Being of "pleasing address" and resonant voice, Dr. Lewis took easily to the lecture field, which the American Lyceum movement, founded by Josiah Holbrook, had spread to all parts of the country, and became one of its most popular speakers. He was so engaged on the Midwestern circuit when he touched off the whirlwind out of which came marching the females, saints and harpies among them, who were to turneth the world of the wicked upside down.

Dr. Lewis's lectures characteristically dealt with a number of things, including temperance; and during this most pregnant season of 1873–74 it pleased him to suggest that if women really wanted to do away with rum, then why did they not organize what he called Visitation Bands of females, who would go into the streets to "pray and sing the saloons out of business." He had broached the idea at lectures in western New York and Pennsylvania, but nothing came of it until he went to Ohio. There in small Hillsboro, two days before Christmas, it exploded into action. Next day Mrs. Eliza J. Thompson, Hillsboro's most prominent woman, told Mr. Thompson she was going to lead a crusade against the thirteen local places where liquor was sold. Mr. Thompson was properly alarmed at what he called a lot of tomfoolery. His wife reminded him that the men had been in the tomfoolery business for a long time, and remarked that "it might be God's will that the women should now take a part." It was obvious the men had done nothing much in Hillsboro, which had "become of late very dissipated."

Although Mrs. Thompson was "a gentle, retiring woman of sixty," she had "received a Call to do the Lord's duty" and she responded. Rallying seventy of her friends at a morning prayer meeting, she outlined the strategy. "We will sing," she said, "that good old hymn, 'Give to the Winds Thy Fears,' and as we are singing, let us form in line, two by two, the small women in front, leaving the tall ones to bring up the rear, then let us at once proceed to our sacred mission, trusting alone in the God of Jacob." And away they went, "this band of mysterious beings," as Mrs. Thompson put it, "singing, praying, a few weeping, in the throes of religious exaltation."

They were not alone. Half of Hillsboro's five thousand citizens were in the wake of the crusaders when they reached their first objective, Dr. William Smith's Drug Store, and watched while the appalled Dr. Smith signed a pledge to sell no more liquor. Their audience grew enormously to follow while visitations were made in turn at other drugstores, at the hotels and saloons. Not all were so craven as Dr. Smith, yet two saloonkeepers signed the pledge, "later shipped their liquors to Cincinnati and sold their fixtures at auction."

It had been a pretty fair start, and if the recalcitrant liquor dealers thought that would be the end of it, they were sorely mistaken. Next day the Crusaders were out early again in force, even noisier than before, and the worst saloon in Hillsboro, the Lava Bed, operated by Joe Lance, surrendered, and Mr. Lance announced he would "go into the fish business." Day followed day, while the hymn singers continued their rounds, and a month later Mrs. Eliza Thompson could announce that the drinking places had been reduced to "one drug store, one hotel, and two saloons, and they sold very cautiously." By then Dr. Dio Lewis's big idea was whirling across Ohio like a tornado.

From Hillsboro he had gone to Washington Court House and there, on the day after Christmas, local women led by Mrs. Carpenter took vigorous action. They invaded one saloon after another, kneeling on the sawdust-covered floors to pray, then rising to read Scripture and to sing hymns. Not one hellhole surrendered. The saloonkeepers detailed a spy to watch the Crusaders, and next day, when the women went forth again, he warned of their approach and they were met with locked doors. They simply knelt in the snowy street, more than one hundred of them, to pray and carry on as before. On the twenty-seventh a new technique was added: The saloon doors were still locked. The women took up their posts by groups, one group in front of each saloon, and there they prayed and sang throughout the day, while others held a continuous prayer meeting in the Presbyterian church, during which the bell was tolled at the end of every prayer.

It was an impressive performance. The crusade was beginning to tell on the rum sellers. On the twenty-ninth the first saloonkeeper gave in. He not only signed the pledge, but went the whole way into reformation, and "nearly one thousand men, women and children witnessed the mingling of beer, ale, wine and whiskey with which they filled the gutters." The bells pealed joyously, boys shouted, the hymns mounted in volume, and thanks for victory were given to God. By January 2, and for the first time since its settlement, Washington Court House was without a place selling liquor. Another great victory was simultaneously reported in New Vienna, Clinton County, where a Visitation Band had so irritated one Van Pelt, "the wickedest saloonkeeper in Ohio," that he doused them with a bucket of beer as they knelt to pray in his barroom. They persisted, however, and at last Van Pelt gave up, saying he had not surrendered to law or force but to "the labors of love of the women."

Dioclesian Lewis was delighted almost but not quite beyond words. Declaring that the Lord, through the Visitation Bands, was going to drive liquor out of Ohio and out of the United States, he canceled the remaining dates of his lyceum circuit, and struck out on a free-lance and free-wheeling tour to keep this "whirlwind of the Lord" rolling over Indiana, Michigan, Wisconsin, Iowa, Minnesota, and half-a-dozen more states. Playing one-night stands, Dr. Lewis did prodigious work organizing women who were already inspired by their sisters in Ohio. In Minnesota the epidemic had the wonderful aid of the Singing Hutchinsons, who had founded the town of Hutchinson and lived there part of the time. These professionals were quick to recognize the great talent of Julia B. Nelson, of Red Wing, who had just written "A Song of the New Crusade," which the Hutchinsons used with mighty effect. This number was significant of the changing attitude of women. In it is none of the pleading to Father to come home. It strikes a new note, that of direct accusation of saloonkeepers. After a few verses relating how savages on the frontier slaughtered women and children, using the knife, the tomahawk, and the poisonous arrow, it tells of a more cruel war, then names it:

> And where are the hands red with slaughter?
> Behold them each day as you pass
> The places where death and destruction
> Are retailed at ten cents a glass.

The Singing Hutchinsons could and did do marvels with such lyrics, and those of Julia B. Nelson of Red Wing, Minnesota, were perfect for the purpose. They were soon added to the ammunition of the Visitation Bands who marched and prayed and sang throughout 1874 before the Women's Crusade petered out almost as suddenly as it had begun.

Like the earlier Washingtonian uproar, the crusade used up emotion too fast. It couldn't last. The crusade may well have closed the twenty-five thousand saloons claimed for it by Dr. Lewis and other interested parties. That is, temporarily. It seems also likely that most of these were open again before 1875 was far along. It is of record that Hillsboro, where it all started, promptly returned to its former wicked ways; and that Washington Court House could count more saloons in 1875 than it had in 1873.

The Internal Revenue Bureau reported that between 1873 and 1875 nearly seven hundred breweries went out of business, and that the loss in revenue ran to more than one million dollars. Yet a year later beer and revenue were soaring above all previous figures. Politicians and the liquor interests obviously had not changed their ways. Neither had the general run of concocters of patent medicines. The next thirty years was a glorious era for the makers of bitters, blood tonics, blood purifiers, and a host of elixirs, most of them carrying a heavy content of alcohol.

The phenomenal rise of proprietary medicines was due in large part to the spread of the temperance movement. It will be recalled that from its beginnings the American Temperance Union had sought to place the use of liquor fairly high in the list of what all good Christians considered heinous sins. It was a blight from which rum was unable wholly to free itself for the next hundred years and more. (If then.) The Women's Crusade intensified the idea of sin, and so did the long campaign of the Woman's Christian Temperance Union. Badgered by his womenfolk and his pastor, the man of the house hesitated to visit lawful saloons or, in dry territory, to visit the joints. Still as thirsty as old Noah, he looked around for succor. The patent-medicine men supplied it.

Until about 1906 the claims of curative values on the labels of many proprietary medicines ranged pretty much all over the field of ills. The warning symptoms to watch for were legion. No matter the actual thaumaturgic effect, the various elixirs did make the patient feel better almost at once. He might continue in that condition so long as the dose was equal to the emergency and was repeated at proper intervals. The curative agent of these remedies ran from 22 to 30 per cent alcohol by volume. Every region of the United States came in time to have a favorite. That of loggers in the Pacific Northwest, during dry periods of local option, was Old Wahoo Bitters, which, according to the late Mr. Wirt Robe, proprietor of Robe's Second-Class Emporium & Sample Room at Granite Falls, Washington, would "turn a man's hat full around on his head." But the national favorite for some thirty years was Peruna.

Peruna was the great discovery of Dr. Samuel B. Hartman, a graduate in medicine of Farmer's College, Cincinnati, who was himself an abstainer. (He didn't even drink Peruna.) Dr. Hartman's advertising was done on a colossal scale, and it stressed the dangers as well as the cure of catarrh, an almost universal ill in that it included catarrh of the stomach, catarrh of the heart, and catarrh of the kidneys. Among the thousands of printed testimonials of Peruna were many from the most eminent Americans. (Wrote Admiral Winfield Scott Schley, a hero of the Battle of Santiago Bay: "Mrs. Schley has used Peruna, and I believe with good effect.") Yet, as Dr. Hartman was fond of saying, "Peruna is its own best advertisement." Possibly because the remedy became an instant favorite in dry Maine and Kansas, both of which have bitterly cold winters, Peruna was well fortified against freezing by a generous 30 per cent of alcohol by volume.

Peruna was also a standard specific in Ohio, where it was made at Columbus and could be had in the drugstores even of Oberlin. For a quarter of a century it went unchallenged into dry country everywhere, but eventually it met trouble in Indian Territory where C. F. Larrabee, the acting commissioner, interdicted its sale because, so he said, "it has been found too tempting and effective as an intoxicant." A little later the Treasury Department notified Dr. Hartman that he had best give his nostrum a little more medical body. Ever ready to please, good Dr. Hartman added a thumping big dose of blackthorn bark to the next batch.

It may have been an oversight, but Dr. Hartman failed to issue any warning in regard to the new and improved Peruna. The results were appalling, for there ensued what a learned member of Dr. Harvey Wiley's staff of federal chemists referred to as the Great Borborygmus Era.* Strong men in Bangor and Wichita cried in perplexity that something obviously had happened to their sovereign remedy. Sales of Peruna dropped alarmingly. They never recovered. One is happy to know, however, that Dr. Hartman, according to his biographer, died wealthy, leaving in Columbus a marble mansion "and the best legitimate theater in Ohio, which he built for his stage-struck daughter."

At least one patent-medicine man played a horse different from the one that ran so well for Dr. Hartman and countless others of the period. He was Joseph Walker, an old forty-niner who in 1874 came into the market with Dr. Walker's California Vinegar Bitters, which the advertisements said were "The Only Temperance Bitters Known." Dr. Walker's splendid almanac used large type to stress the fact that his bitters were "Free From Alcohol"; while interlarded among his descriptions of many ailments were lectures on "Alcohol, The Enemy." Temperance organizations, said he, were fighting against terrible odds with "the nefarious business whose profits were almost beyond computation," and thus it behooved all friends of this great cause to stand shoulder to shoulder "in making war against the General Curse." One way to stand shoulder to shoulder was obvious; but lest the cynical reader chose to believe that the temperance movement was "being used as a means of advancing the sale of Walker's Vinegar Bitters," the doctor swore that "a portion of the profits of this Temperance Medicine will be devoted to the promotion of the Temperance Movement."

It was a noble and daring experiment. It is now impossible to know what sort of reception was accorded these temperance bitters. They seem not to have survived, and inquiry of a number of veteran druggists (in 1956) failed to find one who recalled Dr. Walker and his medicine. One can only wonder, and perhaps muse on the chance that Dr. William Smith, the druggist of Hillsboro, Ohio, who was so shaken and cowed by the Women's Crusade, thereupon stocked up with a case or two of Walker's temperance bitters. The supposition beckons the imagination: Did some thirsty but unwitting customer come in one evening, wink at

* Says Webster: "bor'bo·ryg'mus, *n.* to rumble in the bowels."

the druggist in the manner of sub rosa transactions, and ask for a bottle of bitters; and did druggist Smith, knowingly or otherwise, hand him a vial, not of, say, Old Wahoo Bitters (alcohol 27 per cent by volume) but a vial of Dr. Walker's temperance preparation?

The Temperance agitation may have been responsible for the inspiration of Dr. Leslie E. Keeley, who in 1879 told the press: "Drunkenness is a disease and I can cure it." A graduate of Rush Medical College, he had served as a surgeon with Union forces during the war, then set up as a general practitioner in small Dwight, Illinois. Here he also "continued the study of alcoholics he had begun among Union soldiers." Joseph Medill, editor of the Chicago *Tribune,* challenged Keeley's claim that he could cure drunkenness. Dr. Keeley responded by asking the editor to send him "half a dozen of the worst drunks you can find in your city." Medill did so. When they had completed Keeley's four-week treatment, they returned to Chicago. Medill was amazed. He scarcely could recognize them. "They went away sots," he wrote in his paper, "and returned gentlemen." The future of what became known as the Keeley Cure was assured.

By 1890 Keeley had opened a large sanitarium in Dwight to treat victims of liquor or drugs. He prepared a pamphlet about his treatment which he described as "Double Chloride of Gold, the Only Cure" and started to advertise in newspapers and magazines. Within a year he was coming out with a weekly paper, *The Banner of Gold.* He welcomed investigation by temperance workers and clergymen, many of whom spoke in high praise of his efforts. Among his clients soon were a number of soldiers' homes and hospitals, at least one Army post, and many Indian agencies. The cost of treatment was not exorbitant— twenty-five dollars a week for four weeks. Patients roomed in the sanitarium but were obliged to board out; Dr. Keeley provided that they should "have free access to the best brands of liquor." After the first two days, however, they had lost all appetite for it. They "could not bear the smell of the stuff."

From wet towns and dry, from big cities and hamlets, came thousands of young and middle-aged men who were having trouble with liquor. One wonders if there is a single village in the United States, incorporated before about 1900, which cannot recall at least one fellow citizen who was a graduate of the Keeley Cure. By 1895 some 30,000 of these alumni were organized in 359 chapters of the Keeley League. At that time Dr. Keeley claimed 250,000 cures. By the century's end the number had risen to 400,000, among whom were "17,000 physicians and many hundreds of women."

Although Keeley employed only regular graduate physicians, the organized medical profession objected to his methods, and said that relapses were so frequent as to cast grave doubt as to the value of the medication. Keeley responded with a statement that less than 5 per cent of his cures were followed by relapse. The controversy was of course never resolved. Dr. Keeley died February 21, 1900, of a heart ailment that was being treated, in Los Angeles, by mental-cultists. He was sixty-eight years old. The press reported him to have left an estate valued at one million dollars.

No few graduates of the Keeley Cure were said to have come from the ranks of secret or at least lone drinkers. They never set 'em up for all hands, or even one hand. They took pains to come into a bar only when business was dull; or they might not have drunk in saloons at all, but took a snifter as needed from a bottle cached on a beam in the barn, or in an office desk. In either case they never treated anybody, and in time came to be known as a Dick Smith. Who the original Dick Smith may have been was never determined. One legend has him a professional baseball player, quiet, self-centered, and lonely even in his drinking habits. He was generally looked down upon as of the anti-social type. He certainly was not one of the boys present on/that balmy summer evening when a goodly crowd was there/which well nigh filled Joe's barroom on the corner of the Square.

The Keeley Cure flourished a while longer, then went into a decline. Whether its beginnings can be attributed to the Temperance excitements of the seventies, as was the daring experiment of Vinegar Bitters, the Women's Crusade of that period was clearly responsible for two miracles, namely Mrs. Eliza Daniel Stewart and Miss Frances Elizabeth Caroline Willard. It was Mrs. Stewart of Springfield, Ohio, who went into court to make an eloquent, moving, and successful plea on behalf of a drunkard's wife against a saloonkeeper, which set something of a precedent; and she also founded, in Osborn, Ohio, an anti-liquor group called simply the Woman's League. This body is of singular interest because it amounted to being the first local chapter of what a few months later became the National Woman's Christian Temperance Union.

The other miracle prompted by Dr. Dio Lewis's Visitation Bands was the dredging from the obscurity of the schoolroom the incomparable Miss Willard, queen of the white ribboners.

6.

THE TIMES OF MISS WILLARD
AND MRS. NATION

It is difficult now to appreciate the status accorded to Miss Frances Willard. It was unique. No other living woman quite equaled it, nor was the most sainted female dead quite in her class, though their names might be used effectively to indicate her place in the matriarchy of the ages. Thus in 1891 the chairlady of a meeting of the Woman's Christian Temperance Union made an effort to introduce Miss Willard to the audience. "One day," she cried, "an angel will take a pen of diamond and dip its point in the sun's chosen rays. Then she will write, high above the proud titles of Joan of Arc and Florence Nightingale, the name of our loving sister in Christ's work who is with us this evening."

Before she took up temperance, Christ's work had meant for Miss Willard the education of the young. The Women's Crusade, however, had moved her so deeply that she resigned as head of Evanston (Illinois) College for Ladies to become president of the Chicago chapter of the Woman's Christian Temperance Union. This group had just been organized at the Second Presbyterian Church of Cleveland along plans outlined during the summer of 1874 at Lake Chautauqua, New York. Five years later Miss Willard was elected president of the national body, and to her last day she so devoted her magnetic personality and great energy to reform that her name became almost synonymous with temperance.

Born in 1839 of Vermont natives who attended Oberlin College, she was reared on a homestead in the Wisconsin wilderness. Her father appears to have been a stern man given to dogmatic beliefs, among which was that the reading of novels was a heinous sin. On her eighteenth birthday, however, his daughter calmly seated herself in the living room with a copy of *Ivanhoe* in her hand. The tirade she expected quickly followed, and she interrupted it. "Father," said she, "you forget what day it is. I am eighteen. I am of age. And now I am to do what *I* think right." She was already ripe for the "ideals of independence for women" which she found in the writings of the emancipated Margaret Fuller.

Though an engagement to be married distracted her briefly, it was broken and after schooling under Catharine Beecher, and at North-western Female College, she began teaching in a country school near Evanston. She went on to take posts at Pittsburgh, at Lima, N. Y., and finally at Evanston. She was thus employed when the Singing Bands of the Women's Crusade had their wonderful hour. She had previously become a convert to Methodism, and after marching only once with a Singing Band she "went with zeal into the temperance movement."

As yet the W.C.T.U. had collected little money. But Frances made haste to Old Orchard Beach, Maine, to attend a "Gospel Temperance Camp Meeting," and there met the revered General Neal Dow, who inspired her by relating the story of the first prohibitory law; and one Francis Murphy, who described himself as "a drinking man and saloon-keeper recently reformed."

She went to Boston in order to meet him responsible for this new mania against rum, Dr. Dio Lewis, who "could only tell me o'er and o'er that" if women would go to the saloons they could soon close them for-ever. By this time, however, the temperature of the Women's Crusade was noticeably dropping fast, and Miss Willard felt she should have other and broader counsels than this "considerate and kindly old gentleman whose words had been the match that fired the powder mine." Miss Willard's native good sense told her that the Temperance Union must have money before it could even dent the armor of the minions of hell. That night, in her hotel room, she picked up a Bible lying on the bureau—possibly the gift of some forgotten precursor of the Gideons—and opened it to light on Psalm 37:3: "Trust in the Lord, and do good; so shalt thou dwell in the land, and verily thou shalt be fed." This was all she needed. She set out to find her own place "within the charmed circle of Temperance reform."

That Miss Willard found her place and expanded it is crystal clear. During her long regime, and often through her pervasive influence, the Union achieved notable victories. When Rutherford B. Hayes was elected President of the United States, his wife, a close friend of Miss Willard, announced that as long as she was First Lady, no alcoholic liquor would be served, either at social functions in the White House or at the President's own table. It was Miss Willard, too, who prepared for Senator Henry W. Blair, of New Hampshire, a proposed amendment to the Constitution which, had it been adopted, would have made the United States as theoretically dry as it became in 1920.

In 1880, Kansas shocked the liquor industry by voting for state prohibition by constitutional amendment. Two years later Iowa gave a majority of thirty thousand votes in favor of a similar law, only to have it invalidated by the courts because of an error in the text as printed in the official record. Egged on by the Union, Iowans compelled the legislature to make the state dry by statute. Oregon and Indiana failed to establish constitutional prohibition because of what Temperance Union people said were purposeful errors inserted in the acts by tricky legislators.

The newly organized Prohibition party, even with help from Miss Willard's ladies, failed to attract many votes; and the W.C.T.U. decided to put a little more heat on the Democrats and the Republicans. In 1884, Miss Willard herself appeared at the Republican National Convention to present a memorial urging the inclusion of a prohibition plank in the party platform. She was coldly received, and only after a bitter argument was she permitted to present the memorial. Nothing, of course, came of it, but somebody took the trouble to learn what became of the memorial itself. It was found "amid the litter on the floor of the committee room aslime with tobacco juice," and the Temperance Union promptly published it in facsimile as evidence of Republican disrespect for Christian women.

Neither Miss Willard nor the Union was discouraged because both the Republican and Democratic political machines were hostile. Under her leadership local branches of the group were established in almost every city, village, and hamlet in every state and territory of the United States, and during the last two decades of her life the Union virtually compelled every state legislature to enact statutes providing for compulsory teaching of the dangers of beverage alcohol in all public schools. Thus were the classic colored plates of good Dr. Thomas Sewall's six stomachs inserted by statute in the physiology books of still more generations of potential drunkards, to remind young Americans of the dangers inherent in the most baleful institution in the country—the saloon.

In 1893 the first reform group to ignore the euphemism of "temperance" in favor of an honest name was organized as the Anti-Saloon League of Ohio. It was the legitimate child of the Oberlin Temperance Alliance, which had been formed during the Women's Crusade twenty years before, in the college town where reforms of all kinds had stewed and steamed, including the banning of tobacco, tea, coffee, white flour, and pepper. The Alliance had devoted its efforts to promote a local-option law, passed in 1888. The success may have come too easily. In any event, the Ohio reformers were feeling their oats, and now, at the suggestion of the Rev. David Otis Mears, late of Amherst college and of the Piedmont Congregational Church at Worcester, Massachusetts, they turned the Alliance into the direct-action group that was soon to dominate liquor reform in the United States.

Two years after the Ohio league was formed a call for a national convention in Washington, D.C., resulted in organization of the Anti-Saloon League of America. This was largely the work of the Rev.

Alpha Jefferson Kynett, Methodist clergyman of Iowa, who had discussed it with, among others, Archbishop John Ireland, who appears to have been the first Roman Catholic prelate to join actively with Protestant reformers. Hiram Price, a former Republican representative in Congress from Iowa, became the first president. One of the several vice-presidents was Archbishop Ireland.

Within a short time the Anti-Saloon League of America had strong branches in forty states. Most of its staff, including field agents, were paid employees. Volunteer help was welcomed, but only as long as the professionals could direct the work undertaken. "Temperance" was not discussed; prohibition was. Here was the first hard-boiled, businesslike, and rather cynical outfit to appear in the liquor reform movement since it began. It wasn't long until the more astute saloonkeepers realized they were facing a much greater danger than that presented by "the massed Christian women of the Country." A popular and respected trade magazine, *The Wine and Spirit Circular,* gave them warning and identified the enemy.

The Anti-Saloon League [it said] is not a mob of long-haired fanatics ... but a strongly centralized organization, officered by men with unusual ability, financiered by capitalists with long purses, subscribed to by hundreds of thousands of men, women and children who are solicited by their various churches, advised by well-paid attorneys of great ability, and it is working with definite ideas to guide it in every state, in every county, in every city, in every precinct ...

This warning was no exaggeration. If anything, it was an understatement. Under the direction of Wayne Bidwell Wheeler, who, though not a clergyman, was significantly a graduate of Oberlin College, the Anti-Saloon League of America was to grow swiftly into the holy terror of the liquor business. Wheeler believed that the end justified the means. He had no perspective, and even less of humor; but he was tireless, audacious, and filled—said an admiring friend—"with a passionate sincerity that bordered unscrupulousness." We shall meet him again. But before Wayne B. Wheeler could get into full stride, the saloonkeepers were bedeviled by a female awash with passionate sincerity and who did not "border unscrupulousness." So far as rum was concerned, she *had* no scruples.

She was born Carry Amelia Moore in Kentucky. By the time she came into the public eye she was Carry A. Nation, an amazon five feet eleven and one-half inches tall who kept her weight down to one hundred and seventy-five pounds by exercise for the Lord—the prodigious wrecking of saloons. The odd spelling of her first name was due to the imperfect learning of her father. Her mother lived for many years in the delusion that she was Queen Victoria, and died in the Missouri State Hospital for the Insane.

In 1867 Carry met and married a young physician, Dr. Charles Gloyd, who showed up at the altar smelling of cloves and alcohol. Marriage did not perform a miracle. Six months later he was lowered into a drunkard's grave. Ten years later Carry married David Nation, and together they faced a quarter of a century of bickering, battles, and wandering, while the incompetent Nation almost but never quite made a living with his combined talents as a lawyer, an editor, and a minister of the Gospel.

Meantime Mrs. Nation brooded on her troubles, and often in the dark watches of the night Jesus Himself appeared to comfort her. In their discussions He told Carry she had been chosen to become a martyr to a number of causes which included, not only temperance, but also the doing away with tobacco and with all fraternal orders. (Carry's first husband had done a good deal of drinking in the quarters of his lodge, from which women were excluded.) This was the mental baggage she was carrying when the Nations moved again, this time to Medicine Lodge, Kansas, where her husband, in the character of the Rev. David Nation, preached a while before reverting to law; and Mrs. Nation was elected president of the Barber County chapter of the Woman's Christian Temperance Union.

It was an office that President Nation accepted with the utmost seriousness. Kansas was technically dry by constitutional amendment, and actually pretty wet because of the profound appetites of the farmers for the end product of their handsome fields of corn, wheat, and rye. Medicine Lodge alone, as Mrs. Nation quickly discovered, supported seven drinking places, or "joints," as saloons were popularly known throughout Kansas. She set about to close them by writing appeals to the governor and the attorney general of the state, to the sheriff of Barber County, and to various newspapers. None so much as replied. In this extremity, as she related in her autobiography, Carry Nation had recourse to prayer and divination; and on the afternoon of June 5, 1900, with her eyes tightly shut, jabbed a pin at random into her opened Bible, then looked to see that she had impaled the sixtieth chapter of Isaiah: "Arise, shine; for thy light is come, and the glory of the Lord is risen upon thee."

No scriptural message, not even that which had come to Miss Willard in a Boston hotel, was more fruitful than this received on the far plains of Kansas by Mrs. Nation. Carry was ready to rise and shine, and within a few minutes a musical voice murmured in her ear a command. "Go to Kiowa!" it said. There was a brief silence, then the voice again, "Take something in your hands and throw at those places and smash them!" Only then did she know exactly what the Lord expected of her.

Next day at dawn she bounced out of bed in exaltation. Singing snatches of hymns, she went into the back yard to assemble a creditable pile of stones and bricks. These she wrapped one by one in old newspapers, put them into the buggy, hitched up her horse, and drove out of Medicine Lodge on the jolting and dusty road to Kiowa, nigh twenty miles distant, and destiny. Arrived after nightfall in what was reputed to be "the wettest town in Barber County," she lay low till morning, then hitched up her rig and drove to the joint operated by a Mr. Dobson, there to make history.

With a dozen or more of the missiles stacked upon her left arm, she pushed open the saloon door to find a few hung-over men working hopefully on their eye-openers. They stared incredibly at the apparition of this motherly woman (Carry was fifty-four years old) in a whiskey joint, but they stared only briefly. "Men," said she, "I have come to save you from a drunkard's fate!" Then she let go with her neolithic artillery. She had a powerful arm and, unlike most women, she could throw. Her first missile smashed the large mirror behind the bar. The second was a perfect strike that shattered every glass on the back bar and also broke several bottles. Now sure of herself, she poured a torrent of paper-wrapped stones at the surviving bottles of liquor, then turned to address the poor proprietor. "Now, Mr. Dobson," she said, "I have finished. God be with you." She flounced out of the devastated joint, got into her buggy, and was about to drive off when a happy idea took her. Reaching under the seat, she picked up two more of her neatly packaged stones and heaved them through Mr. Dobson's windows. Then she set her horse to walking briskly down the street.

Kiowa's horrible afternoon was not done, for Carry's ammunition was no more exhausted than she. In a matter of minutes she made desolation of two more joints, improving her original technique by ripping several prints of actresses and sporting figures from the walls, overturning beer tables, smashing chairs, to emerge from the last joint smelling gloriously of the alcohol sprayed by breaking bottles and running in riverlets over the barroom floor. She made no haste to leave the stricken town, but courted the attention of the city marshal and the mayor, of whom she demanded to be arrested. The officials declined, and Carry Nation drove out of Kiowa in what until then was the incomparable triumph of her life.

The Kiowa raid was given only short notice in the Wichita and Topeka papers, but more, much more, was to come. The Madwoman of Kansas was resolved to lay waste to every joint in the state, including what she called "the murder mills of the metropolis of Wichita." She reflected on the glory that had come to an earlier hero, and wondered aloud "if it were perhaps God's will to make me a sacrifice as he did John Brown."

Wichita was notoriously wet. Forty-odd joints ran openly with no concealment other than curtained windows and doors. Each displayed a modest sign, "Sample Room," the current cryptogram for saloon, especially in dry territory. A few more were operated in conjunction with eating places. Another reason Wichita attracted Mrs. Nation was that a majority of Kansas wholesale liquor dealers had their warehouses there.

For her first sortie into Wichita, Carry Nation dressed in the garb she wore as the uniform of a soldier of the Lord to the end of her career: a black alpaca dress fastened by a row of dark pearl buttons extending up the left side from hem to yoke; a broad bow of white ribbon at her throat; heavy, square-toed shoes; black cotton stockings; a black poke bonnet with a silk ribbon tied under her chin; and, except in hot weather, a heavy cape of navy blue cloth. Almost always she carried an umbrella. Cartoonists, with whom she was for many years a favorite character, found her getup perfect for quick and easy delineation.

She was thus attired when she took a train of steamcars for Wichita, save that in place of the umbrella she carried her husband's rugged walking stick and a valise in which she had put a foot-long iron rod. The press of Wichita had not been warned of her coming. On her first day in the city she went forth to inspect the sample rooms, and made no comment until she entered the most elegant joint in all Kansas. This was operated in the basement of the Hotel Carey, and its long, curved bar was a splendid thing of solid cherry, carved and polished, that reflected the brilliance of hundreds of electric lights. Mrs. Nation was fairly blinded, but not quite, and on one wall her beady black eyes did not miss an enormous oil painting, *Cleopatra at the Bath*. She stopped dead in her tracks.

Now, Carry Nation had not planned to pass any comment during this her initial tour of Wichita joints, but the naked Cleopatra changed her mind. She reflected—so she wrote later—that women were stripped of everything by the saloons. Her husband is torn from her. She is robbed of her sons. Then they take away her clothes "and her virtue." This reflection occupied Mrs. Nation no more than a moment. She strode to the bar, pointed a quivering finger at the startled bartender. "Young man," she demanded, "what are you doing in this hellhole?"

"I'm sorry, madam," he replied, "but we do not serve ladies."

"Serve ME!" screamed Carry Nation. "Do you think I'd drink your hellish poison?" She pointed at Cleopatra. "Take that filthy thing down," she cried, "and close this murder-mill." Then she snatched a bottle from the bar, threw it to the floor, and ran out into the street.

She returned to her hotel, to muse on the Hotel Carey bar, "this hell glittering with crystallized tears," and to take from her valise the short iron bar. This she bound with stout cord to the cane and, hiding this formidable weapon beneath her cape, returned to the Hotel Carey, pausing in an alley to pick up a fair load of stones, which she wrapped in a newspaper. Now she was ready for Cleopatra.

On cat's feet the enemy of Cleopatra entered the Carey bar to find bartender Parker serving half a dozen men. They had time only to gape before Carry started heaving rocks that smashed the immense gilt frame and tore through the canvas. "Glory to God!" she shouted. "Peace on earth, good will to men!" Then she heaved another stone to crash almost into the exact center of the great mirror behind the bar. ("Cost fifteen hunnert dollars," bartender Parker told the police.) It tumbled in fragments. The drinkers and bartender lammed through the rear doorway, and Carry moved into the second phase of the battle. Bringing forth the wicked tool she had fashioned from cane and iron rod, she tore around one end of the bar and began slashing at the orderly array of bottles, decanters, and glassware on the back bar. All disintegrated with a most satisfying noise. When Detective Park Massey, followed by curious guests, walked into the saloon, Carry had lifted one of the finest and biggest brass cuspidors in Kansas to the top of the cherry bar and was beating it furiously.

"Madam," said the officer, "I must arrest you for defacing property."

"Defacing?" she screamed. "Defacing? I am defacing nothing! I am *destroying!*" The general appearance of the Hotel Carey bar indicated Mrs. Nation had a better understanding of the niceties of the language than did Detective Massey. When she was taken before Judge O. D. Kirk, the charge was read and Mrs. Nation was asked whether she pled guilty. "I'll have nothing to do with this court," she snapped, "until that man over there throws away his cigar. It's rotten and it poisons me." And "that man," who happened to be the prosecuting attorney, dropped the offending cigar into a cuspidor.

There was a terrible to-do about Carry Nation in the Kansas courts before she was released on bail, and at last the charges were dismissed because, said the prosecuting attorney, he feared for the crusader's mental condition. The crusader's mental condition was unchanged, or perhaps it was intensified, by the hundreds of congratulatory telegrams, letters, and callers that had arrived. There were many requests for help from women in towns and cities all over Kansas, and from other states. "For God's sake come here," was the request. Carry Nation was delighted. She felt she was on the way to the martyrdom and fame she strongly wanted. Even New York City and Boston papers had given front-page notice of her destruction of the Hotel Carey's saloon.

There is no need to tell of more than one of the score or more subsequent raids, all during 1901, which by year's end had made her incomparably the most notorious female character in the United States. The raid in question gave her the symbol by which she is best remembered half a century later. It also shows graphically the perfection of technique she had achieved after no more than half a dozen raids.

This attack was in Topeka, to which Carry had come in order "to free the Capital of Kansas from the shame of its saloons." With her she brought four brand-new hatchets that cost eighty-five cents each and were of the same fine quality as one she had used with terrible effect on the Douglas Avenue Sample Room of James Burnes, in Wichita.

Snow was falling heavily in Topeka when, at the ungodly hour of six in the morning, Mrs. Nation, a Mrs. John White, and a Miss Madeline Southard, a local evangelist of some power, met on Kansas Avenue and proceeded to the restaurant (and barroom) of E. C. Russam, who had got word that the now-famous enemy of whiskey was in town. At the entrance of his place, even at this early hour, the three women ran head-on into a couple of surly guards and were defeated after a brisk contact during which Mrs. Nation sustained slight wounds from her own weapon on forehead and one hand.

Pausing only long enough to stanch the flow of blood with handkerchiefs, the three raiders plodded through the deepening snow across Kansas Avenue, to note there were no guards on duty at the elegant entrance to the Senate Bar, Topeka's finest drinking establishment. Whereupon Mrs. Nation, Mrs. White, and Miss Southard pushed open the door and entered without disturbing Benner Tucker, the popular and efficient bartender, who was busy polishing glasses. He became aware of his visitors when he heard pounding and the tinkle of breaking glass.

Mr. Tucker turned instantly to see Miss Southard at work with bright shining hatchet on the cigar case, while Mrs. Nation and Mrs. White were chopping away at the glossy-smooth bar, raising chips of a size and depth beyond the ability of most women. Tucker knew instantly who his callers were. He grabbed the house revolver from behind the bar and advanced with the idea he would frighten these vixens. Frighten? Mrs. Nation met him halfway, lunged, and swung her weapon viciously at his head. Tucker dodged, snatched the hatchet from her hand, fired two shots into the rococo ceiling, then went through the rear door at a dead run, shouting for the police.

Carry Nation gave a bellow of triumph. "For Your sake, Jesus," she cried, and from beneath her cloak brought forth her spare hatchet and attacked the big mirror. While glass was still falling, she swept her weapon, much like a stick on a picket fence, along the long row of glassware on the back bar, and shouted her special kind of abuse at the absent bartender. "How do you do?" she called. "You maker of drunkards and widows?"

While the acolytes, Mrs. White and Miss Southard, continued to perform as well as their limited imaginations permitted, Mrs. Nation went ahead with feverish experimentation. "The arm of God smiteth!" she cried, and grabbed the cash register from its moorings on the bar. With little more than a genteel grunt she lifted the heavy machine above her head, then heaved it halfway across the saloon, to watch it crash to the floor, with its bell ringing No Sale as never before, while tiny wheels and bolts and silver rolled in happy confusion. It had been a mighty effort. She had been granted the strength of giants.

Mrs. Nation paused only to badger the still-absent bartender again. "Good morning," she shouted, "you destroyer of men's souls!" then turned her attention into demolition channels. First she strode up to face the monstrous refrigerator. With the hammer end of her hatchet she smashed the lock, opened its vast door, which she grasped firmly in her two hands, and tore it fair from its hinges. Taking up her hatchet again, she cut the rubber tube which conducted the beer from the tanks to the faucets, and then, using the tube as a hose, sprayed good St. Louis beer over the walls and ceilings, to cascade down and drench herself and co-workers in malted foam. A squad of police entered to arrest the three crusaders, after disarming them.

The whole gorgeous story went out over the wires, and Carry and Hatchet went into the folklore of the nation. Cartoonists got busy. Almost before one knew it, too, miniature hatchets labeled with her name were being hawked in cities from coast to coast and offered for sale by news butchers on trains.

Other hatchet women appeared as if by magic. In Danville, Kansas, a tall, lean female named Mary Sheriff wrecked a local joint with a hatchet, collected a group of women she called the Flying Squadron of Jesus, and swept through Harper County like a plague, attacked sample rooms in Attica, Anthony, and other towns and left them in dreadful condition; while in Elk County there arose a smasher fit to talk with Mrs. Nation herself. She was Mrs. McHenry. In a brief war she laid waste to every joint in the county, then moved on to new successes all over the state. Other imitators of the Lioness of the Lord erupted, if only briefly, in Illinois, Indiana, and Ohio. These plagiarists had no effect on Mrs. Nation's fame save to enhance it.

In that day a character of the celebrity of Carry Nation was headed as surely for the lyceum circuit as for heaven. Billed variously, according to neighborhood, as The Home Defender, The Smasher, The Wrecker

of Saloons, The Woman with the Hatchet, she toured much of the
United States. She began publication of a weekly paper, *The Hatchet*.
She went to Washington for the express purpose of talking to—not with—
President Theodore Roosevelt, to warn him of the hideous example his
daughter Alice was setting for pure womanhood by smoking cigarettes.
The White House guard was polite but firm. He met Mrs. Nation before
she got to the door to inform her it was not possible to see the President.
When she began a harangue about cigarette fiends, the guard broke in.
"Madam," he said, "do not make a lecture here." Mrs. Nation sighed,
and left with a well-turned phrase. "I suppose," she said, "you have the
same motto here in the White House that they have in the saloons, 'All
Nations Welcome Except Carry.' " She went away to tell a newspaper
reporter that Roosevelt's predecessor, President McKinley, might have
recovered from the wounds of his assassin "had not his blood been
poisoned by nicotine," and left such dark inference as the reporter cared
to form in regard to what might well happen to the Roosevelts.

Though a few individual members of the W.C.T.U. considered
Carry Nation a true hero-martyr in the John Brown tradition, she was
treated coolly, then with increasing hostility by virtually all of the Union.
The excitement she created gradually died in the United States. She
went abroad to lecture in the British Isles, where she appeared in the
music halls and was greeted by large audiences and often with showers
of eggs and vegetables. Finding on return that she was in great danger
of being wholly forgotten, she attacked the barroom in Washington's
Union Depot, late in 1909, and wrought fearful havoc with *three* hatchets
she told the police were Faith, Hope, and Charity. In the following
January she made her last attack. It was properly enough in Butte,
Montana, then, as now, a lively town, and it was directed at May Maloy's
Dance Hall & Cafe. For the sake of the record, it was on January 26,
1910, when Carry Nation entered Miss Maloy's place with the avowed
intention to destroy a painting, and was met at the entrance by the
proprietor herself, a young and powerful woman, who went hammer-
and-tongs at the astonished crusader. The encounter was brief, terrible,
and one-sided. The old champ went down, and went away to Arkansas.
On January 2, 1911, she was stricken while speaking against joints
and jointists at Eureka Springs, and died June 9 in Evergreen Hospital,
Leavenworth, Kansas.

In Mrs. Nation's day almost nobody had a good word for saloons.
The brewers and distillers were inclined to let the saloonkeeper fight his
own battles, smugly confident that more genteel vendors of their wares
would take his place. Though the Anti-Saloon League ignored Carry
Nation, her furious onslaught focused publicity on the liquor outlets, and

she also forced Kansas and other pseudo-dry states—as one commentator put it—to "live up to their pretensions." He thought that "a whole host of temperance workers were unequal to her influence."

Carry Nation was a unique character in many ways, including the fact that she is best remembered by the symbol she made her own, much as an earlier American female, Miss Lizzie Borden of Fall River, Massachusetts, is remembered for a slightly larger symbol, which was the ax.

7.

TRIUMPH AND THE GREAT ILLUSION

SURVIVORS of the prohibition era in the United States may be excused if in retrospect they recall the Anti-Saloon League of America as led by a group of hard-boiled fanatics who believed that almost a century of temperance effort had proved moral suasion to be worthless and set about to ban liquor by police action. This may be a simplification, yet it is near enough to pass muster.

If objection be made to identification as hard-boiled fanatics, it is well to recall a statement made in 1926 by Wayne B. Wheeler, the League's incomparable counsel and superintendent. Six years after prohibition became law, and deaths from drinking alcohol denatured by federal act had increased alarmingly, Mr. Wheeler was happy to defend the use of poisoned alcohol. The government, he pointed out, was under no obligation to furnish people with potable alcohol when the Constitution forbade it. "The person who drinks this industrial alcohol," he added with obvious satisfaction, "is deliberately a suicide." This ex-cathedra statement of the Anti-Saloon League seemed a notice that the Christ and Temperance of Miss Frances Willard had lost out and that an Old Testament God of savage determination had taken over the business in characteristic style.

The change of attitude and direction was at first subtle. The clear-thinking fanatics of the League knew well enough that they must have the churches and the temperance people on their side. This alliance was virtually guaranteed by the League's officers, among whom were the Rev. George Young of Kentucky and the Methodist bishop of Virginia, James Cannon, Jr., a man to reckon with in church affairs, in legislative halls, and in the field closely allied to that of legislation, which was money. No one understood more clearly than the Anti-Saloon Leaguers that because a majority of laws have some economic aspect or other their introduction and passage are not often accomplished without the expenditure of money, both by those who want the laws passed and by those who would be injured by their passage. Superintendent Wheeler testified that in less than thirty years the League had spent thirty-five million dollars "to create and to sustain public interest in its cause."

An idea of how public interest was created and sustained was made fairly clear by the most illustrious of the League's army of field agents, William E. (Pussyfoot) Johnson, who recalled with apparent enjoyment his supervision of successful campaigns for constitutional prohibition in many states. He described his work specifically as "publicity and underground activities," to which end he boasted, "he had drunk gallons of whiskey and told enough lies to make Ananias ashamed of himself."

The enormous sums raised and spent by the League came in some part directly from church organizations, in some part from the Woman's Christian Temperance Union, but in much greater part from wealthy industrialists who had become convinced that liquor was not of any help to the speed-up incidental to mass production. It would appear also that the League received much greater return for money spent than did the liquor interests, whose war chest was variously estimated from five to twenty million dollars annually. For instance, the League managed to keep the moral suasionists of the temperance societies in hand by establishing, at little more cost than for letterheads and neat buttons, a Lincoln Legion of total abstainers who liked the idea of signing a pledge allegedly written by Abraham Lincoln in 1846. When the Lincoln Legion failed to interest the South, the alert researchers of the League suddenly discovered that Robert E. Lee had also been "a firm advocate of temperance," the Legion was converted promptly into the Lincoln-Lee Legion, and some two million Southerners signed up for prohibition.

Meanwhile the legislative and "undercover" departments of the Anti-Saloon League were hewing to the line of drying up the country by law. In 1907 Georgia voted dry, and was in quick succession followed by North Carolina, Tennessee, Mississippi, West Virginia, and Oklahoma. The League refused to endorse either political party, and even considered William Jennings Bryan, noted as a dry orator, to be an antique nuisance. What the League did was to choose carefully the candidates for political office, then put the weight of its financial and moral support behind them. It paid off. In 1913 some five thousand men and women were summoned to Washington to observe a celebration of the alliance between the Anti-Saloon League and the W.C.T.U. Wearing white satin badges and carrying banners inscribed "National Constitutional

Prohibition," they paraded the capital, then held a mass meeting at which was presented to Senator Morris Sheppard, of Texas, and Representative Richmond P. Hobson, of Alabama, a petition asking Congress to submit to the people a constitutional amendment prohibiting the traffic in intoxicating liquors for beverage purposes. It was a shadow of things to come. That very afternoon, which was the tenth day of December, both Mr. Sheppard and Mr. Hobson introduced submission resolutions in Congress.

The Anti-Saloon and Temperance Union songsters cut loose with a favorite number entitled "A Saloonless Nation in 1920." Women wept for joy, and the male delegates cheered. Wayne B. Wheeler did neither. There was work to be done. "Congressional elections were to be held in November, 1914," he later wrote, "and we planned to concentrate on them and the preceding primaries." Wheeler soon had the League's big printing establishment at Westerville, Ohio, running three shifts. "It was no uncommon thing," he said, "for whole carloads of printed material to roll out of the plant in a single day." No less than twenty-thousand speakers, mostly volunteers, took the field, "directing their fire upon the wets in every village, town, city, county and state." Their number was later increased almost threefold. "We went into every Congressional district where there was a chance to elect a dry . . . we were also bombarding the House and Senate in Washington. . . . We kept our field workers advised of the attitude of every individual member of Congress. "And," he added meaningly, "we suggested ways to the local workers of winning converts."

There was to be no letup. The first intimation that a constitutional amendment was not a joke came late in 1914 when the House voted 197 to 190 in favor of Mr. Hobson's resolution. A two-thirds vote was necessary, but the trial run was encouraging.

The wets roused at last. They expected the drys to make another attempt in 1915 and 1916, but they did nothing of the kind. "The strategy of the day," Mr. Wheeler remarked, "dictated that we hold off until we were sure of the necessary two-thirds majority." And "we laid down such a barrage as candidates for Congress had never seen before." The coming of war in April 1917 caused President Wilson himself to request that resubmission of the prohibition act be delayed so that Congress could get on with the war, which seemed to many to be more important even than dry legislation. The Anti-Saloon League gracefully agreed not to press the matter. They could afford to. No matter who won the battles in Europe, the war was on the side of the Anti-Saloon League and its allies.

The war, as Charles Merz pointed out in his study of *The Dry Decade,* did three things for prohibition in the United States. It centralized authority in Washington. It stressed the importance of saving food. It sought to outlaw all things German. The first change was inevitable, for the restraints normally imposed on Congress were brushed aside, while the government seized the railroads, took over mines, fixed prices, punished careless use of fuel. Secondly, the importance of food was clear. The Anti-Saloon League was ready with figures alleged to show the infinite number of loaves of bread which could be made from the grain "wasted in a single day by the brewing of beer and distillation of spirits." And as early as November 9, 1917, Wayne B. Wheeler, in a New York *Times* interview, was happy to pass a few remarks about the enemy in our midst. "The liquor traffic aids those forces in our country," smeared he gravely, "whose loyalty is called into question at this hour. The liquor traffic is the strong financial supporter of the German-American Alliance." Pausing a moment to contemplate the horrible dangers on every hand, he mentioned that the chief purpose of the Alliance was to promote German ideals and German *Kultur* "and oppose any restriction or prohibition of the liquor traffic."

This was hitting well below the belt, which is just where Mr. Wheeler liked to catch an antagonist. He was glad to leave to the clerical arm of the Anti-Saloon League the opportunity to bring God into the matter. This was done promptly by an official statement from the League's headquarters, possibly written by Bishop Cannon, who was good at such things. Said the statement: "The spirit of service and self-sacrifice exemplified in our wonderfully efficient and loyal staff made it possible to take advantage of the war situation and the confusion which He whom we serve has wrought among our enemies." This pious comment had reference to the Food Control Act, a war emergency measure just passed which closed the distilleries and was, only a bit later, to close the breweries as well. It was understood that the closures were for the duration of war only.

The confusion which He-whom-we-serve and the Anti-Saloon League had wrought seemed to palsy the hands and minds of the liquor lobby in Congress. Even before the breweries could comply with the shutdown order, the House overrode the last defenders of states' rights and voted, 282 to 128, to adopt the Eighteenth Amendment, subject to ratification by thirty-six states. The League doubled its pressure on various state legislative bodies. Its hatchet men were dispatched to see the boys in the chambers of capitols all the way from Concord to Carson City, from Tallahassee to Lincoln, and to tell them, subtly or otherwise, what happened to bad men who did not "Vote Patriotic." The results were fantastically successful: On January 8, 1918, Mississippi ratified, and other legislatures fairly fell over each other in haste. At 10:32 on the morning of January 16, 1919, Nebraska's upper house voted 31 to 1 to ratify. It was the thirty-sixth state to do so.

Meanwhile the thoughtful Wayne B. Wheeler had written an enforcement act for Congressman Andrew Volstead of Minnesota which readily passed both House and Senate. When later in the year President Woodrow Wilson vetoed the bill, House and Senate promptly swamped the veto; and Congressman Volstead was assured of immortality for at least fourteen years. The great lid was now ready to be clamped down. The clamping shut was set for January 16, 1920. The Anti-Saloon League's high command prepared a nice greeting to mark the occasion. This was proper enough. Who, after all, had laid strong hands on the great dream of generations of well-meaning if ineffectual temperance people and congealed it into the hard fact of the Eighteenth Amendment?

"It is here at last—dry America's first birthday," said the League's greeting, given to the press on January 15, 1920. "At one minute past twelve tomorrow morning a new nation will be born ... Tonight John Barleycorn makes his last will and testament. Now for an era of clear thinking and clean living! The Anti-Saloon League wishes every man, woman and child a happy Dry Year."

In view of what happened it seems unlikely that a more preposterous statement than this could have been composed. The era of clear thinking and clean living turned out to be fourteen years of a titanic farce, tragic and costly beyond calculation. The manufacture, transportation, and sale of liquor became the biggest business in the country. It was protected by corruption the like of which has not been seen before or since. Gangsterism flourished. The wars of bootleggers and highjackers made the tommy-gun a symbol. The United States had never been a particularly orderly country, but prohibition turned us into the most lawless nation on earth. It is not the plan of this book to remind us who suffered through it, or to warn younger generations, what the Anti-Saloon League's "happy Dry Years" were like. They went into history as the Great Illusion, and one can be happy that Frances Willard, who after all was a gentle person and in spite of only too many of her admirers a modest one, did not live to see the ultimate flowering of temperance. It was as foul a species of flora as ever bloomed.

The Great Illusion disappeared into the mists of bygones on December 5, 1933, when it was repealed by adoption of the Twenty-first Amendment to the Constitution. It is worthy of notice that the women of the United States, to whom the Nineteenth Amendment had given suffrage, had a hand in voting to repeal the Eighteenth, which had been passed when women were voteless. That many of them must have voted for repeal seems assured if only by the fact that several hundred thousands of them were hard-working members of the Women's Committee for Repeal of the Eighteenth Amendment, organized in 1927, whose slogan was "The Restoration of the Bill of Rights."

Whether Americans are a more or a less temperate people than they were forty years ago, they are no longer doing their drinking in woman-less saloons. The heroic efforts of the Anti-Saloon League had one last-ing influence. Americans today do their drinking in bars, taverns, grills, beer parlors, and cocktail lounges, where the principle of equal rights for women is respected.

Part Four

GOD MADE THE LAND FOR USE

1.

A MOST VEXING PROBLEM

THE most vexing problem facing the new United States of America, at the end of the Revolutionary War, was neither eugenics nor rum. It was land—the same hoary old subject that had troubled kings and prophets through the ages. Down the years still echoed clear the great discontent of Isaiah. "Woe unto them," he had cried in warning, "that join house to house, that lay field to field, till there be no place . . ."

With the United States it was scarcely a matter of there being "no place." The new nation set up in business with an immense domain. It was soon to add another empire by the purchase of Louisiana. It was to acquire new lands steadily until it occupied the Pacific coast and a grand total of more than three million square miles. What troubled the Founding Fathers was not a dearth of vacant land but how best to distribute it to the everlasting glory of the republic.

There it lay beyond the first mountains, a world of land extending beyond the feeble imaginations of a people who for generations had thought in terms of room for a cottage and garden, with all else enclosed for the use and pleasure of kings and barons. There it lay, fallow and waiting for the ax and plow, a wilderness of forest night and sunny plain, of remote rivers flowing through an illimitable silence that was broken only, wrote a wilderness poet, by the melancholy cadences of the owl.

The poet seems not to have heard them, but the wilderness was also broken here and there by the cries of surveyors and agents of men already known as land sharks, land jobbers, and even worse names. Indeed, it had been controversies between states, often instigated by land sharks, that had been delaying ratification of the Articles of Confederation and perpetual union. When confederation was completed, the need of federal revenue was so urgent that Congress began almost immediately to sell vast tracts of wild lands at less than bargain rates. These sales were made through the Land Ordinance of 1785, which was to remain the basis for American land policy for three quarters of a century, or until the Homestead Act of 1862. The Homestead Act was incomparably the more equitable system, but it, too, was subject to gross abuses. By then the circumvention of laws relating to disposition of public land had been raised to an art.

From early colonial times land sharks proved equal or superior to any act of crown, province, state, or federal government. More than one legislator, honest or otherwise, came in time to believe that quicksilver was more easily controlled than were the so-called wild lands.

Our first Congress was far from naïve in the matter of public lands. These were men well acquainted with the history of land acquisition by private companies and individuals. No few of them themselves had had a hand in real estate transactions of doubtful legality. It was much the same with the legislative bodies of the thirteen new states. They were prompt to confiscate the crown lands, those of Tories, and the princely estates of proprietors like the Penns, the Calverts, and others. These were redistributed, though only in part, to small farmers and war veterans.

The first state and federal legislators faced an aggressive electorate that was in a terrible hurry to taste the material fruits of democracy. The war veterans wanted the pay they hadn't got. And nearly everybody else wanted something. More often than not it was land they wanted, for the right to vote was still the privilege of men of property. They got land, too, but mostly, so it turned out for many years, they had to get it from a private land company. They had to *pay for it*.

For generations we have cherished the romantic idea that in colonial times, and early days of the republic, all a man who wanted land had to do was to strike out in any direction into the wilderness to cut himself a clearing, build a cabin, then lay a fence, or merely blaze a line of trees to encompass such land as he thought he wanted. Whereupon he was not only a freeholder, but something of a baron who owed nothing to king, church, or state. Without asking leave of anybody here he was, lord of a domain by right of peaceful conquest. We fancy him raising his first corn among the stumps, pounding it to meal; shooting or catching his meat and clothing; teaching his children to read with the Bible as textbook and bullrushes for illumination.

This pleasant myth, based on the sovereign American squatter, is one of the most satisfying we have. It has, however, little substance of fact, for it usually turned out that land sharks in one shape or another had got there ahead of him, not necessarily in person but in the form of a grantee-lord of whom he never heard, or of a corporation he did not know existed. In either case, the squatter was heading into trouble.

It was so from the first. When in 1624 the London-Virginia Company gave up its charter, its huge landholdings reverted to the crown and were administered as a crown colony. Every immigrant who paid his own passage was entitled to fifty acres of colony land; and anyone who imported a laborer was entitled to fifty acres additional, provided that within a reasonable period he was living on the land and had done some clearing. This was called a head right, a system that virtually invited the land jobber. Captains of ships secured land in the names of the sailors of their crews who had no intention of remaining. In exchange for a drink or two of rum the sailor was glad to transfer his right to the captain. In this manner the skipper of a ship carrying a crew, say, of twenty, and with a little collusion of shore officials, might quickly and at small cost become the owner of a thousand acres of the finest tidewater lands in Virginia. He could either sell the tract before he quit America or hold it for sale later. By the middle of the seventeenth century estates of ten thousand acres and more, acquired by fraudulent head rights, were common in the Old Dominion.

The English custom to establish colonies in America was usually to secure from the crown a charter by which immense tracts were bestowed upon favored individuals who were willing to risk their fortunes, or possibly the fortunes of investors, in the hazardous enterprise of foreign development. The original rights to these lands were seldom recognized, though some few grantees thought it worth while to distribute gewgaws to the Indians and go through the form of a treaty-purchase with these natives who had no conception that an individual, red or white, could actually *own* a piece of land. As a usual thing the title passed from king or queen direct to the proprietors, who could then dispose of the land as they saw fit. The leading officials of a proprietary land company seldom troubled to cross the ocean to visit, much less to live on their domains. The business of locating the actual settlers was left to resident agents who were also responsible for collection of the quitrents and almost everything else having to do with the proprietary colony.

Although the term was not then in use, what the settlers had to do was to "work out," or to "work off," what amounted to the mortgages on their farms.

Between the crown and the sweating settler was not only the proprietor or company, but his agent and more often than not a bewildering series of baffles represented by subproprietors, colonial or provincial judges, town officials, surveyors, and even tithe collectors. To say that these numerous agencies presented opportunities for profitable dishonesty is not to speak libel. There at the very end of the line was the settler. When at last he had worked off the mortgage and became a freeholder, he was likely to hold the belief that of the many prophets of biblical times the clearest seer of them all was Isaiah, he who warned of land sharks.

The complexities of a bona fide settler's getting a clear title to his little patch of ground can be judged by the experience of families who made their pitch in what in good time became the town of Palmer, in Massachusetts Bay Colony. In 1727 a group of speculators, basing their claim to the tract on an old illegal Indian "purchase," petitioned the provincial general court, or legislature, for a confirmation of title. It was refused, and it well should have been. Despite this the speculators went ahead with their plan. In formal meeting they voted to warn off all squatters and to come to an agreement, with such as had settled, to become their tenants on lease. They sent a surveyor to lay off six miles square. They gave deeds to the fifty-odd families who agreed to pay for their lands in cash, or kind, or labor. But then, because they could not secure a confirmation of their doings from the court, the speculators simply dropped the matter and, by political influence that unquestionably included bribes, managed to get another tract for their subdivision activities.

The poor settlers of Palmer were left without title to the farms they had cleared and were tilling. They petitioned the general court, pointing out the fact that they had been hoaxed, that they had nothing between them and starvation save their farms, and asked to be given clear title to the wild lands their labor had turned into productive fields. Even the petition itself had cost them £16, a considerable sum. The general court appointed an investigating committee, which reported back that the settlers of Palmer were a God-fearing and law-abiding people. For above three years they had supported a minister of the gospel. They had, indeed, been hoaxed by the land company. They had already expended "the chief part of their Small Fortunes." To remove them now, said the committee, would make them paupers.

The general court considered the hard times of these settlers and voted they should be granted clear title to one hundred acres each, but only on condition that they pay to the court the sum of £500, plus £67 more "for expense of the Committee." To the settlers this seemed an enormous sum, as indeed it was, yet the court had spoken. There was nothing else to do but to try to meet the court's demands.

Meanwhile the land sharks who had saddled the Palmer settlers with bogus titles had been granted by the same court a wholly new tract without costs—except for such gratuities as the speculators gave secretly to the legislators. It seems not to have occurred, either to the court or to the duped settlers, that the speculators could be brought to justice. They went their way freely.

As for the unfortunate settlers, they were not permitted to organize the town of Palmer until 1776, when the revolution had begun to settle a lot of things. For forty-nine years the people of Palmer had lived under a worrisome cloud as voteless orphans. The bitterness engendered by this and uncounted other land frauds, so many American historians have written, was evident in the geographical distribution of radicalism which became increasingly apparent as the revolution neared. These were the regions most anxious to fight.

A full century before the thirteen colonies declared their independence Nathaniel Bacon led a rebellion of small farmers against Governor Berkeley's regime in Virginia. They had tired of the more-than-sharp land jobbing of the big planters. A little later philanthropist James Oglethorpe, who meant that his colony of Georgia should be a true Utopia (slavery and rum and land jobbing were prohibited there), was suddenly shocked to discover that land jobbers had slickered both him and his settlers. The fifty-acre farms of the settlers had disappeared as if by magic and reappeared as pieces of the huge new plantations. The plantations were being manned by slaves, red, white, and black, who —as if to make complete hash of Utopia—managed to get all the rum they needed, and more.

The Carolina colonies were turbulent with troubles due in the main to activities of land jobbers engaged in putting together the large estates needed by the rising planters. In 1719 the largely dispossessed small farmers of South Carolina backed a rebellion led by Colonel James Moore, only to discover too late that they must still deal for land with the jobbers.

Again and again, and in all of the thirteen original colonies, it must have seemed to the actual settler of small means that every hand was turned against him to prevent his becoming a man of property, the owner of at least fifty acres, and thus a freeman who could vote. Meanwhile the big estates grew steadily bigger. The first Lee in Virginia had by 1663 accumulated 20,000 acres. One of his several children was able to bequeath 50,000 acres. The original estate of Lord Fairfax ran to 6,000,000 acres. To Lord Baltimore was given by Charles I the entire region that is now the state of Maryland, and with it went the power to coin money, appoint judges, pardon criminals, and grant titles of nobility. It was a pretty fine deal. The colony flourished under several Lords Baltimore, who for a time were Catholics, then turned Protestant, and just before the revolution the lord proprietors were receiving more than £4000 annually as quitrents from settlers.

The proprietors of the Dutch West India Company, who came to operate along the Hudson River, favored settlement under the patroon system. A patroon was a man who would guarantee a colony of fifty persons, and to him the company was glad to grant sixteen miles of waterfront along a navigable river, plus as far into the interior as he could settle. When the English took over in 1664, the existing feudal system was expanded, and in time it ran into the rebellion that was long overdue. The first protest was organized and led by William Prendergast, described as "a Kilkenny Protestant," who raised an army of Levelers among the renters and marched them to such purpose that they scared the daylights out of New York City's burghers and out of patroons up the river. The military had to be called to put down Prendergast and his mob. Had it not been for his Quaker wife, who made a dramatic ride to secure a pardon for him, he would have been hanged. The renters were so discouraged by defeat that they did not organize another protest for close to a century. Sabotage continued, however, and the patroons never slept so soundly as before.

The best-governed and in many ways most successful of the colonies was that of William Penn, a remarkable man who accepted, in payment of a debt owed his father by Charles II, a good part of present Pennsylvania and Delaware. Penn was a publicist well ahead of his times. He wrote advertisements to obtain settlers which were printed in four languages, and must have been most appealing, for Pennsylvania grew faster than any other of the colonies. It had little or no trouble with the Indians, not only because Penn treated them well but because the Delawares were a weak tribe and little more than vassals of the powerful Iroquois, who at that period were friends of the English and would not permit a subject tribe to attack even the German (or Pennsylvania Dutch) settlers who were friends of Englishman Penn.

Though Pennsylvania was the most tolerant and perhaps the best governed of all the colonies—and for many years the land sharks were controlled by strict discipline—it even so came to have troubles over land which flared up in the Wyoming Valley and reached the shooting stage before it was settled.

The Wyoming Valley affair, and much of the violence that broke out elsewhere, both before and after the Revolutionary War, was due to the opportunities presented, to a few alert men, by conflicting grants to wild lands. Perhaps the most celebrated of these concerned the so-called New Hampshire Grants, which since 1791 have been called Vermont.

2.

THE GODS OF THE HILLS

THE long and bitter conflict that resulted in the Independent Republic of Vermont and much later the fourteenth state of the Union, was waged between two sets of land jobbers and involved two incompatible theories of land ownership and development. The province of New York fostered great manors granted to a few wealthy men and cultivated by tenant farmers whose condition and opportunities approximated those of European serfs. The province of New Hampshire, like most of New England, favored dividing the land into small farms owned in fee by the actual settlers. The controversial territory extended west from the Connecticut River to Lake Champlain and an imaginary line from the south end of the lake to the northwest corner of Massachusetts Bay Colony.

The person responsible more than any other, not for starting, but for waging and winning the land war for the New Hampshire grantees was Ethan Allen, a man, surely, of many parts, not the least of which was his role as president, general manager, and general factotum of the Onion River Land Company, an outfit whose 45,000 acres, according to an announcement written by Allen, who was also the advertising manager, comprised land "rising from the intervales, in graceful oval hills, to spread into swails of choice mowing ground." For the purpose of modern identification it may be of interest to know that this milk-and-honey Canaan Allen described so charmingly now includes parts of several towns and the handsome city of Burlington, overlooking Lake Champlain.

The troubles of the so-called New Hampshire Grants had their inception in the infinite ignorance of North American geography possessed by the English king and his so-called advisers. In 1741 the King appointed Benning Wentworth to be the royal governor of New Hampshire province. With the office went the right, even the duty, which all crown governors were expected to exercise—that of the granting of wild lands in his jurisdiction for the purpose of encouraging settlement.

Royal governors first and last enjoyed nothing quite so much as the granting of lands, and Governor Wentworth held true to form. He was untroubled by the apparent fact that the western boundary of his New Hampshire province seemingly had never been described in a legal manner. New Hampshire simply extended westward until, as the phrase stated, it "met other lands of His Majesty." In this case the other lands of His Majesty were the province of New York.

New Hampshire had once been a part of Massachusetts Bay Colony, and the western boundary of that province had long been established as "a line twenty miles east of Hudson River." Hence, so Governor Wentworth logically reasoned, New Hampshire must extend the same distance. It looked very simple, and Wentworth went happily to work granting lands. His fees were comparatively small, but he was an astute businessman and in all deals he stipulated that at least two choice lots be set aside for himself. He also had a strong leaning toward nepotism, and seems to have granted a lot of the better lands to relatives and friends. So much so that he was long a source of complaint and in 1765 was permitted to resign, though not before an understanding was made that a nephew, John Wentworth, should succeed him as governor.

Before the elder Wentworth resigned, he had granted a large number of townships east of the Connecticut River, and many more west of that stream. One of these west-side towns, Bennington, soon became a flourishing settlement and presently caught the eye and the imagination of Cadwallader Colden, lieutenant governor of New York, who happened to be as astute an operator as Wentworth and like him had been doing a brisk business in land grants. He promptly began a study of the ancient records to discover that in 1664 the grant of King Charles II to his brother, the Duke of York, seemed to describe the eastern boundary of the ducal province as the Connecticut River.

This looked to be a matter well worth following up, so thereupon Colden referred the business to the King, who was now George III; and the King, on July 20, 1764, issued an order in council saying, in effect, that the one-hundred-year-old grant to the late Duke of York was still valid and that its eastern boundary was indeed none other than the Connecticut River. The matter might have rested there except for one thing, which was the conflicting interests of two sets of land jobbers, namely the holders of New Hampshire Grants west of the Connecticut River, and the friends and catchpoles of Lieutenant Governor Colden of New York.

Colden was quick to publish a proclamation warning all squatters off the disputed territory, and simultaneously began making grants within it. Rumors flew about that Colden planned to make the King's order in council retroactive in its effects, which meant that the settlers of Bennington and other new towns west of the Connecticut must abandon their homes and the lands they had bought and cleared. Either that or these pioneers must pay again "in fees and exorbitant charges to New York officials." In confirmation of the rumors New York grantees appeared on the debatable ground in the summer of 1765. They brought with them surveyors who busied themselves running lines, blazing trees in the woods, setting up stakes in the openings.

Faced with moving off or paying a second time for their farms, the people in Bennington and vicinity did neither. They sent one of their number, old Samuel Robinson, Bennington's first settler, to London to place before the King himself the fact of the appalling injustice they seemed about to suffer. The King, or someone in authority, was touched by the plea of the aged and well-spoken man, and New York was commanded to cease and desist until the matter could be looked into by the crown. The King's order was not obeyed. New York's lieutenant governor continued to grant lands in the disputed region.

First signs of the coming storm were to be seen when a party of "foreign" or New York surveyors, in which was John Munroe, a Yorker justice of the peace, came to the farm of James Breakenridge, near Bennington village, to run lines and, if need be, to eject Breakenridge, an honest if mulish man who had paid the governor of New Hampshire for his land and did not plan to pay again to New York. That he was an actual settler was clear from the fact of his field of waving corn, his modest home, and fine barn. That he also intended to remain there was made clear to the Yorker party when they found the farmer's place occupied by a much larger group of men than was needed to harvest his small crop of corn. But that, said Breakenridge, was just what the men were there for, even though every last one of them carried a gun instead of a corn knife.

Justice of the Peace Munroe stepped forward to read the riot act, calling upon the mob of alleged corn tossers to disperse. He might have been talking to the tall pines around the field. The backwoodsmen sat around on stumps, guns between knees, and gave no sign of moving. They simply sat there. Farmer Breakenridge suggested to the Yorkers that they be gone. "I hope," he added for the benefit of Munroe, "I hope that you will not try to take advantage of us, *for our people do not understand law.*" The Yorkers went away.

The next move of Acting Governor Cadwallader Colden was to prepare ejectment suits against Breakenridge and many other holders of New Hampshire titles. No few of these were speculators who had purchased whole townships. One such group lived in and around Salisbury, Connecticut. They were so alarmed for their investment that they called a meeting and voted to assess themselves to provide a defense fund. Someone suggested that Ethan Allen, who was known favorably or otherwise to the group, might be a good man to put in charge of defending the New Hampshire title.

Young Allen, who had just turned thirty, had the reputation of an energetic, contentious, and somewhat rowdy character who had been in and out of the police courts of Connecticut towns on charges that could be summed up as acting "to the disturbance of his Majesty's good subjects." He had established and operated a "furnace" for smelting iron ore, sold out, and tried lead mining, but appears to have spent more time in taverns than at the mine. Only recently the selectmen of Northampton, Massachusetts Bay Colony, had called in a body upon him and asked him to leave town for the town's good. This time the charge was laid by the Rev. Mr. Judd, and it was serious—impious and profane scoffing. Young Allen loaded his wife, one child, and possessions into an oxcart and removed to comparatively liberal Salisbury. (He could reflect that even the great Jonathan Edwards, "the first mind in New England," had once upon a time been exiled from Northampton.) At the time the Salisbury speculators met to discuss their imperiled land in the New Hampshire Grants, young Allen had just returned from a winter spent in that wild region with one of his brothers, Ira. Both Allens were impressed with this new frontier.

When Ethan Allen accepted the invitation to attend the Salisbury meeting of the land speculators, they saw an impressive figure, approximately six feet six inches high. His countenance in repose was grave, perhaps sullen, though he was commonly jovial. His mind was probably as alert and quick as that of the shrewdest speculator present. His general bearing, if we are to credit contemporaries, was that of a born leader of men. Whatever the case, he must have struck the Salisbury group as one fit to defend their cause. They gave him a modest sum and suggested that he be on his way to the scene of action.

Astride a horse, Allen rode first to Portsmouth, capital of New Hampshire province, to confer with John Wentworth, who had succeeded his uncle as governor. From him he got a copy of the charters of the towns concerned. He also did a little business on his own, by purchasing one right each in the towns of Poultney and Castleton, both of which were in dispute. Allen next rode to New Haven to engage Jared Ingersoll, a leading attorney, to accompany him to Albany, where the ejectment suits were to be tried. When lawyer Ingersoll saw who was to be the presiding judge, he knew what to expect, for Judge Robert Livingston was one of the largest Yorker grantees of the lands in question. The trial was a farce, the judge holding that the land had never been a part of New Hampshire, hence could not have been granted by Governor Wentworth.

That evening Ethan Allen had callers at his tavern. One was John Tabor Kempe, attorney general for New York, the other James Duane, a lawyer. Both men were real estate operators who were fairly loaded with lands in the disputed region. Kempe, knowing a likely man when he saw one, tried to entice Allen to the New York side of the controversy, offering him as bribe a fine, large piece of land. Allen refused, whereupon Kempe started to get tough in the matter. "You should be advised," he warned Allen, "that the people settled on the Grants will do well to make the best terms possible with the rightful New York landlords." He let that sink in a moment, then told Allen: "We have might on our side, and you know that might often prevails against right."

"Sir," replied Ethan Allen with a line that is often quoted in Vermont these past one hundred and eighty-six years, "sir, the gods of the hills are not the gods of the valleys." It had that something about it men remember; nor was it the last quote from Allen that was to go into history.

Allen returned to the grants and to the Catamount Tavern in Bennington, to find a crowd of anxious settlers and speculators waiting to hear his report of the Albany case. One may judge it, from the fragments of it that have survived the years, to have been a ripsnorter. He referred to the Yorker courts, officials, and even plain citizens as "a junto of land thieves" and said there was nothing left for the honest New Hampshire grantees but to prepare to defend their lands by force. Then and there in Stephen Fay's tavern, amid the heat generated by Allen's inspired harangue about land thieves, and a bowl that was both stout and flowing, the farmers and proprietors of the Grants formed a band of backwoods militia sworn to defend New Hampshire titles against the Yorker junto and all else. They called themselves the Green Mountain Boys; and possibly because they elected Ethan Allen as their colonel commandant, the Green Mountain Boys went into legend.

For almost two decades, or until 1790, when the state of New York and the still-independent republic of Vermont came to an agreement by which the New Hampshire titles were permitted to stand, the Green Mountain Boys were intermittently active as a sort of internal police, and also fought as a regiment in the American army. There is neither room here nor need to give an extensive account of their doings, except to indicate the methods they used to prevail over what Commandant Ethan Allen called the infernal projections of that despotic fraternity, the Yorker junto of land thieves, scalpers, and murderous scoundrels, to the end that what he termed the honest and industrious peasants of the New Hampshire Grants should live in peace and the enjoyment of their rightful farms. The Bennington meeting closed with hand shakings and vows that the New Hampshire titles should prevail.

Action came at once. The Green Mountain Boys had little more than organized when a mounted spy tore into Bennington to report the approach from Albany of High Sheriff Ten Eyck and an army of three hundred armed men. Runners were at once dispatched to notify the Boys to hasten to the Breakenridge place, which was believed to be the object of the invasion. The Boys rallied with such speed that, by the time the Ten Eyck gang reached the farm to eject Breakenridge, that determined man remarked that his place was now under protection, then waved his hand eloquently toward a bushy ridge nearby from which the heads and guns of what looked to the sheriff to be hundreds of men were peering and pointing. His own gang had already begun to disintegrate. No more than twenty remained by his side as he read the writ of ejectment. He and they returned whence they came, to report

to the governor of New York that the Grants were in armed revolt
against authority.

During the summer and fall—it was 1771—Yorker sheriffs and surveyors kept the Grants boiling. They were run off by prompt forays
of the Boys, who had already organized a workable system of communication by signalling with gunshot or blasts on a conch shell, and
by runners to the more remote farms. Threats but no violence so far
proved sufficient in removing the invaders. On the last engagement
of the season, however, Colonel Allen thought it was time to make an
example of these foreigners who would steal the land of honest farmers.

Three Yorker families had gone so far as to build houses on what
New Hampshire designated as the town of Rupert and New York said
was New Perth. They were busy cutting fuel for approaching winter
when suddenly, one day in October when the woods were ablaze with
color, Colonel Allen and a small party of the Boys appeared and proceeded to set fire to the three houses. Then Allen told one Hutchinson,
who seemed to be spokesman for the Yorkers, what they could do
about it. "Go your way now," said Allen, "and complain to that
damned scoundrel your governor." And he added a shocking oath:
"God damn your governor, your laws, your king, council and assembly."

Hutchinson, a pious man, was astounded at such blasphemy. "Colonel
Allen," he said, "you curse most horrible!"

"Damn your soul!" shouted Allen. "Are you going to preach to us?"
From that day on "New Perth" became and remained Rupert.

An immediate result of this affair was that the governor of New York
posted a reward of twenty pounds for the arrest of Ethan Allen. As
a response Allen prepared a poster offering, in his name, fifteen pounds
for the arrest of James Duane and ten pounds for John Kempe, New
York officials, whom he termed "common disturbers of the peace."
He drove to Hartford, had the poster printed, then distributed it on
the Grants, and in person took one copy to Albany, where Allen was
an outlaw, and gave it to landlord Benedict with the request it be tacked
up in the tavern. This piece of bravura made a great noise.

During the winter when even the most determined Yorkers made
little effort to settle on the Grants, Colonel Allen turned propagandist
and kept the friendly Hartford *Courant* lively with harrowing letters
about the "Diabolical plotters" who "by the handle of jurisdiction aim
at the Property" of the "hard laboring peasants" who were engaged
in "cultivating a howling wilderness." He magnified every incident
of contention between Yorker settlers and "lawful settlers" into atrocities
on the part of the former. He gave thought to the poor families of the
latter. He listened and indeed he could hear quite plainly the "women
sobbing and lamenting, children crying and men pierced to the heart

with sorrow and indignation at the approaching tyranny of New York."

This was the stuff to make heroes, something to pump the blood faster through the arteries of the folks on the Grants, something to raise even the fainthearted to fighting pitch. Colonel Allen followed it with a story intimating that New York Governor Tryon himself was about to lead an immense body of troops to the Grants; then, when the Grants were thoroughly alarmed, he called out the Green Mountain Boys to parade on the common at Bennington. Governor Tryon and his army did not appear. The governor was in fact ready to try diplomacy. He dispatched a conciliatory letter to the Rev. Jedediah Dewey and "other leading inhabitants of Bennington," in which he suggested that representatives of the Grants be sent to confer with him on a peaceful settlement of the controversy. Allen, the outlaw, was expressly barred from serving on the committee, but two good men, landlord Stephen Fay and son Jonas, were elected to go.

While these commissioners of peace were on their way to meet the New York governor, word came to Colonel Allen via the Green Mountain grapevine that a "notorious" Yorker surveyor, William Cockburn, had returned to the Grants. Allen and a party set out to find him. Allen thoughtfully selected a route which would take them past the mouth of Otter Creek, near which he had purchased, from Governor Wentworth, five hundred acres but which he had never seen. Other Connecticut men had also bought several thousand acres, on New Hampshire title, and hired a few "settlers" to live on the ground and do a little clearing. At almost the same time a Colonel John Reid, late commander of His Majesty's 42nd Regiment of Foot, had acquired the same land under a New York title. To hold fast to what he thought was his land, Reid moved in with several families and drove off the New Hampshire settlers, and also erected a gristmill.

Now came Ethan Allen and party looking for surveyor Cockburn but also ready to perform any other service to clear the Grants of Yorkers. They ordered Reid's settlers to be gone, and watched them depart while their homes were burning. The Allen party broke the millstones in two, set the structure afire, and went on to catch up with Cockburn running lines on the Onion River. They broke his fine compass and chains, and took him prisoner to Castleton. Colonel Allen was about to hold a drumhead court-martial when a runner arrived from Bennington to say that the peace mission to New York had returned with a message from Governor Tryon of truce and conciliation. Cockburn was turned loose with a severe admonition to stay away from the Grants.

On return to Bennington, Allen and party found the assembled citizens holding a jubilant meeting to approve the peace offering and salute Governor Tryon with a discharge "of the whole Artillery of the town," which consisted of one old mortar. Colonel Allen did not approve of such doings. After all, was not Tryon the very hideous head of New York tyranny? Allen need not have worried overmuch, for the feeling of peace was shattered just as soon as the dispossessed settlers of Colonel Reid reached Governor Tryon to report the outrage, and to garnish it with numerous "atrocities," alleged or real. The much harassed governor sent an angry letter to Bennington, charging a breach of faith and honor and demanding immediate reinstatement of the evicted settlers.

This letter put the New Hampshire leaders on the spot. Colonel Allen knew that if they gave in and allowed re-establishment of Yorker Reid's tenants, the Green Mountain Boys would lose the faith of their followers, who, as Allen recognized, were ever ready to jump with whatever promised to be the strongest wind. Working swiftly to prevent any such white-livered submission, Allen himself composed a letter to Tryon stating that the dispossession of Reid's tenants had occurred before the truce was made, and as for the truce, it was conditional on the cessation of any attempts by New York to make settlements or *surveys* until the King had been heard from. He subtly implied that Cockburn had been caught red-handed in not only breaking the royal order to cease and desist, but in breaking the truce as well. In the matter of Reid's tenants, Allen went on, re-establishing them was manifestly unthinkable, for Reid had "violated all the laws, restrictions and economy, both of God and Man"—a piece of rich bombast typical of Allen that made good propaganda for home consumption.

The controversy was obviously coming to a head. Nothing can be clearer than that the leading spirits on both sides were those who owned, or claimed, the most land. If the speculators holding New Hampshire titles could not make their titles stick, all was lost. If New York's wealthier and more influential claimants permitted such titles to hold, then they had lost everything. The issue was clear enough to the vitally interested parties. Whether or not the actual settlers realized the true condition of things at this period can only be guessed. It did not matter too much, anyway. All depended on who were the more forceful leaders. Possibly the most forceful of them all was Ethan Allen. In the brief moment of indecision during the abortive peace he went into furious action.

In the Hartford *Courant* appeared a series of abusive articles in which the writer, who was Allen, called the New York officials all the names the *Courant's* editor would allow in print. The articles were far from factual, but were fashioned to make men see red from contrasting the monstrous and cruel Yorkers with the simple, home-loving people who happened to have New Hampshire titles. Meanwhile Allen, whose spies were working well, sent a party to take care of a new invasion headed by surveyor Benjamin Stevens, reputedly a hard and warlike man, who had come with a bodyguard of Indians to do some land-looking along the Onion River. In a brief set-to Allen's Boys put the redskins to flight, then fell upon Stevens and his compass men and chainmen. In a rough-and-tumble fight one of the Yorkers was thrown into a campfire and badly injured. The others were beaten up, then tied to trees, while the Green Mountain Boys sat around, drinking the surveyor's rum and debating audibly the proposition of roasting the whole lot of Yorkers over a slow fire. The Yorkers begged hard, and were finally turned loose and headed west.

Now came news that Colonel Reid had returned to the Grants with a new crowd of tenants armed to the teeth. They had hooped the broken stones of the old gristmill, erected new cabins, and looked dangerously well settled. Colonel Allen, who recently had taken to the custom of wearing a sword, buckled it on and set out at once. "We're going on a big wolf hunt," he shouted as he came to clearings along the way, and from each cabin soon appeared a Green Mountain Boy, gun in hand, a powder horn at his side. Next evening the men, women, and children in Colonel Reid's settlement could have heard hoot owls in the woods all around their clearing, signals of the Boys, moving in on all sides. They suddenly burst, a good hundred strong, into the open, to capture the settlement before defenders could get musket to shoulder.

Colonel Allen bid the settlers go get their household effects out of the cabins. The cabins were set on fire. One settler, Angus McBean, said he intended to hold his house and property. "Damn your soul," Allen told him. "If you attempt such a thing I'll tie you to this stump and skin you alive." He made this promise, so McBean testified later in a New York court, with "evil countenance and angry gestures." He told McBean that if he ever "laid hands on your Colonel Reid I'm going to cut off his head." Then, while the Boys were breaking the millstones into small bits, Allen sent the Reid foreigners on their way with a warning. "My authority," he said, pointing to his long rifle, "is this gun, and we are a lawless mob. I've run these woods these seven years past and never was catched yet; and by God, if any of you hereafter attempt to build houses here, the Green Mountain Boys will burn them up and whip you into the bargain."

Such, according to testimony of the settlers, was what the outlaw Allen told them. When the depositions were received by Governor Tryon, he increased the bounty on Ethan Allen's head to one hundred pounds. What the ousted settlers did not report to the New York court, only because they could not know it, was the action taken by Allen and his crew *after* the Reid tenants had left. Felling timber right and left, and using the remnants of the gristmill, they put up a blockhouse fort, and Colonel Allen detailed a small party to remain, just in case Colonel Reid had not had enough. Then he and the rest of his party moved on to Onion River, where a spy said still another Yorker surveyor was at work. He was hard to find. The Boys cruised through Waterbury, Middlesex, Kingland, and so across the Green Mountains to Bradford and Haverhill on the Connecticut River, seeing signs of the intruder's work. Stocking up at Haverhill with provisions and "sperits," they chased back to the west side to learn that the hunted man, apprised of the posse, had driven his last stake in Montpelier township and fled to New York.

But there was more work for the Boys. A crowd of Yorkers headed by Judge Benjamin Spencer were putting up houses in Clarendon (New Hampshire title), which New York said was Durham. At about eleven o'clock one frosty night in November the front door of Judge Spencer's home was battered in by men using a pine log for a ram. Colonel Allen followed the ram into the house and started shouting for "that damned old offender Spencer." Spencer was ordered to rise and dress, but went about it with too much deliberation. Colonel Allen whaled him, smartly it is said, over the rear to speed matters, then took him out of the house and tried him on the serious charge of "cudling with the Land Jobbers of New York." Judge-Colonel Allen declared him guilty and ordered that the Spencer house be burned. Spencer pleaded the great hardship this would put on his wife and children, who were tearfully present. Judge Allen softened, and decreed that the roof should be removed, then replaced, and the case considered settled, provided that Spencer declare henceforth it was a New Hampshire and not a Yorker house. Spencer agreed, and the sentence was carried out, leaving the house intact. How the title was settled is not known. In any case, the bystanders declared Judge-Colonel Allen to have shown great moderation, as well as ingenuity of thought.

Of more significance than the raids during this campaign by the Green Mountain Boys was the building of a second fort, this time at Onion River falls. Ira Allen, youngest brother of Ethan and the most notable landlooker and businessman of the clan, had had his eye on the lower Onion River for more than a year. He thought this land to be the finest on the west side of the Grants. Again and again he urged Ethan to go with him to see it, but Ethan, who calculated he already had as much if not more land than he could hold onto, put him off. But finally he succumbed to Ira's eloquence. The two brothers made a trip to the falls. Ethan was enchanted with what he saw. Ira knew who owned this tract, one Edward Burling of White Plains in New York province. It could be had for a song, or less.

Then, only a little later, after leading the Boys on the raid of Reid's settlers, and the other efforts to discourage Yorker invasions, and coming again to Onion River, Colonel Allen was struck once more with this region. He had just built a fort not far off to prevent a resumption of Reid's persistent attempts. Why not another fort here on Onion River? It would give pause to any Yorkers who might pass this way. Ninety-odd good men were with him . . .

Up went the fort on Onion River—a staunch affair, twenty by thirty-two feet, of large logs and timbers, with thirty-two portholes in the top story that jutted out four inches over the lower, to permit firing down close to the walls. The roof was so constructed that it could be cast off entire, should it be fired by attackers. Every door was double. Heavy wood blocks were shaped to fit the portholes. Beneath the ground floor was a fine spring. Here was a challenge to Yorkers. (It may have occurred to Colonel Allen that it might also become a good outpost, when and if the fine Onion River lands should be put on the market.)

Quite soon the Hartford *Courant* carried an advertisement of the Onion River Land Company which stated there was no other "tract of land of so great quantity Between New York and the Government of Canada that in a state of Nature can justly be denominated equally Good." After expressing admiration for the "graceful oval hills" the "choice mowing ground," and the absence of timber except for "a few scattering buttonwood, elm and butternut trees," the company mentioned that the Onion River itself abounded "with a diversity of excellent Fish particularly the Salmon." This superb land was, moreover, offered for sale "at a moderate price." Of even greater importance, considering the trouble with Yorker land thieves, was the Onion River company's guarantee at the end of the advertisement. "N.B.," it said. "Purchase and settlement is insured on a title derived from under the Great Seal of the Province of New Hampshire."

If the junto of Albany land sharks had really known the men they had to deal with, they might well have given up the struggle when the Onion River company announced it had for sale 45,000 acres of land *insured by a New Hampshire title.* The use of "insured" had a sinister connotation to anyone acquainted with Ethan Allen, who was not only the president of the Onion River Land Company but colonel of the Green Mountain Boys, sometimes vulgarly called "the Bennington Mobb."

The advertisement was based on the fact that Ira Allen's suggestion to Ethan had been acted upon: Edward Burling's tract had been purchased by Ethan, Ira, Heman, and Zimri Allen, brothers, and a first cousin who was Remember Baker. Little cash could have changed hands. The Onion River company had little. But land deals in that time and place could be made for a few pounds on the barrelhead, the rest on the cuff. The company started immediately to survey the tract, which already boasted a fort, and were making sales while Ira was still running lines. Among the first customers was Thomas Chittenden who was soon to be elected governor of the Independent Republic of Vermont.

Paying no heed to the Onion River company's "insured" titles, the New York governor now proclaimed that a gathering of three or more persons on the so-called Grants was prohibited, punishable by death. Officers of New York were absolved from any penalty if they found need to injure or kill while enforcing the law. Ethan Allen sensed a fine opening. He signed a letter for printing in the *Courant* in which he called upon all decent men to resist and to violate this "Bloody Law," describing Governor Tryon and his men to be "insatiable, avaricious, overbearing, inhuman, barbarous, and blood-guilty," which will indicate Colonel Allen's vocabulary when he was in good form. He followed it with a pamphlet that became famous. In it he aired his astonishing knowledge of "Draco, the Athenian law-giver," who, it seems, had "caused a number of laws to be written in blood." But, he went on, "our modern Dracos determine to have theirs verified in blood." There was more, much more, all in defiance of New York. When Allen had completed this inflammatory pamphlet, and went to Hartford to have it printed, a Yorker agent named Robert McCormick made an attempt to capture the Green Mountain firebrand and rush him in a waiting sleigh to Albany, there to collect the "premium" (reward) of one hundred pounds. Allen drew a pair of horse pistols and told the fellow to begone.

Allen's incendiary pamphlet got an immediate and wide distribution. It was followed by the "trial" of the Rev. Benjamin Hough, a doughty Anabaptist preacher from New York who had defied the Green Mountain Boys to remove him. He was found guilty, tied to a tree, brutally whipped, and escorted out of the Grants. Ethan Allen then staged a meeting at which forty-six settlers (with New Hampshire titles) signed a written compact to defend their "liberty and property, the household gods of Englishmen." Shortly after this meeting Allen wrote a letter to a friend revealing what was uppermost in his mind. It was nothing less than the carving of a new and independent state out of the New Hampshire Grants. It was the first intimation of Vermont in the making, though Allen did not then suggest a name for it.

It was now 1774, and the troubles that had long been brewing in Boston, New York City, Philadelphia, and other places were being discussed by a Continental Congress, meeting in Philadelphia, which had passed resolutions denouncing certain acts of His Majesty's government. Copies of the resolutions were forwarded and read to meetings in all the thirteen colonies, even in the town of Westminster on the Grants. The people of the Grants declared themselves in favor of the resolutions, and also formed a committee of correspondence, like the groups which had long since been formed in the several provinces.

It was obvious, even here on the backwoods frontier, that the American colonies were fast approaching an organized revolt against the crown. This same settlement of Westminster happened to be the only town on the Grants dignified by or cursed with a King's Court. On March 13, 1775, when the court attempted to meet, to dispose of a number of civil suits seeking ejectment for non-payments due on lands, the judge, sheriff, and other crown officials found the courthouse to be in possession of a large group of men who refused orders to leave. The sheriff commanded his men to fire. They did, wounding ten men, two of whom died.

Although the "Westminster Massacre," as Ethan Allen and others delighted to call it, was not strictly a part of the New York-New Hampshire land war, it was used by the president of the Onion River Company to base a demand that the Grants "be taken out of so oppressive a jurisdiction, and either be annexed to some other government or erected and incorporated into a new one." Vermont was taking shape in Allen's mind.

Shortly after the affair at Westminster, Ethan Allen called a meeting, apparently the first, of the Onion River company's board of directors. The bookkeeping seems to have been somewhat vague, but the directors figured they had sold 16,793 acres of land, and still held what was described as "rights" to 60,289 acres. The cost of printing Ethan's violent pamphlet against New York was, significantly, charged to Onion River account. It seems probable that another subject was discussed by the board, for directly afterward Heman Allen went to Hartford and told the committee of correspondence, the revolutionary group there, that the people on the Grants believed the British outpost on Lake Champlain, Fort Ticonderoga, could be seized by the Green Mountain Boys.

Right on the heels of the Onion River Company's meeting, word arrived on the Grants that the King's troops had marched on Lexington and Concord, in Massachusetts Bay Colony, and had horribly killed poor and honest farmers. A few moments after he got the news, Ethan

Allen jumped on a horse and rode to landlord Fay's Catamount Tavern in Bennington. The taking of Fort Ticonderoga followed.

There, for a moment, American history paused long enough to catch sight of a tall man on the barrack stairs, waving a sword and shouting one lurid sentence fit to echo from school books and Fourth-of-July orations with the best that America has to offer. Then the mists close around the tall man, and he is seen no more on the great pages of history. This is regrettable. Colonel Ethan Allen was just beginning his career.*

Three years later, by an exchange of prisoners of war, Colonel Allen, now broken from exposure in the field, and incarceration in hulks, and in Pendennis Castle, Falmouth, England, returned home, to find it no longer the Grants but "a free and independent state capable of regulating their own internal police in all and every respect whatsoever, and that it should thereafter be known by the name of Vermont," a word coined by Dr. Thomas Young, an old friend and mentor of young Ethan Allen in his Connecticut days. The governor of this odd anachronism, which Congress had refused to recognize, was Thomas Chittenden, who had been an early customer for lands of the Onion River Company. The company was no longer in existence, but all Tory lands, as Vermonters described any property not "insured of New Hampshire title," had been confiscated. This was happy news to the returned hero. So was the report that the Green Mountain Boys had fought well at Hubbardton and Bennington and other battles with British and Hessian troops.

A celebration to welcome Colonel Allen was staged to coincide with the June session of the Vermont Assembly. The combined affairs required several days, and called for considerable drinking of toasts. Colonel Allen looked about him to note that "rural felicity, sweetened with friendship, glowed in each countenance." Yet the war with Great Britain was not done, nor had New York quite given up the struggle for its stake in what many Yorkers still chose to call the pretended state of Vermont.

The Vermont Assembly voted to commission Ethan Allen brigadier general in charge of its militia, and as such he rode herd on all Yorkers and Tories—the terms had become interchangeable—who in any manner opposed Vermont's authority. His last tour of duty was to subdue the hotbed of Tories in Guilford who hoped to attract the attention of Congress to the end that Continental troops would be sent, possibly to make the pretended state of Vermont a part of New York.

---

* Later in 1775 Allen conceived a bold plan to capture Montreal. Leading a motley force of 110 men, he was met by Sir Guy Carleton and 500 troops, badly defeated, and himself captured and sent in chains to England.

The Guilford revolt was of course inspired by New York grantees as a last-ditch stand against New Hampshire titles. It was led by a Timothy Phelps, an able and courageous man who held a New York commission of sheriff and deputized virtually every male settler in Guilford and adjacent Halifax. General Allen wanted to enter Guilford with such an overwhelming show of force that the citizens would give in without bloodshed. He rode into the village at the head of four hundred mounted men. Phelps was arrested and taken before General Allen, whom he abused roundly, terming him and his troops a pack of rioters and outlaws. General Allen said nothing but acted promptly and with unusual gentleness. When the pseudo-sheriff paused for breath, the general reached out with his sword and with one mighty swipe cut Phelps's hat neatly from his head. "Take the damned rascal away," he commanded.

The arrests in Guilford village were made without bloodshed and with little violence. Late in the afternoon Allen, with a part of the troops and all the prisoners, set out for Brattleboro. A little way out of Guilford the advance guard was surprised by an ambush. Volleys of gunfire rattled. Several soldiers were wounded. General Allen dismounted. Taking a squad of troops with him, he strode back into the village, and at its center paused to deliver a brief proclamation that remains fresh in Vermont legend. Said he:

"I, Ethan Allen, do declare that I will give no quarter to the man, woman, or child who shall oppose me, and unless the inhabitants of Guilford peacefully submit to the authority of Vermont, I swear I will lay it as desolate as Sodom and Gomorrah, by God!" It was an ear-filling threat by a master of such things who knew the Guilfordites to be pious people who read their Bibles and were acquainted with what had happened to the biblical cities named.* All of those arrested at Guilford were either fined, jailed, or banished. It was the last armed rebellion against Vermont authority.

The peace with Great Britain found Vermont in 1783 still an orphan. A year later she had established her own post-office department, her own mint, and elected an ambassador to treat "with all foreign powers," which included the United States of America. In 1790 she came to an agreement with New York by which Vermont appropriated $30,000 to settle Yorker claims to Vermont land. On March 4, 1791, Vermont entered the Union as the fourteenth state.

But the question of the legality of the New Hampshire titles, on which

---

* In 1943 many New England newspapers carried a dispatch dated at Guilford which quoted Allen's dreadful proclamation, then remarked that "Guilford is the only Vermont village whose population has shown a decrease in every census since 1790."

so much of Vermont's land was based, was not settled for one hundred forty-one years after the state was admitted to the Union, when the United States Supreme Court found that the jurisdiction of New Hampshire never extended west of the Connecticut River. "Thus was demolished," wrote Matt B. Jones, a native of Vermont and one of the great legal minds of New England, "thus was demolished the legal theory by which the claimants under New Hampshire grants west of the Connecticut River sought to justify their appeal to force." One can only muse whether this region would not today be a part of New York State if it had not been for the Onion River Land Company and the genius of its head man. One hesitates to call it a "reform" of land distribution. It was a land jobbers' war, with the honors going to the more determined jobbers.

3.

REBELLIONS ON THE MANORS

THE agreement of 1790, by which Vermont paid a modest indemnity to New York, settled the business of the New Hampshire Grants except, as indicated, as a matter of academic interest. Yet New York was not done with internal troubles relating to land. The great manors of the Hudson River Valley and adjacent counties remained. Not all of them, for many of the patroons, or manor lords, had guessed wrong and stayed Loyalist. But a few of the greatest landowners fought with the patriots and came out of the war with their estates intact. In several instances, indeed, the estates were larger than before by addition of the confiscated lands of the Tories.

As the new Republic of the United States came into being, none of its basic legislation affected the manors. The medieval patroon system survived to saddle the valley with a hoary anachronism, a threat to the principle of equal rights for all. For instance, the lands of the Van Rensselaer family embraced all of Albany and Rensselaer counties and part of Columbia. By 1838 somewhere between sixty thousand and one hundred thousand tenant farmers lived on Van Rensselaer lands. The Livingston Manor covered most of Columbia County. Other immense estates belonged to families named Morris, Jay, Van Cortlandt, and Schuyler. During more than a century there had been considerable intermarriage of patroon sons and daughters, although one of the Schuyler girls saw fit to marry outside the landed gentry. Her husband was Alexander Hamilton, who thus became a kinsman not only of the landed Schuylers but also of the Livingstons and Van Rensselaers.

Hamilton was one of the young republic's most brilliant statesmen who, among other things, had helped to frame the new constitution; and it was only natural that one of his in-laws, Stephen Van Rensselaer, should turn to him for help in drawing up a suitable contract for his thousands of tenants to sign. This seemed necessary in view of the fact that New York State had in 1782 outlawed feudalism by abolishing entail and primogeniture.

Young Hamilton was glad to oblige. He drew up a "lease" that would bind all new tenants permanently to the estate. In effect it differed little from the leases given back in colonial days by the original Van Rensselaer to his tenants. Yet the new lease made it appear that the patroon *sold* the property to the farmer and his heirs and assigns forever. Indeed, the contract Hamilton drew up was on the face of it described as an instrument of "Incomplete Sale." Generations of attorneys have been unable to conjure up a finer euphemism for perpetual lease. Hamilton's incomplete sale meant that the tenant could not sell his property, but only his contract with its terms unaltered. The land remained in the ownership of the patroon.

The contract stipulated that the so-called "purchase" price of the title and the use of the soil was "ten bushels of winter wheat and four fat fowls" annually. In addition, the tenant was to give one day's work each year with horse and wagon. The ironclad instrument specified that the tenant must have his grain made into flour only at the mill of the manor, for which the usual grist was charged. The tenant was to pay all taxes. He was to use the land for agricultural purposes only. The patroon reserved for himself all wood, mineral, and water rights.

This remarkable contract, as historian Henry Christman observed, "was an expression of Hamilton's theory of government." He proposed to save the nation from democracy by putting the wealthy in a position to check the "unsteadiness and imprudence" of the common people. He wanted to "preserve the old class distinctions by preserving the institutions which made them possible." To this end nothing could have been more purposeful than the incomplete sale, devisd by Alexander Hamilton and quickly plagiarized by other patroons, which was still in effect more than half a century after Yorktown.

That in fifty years the tenants had not revolted did not mean they were content with their lot. The fresh winds of the Revolution had fanned through the great estates and stirred great hope in the minds of the more imaginative tenants. Many of these men had fought at Saratoga or suffered at Valley Forge. They believed the war had been fought as much for them as for the men of property. But now time had passed.

The perpetual rents remained. A new generation of tenants found themselves no better off than their fathers before them, or their grand-fathers. That they continued serf-like to work their rented acres with no more than an occasional mild protest was due to apathy and fear. The more aged among the tenants could remember the time when, just before the Revolution, William Prendergast had organized an anti-rent movement that swept the manors like fire, and was put down only by General Gage and his redcoats. Yet, when the excitement was over, the whipped tenants returned to their leases, rebel Prendergast was in prison, and everything was the same as it had been before.

But not quite everything. The Cromwellian Levelers, as Prendergast liked to call his anti-rent army, had left more than a residue of resent-ment among tenants. It smoldered until the 1840s, when another rebel appeared to lead the manor serfs in what went into New York history as the Tin-Horn Rebellion.

This new hope of the tenants was young, soft-spoken Dr. Smith Boughton, born in 1810 on his father's leasehold in Rensselaer County but, surprisingly enough, sent to be educated at Middlebury College in Vermont. He set up in medical practice at Delhi in the Catskill Moun-tains of New York's Delaware County, much of which was held under semi-feudal leases, a condition he had been familiar with since boyhood in the East Manor of the Rensselaer estate. He often recalled the sight of his father driving once a year to the manor seat "with his load of wheat to ransom his right to live on the land and cultivate it."

Young Boughton was not to be the first rebel in his family. His Huguenot forebears fled France in the seventeenth century. His father and two uncles fought in the American Revolution. The young man him-self had displayed insurgency at Middlebury College, where students were required to attend Congregational services until Boughton led some forty-odd of his mates on a march of protest to authorities and argued that they had no right to impose theological tenets. He won his case. Even after he had settled down to medical practice the fires of revolt still burned within him. In 1837 he dropped everything and went to Canada to enlist on the side of Louis Papineau and William Lyon Mackenzie in the so-called Patriots' War against the government. Boughton got into the shooting too, and was captured, imprisoned, then deported.

On return to his native region Dr. Boughton married and settled in the village of Alps in Rensselaer County. During his absence in Canada several of his boyhood companions, including blood cousins, had been sent to jail for anti-rent riots on the West Manor of the Rensselaer estate in Albany County. Boughton visited them and returned home convinced that, though the American Revolution had done nothing to unfetter tenants from the thrall of Hamilton's incomplete-sale illusion, it might be possible to stage a home-grown rebellion in the manor counties.

At this period the still-young Dr. Boughton was a tall, slender man, with fine eyes, a reflective face, and white hair. He also possessed a quiet eloquence. Having made up his mind that the only hope for an effective revolt was first to bring all tenants into a group pledged to pay no more rents, he made use of his professional rounds to instill the idea among patients. He presently met up with Thomas Devyr, a warm-hearted, fiery agitator who had battled landlords in his native Ireland, from which he fled to England and there became embroiled in the abortive revolt of the Chartist radicals. Fleeing again, this time to America, Devyr almost automatically was attracted to Albany by the anti-rent troubles in the West Manor. Boughton liked him instantly.

With Devyr's help Boughton drew up a formal "Statement of Grievances and Proposed Redress," which, after recounting the wrongs of the tenants, expressed grave doubts that the titles to the large estates were legal and demanded a constitutional amendment to end the leasehold system. The signers of his bold document pledged themselves to pay rent no longer. They committed themselves, if need be, to "a ten-year war for justice."

On the first day of January, 1844, Dr. Boughton rode down from the hills and across the Hudson to Albany and the Capitol, to present the Anti-Rent association's petition, which had been signed by several thousand manor farmers. By a slim majority the Assembly voted to refer it to a judiciary committee, and Boughton was asked to supply legal opinions in support of his contention that a legislature had the power to interfere with the tenures. Boughton took off for Boston and there had a talk with the aging but still formidable Daniel Webster, whom he found to have the mouth of a mastiff, a brow like a mountain, and "eyes burning like anthracite." The great man encouraged Boughton. "If I had the time," he rumbled, "I would tear that manor apart." He sent Boughton to New York City to see Ambrose L. Jordan, known in legal circles for his corrosive skill as Old Aqua-fortis (nitric acid). We shall meet him again.

With supporting opinions from both Webster and Jordan, Boughton returned to Albany to bolster the anti-rent case. The committee was notably impressed. All appeared to be going well when suddenly the committee voted to defer action of the matter until the state comptroller had time to look into it. This meant a long delay. It meant to Dr. Boughton that the petition had been scuttled by "a handsome sum" paid certain committee members by agents of the Rensselaers.

As Dr. Boughton saw it, only one course was left to the anti-renters. They had sought relief by legal means. Now they would seek relief by whatever means seemed most effective.

None of the manor lords lacked casual informers or active spies. Someone or another who served the Rensselaers came in to report that Dr. Boughton was not only a dreamer of dangerous and quite impossible dreams, but also a sort of cloak-and-dagger romantic. He was organizing a secret order of renters called simply "The Indians" or "The Natives," complete with passwords, countersigns, outlandish titles for its officers, and fantastic disguises. If all this sounded to the patroons like little more than rustic horseplay, foolish yet harmless, they changed their minds soon enough when a spy related what he had seen and heard with his own eyes and ears.

While riding a back road in Taghanick Township, said the informer, he heard the sound of fife and drums, and soon came to a scene that staggered his imagination. Marching up and down, in military formation, were hundreds of men, all masked. The masks covered head and neck, and were hideously painted with popeyes, cockeyes, clown noses, and contorted mouths. The uniforms were a sort of smock of brilliant calico of garish stripes, bold designs, or solid colors to match the rainbow. From every belt hung a bright tin horn. In the hands of each marching man was a weapon—spear, tomahawk, club, pitchfork, pistol, or gun.

When the astounded spy could take his eyes from the marching men, he looked around to note that a crowd of spectators in everyday dress and numbering more than a thousand had gathered at one end of the field near a raised platform. The parade of the masked army came to a stop fronting the platform, onto which presently climbed a masked figure. The calico soldiers greeted him with a shout. "Big Thunder!" they yelled.

Big Thunder responded with what seemed a war cry: "Down with the rent!" The lurking spy bent his ears to hear Big Thunder say a shocking thing. "The Livingstons and the Van Rensselaers," he cried, "have taken from us and our fathers in manor rents many times what the land is worth." The voice was calm, yet had an undertone of suppressed emotion. It continued: "It is treason to pay rents to robbers who forfeit citizenship by calling themselves lords and refuse honest citizens the right to own their own homes." The calico soldiers shouted and blew a blast on their tin horns. The speaker went on: "Do not pay the rents," he admonished. "Be still and do nothing. The Natives you see here will take care of you." (More shouts.) "When the sheriffs come to take your farms, the Natives will come out of the rocky glens and caves in the mountains and drive them off. They will come in the night and depart before day. No one will know whence they came or where they went."

In Big Thunder's harangue was more than an echo of Ethan Allen, who, on one occasion said he was "determined to defend the independence of Vermont" and that, rather than fail, "I will retire with hardy Green Mountain Boys into the desolate caverns of the mountains, and wage war with human nature at large." It is improbable that Big Thunder's audience recognized the echo, but if Big Thunder was Dr. Smith Boughton, then he was surely acquainted with Colonel Allen's famous defiance, which was still a popular quotation in the Green Mountains, where the doctor had been educated at Middlebury.

When Big Thunder had finished, the calico men blew their horns, waved their weapons, and chanted, "Down-with-the-rent . . . down-with-the-rent." Then they and the spectators joined to sing a doggerel song that had something to do with tarring and feathering sheriffs. Sensing "the rise of a more dangerous mood" in the immense crowd, the spy took off to report to his patroon employer.

The spies and informers of all the manor lords were to have a busy year, for the Anti-Rent association grew almost as fast as members could be listed on the protest petitions. The secret bands of Indians or Natives multiplied. The time was ripe. What was called agrarianism was in the air, not only the air of the manors but of the country at large. Reformer Albert Brisbane was helping to establish socialist communities advocated by the Frenchman Fourier. The influential Horace Greeley was whooping up this idea. And George Henry Evans, who for two decades had been advocating free homesteads for all, along with a system much like what later was called the Single Tax, revived his *Working Man's Advocate,* specifically to support Dr. Boughton's anti-rent war.

The Van Rensselaers and Livingstons went into action almost simultaneously. The former, toting up rents in arrears, discovered that their renters of the East Manor alone owed them more than two hundred thousand dollars. Sheriffs were given a stupendous number of writs to dispossess, but were met along the way by masked men blowing tin horns and finally by a small army of masked Indians. One officer was tarred and feathered, the others told to begone. In Columbia County, Sheriff Henry Miller and deputies set forth to evict leasehold farmers Steve Decker and Abe Vosburgh. They, too, were met by a long column of The Natives, masked, decked out in bright calico, and accompanied by possibly "two thousand undisguised spectators." The entire crowd followed the officers to the Vosburgh place.

Just as Sheriff Miller started the legal process of eviction and sale, Big Thunder appeared. He ignored the officers, but addressed the Indians.

"Shall we take their papers and burn them?" he asked. The calico maskers raised their left arms in a silent vote. Big Thunder turned to the spectators. "Do you Palefaces agree?" he asked, and was answered by a shout of approval. There was a mean quality to the shout. Sheriff Miller turned the papers over to Big Thunder, who thereupon led the entire mob down the road to Sweet's Tavern, where a barrel of tar was blazing in the yard. He tossed the offending papers into the fire. The officers could hear talk in the crowd of tar and feathers, but they were allowed to depart, to "ride disconsolantly back to the town of Hudson," the seat of Columbia County.

For reasons not clear no arrests followed the affair at Sweet's Tavern, but the anti-rent agitation was spreading. The fiery Irish radical, Thomas Devyr, who had helped Boughton to draw up the "Statement of Grievances," was loose on the manors, shouting "For the Land is Mine, Saith the Lord," moving swiftly through Rensselaer, Albany, and Green counties, then over the hills into Schoharie and Delaware counties. When one day calico Indians attempted to halt the carriage of General Jacob Livingston, he drew two pistols and shot at the masked riders.

The Indians were growing bolder everywhere, and in Columbia County they distributed handbills announcing that Big Thunder was to speak at a rally of renters on "the faulty titles of Livingston Manor." This time a monstrous crowd, described by informers as "thousands of people" gathered at Bam's Tavern. To warm up the crowd, several hundred calico Indians staged a wild performance of leaping, yelling, blowing horns, and discharging firearms. During this preliminary some careless Indian fired a gun that held not a blank charge but a bullet. It killed young Bill Rifenburg, son of a nearby renter. Big Thunder hastened to the tavern's upper veranda to explain that the fatal shot was a regrettable accident, and that the meeting was dismissed. The vast crowd, shocked at the tragedy, milled around and started to drift away in silence. Big Thunder and a few other leaders of the Indians gathered within the tavern to discuss what to do next.

They were still talking when Sheriff Henry Miller with four deputies and the district attorney of Hudson entered the taproom. "You are under arrest, Dr. Boughton," Miller said. Boughton made no protest, and left the room with the sheriff's party. Before they could enter the sheriff's carriage, however, a good dozen of the Indians came tearing out and attacked the officers. The sheriff's men prevailed, and drove off with Boughton and also Little Thunder, who was Mort Belding. Though no attempt was made to halt the sheriff and his prisoners, the carriage was trailed to the outskirts of Hudson by a growing band of calico men blowing the daylights out of their tin horns.

The citizens of Hudson had no sympathy for the anti-renters. They were elated when their sheriff returned to lock up the two Indian leaders in the town jail. With nightfall, however, came a feeling of unease brought on, perhaps, by the sound of horns from the surrounding countryside. The sounds rose and fell on the changing winds, but they were almost continuous. Across the Hudson River, too, torches could be seen moving, as if in an endless parade, in the vicinity of Athens. Coupled with Sheriff Miller's report of "several thousands" in the anti-rent mob from which he had taken the two leaders, plus the moving torches and the far-off but repeated blowing of horns, Hudson people had an ominous feeling they could not shake off.

Into the town next morning came a messenger from the Indians bearing a demand that Boughton be released. Otherwise a thousand calico soldiers would march in to put the town to the torch. Mayor Cyrus Curtis and his councilmen panicked. A horseman was sent flying upriver with an appeal to the governor for immediate troops. The men of the Albany Burgesses Corps were mustered, put aboard a railroad train, and dispatched to Hudson, to make a splendid entry in their handsome uniforms, flags waving, drums beating. After conferring with the mayor their colonel and a detail of the corps set out to find and arrest the most dangerous of the calico leaders still at large. This was White Chief —born Walter Hutchins—who was believed to be hiding in a tavern south of Hudson. After a night of futile wandering in the field the detail returned to find Hudson loaded with four more companies of Albany militia, while before long, a steamboat hove in from New York City bearing the men and horses of Captain Krack's Cavalry.

Even these gallant troopers were not enough to stem the fear that seemed to have taken firm hold of Hudson, for the townsmen mustered a large company of home guards, a couple of pieces of artillery that were paraded with field music, then busied themselves by patrolling what was virtually a town in siege.

Captain Krack's troopers meant business. They dashed out to run the elusive White Chief to earth, and found him hiding in a house in Minkville. The astute captain knew how to deliver a notorious criminal. He loaded White Chief Walter Hutchins into a requisitioned farm wagon, took pains to send a courier ahead to alert Hudson to the wonderful news, then rode into the waiting town with his prisoner riding in the midst of twenty superb horsemen.

This turned out to end the siege of Hudson. The excitement died almost as suddenly as it began. The swarming militia returned to their homes; and the town, which for more than a week had been in the national spotlight, returned to its usual quiet. It is likely that the townsmen thought they would hear no more of Dr. Smith Boughton. They were mistaken.

While Boughton remained without recourse to bail in Hudson, his allies, George Henry Evans and Thomas Devyr, worked valiantly to build the doctor into a martyr-symbol of some stature. At his first trial the jury did not believe he had been properly identified as being the Big Thunder of the riots. They disagreed as to his guilt. He was released on bail. By the time Boughton came to trial again, in the autumn, he was a national character, talked about from Maine to Illinois.

Two days before the trial was to start Hudson filled again, this time with the wagons and buggies of anti-renters come to town for what was widely heralded as the greatest struggle to date between the patroons and the leaseholders. The little courthouse seemed lost in a crowd of silent and sullen farmers.

The trial was considered so important that the attorney general himself, who was handsome John Van Buren, the son of a recent president of the United States, came to prosecute. In charge of the defense was white-haired and crusty old Ambrose L. Jordan. When Jordan learned that the judge was to be John W. Edmunds, a close personal friend of the Van Burens, he knew well enough that this was to be no impartial court; he expected Edmunds to prove himself as "effective a landlord's agent" as could be found. "Judge Edmunds," wrote historian Christman, "knew almost everybody in the county and used this knowledge freely to help Prince John [Van Buren] to hand-pick the jury."

The long trial was enlivened by forensic bouts between Jordan and the prosecutor, and once turned into a brawl when Jordan remarked that "Van Buren has not contended for justice, but is here to exhibit himself, to pander to the miserable ambition which was the curse of his father," then went on to compare the two Van Burens. "Though the father," he said, "had brains to temper his wild ambition to some degree, the son has none to temper his, and it breaks out everywhere in puerility and slush."

Attorney General Van Buren swung and caught Jordan full in the face. Jordan shook his white head and tore into the younger man furiously. Officers broke it up before much damage was done. Otherwise the affair proceeded evenly to its foreordained conclusion. Dr. Boughton was convicted. The charge against him was robbery. Yet when Judge Edmunds delivered sentence, he remarked that "the offense in fact is high treason, rebellion against your government, and armed insurrection." He termed Boughton "the leader, the principal fomenter of all these disturbances." Then he declared to the prisoner that he "should be confined to prison for the term of your natural life."

The hardness of the sentence staggered almost everybody except the patroons, their agents, and their friends, personal and political. Boughton, however, agreed with counsel Jordan that it would be useless to appeal. "By submitting to my fate," said the prisoner, "I will win public opinion and help our cause."

The more than five thousand leasehold farmers who crowded the square around the courthouse made no demonstration. They had lost their incomparable leader. They were discouraged beyond telling. Grim, many of them weeping, they made their way back to their homes and the unpaid rents that had steadily been mounting. That same night Dr. Boughton, heavily ironed, started the first lap of the journey that ended at Clinton Prison, in Dannemora, Clinton County.

Meanwhile other courts of the manor counties were convicting local leaders of the Anti-rent association. In Delaware County, anti-renters O'Connor and Van Steenbergh were sentenced to be hanged in connection with the killing of a sheriff. Four more were given life, and nine others sent up to serve from two to ten years. The death sentences were commuted to life imprisonment. Dr. Boughton was to have company in Dannemora.

Still at large were Boughton's two staunch friends, Thomas Devyr, now editing a new paper, *The Anti-Renter,* and George Henry Evans, editing *Young America,* the new style of his pioneer *Workingman's Advocate.* Remarking that Dr. Boughton had "committed no sin against morality or the principles of the American Revolution," Evans declared that henceforth his paper would carry on its masthead a line in boldface: "Liberation of Dr. Boughton." Editor Devyr reminded his readers that there was never a great reform that didn't demand its victim. He bid them to be of good cheer. He advised them to "Keep within the bounds of the law. But be up and onward."

The savagery of the sentences put an end to the calico Indians. They quietly disbanded, and most just as quietly got rid of their uniforms. Many years later John Burroughs, the naturalist, recalled discovering, as a youth on his father's leasehold in Delaware County, a "hideous mask of stained leather with horns" buried under a stone pile.

It seems improbable that all save the most ignorant of the anti-rent men had realized from the first that they could not win against the government by violence. They had resorted to violence in desperation. It had seemingly failed. Only the ballot was left to them. Yet the calico tribes had not been in vain. They kept the sheriffs and other agents of the landlords at bay until the movement could grow into a powerful political force. The national publicity attendant to the riots, and shootings and trials over much of New York during several years, had focused attention on a condition that was shocking to most Americans. The patroons could respond to every attack of the anti-rent army with a reprisal. But the patroons were not equal to defending their status as feudal lords.

In his paper George Henry Evans spoke of the "inordinate stupidity" of anyone who still believed that "Patroon law and Landlord judges" had a leg left to stand on. The way was clear now. The bloodless but effective weapon of the ballot would soon remedy the wrongs of two centuries.

That was the way things worked out. At a convention called to revise the state constitution, none of the great names of New York was in dominance. For the first time in state history more than fifty of the delegates were either farmers or "mechanics," as factory operatives were known. They were there to take care of a number of things, including feudalism. After weeks of powerful and often bitter debate the framers of the new constitution agreed on a clause providing that no more "incomplete sale" leaseholds could be issued. Many of the worst features of existing leases also were eliminated. All restrictions on the transfer of titles were outlawed.

The anti-renters had meanwhile been working to replace Governor Silas Wright, long the villain in the calico army's doggerel songs, with John Young, who took office on the first day of 1847. One of the first acts was to pardon Smith Boughton and a score more anti-renters who were still in prison. Not all of the patroons were yet giving in, but John A. King, one of the great landlords of Schoharie County, accepted $25,000 as a cash settlement from leaseholders of Blenheim, for fifteen thousand acres. It was a cheering omen, yet the manor walls were going to crumble slowly under the constant pressure of laws and courts.

On the counsel of Samuel J. Tilden, a young lawyer, tenants brought suit against the Van Rensselaers, charging that their titles were invalid, and won. In 1852 counsel for the Van Rensselaers admitted that the end had come. They gave up the struggle. So did the Livingston lawyers. There were troubles ahead, and a few more riots, and at least one shooting, because of speculators who bought manor lands and tried to make fortunes. It was not until 1880 that the great majority of leaseholds passed into the hands of farmers. In that very year Dr. Smith Boughton, aged seventy and still making his rounds as a country physician, decided to retire from practice. "It is time," he told his friends, "not to mix any more in the turmoils and busy scenes of life." He had known more than his share of turmoil, but he had the great good fortune, not given to many dreamers, to live out his dream, to see it set down in hard legal phrases. The patroons had passed.

In his retirement at his old home in the village of Alps, on what once was the great East Manor of the Rensselaers, Dr. Boughton liked often to take his cane and walk across the meadow, to look up at Pikes Hill and recall the exciting times when, wrapped in the calico smock of flaming colors, he had become Big Thunder and told his neighbors to "strike for the green graves of their sires." He lived on to die at the age of seventy-eight, in 1888, a time when to a new generation the days of the patroons seemed to be as far in the past as those of the Bible. By then, too, thousands of men and women who had been born and reared on manorial leaseholds were rearing their own families on lands acquired through the national Homestead Act, a law, incidentally, which Dr. Boughton's good friend and agitator, George Henry Evans, had been the first to propose.

4.

FREE HOMESTEADS FOR ALL

THE two Evans brothers would have been given notable dreams in any age, but because they grew to manhood in the United States during the early nineteenth century their dreams almost automatically called for some reform or other, or at least a radical departure from established ways. The lure of the untried has perhaps been never so general, or so urgent, as in that period.

New homemade religious sects were offering new routes to heaven. The United States Patent Office was deluged with drawings and models of new machines. The whole country was fairly yeasting with ideas for improving him called the common man. No little of this abounding optimism came with the realization of the unlimited resources of virgin land.

It is astonishing still to reflect, in so young a nation, how assured and widespread was the belief of Americans, no matter where born, that they were the hope of the world, that their institutions were based on the laws of Nature, which was always written with a capital, and that they were engaged in perfecting a refuge for the oppressed everywhere. It was their plain duty to live up to the ideals that had been so eloquently declared by the Founding Fathers. Not only to live up to them, but also, if any of these magnificent promises seemed to be corroding from the abuse of self-interest, to act. Among the more idealistic of these Americans were the English-born Evans boys, George Henry, born in 1805, and Frederick William, born in 1808, who had migrated to central New York in 1820.

Both lads were omnivorous readers. George was apprenticed to a printer, Frederick to a hatter, and both continued to read. At this time Thomas Paine was their favorite author as well as authority on matters spiritual and material, and the strong provender they got from *The Age of Reason* and *Common Sense* turned them, on the one hand, into infidels and, on the other hand, into devout believers of the proposition that every man has an inalienable right "to the materials of Nature," such as light, air, water, and soil.

Within two years George Evans was editing at Ithaca a radical paper called simply *The Man*. He followed with interest the attempts of factory hands and other urban labor to organize unions in the larger cities, and presently went to New York, where he became active in the movement. At this time he regarded equal educational opportunity as the basic need of the poor, but gradually saw that "the primary social injustice from which all others sprang" was unequal distribution of land. When a Workingman's Party was organized in the seaboard cities, Evans was made editor of its official organ, *The Advocate*. Brother Frederick had meanwhile walked eight hundred miles from central New York to Ohio, to join an Owenite community of reformers which disbanded almost immediately. He came on to New York to work with George on *The Advocate*.

The Workingman's Party grew steadily until 1836, when it was disrupted by factionialism and went to pieces a year later in the widespread financial panic and depression. Frederick Evans, in the eyes of his still-infidel brother, went to pieces too. He joined the United Society of Believers, commonly called Shakers, at Mount Lebanon, New York, to remain for sixty years and become the presiding elder. In ill health, and embittered at the failure of the Workingman's Party and the defection of his brother, who had "turned to heaven and the spirit of departed friends for guidance," George Henry Evans bought a farm in Granville, New Jersey and retired there to revise his social thought. He regained his health. From time to time, as money permitted, he published a little paper, *The Radical,* in which was aired the agrarian philosophy he believed was the answer to almost everything.

Declaring that every citizen had an inherent right to a piece of land, Evans demanded that the federal government pass an act permitting actual settlers to stake out portions of the public domain for their own immediate use. He thought that this "inalienable homestead" ought to be one hundred and sixty acres. The proposal began to attract the attention of all manner of active radicals, and of others who merely dreamed. Encouraged by letters and comment, and with his health restored, Evans roused himself and returned to New York City. Gathering a group that numbered many of the extinct Workingman's Party, he organized the National Reform Association, and revived the old *Advocate* as its organ.

Evans's backing of Dr. Smith Boughton and the anti-renters, which has been covered in the previous chapter, was a deciding factor in breaking up the manor leaseholds. Evans was also keeping an eye on the national scene. Nothing was attracting more attention just then than the dispute between the United States and Great Britain over the sovereignty of the Oregon country. Serving his first term as a congressman from Indiana was one of Evans's old radical friends, Robert Dale Owen. Drawing up a petition seeking to dispose of Oregon lands free to settlers, Evans asked Dale to introduce it in Congress. He did so, and five months later presented to that body a formal request for a general homestead law.

Both memorials died in committee, but the idea did not die in the *Advocate,* nor in *Young America,* nor in the *Daily Sentinel,* all of which were edited by George Henry Evans almost to the time of his death in 1856. By then a new champion had appeared to carry the banner of free homesteads for all. But let us not leave Evans without recalling the homage paid his memory by reformers who had known him in the flesh. In 1874 a group of his comrades of the anti-rent wars sought out the grave of "this pure-hearted man who had done so much for the cause." They found it on his farm by a little path "amidst a wild growth of herbage, while the moaning breeze waved the branches of the overhanging trees like a banner, as if still inviting the landless and the pauperized masses to strike for perpetual and not a mere transient share in the soil."

The new champion of free homesteads was Galusha Aaron Grow, something of an Old Testament character, who weighed two hundred pounds, stood six feet two inches, and in youth had been a prodigious man with an ax. He was born in 1822 in Windham County, Connecticut, where four years later his father died, leaving a widow and six children. Mother Grow was happily a fearless and enterprising woman. In 1834 she set out for "The West," meaning Pennsylvania, where new settlements were being opened up in the Tunkhannock Valley. Here she bought four hundred acres of wild land, near what became Glenwood, and also opened a store. Young Galusha and an elder brother went to clearing and farming. A sister or two helped in the store.

Both farm and store prospered so well that the Grows began to deal in lumber and hemlock bark, which was used in tanning leather. At the age of fourteen Galusha was competent to fell timber, and was a very fiend with a spud, the tool used to peel hemlock. He must also have been wise beyond his years, for in the same year Widow Grow permitted him to take a boatload of bark and lumber down the Susquehanna for sale at Port Deposit.

The Grows' operations flourished. Galusha prepared for college at Franklin Academy, Harford, Pennsylvania, then entered Amherst, from which he was graduated in 1844. In that year he campaigned for

James K. Polk, then entered the law office of Governor Chauncey Cleveland of Connecticut. After admission to the bar in 1847 he formed a partnership with David Wilmot at Towanda, Pennsylvania, whose name was to become historic in connection with the Wilmot Proviso. In 1850 Grow ran for and was elected to Congress, taking his seat as its youngest member.

His first speech was significantly on the subject of man's rights to the soil. His ideas had been formed, not only by the efforts of George Henry Evans and the National Reform group, but by his own experiences on the frontier, where he observed the activities of land speculators, a majority of whom he considered to be the most rapacious and unconscionable men at large. Grow knew at first hand of the sufferings of, and even the disasters to, settlers that were largely brought about by dishonest land sharks. These things had made him in fact if not in name something of a single-taxer.

Grow was returned to Congress for a second term, during which he drew up and introduced a bill providing that every applicant be given a quarter section, or one hundred and sixty acres, of the public domain, with the stipulation that he himself should settle on the land. It did not pass. Neither did its failure discourage its sponsor. Again and again, in the next decade during which he was re-elected continuously, Grow introduced his homestead bill, and took every occasion to talk it up both in Congress and elsewhere.

As the crises between North and South approached, Southern members grew implacably opposed to Grow's bill, while Northern members just as firmly favored it. Congressional sessions grew in turbulence. There were fist fights in both the House and Senate, and occasionally a hot-tempered Southerner issued a formal challenge to a duel. This practice, however, was memorably discouraged when Senator Ben Wade of Ohio, who had called a Southern gentleman a liar on the floor of the Senate and was challenged to choose his weapons, was waited upon by the fire-eater's friends. Would he accept, they wanted to know? Senator Wade leveled at the intermediaries as mean a pair of small, beady black eyes as they ever saw. "I am here," he answered coldly, "in a double capacity. I represent the State of Ohio and I represent Ben Wade. As a Senator I am opposed to duelling, but as Ben Wade I recognize the code. I say your friend is a foul-mouthed old blackguard, but you will find that he will not notice what I have said. I will not be asked for retraction, explanation or fight." Nor was he. From that day until secession the tendency of Southern gentlemen to toss challenges was notably lessened.

In the House it was Congressman Grow who did something to tame members from the South. Being a dyspeptic, he shunned all drink at a time when many senators and congressmen drank too much for their own or their country's good, Grow could be "counted on to take the offensive at any time" and "his coolness and strength made him one of the most aggravating Northerners," one who could easily goad an impulsive Southern gentleman to desperation. He delighted in doing as much, and soon became celebrated for a rough-and-tumble fight with Congressman Laurence M. Keitt, a notorious fire-eater.

Although abolition and states' rights absorbed much of the attention of Congress, Grow found it necessary to devote no little of his energy to detecting and defeating the endless parade of dubious or patently fraudulous land-grant bills introduced by the creatures of smart lobbyists. He could scent a land-steal bill quicker than anyone else in House or Senate. Because of his knowledge of the schemes and methods of land sharks he was quite able to expose seemingly innocent and meritorious bills as bogus.

When at last secession cleared the House of its Southern members, Grow knew that his chance had come. He was elected Speaker at the special session of the War Congress in 1861. During his term he had the superb joy of watching passage of the Homestead Act, which was later signed by President Lincoln. The act was not Grow's original bill, nor was he wholly responsible for it, or even for its passage. But his was surely the greatest single influence in connection with it.

Defeated in the next election, Grow became active in various business enterprises in lumber, oil, and railroads, and for four years was president of a Texas railroad. In 1893 he returned to Washington as congressman from Pennsylvania, to serve another ten years, becoming the veritable Nestor of the House, yet still active in extending and improving homestead legislation. At his death, in 1907, Galusha Grow was mentioned in obituaries as "The Father of the Homestead Act." One saw him as "among the last remnant of that veteran corps whose ranks have been decimated by the grape and cannister of Time . . . who has now been compelled to take the achievements of a long life for a pillow and seek rest in that sleep whose night giveth place only to the morning sunlight of immortality."

The first effects of the Homestead Act were all that the most devoted land reformer could have wished. It set off an immediate wave of migration westward. Before the war was over more than fifteen thousand homesteaders were actually settled on two and one half million acres. And in 1872 alone homestead entries totaled almost five million acres. The measure seemed foolproof: Any adult citizen or any alien who had filed his first papers could claim 160 acres of the public domain. He must live there for a term of five years. He must erect a dwelling, the minimum specifications of which were stipulated in the contract.

He must also "improve the land," which meant clearing or plowing, according to the character of the homestead. These things accomplished, the settler was given title.

Though drawn up and passed with the best of intentions the original Homestead Act was seen, after a few years, to be faulty in practice. One of its inadequacies was due to the fact that the law's framers, whose "experience was gathered in the humid East," had drafted a measure unworkable in the semi-arid West. A land unit of 160 acres was generous anywhere in the Mississippi Valley. But he who sought to make a living on the Great Plains needed much more land, or much less. "If he were a cattle rancher," wrote Ray A. Billington, "he should have from 2,000 to 50,000 acres, and at least 360 acres if he practiced extensive agriculture," although a mere 60 acres would do if irrigation were used. But nowhere west of the 98th meridian was 160 acres a workable agricultural unit.

From time to time, beginning in 1873, experimental amendments to the Homestead Act were adopted. The first of these was an honest attempt to adjust the law to Western conditions and permitted the homesteader to apply for an additional 160 acres. Later came amendments called the Desert Land Act (1877), the Timber and Stone Act (1878), and other modifications of the original homestead law. Meanwhile the Morrill Land-Grant College Act gave each state 30,000 acres of Western land for each senator and representative in Congress. Other grants went to subsidize railroad construction. Still in circulation up into the eighties were land warrants called soldier's script, issued to veterans of the Revolution and all other conflicts. These could be bought for much less than face value, then exchanged for land. Coupled with direct sales by the General Land Office, the many outright grants comprised by 1887 the impressive total of half a billion acres. These lands, as Billington points out, "were surrendered to monopolists," by which he meant speculators, "in an era when orators boasted the United States was giving land free to its poverty-stricken masses." Despite which almost one hundred million acres were in perfected homestead entries by the turn of the century.

The failure of the Homestead Act to live up to the hopes of its sponsors was due in part, as said, to deficiencies in the law, and in larger part to the myriad speculators who had been learning their business ever since 1624, when the first ship's captain entered the names of his crew for a head right of fifty acres each of crown-colony land in Virginia.

5.

THE POPULIST REVOLT

TRY as they would, generations of dedicated land reformers were never able to devise an equitable and foolproof system for distributing the public domain. Granted an imperfect world, it is improbable that such a distribution was possible. The Homestead Act was a noble try. That it did not achieve even near perfection was due not only to land speculators but to the all-but-universal venality of him for whom specifically the Homestead Act was passed—the so-called common man. It seems odd that attention to this moral defect is seldom if ever drawn in the immense literature dealing with the fraudulent acquisition of land.

Gustavus Myers tells of "entire trainloads of people, acting in collusion with the land grabbers," who were brought from cities and towns out into the homestead belt to act as dummy applicants for the lands coveted by the conscienceless speculators. Well, who *were* the passengers that packed these trains? They were the common man eager to aid, at the going rates for dummies, in the plundering. Sometimes the dummies could perform their simple duties without an exhausting ride on the steamcars, as was made clear when evidence was taken in the monstrous fraud known as the Oregon Timber Ring.

Much of the evidence came from an ebullient character, Stephen A. Douglas Puter, who called himself "King of the Oregon Land Fraud Ring." Born in the California backwoods, he found two terms of schooling sufficient for his needs, and at seventeen was "running compass" on a United States surveying crew. "By reason of my field work on the survey," he recalled much later, while relaxing in jail awaiting trial, "I gained a knowledge of all the desirable claims." So he did, and at the age of eighteen, he charged $25 for "locating" such a fine claim and offered, for an additional $25, to erect a shack on the claim. This was the only "improvement" any of these claims were ever to know, for the entry men were dummies. Within a short time young Puter was taking charge of groups of as many as twenty-five applicants, whom he marched to the courthouse in Eureka, where they declared their intention to become citizens, got their first papers, and were then led directly to the land office to file their entries for homesteads. The location papers were all ready for them. A notary public helped them to execute acknowledgment of a blank deed. Then Puter gave $50 to each, who thereupon had completed his part of the deal, went away, as often as not to one or another of the saloons and dives which made Eureka something of a reservoir for the common man.

"The description of the tracts filed on," Puter explained, "was afterward inserted in the deed and transfer of title made to the corporation." The corporation was of course the outfit that wanted the virgin redwood standing on the claims so closely that the sun had never penetrated to the soil in five hundred and more years. Puter figured that the timber alone was then worth from $200 to $300 an acre. As for himself, Puter pocketed $1250 for each batch of dummies as processed.

Seeking fresh pastures, Puter moved to Oregon, where he found what he called the land business fairly booming. "Every hotel in the timbered sections of the state," he recalled, "was crowded with timber speculators, cruisers, and locators. Moneyed men were here from Michigan, Wisconsin, Minnesota and other states, eager to make investments and grasp the unlimited opportunities of reaping big returns." So were thousands of locators and, of course, prospective entrymen. Puter was not at all discouraged at the competition of locators, while the surplus of dummies brought *their* fees to a new low. One of Puter's agents, Spider Jackson, whose stated occupation was that of head bouncer at Erickson's vast saloon in Portland, signed up several dozen denizens of the North End at "fees" ranging from a high of twenty-five dollars to a low of a ten-dollar gold piece. Although most of the dummies were loggers, sailors, or itinerant workers, Spider saw no reason why women should not get in on a good thing, and acted accordingly. At the jolly resorts operated by dainty Mary Cook and Elizabeth (Liverpool Liz) Smith, he induced a total of six inmates to apply for homesteads in the foothills of the Cascade Range, giving each a ten-dollar gold piece for her trouble. They were delighted. Although there seems to be no official record of such things, Spider Jackson may well have been the first subagent of a locator to provide dummy entrywomen from Below the Line.

Stephen A. Douglas Puter went onward and upward to become the leading locator in Oregon's timbered counties. His opposite number, in the range country east of the Cascades, was Henry Owen, who, even in that remote and sparsely populated region, could somehow whump-up, on short notice, an astonishing number of entrymen to file on homesteads. It was told of Henry that he'd ride out into the great loneliness of the short grass, shoot his Winchester into the air three times, and entrymen who swore they were trappers, hunters, sheep-herders, cowboys, or merely geologists would pop up from the ground.

But his really important contribution to the technique of fraud awaited passage by Congress of a land measure entitled the Swamp & Overflow Act. This permitted the purchase of marshland at $1.25 an acre. The purpose of the act, of course, was to cause the buyer to drain and improve what otherwise was worthless land. As soon as he had read an official copy of the new act, Henry Owen dropped his efforts to fill homesteads to specialize in swamp-and-overflow. Procuring a small, flat-bottomed rowboat, he hitched it behind a team of horses, and was hauled across the best grazing land he could find. Then to the nearest land office, where he could, and did, take oath that he had covered the area in a boat. This sounds just a little too cute, yet it is of record that he filed on and bought so much land designated as swamp-and-overflow that he became famous as the Oregon Swamp Rat.

Techniques similar to those described were being practiced at one and the same time in all of the Western states and territories. In Alabama speculators in coal and ore lands got entire families to file on homesteads, and there were instances where the father was alleged to be living on one quarter section, a son on another, and the mother and unmarried daughters on others. In the lake states there were locators who built a claim shanty on an ox sled to be hauled about from one claim to another for a series of dummy settlers. There is no need here to say more than that, between 1862, when the Homestead Act was signed, and the end of the century, for every free homestead entered and retained by a bona fide settler, nine others were bought from railroads, or speculators, or from the government itself. So far as the outright frauds were concerned, the government roused, now and then, during these three decades, to feeble efforts at retrieving stolen lands, and to indict and sometimes to fine guilty operators. Not until the new century came in did a man eminently fitted to deal with corruption appear. He was Ethan Allen Hitchcock, a great-grandson of the president and general manager of the Onion River Land Company. We shall come to him presently.

The Middle West had been filling up with settlers a full decade before the Homestead Act was signed. They were attracted by the expert publicity put out by the new railroads of Indiana, Michigan, Illinois, Wisconsin, and Iowa, each with a land grant to dispose of. In the van of those to Minnesota was a young Philadelphian named Ignatius Donnelly, who in 1856 purchased eight hundred acres of wild land on the west bank of the Mississippi below the territorial capital of St. Paul. He wanted to found a town.

Young Donnelly's wild acres were no wilder than Donnelly's imagination. His town, which he christened Nininger City for a friend, was not a real estate affair. He was no promoter seeking to make a quick fortune by unloading lots on the gullible. Nininger City, to his mind, was to be a community where artistic and intellectual pursuits went hand in hand with agriculture and industry. A city of course must have citizens, and Donnelly's first move was to establish *The Emigrant Aid Journal,* unquestionably the oddest and possibly the most intellectual periodical ever issued in connection with land acquisition. Its logotype was magnificent, one of those teeming, old-fashioned trade-marks one can study for an hour, like a Hogarth drawing, and still discover things.

Here across the top of Donnelly's paper were steamboats racing like mad to the great terminal of Nininger City; railroad trains were belching smoke across the prairie; covered wagons were coming on out of the East; men were plowing, wheat growing. Fruits and vegetables of startling girth clustered around the houses. Thus far the paper displayed the characteristics of virtually all town-promotion literature. But beneath the dazzling picture was something wholly out of character. It was a question and an answer:

> Dost thou know how to play the fiddle?
> No, replied Themistocles, but I under-
> stand the art of raising a little village
> into a great city.

Classic Athenian figures were not commonly associated with the opening of the American West, but neither was the sort of city Donnelly had in mind. Right away you learned that lots here were sold at cost, which Donnelly reckoned to be no more than six dollars. Yet there could be no speculation, none of the quick turnover in land that fetched the usual shark. Donnelly's contract stipulated that the purchaser must "begin improvements" within six months and complete them within two years. Until then the lot could not be resold by the original purchaser. Such unthinkable restrictions alone would doubtless have been enough to prevent Nininger City from having a glorious future. But Donnelly had gorgeous dreams far beyond those of most men. He wanted only those settlers who had their hearts set on erecting the finest, most intelligent commonwealth possible.

Nininger City got off to a good start. By the end of 1856 the town was still abustle with new arrivals and a great noise of hammers and saws. *The Emigrant Aid Journal* was coming off the press in thousands of copies, many of which were being "placed in the reading rooms of all transatlantic steamers." A bounteous hotel, the Handyside House, was open, offering a menu listing nine kinds of meat and fowl, four kinds of pie, ice cream, blancmange and charlotte russe. In the Handyside's cellars were eight kinds of imported wines, including champagne. Little wonder if Nininger City's hotel astounded visitors.

A literary society, the Atheneum Company, had been organized. So had a musical society. And the erudite editor of the *Journal,* who was Donnelly himself, was indicating the sort of place its founder yearned for. Between helpful accounts of how to make good butter and the care of farm machinery were interspersed a poem by John Greenleaf Whittier, a piece against spiritualism signed by Harriet Beecher Stowe, and a forthright indictment of slavery by the editor. In another issue Donnelly discussed lavender farming, tore off a rousing account of the Battle of Balaclava, and wound up with a lengthy obituary of James G. Birney, the abolitionist. In still another he hailed the first number of a magazine called *The Atlantic Monthly;* announced organization of a co-operative society by which prospective immigrants of the British Isles could pay their fares—doubtless to Nininger City—in more or less easy installments; and then he let go a thunderous blast consigning all bankers to the lowest and hottest chambers of hell, which he intimated was in charge of Adam Smith, and good enough for him. In it was a promise of things to come—to come rolling in threatening dark clouds out of the West and to waft an enormous feeling of unease to Eastern United States.

The year now was 1857. Just as Nininger City went blooming into its second year a sharp, sudden panic hit the country. Banks closed, many never to reopen. Factories shut down. Wheat rotted in the fields. Nininger City's pulse slowed, then all but stopped when it became known that the railroad, which Donnelly had been assured would pass through his city, chose another route that would put nearby Hastings beside its tracks. It was a blow Donnelly's town could not survive. By May its population, which had risen to near one thousand, picked up and left.

But not Donnelly. That stouthearted man and his wife remained, to live another half century in the big rambling house they had built in the city of culture. And at least one thousand prairie dogs returned to their old homes in Nininger's now empty lots, and the big harvest moon of 1858 revealed tall grass, high enough for hay, growing thick in the doomed city's main street.

Ignatius Donnelly had lost everything in the crash, save his resiliency, which was that of rubber. He leaped into state politics to be elected lieutenant governor, then was sent to Congress, where he sat in the House and made an excellent record. Yet he was hard to handle. The republican bosses of Minnesota found they could not manage him, so the skids were greased, and he retired to his old home amid the melancholy ruins of Nininger City. Here began work on a book that was to live.

He named it *Atlantis: The Antediluvian World.* It appeared in 1882 from the House of Harper, and turned out to be a serious if popular work to "demonstrate the truth of Plato's story of a sunken Atlantic continent." First and last, it sold more than a million copies and was in print seventy years after publication. The sales put Donnelly on his feet, and took him to the national lecture platform. He continued to write, and soon came *The Great Cryptogram,* a book that stirred an uproar to last a long time. This book—said its author—proved beyond doubt that Francis Bacon wrote all the works attributed to Shakespeare. After touring the United States again Donnelly toured England, and when he returned to Nininger City this time, he was an international literary character.

Meanwhile the now famous author had been editing an independent weekly paper, *The Anti-Monopolist,* and took out after an imposing number of "enemies of the people." These included land grabbers of all sorts, banks and bankers, railroads, high-tariff men, hard money, and minor menaces as, if, and when they were recognized for what they were. He welcomed the new Patrons of Husbandry, called the Grange, and did a good deal to change what began as a mere social order into a powerful group numbering one and a half million members who sought relief from the "oppression" of railroads and banks.

By 1890 Donnelly, hailed as the Sage of Nininger, was ready to enter his period of the Apostle of Protest. True, he had already been protesting sporadically for thirty years, but now he turned every effort to capitalize on the fame his books had brought him. His next book was a charge of dynamite which the author hoped would waft everybody into the Utopia he outlined in the closing pages of a novel entitled *Caesar's Column.* The plot of this fantastic story seems to have occurred to Donnelly, so writes Richard Hofstadter, "in a moment of great discouragement, when he was struck with the thought of what might come to be" if what he considered the worst tendencies of the 1890s "were projected a century into the future."

Readers of *Caesar's Column* were given a graphic picture of the hell of the United States in 1990. The country is controlled by an inner circle of plutocrats who demolish all opposition with machines which Donnelly had to invent for the purpose, there being at the time he wrote no such things as radio, television, or a fleet of huge dirigibles ready to drop poison-gas bombs. To operate these weapons for detection of subversive plots and the destruction of their perpetrators, the Plutes have in their hire a police force called Demons. The honest, simple American farmers have been turned into savage serfs. The honest, simple American workingmen of the cities have become a sullen, silent proletariat.

When at last the farmer-serfs and the proletariat rebel, they manage, through a secret revolutionary group called the Brotherhood of Destruction, to buy off the Demon police, and then ensues a monstrous round of looting and massacre beside which the Terror of France's revolution seems almost bloodless. So great is the carnage that the disposal of corpses becomes an immense sanitary problem. It is solved by piling the dead, under the command of one of the rebellion's leaders named Caesar, into a gigantic pyramidal column and covering it with cement.

Such was the end of the United States of America. Donnelly's climax was a gorgeously hideous affair, and one can wonder if its visual possibilities have never been considered by the Caesars of motion pictures and television.

There remained, of course, Donnelly's message, his reason for writing the book: When the awful carnage was done, and the corpses piled higher than one could well imagine, a remnant of decent as well as intelligent Americans escapes by dirigible to the mountains of Africa, where they start all over again, this time founding a sort of patented Utopia, in which Donnelly's program is adhered to. Land is distributed equitably. There are no banks. Interest is illegal. In other words, all is well in the first Christian socialist state the world has known.

The appearance of *Caesar's Column* was perfectly timed. It was a dark period. The optimism of the pre-war generations in the United States had been tempered by and almost disappeared in the troubles accompanying the rising industrialism and the plight of Western farmers bedeviled by mortgages and the "grasping and domineering railroads." Donnelly's was a desperate work. It came at a desperate moment when, as Hofstadter, a historian of reform, put it, "the threat of a social apocalypse seemed to many people not at all remote."

The threat was given direction by the forming of the National People's Party, whose members called themselves Populists. The Populists included some twenty-odd dissident or rebellious groups that were seeking reforms beyond number. Though a majority of these were already indoctrinated as Greenbackers, Socialists, Single Taxers, Knights of Labor, Farmers' Alliance men, Grangers, and even Prohibitionists, Donnelly's book about *Caesar's Column* had scared all hell out of thousands of conventional and conservative Democrats and Republicans, convincing them that the United States faced major economic reform or dreadful apocalypse.

Donnelly leaped joyously to the platform to speak for Populism. Long identified with the Grangers, he reminded farmers that the crowning infamy of the railroads was their theft of the public domain, and pleaded for both political and economic action. Otherwise, he said, "we will be making a gun that will do everything but shoot." He sought to combine the fears and hopes of city and country as the basis of a religion to defeat the baleful influence of the plutocrats. Eloquence flowed from him like fire from the open hearths of Pittsburgh and Johnstown, like the fires Kansas farmers were feeding, in their own mortgaged stoves, with ten-cent corn because it was cheaper than coal. Paced and inspired by this rotund and magnetic man who, so wrote John D. Hicks, "was at his best in unsparing denunciation," Populism did become a virtual religion to millions of Americans in the West and South.

Up out of the rotting wheat and burning corn of Kansas suddenly appeared an apparition named Mary Elizabeth Lease, a tall and stately woman with the voice of a bass trombone, to stump villages and crossroads in the grain belt, telling her audiences: "What you farmers need to do is to raise less corn and more hell." Ranging the cow country came Sockless Jerry Simpson, a terrific rouser, demanding the single-tax, and government ownership or control of almost everything except cows, range cattle, and ensilage cutters.

Down in Georgia, Tom Watson, a small wizened demagogue, moved across the red clay with shouts against the jute trust. Dripping venom like a cottonmouth moccasin, he struck at industrialists who were "importing the scum of Europe to work for nothing in their factories"; while Pitchfork Ben Tillman operated in the Carolinas, an agrarian jihad with a brass throat, fighting what he called oligarchy for his followers, the woolhats.

There were many others, too, who appeared with "the frightening banners of revolt," and Donnelly himself kept up an ominous drumming in Grange halls, in churches, and from the tail gates of farm wagons, all to the end that fourteen hundred Populist delegates, representing every possible shade of reform, and even more conflicting ideas as to how the reforms were to be achieved, met in convention at Cincinnati. There, with a tact that matched his eloquence, Donnelly took charge of this disparate mob of the discontented, to work out a compromise platform.

In 1892, in Omaha, four thousand Populists let go a cheer that "rose like a tornado" as Donnelly took the platform. It lasted for thirty-four minutes. Then the delegates nominated James B. Weaver of Iowa, a former Union general, for president of the United States, and for vice-president a former Confederate general, James G. Field of Virginia. "The Blue and the Gray," cried Donnelly, "are woven together to make our banner."

Now Donnelly turned to write most of the new party's platform, a document singular for the clarity of its prose. The Populists polled a surprising 1,027,329 votes in the election that year. It was in reality one of the most influential protests in our history, for nearly if not all of the dreadful heresies Donnelly put into the plank were to be made into national laws during the next forty years. In his masterly summary of what he termed *The Populist Revolt,* John D. Hicks remarked "that much of their Program has found favor in the eyes of later generations." He quoted Mary Elizabeth Lease, who was proud, thirty years after, that "the seed we sowed out in Kansas did not fall on barren ground"; and William Allen White, who believed the Populists "had abolished the established order completely and ushered in a new order."

But as a distinct political group the Populists disappeared. They went underground to reappear four years later as Democrats, when the astute fixers of that old party listened, incredulous at first, to a new drum, the "drum incarnate" of William Jennings Bryan, the silver-toned wonder boy of the Platte, who was to run and run again as the champion of the downtrodden. Bryan and his managers were a pale substitute for Donnelly and his bearded wild men, but a residue of Populism remained, heaving turbulently under blankets labeled "Free Silver, 16 to 1," until it could be aired and given physical form in the next century.

Strangely enough, it was left to conservative William McKinley to appoint as his Secretary of the Interior the first cabinet officer to tackle head-on and without gloves the systematic robbery of government lands. This was Ethan Allen Hitchcock, mentioned earlier, a great-grandson of Colonel Ethan Allen of the Green Mountain Boys. At the time of his appointment to the Cabinet in 1898, Secretary of the Interior Allen was sixty-three years old. Long since well-to-do, by reason of the first successful plate-glass manufactory in the United States, which he established near St. Louis, and extensive interests in iron and steel, he had served as our Minister to Russia, from which he returned to accept the Interior post.

Secretary Hitchcock began his long regime with a quiet and most thorough investigation of the countless problems presented by an empire of public land which hordes of cleverly sharp men were determined to obtain or at least use for their own benefit. He was still so engaged when President McKinley was killed by an assassin and Vice-President Theodore Roosevelt took the executive office. Within a short time Hitchcock was ready. He could hardly have had a chief more in accord with his plans than Roosevelt.

Corrupt and merely incompetent Interior officials and agents began falling like leaves in autumn. A vast plot of corporate interests to get control of Indian lands of the Five Tribes was prevented and "a magnificent inheritance of oil and gas resources" was preserved for the red men. Secretary Hitchcock also suggested what proved to be effective restrictions and qualifications in regard to leases, timber-cutting, mineral rights, and many another improvement in departmental procedure. Few if any of these changes were made without pressure to stop or hamper the Secretary. Demands were made on the President to remove him. Roosevelt refused. Hitchcock, frosty in manner, collected in speech, went ahead, utterly impervious to the influence of men high in government counsels.

Early in 1903 the Secretary suddenly dismissed his commissioner of the General Land Office. Almost simultaneously he instituted a relentless investigation of frauds based on the Homestead Act, and one of the great scandals of the period came in for an airing. More than one thousand persons in twenty states were indicted, among them several United States senators. Stephen A. Douglas Puter, King of the Oregon Timber Fraud Ring, decided to tell all, and unfolded a tale of corruption that is said to have bemused even the veterans of Crédit Mobilier. In 1906 alone one hundred twenty-six land sharks went to prison.

Exhausted by almost a decade of defending his actions, and attacking frauds at the same time, Ethan Allen Hitchcock resigned in 1907 from the Cabinet, soon to die at seventy-two. He left a public domain incomparably safer from raid than it had ever been before. It is to be hoped that some obituarist suggested the possibility that, if any reward were to come to Secretary Hitchcock, it must come from the hearts of a grateful people. Possibly it did, though one doubts it; and fifty years after his death, he who "throttled the land-grabbers with the iron hand of government" is so forgotten that most if not all of the many recent books on the history of conservation in the United States fail even to give him so much as a footnote.

6.

HENRY GEORGE: THE NOBLE FAILURE

IF, after putting the fear of the law if not of God into the hearts of the land grabbers, Secretary of the Interior Ethan Allen Hitchcock is forgotten, this is not true of Henry George, whose herculean efforts of a lifetime were rejected first and last by his countrymen. Perhaps he is remembered chiefly because he was a splendid dreamer and a magnificent failure; and also because a magnificent failure to achieve the impossible strikes a responsive chord of sympathy in men, most of whom come in time to recognize their own failures.

Henry George was the Single-Tax Man. More than half a century after his death his name, and often many pages about him, appear in all books dealing with reform in the United States, and quite as often in England. Even while he lived, and for decades after, an excellent five-cent cigar bore his name and its handsome band bore his likeness. This was fame to put him with other immortal Americans like Clay and Webster. In spite of which his countrymen could not quite bring themselves to accept the remedy he offered for all their economic and social ills. He called it the single tax. It had nothing in common with communism, socialism, populism, or any form of collectivism no matter its trade-mark.

Henry George's plan was based on the premise that land monopoly was an ancient curse that had laid its blight on every civilization. The expropriation of natural resources was the origin of rent. Rent was a social tax parasitic in nature. It increased in proportion to the rising value of the land. The rising value of the land increased with "progress," or the incoming of people and the upbuilding of civilization. Yet poverty grew hand in hand with progress simply because land monopolists kept the entire rent or gain for themselves. This condition could be righted by a single tax on increments in the value of land. Such a tax, George believed, was equitable because it assigned to the public that part of the value of any given piece of land which the public had created.

The single tax would, in short, reduce all real estate to common property by the imposition of a tax equal to the total rental value of the land. It aroused both horror and admiration. "It was even denounced," Thomas Beer ironically remarked, "by the Duke of Argyll." And denounced also by many American men of property, though the industrialists with factories could see in it no disturbance to their economic operations. Some industrialists went so far as "to patronize Henry George." To the common man, however, the great appeal of George's proposal was, so Merle Curti pointed out, "the argument that the receipts from the social acquisition of the unearned increment . . . would be sufficient for all purposes." Hence "The Single Tax" was a magic phrase. It would relieve the public of all other taxes.

There was something almost magic about Henry George himself. There was nothing of the intense and often sour fanatic about him. The defeats of a quarter of a century left him the same gentle, sympathetic, affable, and even humorous man he had always been. It is doubtful if any other American radical, unless it be Eugene Debs, appealed so warmly to those who knew or only met him. On one occasion Charles Dana, editor of the New York *Sun*, sent a reporter to interview the single-tax advocate but did not print the result. Instead he called the reporter into his sanctum, telling him, "You sound like Wendell Phillips reporting Saint John the Baptist. I told you to see a Mr. Henry George."

He was born in Philadelphia in 1839, one of ten children of first-generation Scottish and English parents. At sixteen, after little schooling, he went to sea; and on a later voyage to California got a job setting type in San Francisco, an occupation he followed off and on for many years.

He married, then drifted from one California paper to another. An attempt with five other printers to found a daily paper quickly failed. Occasionally he sought wealth by the almost standard method of the time and place, which was to put a few dollars into mining stock; and the return were also standard, being assessments "for improvements." He failed as a house-to-house salesman, failed again with a job-printing office; and on at least one occasion was obliged to pawn some small jewelry to get food for his wife and two children. His early years were filled with hardship and failure which he later conjured up to describe a sort of generic House of Want for the many, while the buccaneers of enterprise were "pre-empting the virgin resources of California."

In about 1865 he started contributing, mostly to obscure local periodicals, on various subjects, and joined a debating society. This was the point, he afterward said, at which his career really began. He spoke with ease in what one listener described as a lyrelike voice. His prose, too, was clear, natural, and effective. His mind turned, naturally enough, to the subject of poverty. In George's time poverty existed by divine right, as monarchy did in earlier days. Indeed there were few to question the status of poverty. Charity toward the poor was of course a Christian duty. But to propose a radical interference with the incidence of poverty was both impious and dangerous.

At this period the big subject of discussion in California was the impending completion of the long-awaited transcontinental railroad, which fired the imagination of all Californians. It would put the state "on a par with New York." It would bring a huge population to the West Coast. Land would boom. So would industry. The prosperity would be so great as to bring riches to all. In the *Overland Monthly* for October 1868 appeared an article by Henry George entitled "What the Railroad Will Bring Us." It was a daring thing to write, or to publish. In it the author took an almost sacrilegious view, namely that the increasing population and business activity would bring California "wealth for the few and greater poverty for the many." It was shocking. George followed it with a pamphlet about "Our Land Policy," which, though written in a low key, contained the essentials of the philosophy he was to expand and refine in his major work almost a decade later.

The Central Pacific Railroad knew an enemy when it saw one. Noting that this typesetting tramp opposed the various subsidies the railroad was demanding, its catchpoles were ordered to take steps.

George was defeated for a seat in the California Assembly, and as a delegate to the state constitutional convention. The newspaper he was editing was taken over by its creditors.

This was most unfortunate for a heretical man who doubted that poverty was ordained by divine right and meant to discover the actual reasons for it. There were then no "foundations" to support the work of impecunious scholars; the newly wealthy of the Gilded Age were still busy erecting quite remarkable palaces to indicate their status. But Henry George prevailed on his good friend, Governor Irwin, to appoint him state inspector of gas meters, a post not overly onerous which permitted him to get on with his work on what he called land taxation.

The Moses of single tax started writing *Progress and Poverty* in mid-1877, a year of incomparable riots involving labor and most of the railroads east and west. The violence brought out thousands of regular troops and militia before anything like peace was restored. It was a sullen peace, too, which left neither labor nor capital content. In California appeared Denis Kearney, a labor agitator called the "Sand-lot Man," who wanted a large number of reforms put into effect immediately. Out of his vehement oratory came only the anti-Chinese movement, which from San Francisco spread up and down the West Coast and grew into riots.

Henry George wrote on, pausing only to reflect that time was proving even sooner than he had thought the rightness of his theory about the basis of poverty. The manuscript began to pile up, and his teen-age son, Henry, was set to copying it fair for the printer. It was done early in 1878, and it was rejected by the several Eastern publishers to whom it was submitted. A friend and printer, William M. Hinton, offered to make plates for the book. He did so, and brought out a small edition, in San Francisco, in 1879. When a copy was received by Appleton's in New York, that well-established firm changed its mind, and agreed to bring out the book if the author would supply the plates. *Progress and Poverty* appeared early in 1880.

Publication brought no great noise. It fell from the press as "dead as Julius Caesar." A friend wrote from New York to suggest that George come there to stir up interest in the book. He backed his suggestion with cash for railroad fare. Late in the summer the author arrived in the metropolis, while his wife took in boarders in California and his son got a job setting type in a San Francisco shop. But George himself could find no work in New York. The Garfield-Hancock presidential campaign was getting warmer just then. George was an experienced speaker. One of the three friends he had in New York got him a long list of engagements to stump for the Democrats, who were backing General Winfield Scott Hancock. The Republicans had tossed that old favorite, the tariff issue, into the campaign, and were stigmatizing the Democrats as free-traders. The Democrats wanted speakers to go out and tell labor that the Democrats were every bit as favorable to a tariff as the Republicans. Having thus been briefed by candidate Hancock's managers, Henry George took to the road to enlighten honest workingmen.

What the politicians apparently did not know was that Henry George was an idealist and that a tariff of any kind was not among his ideals. His first talk was his last. At his first appearance he told his audience he had heard of high-tariff Democrats and revenue-tariff Democrats, but that, speaking for himself, he was a no-tariff Democrat. Before anybody could stop him, he went on to call upon the Democrats "to sweep away all custom-houses and custom officers, and have Free Trade." Cheers and cheers, but the professional boys on the platform with him were too shocked to speak at all. "I took my leave of them," George reported at headquarters, "without a man to shake my hand."

Convinced that George was either a dirty traitor to the Democrats or a simple-minded rustic, innocent of all political knowledge, the high command of General Hancock instantly relieved him from duty. Yet his next job was ghost-writing for Democratic Congressman Abram S. Hewitt, for which he was paid the enormous salary of fifty dollars a week. He must have proved competent, for he worked at it more than four months, saving enough money to bring out a small book, *The Irish Land Question*, he had found time to write while on Hewitt's payroll. This pamphlet was the turning point in George's career. It did for *Progress and Poverty* what neither author nor publisher had been able to accomplish; it started the major work on its way toward becoming a world-wide best-seller.

Curiously, as Albert Jay Nock was to point out, "this simple-hearted man wrote the pamphlet on *The Irish Land Question* with no notion whatever of the effect it would have on his personal fortunes." The trouble in Ireland over land and landlords was just then an outstanding subject in the English-speaking world. Everybody was talking about it. New York even then held more native Irish than the City of Cork. And the next thing Henry George knew "a prodigious rabble of charmed and enthusiastic Irish had hoisted him upon their shoulders and borne him to fame." Irish-like, their enthusiasm and loyalty were personal, unreasoning, unquestioning. They might be wholly unimpressed by George the philosopher, or his logic. It was enough that he was against the landlords. From that moment, said Nock, "Henry George, the protagonist," was a made man.

In New York City, George's status went up like a rocket. The bolted doors of opportunity seemed to open of their own accord. Sales of the slowly moving *Progress and Poverty* doubled, and doubled again.

Nothing could stop it now. The influential *Irish World* of New York sent the bemused author on a speaking tour of the British Isles, where he was a hero to the Irish and to the workingmen of London and the provinces. He returned to New York to find himself a hero there, with a gigantic welcome meeting at Cooper Union and a high-toned dinner at Delmonico's. The "Henry George" cigar was selling as fast as *Progress and Poverty* in new and huge paperback editions. Fame could hardly go further.

Fame, however, could not offset the machinations of professional politicians plus an event in Haymarket Square, Chicago. This was in 1886. Henry George was the candidate for mayor of New York sponsored by organized labor in that city. The Democrats, operating as Tammany Hall, as well as the machine Republicans, were dismayed. They saw their comfortable alliance in danger. The Tammany chief, Richard Croker, acted quickly and skillfully. He forced his crowd to agree to the nomination of Abram S. Hewitt, generally described as "an independent Democrat of great wealth." This was the same Hewitt for whom George had done a stretch of ghost-writing. Croker wisely believed that Henry George would scare large numbers of Republicans and independent Democrats; if the single-tax Moses could be made into a fearsome enough menace, their votes would go to Hewitt.

The Republican bosses, had they been interested only in defeating George, would logically have endorsed Hewitt. "But the bosses had more fundamental interests," as Henry Pringle has pointed out. "It did not seem possible, with so honest a man as Hewitt running for Tammany, that the usual division of spoils with Tammany could be made." The Republican bosses figured also that George would draw more heavily from the Democratic side, "which pretended to be the party of the workers." Hence young Theodore Roosevelt, aged twenty-eight, was nominated.

Then, in Chicago, at a street meeting called by a radical labor group, a bomb exploded. Sixty police were wounded, seven fatally. Who heaved the bomb was never known, but the tragedy was believed by most "respectable people" to have been the work of labor, and that, as far as the New York mayoralty campaign was concerned, took care of Henry George. Laborites, in fact reformers of all sorts, were at once seen to be anarchists bent on destroying the American way of life. Though George ran second in the three-cornered election, his former employer, Hewitt, won handily.

The rest was anticlimax. Henry George toured the British Isles again, speaking to larger audiences than before. He took Australia and New Zealand by storm. He talked his way across the United States and back to New York. But nothing resembling a single-tax party was ever formed. He died in New York City, worn out at fifty-eight, in 1897. His body lay in state in the Grand Central Palace, where more than one hundred thousand persons passed the bier, many of them weeping for the Great Dreamer, who thought ill of no man but merely wanted to destroy the temple of Moloch, out of which issued the corruption of man.

Historians seem agreed that single-tax doctrines had little or no influence on the taxation of land in the United States. Yet none has cared to say Henry George did not make rubble of the stoutly held dogma that poverty was ordained by Almighty God. When he was done, his countrymen could see clearly why the poor were always present; the reason, just as George had said, was because land given to man for his own use had been "prostituted to parasitic gain." Henry George's failure was in no manner due to any imperfections of his single tax, but to the seductive nature of capitalistic society.

Part Five

THE RIGHTS OF WOMAN

EARLY AMAZONS

IT IS probable that Henry George, once he had perfected his single-tax idea, felt there was little or no need to trouble with minor reforms. Was it drunkenness? Or crime? Both stemmed from poverty. So did almost any other social evil you cared to name. All of them would disappear when the one single and certain therapy was applied. . . . That was the way it went even with gentle dreamers like George. Obsession created a mirage with a halo so bright as to dazzle the vision; the eye could not penetrate through and beyond the gorgeous illusion.

True, until recently there had been the black page of slavery, but that ended with the war in 1865, when the single tax was not quite ready. Another fifteen years must elapse before George considered it ripe to offer to the world, and its creator, if ever he thought of it at all, certainly never recognized what in that very year of 1880 was described by a Miss (or a Mrs.) Lucy Stone as the "darkest page in human history." This gloomy phrase was the mildest she cared to use in respect to the "prolonged slavery of Woman."

Miss Stone was not the first of her sex to remark on the injustice which since biblical times had "brooded over the character and destiny of one-half of the human race." She was merely one, if perhaps the most thorough, of the early band of female agitators in the United States who wanted a whole slew of things called "woman's rights." Before Miss Stone there had been, here and there, a lonely woman who had spoken about these alleged rights, and they bequeathed to their younger sisters a sort of apostolic blessing, as well as knowledge. But they did not found anything that could be called a movement. That remained the task of a later generation.

Chief among the many rights women wanted was the right to vote, a goal that was not achieved until the last of the pioneer feminists was in her grave. Many minor triumphs were won along the way, but seventy-two years separated the first organized meeting for Woman's Rights, and passage of the Nineteenth Amendment in 1920, which declared that the right of citizens of the United States to vote should not be denied or abridged by the United States or by any state on account of sex.

The dedicated women involved in this long struggle meant that their efforts should not be forgotten by future generations, and to this end they began to write in 1880, and finish in 1920, a *History of Woman Suffrage* which now occupies six great volumes and may with good reason be called monumental. Each volume of this work, the total of which weighs a little more than twenty-four pounds, has a frontispiece. The frontispiece of Volume 1 is a handsome steel engraving of Frances Wright, a Scot who with the American Margaret Fuller is generally conceded to have inspired women of the United States to the belief that their only weapon of self-defense and self-protection was the ballot.

Whether or not there is any special significance in the choice of Miss Wright rather than Miss Fuller for the honor is not clear from anything in the text; yet Miss Fuller's picture does not appear anywhere in this volume or in any of the others. One can only wonder if the editors were a little self-conscious because of the gibes of menfolk—and womenfolk, too—concerning the alleged masculinity of these woman's-rights agitators, these "trousered females," with their lack of dainty charm, the seemingly studied indifference with which only too many of them regarded appearances, including clothing, hair arrangement, and complexion. Miss Fuller may have been no beauty, though near the close of her short life she had an affair that ended in an unconventional marriage "after her situation rendered it necessary." But Miss Wright was not only good-looking. She was obviously all woman with "a beautiful, high-bosomed figure who carried her nearly six feet of height superbly, like a ship in full sail," wrote Helen Beal Woodward of this *femme fatale* who bowled men over like ninepins. Even the aged General Lafayette was roused to such a pitch by this young woman that his plan to adopt her as his stepdaughter was abandoned only because of immense pressure by the French-American hero's scandalized family.

Perhaps it was for these reasons that Fanny Wright peers forth at the reader from beneath pretty curls and above the smart fichu of lace that reveals the neck which strong men who were not poets nevertheless likened to a swan's. When one comes to the text of Volume 1 of the *History of Woman Suffrage*, however, one learns it was Margaret Fuller, late of Cambridgeport, Massachusetts, who was "the precursor of the Woman's Rights agitation, and had more influence upon the thought of America than any other woman."

To an unbiased male reader of the nearly nine hundred pages of Volume 1 it seems likely the editors chose well enough. Fanny Wright got the frontispiece; Margaret Fuller got not only generous space in the main text, but an Appendix to boot. Both deserved everything their disciples could give to the memory of this pair of early amazons who were fit to deal with the despots called men.

Fanny was first in the arena. Dundee-born in 1795, she was in full bloom when she came to the United States twenty-three years later, bringing with her a complete materialistic viewpoint coupled with a rebellious nature and a most magnetic personality. In her mental baggage was a terribly urgent dream to set free the victims of chattel slavery and the far more numerous victims by which an idiotic and cruel legal system made woman the slave of her menfolk. It may be of interest to scoffers of the theory of inherited instinct that Fanny's well-to-do father, who died when she was two years old, had been a devout and militant disciple of Thomas Paine, whose *Rights of Man* he had been active in circulating throughout Scotland.

Reared by conventional relatives, Fanny was a difficult child who read what she wanted to and not what her governesses prescribed, and at eighteen wrote a play, published later as *A Few Days in Athens*, which a biographer said "contained the well-worked-out philosophy" she followed the rest of her life. With a younger sister, Camilla, Fanny chose not to make the grand tour of Europe, but preferred to see the young republic of the United States. The sisters spent two years touring America, returning home in 1820, where Fanny published an appreciative travel book. This led to friendship, as said, with General Lafayette. Fanny's next visit to the United States, as a biographer accurately remarks, was "timed to coincide with that of the French-American hero of the American Republic."

Lafayette's farewell tour was a sensational sequence of celebrations marking the triumphal progress of the Frenchman from city to city, from town to town, each community doing its utmost for him who had been a staunch friend in time of need. In his entourage, wherever he went, was Fanny Wright. She was by his side to visit Thomas Jefferson and James Monroe, with whom she discussed Negro slavery; but to the mass of Americans she was still a face in the crowd, albeit a pretty one, and never far from the guest of honor, who at sixty-eight was yet a gallant in the best traditions of his native country. Fanny remained in the United States when the Marquis sailed for France, leaving legends that are cherished one hundred and thirty years later, as witness the many taverns, hotels, and homes labeled "Lafayette slept here."

Where Fanny Wright slept was left to conjecture, yet she immediately began to make Americans conscious of her presence. In western Tennessee she invested much of her inherited fortune to found an experiment she called Nashoba, a Utopia to be cultivated by a few white families, and Negro slaves she purchased and freed. As usual with Utopias, with which the United States was beginning to swarm, Nashoba attracted an assortment of eccentrics, reformers, and mere lazy louts who were quick to recognize the welfare state in whatever form it appeared.

Nashoba went utterly to pieces. The poor blacks, so suddenly removed from bondage, had not the least idea of what Nashoba was supposed to prove and were, wrote an observer, "more than passively useless"; while the white colonists bickered, sulked, or fought each other over doctrine and the division of labor. Nashoba failed even sooner than the more pretentious New Harmony colony of Robert Dale Owen. When both experiments expired, Miss Wright and Mr. Owen sailed together for Europe, there to relax and to reflect on the difficulties of creating a new society based on rational thinking.

On their return to the United States they were chagrined to learn that one of Miss Wright's so-called managers at Nashoba had written an article dealing in part and in specific detail with the domestic life of the freed slaves and even freer white people of the colony. The details had to do with what was becoming known as "free love," and were read avidly. The whole thing was a scandalous exposé of the "licentious living" said to have been encouraged by Miss Wright, and was to be a lifelong plague to her. To answer these charges of "gross immorality," and explain "a rational mode of living," Miss Wright and Mr. Owen founded the Free Enquirers, whose official organ made clear that the group was opposed to organized religions and favored liberal divorce laws, together with a host of other items that included national, practical education which seemed to be the only "regenerator of a profligate age."

The Free Enquirers were of course strong for the total emancipation of woman, and one of their number, Abner Kneeland of Boston, held emancipation to include the control of conception, a subject on which he published a pamphlet engagingly entitled "The Fruits of Philosophy: or, The Private Companion of Young Married People." It seems to have been the first treatise on birth control in the United States, and was written by Dr. Charles Knowlton, a friend of Kneeland's, who advocated his suggestions on social, medical, and economic grounds. Free Enquirer Kneeland was arrested and indicted, not for publishing Knowlton's pamphlet, but indirectly on the charge of publication in his little paper, the *Boston Investigator*, of a "certain, impious and scandalous libel of and concerning God." For the next five years Kneeland's case was never out of the public eye. After three trials and two appeals he was convicted and spent sixty days in jail.

The uproar made Kneeland a celebrity. The pamphlet, which was never mentioned during the affair but was rightly considered to have been the cause of it, became a best-seller of 1832 and for a decade afterward. Miss Wright and Mr. Owen, along with nearly all of Boston's intellectuals, signed a petition for Kneeland's release, and Theodore Parker observed that "Abner will come out of the jug all foaming, and will make others foam, too." Parker was right. Abner came out swinging both arms. He resumed printing of the pamphlet and it was not long before he could with great satisfaction add up the editions to a total of two hundred and fifty thousand copies. He felt vindicated, and thereupon gathered a company of Boston and New York radicals and emigrated to establish in Van Buren County, Iowa Territory, a colony for the First Society of Free Enquirers. It was characteristic of him to name this haven Salubria, and typical of such places that it promptly failed.

By the time Kneeland was starting a new Utopia, Robert Dale Owen decided that the best way to reform was through legislation, and was sent to Congress from Indiana. Fanny Wright took to the lecture platform, an occupation for a woman almost as scandalous if not so common as that of engaging in prostitution. From the platform and in interviews with the press she lambasted men for keeping women in slavery. She was both lively and brilliant. Men especially liked to see and hear her. She became a favorite with the men of the press, who gave her, as the saying is, all the breaks possible.

But to clerics and those commonly described as solid citizens Fanny Wright was a shameless bawd. Lights were mysteriously turned out in halls where she was to speak. Vegetables were heaved at her from audiences. Boycotts were used. On one occasion, in New York, a smudge was set to burning in the Masonic Hall in an attempt to smoke out the customers. She talked on. She warned against the clergy who, she said, relied upon women for support of their insidious campaign to hold female human beings in a state of subjection and degradation. The clergy's strength, she explained, depended on their ability to keep woman "ignorant, devout and superstitious." She must have spoken most effectively, for there is more than a tinge of anti-clericism to the early leaders of organized agitation for woman's rights. The editors of the *History of Woman Suffrage* were speaking ex-cathedra when they wrote that "in the union of Church and State mankind touched the lowest depths of degradation."

Frances Wright lived up to her doctrines that a woman should try matrimony, become a mother, and then, if unhappy with her husband, get a divorce. In 1831 she married a fellow reformer, gave birth to a daughter, and soon after the marriage was terminated by divorce. She died in Cincinnati in 1852, a year when woman's-rights agitation was becoming well enough known to warrant and receive the ridicule of all right-thinking males.

By then, too, Margaret Fuller was gone, and recruiters for the feminist forces were using her best-known work as a sort of Declaration of Independence to indoctrinate embryo agitators. This was *The Great Law Suit; or, Man vs. Woman,* which may well have proved hard going for no few of the sisters, for its author was commonly looked upon, even in Boston, as an intellectual monstrosity. Yet it touched on every issue that was to form the program of the woman's-rights campaign. It considered the question of political equality, but did not stop there; it went on to sex equality, even to frank discussion of physical passions such as few if any American women, or for that matter men, had ever seen in print. Though *The Great Law Suit* was never shrill, it made clear that Miss Fuller was a dangerous rebel against man's inhumanity to woman.

Like Frances Wright, the Yankee girl came by her rebellious nature right enough. Her father, Timothy Fuller, while still an undergraduate at Harvard lost his place as first-honors man by leading a protest against certain hated regulations of the college; and later, while serving four terms in Congress, his non-conformity was notorious. A biographer of the Fullers characterized Timothy as "a stubborn oak that might break but would not bend" and believed Margaret's life had been sketched by her father.

The rather grim Timothy was proud of his precocious daughter. At the age of six he set her to studying Latin, and two years later she was reading Ovid. At twelve she was also familiar with Shakespeare, Cervantes and Molière. A decade more and she was accepted as an intellectual equal in the Transcendental set of Emerson, Parker, Alcott, and Thoreau. But the Brook Farm experiment, which she did not join, repelled her. She did not think the road to Utopia could be opened with a common plow.

The psychiatrist-biographers of later years have been fascinated by Margaret Fuller. She had been "forced into the rigid grooves of classical learning" when she "should have been playing with her dolls." Overstimulation broke her health. She became a victim of "somnambulism and freaks of imagination." She developed into "a female counterpart of Cotton Mather, domineering, moody, visionary." Yet to conceive of her as sexless is to miss the point "of her ardent nature." Had she married early, her "excessive energy might have been turned into domestic channels." Emerson thought her great tragedy was that "behind the poet was the woman, fond and relying," yet her heart had been unable to find a home.

When she "crossed the threshold of an evening party," Margaret frightened men "with her magnetic powers, the depth of her eye, the presence of the mysterious fluid of genius." In New York City, Horace Greeley felt it in her writings for the *Dial*, which she edited, and invited her to join his staff of the *Tribune*, for which she was soon writing literary judgments on the works of Carlyle, Browning, and lesser whales of letters. Then she took off for Europe, where she met Mazzini, the

Italian revolutionary, and began a book about his efforts to found the republic of Rome. This was the brief period when the Yankee intellectual proved Emerson was right—she *was* a woman. After an affair with Angelo Ossoli a marriage was announced following the birth of a child. Father, mother, and child all were drowned, in 1850, when their ship was wrecked by storm off Fire Island, New York. Washed up on the beach was Margaret's desk and the body of the child. No trace of the tragic lovers was ever found.

It was a romantic end to satisfy the emotions of the most addicted reader of current novels, and it doubtless had an influence in attracting readers to *The Great Law Suit,* which had been brought out under the stark title of *Woman in the Nineteenth Century*. What was more, it was easy now for her sisters to recognize Miss Fuller as the veritable Joan of Arc of woman's rights:

> They never fail who gravely plead for right,
> God's faithful martyrs can not suffer loss.
> Their blazing faggots sow the world with light,
> Heaven's gate swings open on their bloody cross.

No American woman's-rights agitator was to be burned at the stake. Yet there has never been a struggle, in which emotions run to high pitch, that has not developed a martyr complex. Martyrs do not always win, but they can be excessively dangerous to the opposition.

2.

THE MORNING STAR OF LUCY STONE

OF ALL the rebels against male dominance none has survived the erosion of years more engagingly than Lucy Stone. None was readier, if need be, to face those blazing faggots of suffrage verse, none was quite half so consistent in the demand for equal rights before the law. When late in life, or at thirty-seven, she took a husband, she did not become Mrs. Henry Blackwell but remained Lucy Stone, either Miss or Mrs., it was all the same to her, the first married woman to keep her name. It was one way to give point to the claim that she was an individual human being and dramatically effective to register protest that *this* woman was not to be "sold like a beast to the highest bidder." She had been heard to remark that no more legal respect was paid to a woman's marriage "than a farmer pays to the conjunctions of his swine."

Lucy Stone was a sprite who, full grown, weighed one hundred and four pounds with all her many clothes on, and was so discontented with cooking, weaving, spinning, milking cows, and making butter as to cry aloud in her dejection. "Is there nothing," she asked her mother, "to put an end to me?" But there wasn't, and little Miss Stone went away from home to shine, and often to glitter as a morning star in the dreary night of an all-male world.

Born in West Brookfield, Massachusetts, of Revolutionary stock, Lucy's great-grandfather Stone also had led four hundred discontented farmers of Shays' Rebellion. Her father was a well-to-do farmer and tanner, a man of strong opinions among which was the belief in the divine right of a husband and father to rule his wife and family. His sense of humor was fairly primitive. Though his daughter was quite attractive to most men, he thought her plain if not downright ugly because she had failed to marry at the conventional limit of eighteen, and often gibed her about it. "Lucy's face is like a blacksmith's apron," he enjoyed remarking, and, when he had everybody's attention, he could scarcely contain himself to deliver the roguish denouncement: "Because it keeps off the sparks!"

Somehow Father Stone's humor alone prepares one to accept without reservation the family tradition that Lucy's overmastering purpose in life took possession of her at an early age. There were of course other influences. New England was afire with anti-slavery agitation, around the fringe of which smoldered incipient things like the Unitarian controversy, temperance, and prison reform; while here and there was an oddly reflective female, such as Lucretia Mott, the impulsive Hicksite Quaker schoolteacher, who observed aloud that she was paid exactly half as much as male teachers and wondered if it were not time that some thought were given to the status of women, who, said Mrs. Mott in the clipped accents of Nantucket, were ranked by every state constitution with "idiots, lunatics, criminals and minors . . ."

Right at home, and all around her, young Lucy could see men acting out their parts as the lords of all creation. Her own mother was being worked to death, quite conventionally and without complaining, and once even related that on the very night Lucy was born she had milked eight cows besides getting supper for a haying crew. In other households it was much the same. Some were worse, for in them were sots who never worked but drank that their womenfolk should labor to buy the drams. But even they seldom beat their wives, as was said to be a legal right elsewhere, for Massachusetts, the enlightened, had a strict law against it.

In Lucy Stone's childhood, however, a married woman's property and earnings belonged to her husband. So did her children. Should he die before her, he might will them away from their mother to strangers. The wife could not make a contract. She could not sue or be sued. She could not make a valid will without her husband's consent unless she willed everything to him. There were many other restrictions that seldom or never were questioned.

These things only gradually became apparent to little Lucy, but none was quite so terrible as what she suddenly discovered by herself in Holy Writ. There it was in the big Bible, the Lord God laying down the law unto Eve—"and thy desire shall be to thy husband, and he shall rule over thee." Lucy was filled with horror. She knew that the laws and the customs of New England were against the women, but it had not occurred to her that God, too, was against them. Brooding over this awful revelation, she at last went to her mother for comfort. But the scriptural Mrs. Stone could offer no comfort. "It is woman's duty," said she, "to submit." It was then, according to family tradition, that Lucy Stone cried out for annihilation, and was in despair because a thunderbolt did not bring her wish immediately. In later years she was to learn Greek and Hebrew "in order to read the Bible in the original and satisfy myself as to whether such texts had been correctly translated."

At sixteen Lucy went to teaching district school at one dollar a week, plus a chance to board around free. Within a few years her salary had reached sixteen dollars. She saved most of it, spent three months under the remarkable Mary Lyon at Mount Holyoke Seminary, then, in August 1843, with light purse and scanty wardrobe, she entered the often praised and more often deplored new college at Oberlin, Ohio, the first coeducational place of higher learning in the United States. Here was a beacon in the wilderness to champion many of the noblest dreams of visionaries and almost as many of the whimseys of cranks who pointed the way to heaven by routes variously labeled grahamism, hydrotherapy, gymnastics, down-with-nicotine, phrenology, and, for at least three decades, Sabbatarianism, when Oberlin was solidly against any normal enjoyment of what most Christians—the Adventists excepted —call, with a handsome disregard for the calendar they use, the seventh day of the week.

Her first two years at Oberlin were Spartan. To help with expenses, she taught the Negro pupils in the preparatory department two hours daily, for which she was credited with twenty-five cents. For three cents an hour she did housework in the Ladies' Boarding Hall, where she washed dishes with a Greek grammar propped up in a rack, learning it line by line. In her third year, however, Father Stone mellowed and wrote Lucy that henceforth he would pay for both tuition and board and room—and even "pay the postage on all letters that are sent or received." (Because letter postage was twenty-five cents, it was common practice to send a newspaper and to mark words or letters to form a message.)

Lucy's last two years became a tradition at Oberlin. Contrary to rules she gathered a few classmates and formed a female debating society which met secretly in the home of a Negro woman. She badgered professors with embarrassing questions about "why are women more sunk by marriage than are men?" She thought one reason was because the woman "surrendered her name and in some sense her personality."

Abolition was a chief subject of interest at Oberlin. Lucy was fired by visiting speakers like Stephen Symonds Foster, the abolitionist lecturer, and his eloquent wife, Abby Kelley; and the Grimké sisters, Sarah and Angelina, daughters of a South Carolina planter, who made a deep impression throughout the North and whose printed lectures were publicly burned by Southern postmasters. When the colored people of Oberlin invited Lucy to speak at a celebration of the anniversary of West Indian emancipation, she was delighted. She spoke well, too. Next day she was called before the Oberlin Ladies' Board, who demanded to know if she were not ashamed of herself for "being up there on the platform among all those men?" She replied no, she was not ashamed. The board cited her all of the texts, biblical and otherwise, against public speaking by women, and she was allowed to go with a severe admonition.

Then, in August of 1847, Lucy Stone, garbed in a black bombazine dress that cost $4.66, was given her diploma, and left for home, a quietly seething radical, her gray eyes burning with a desire to free not only the blacks but women, too. Woman's rights? Hardly a female of the time knew that she had any rights. No time was to be lost. Within a month Lucy gave her first talk on the subject from the pulpit of the Congregational Church at Gardner, Massachusetts, where her brother Bowman Stone was pastor. It was probably the first time a lecture devoted solely to woman's rights was given in the United States, and it shocked an audience accustomed to hearing about black slavery.

Until Lucy Stone it had been the fate of woman's rights to be a side show, and a minor side show, to abolition. The Grimkés, the Fosters, Lucretia Mott, Lydia Maria Child and others who had spoken of woman at all did so under cover of the broad principles of human rights for all. Indeed, it was the question of woman's right to speak publicly on any subject that had in 1840 split the ranks of the American Anti-Slavery Society into factions. Lucy Stone understood these conditions perfectly, and within a few months after graduation she accepted an offer to lecture regularly for the Massachusetts Anti-Slavery Society.

Hers was a voice of great and singular beauty, low, vibrant, as haunting as an echo in a mountain valley; and she was to use it most effectively to hasten abolition and always to arouse the silly dolts who called themselves females. One of her first meetings, at Harwich on Cape Cod, was broken up by a mob who drove off the speakers, including Miss Stone, then wrecked the platform "making demoniac yells which were heard a mile away."

Lucy Stone was to speak in every city and most of the hamlets of the East and Middle West. She was mobbed many times. Once she was felled by a thrown missile. Hoodlums made charivari of her meetings. She talked on, and first and last woman's rights was her chief message. She stood under the withering sun of Kansas and demanded that its new constitution should give women a say in government. Kansas turned her down. So did New Jersey, where she went to live a while and where, because she refused to pay her taxes, the sheriff came and sold her household goods. It was faint talk to say she was devoted to "The Cause." When threescore and fifteen she stood on a platform at the World's Fair in Chicago and there, her liquid voice still like a harp of many strings, she spoke of woman's rights to females who had come to see the sights and their consorts who had come to see a female called Little Egypt, who weighed many pounds more than Lucy Stone and could dance, it was said, merely by use of her hips and stomach muscles. And *what*, pray, were woman's rights compared to a ride in a gondola poled along the Chicago River by a romantic Venetian or a sight of the hootchy-kootchy?

Meantime Miss Stone made two notable converts to woman's rights, none other than Susan B. Anthony and Julia Ward Howe. She also became the wife of Henry Brown Blackwell in a marriage that was unique in or outside the suffrage agitation and made "Lucy-Stoner" virtually a common noun to describe any woman who, as the possibly too apt phrase has it, possessed a mind of her own. Single or married, Lucy seems never to have approached either in looks or in actions the grim and mannish creature of the cartoons that plagued woman agitators until the Nineteenth Amendment was won.

The most widely known marriage of 1855 was a quiet event on May Day, held in the home of the bride's parents in West Brookfield, Massachusetts. The groom, Mr. Blackwell, had just turned thirty and was thus seven years his bride's junior. He was doing well in the hardware business in Cincinnati, but devoted much energy to the anti-slavery movement, and first met Lucy when he heard her speak at a meeting in the State House at Boston. He appears to have been of marked personal charm and a good businessman to boot. (His younger sister, Elizabeth, had already become in 1849 the first woman doctor of medicine in the United States.) The ceremony was performed by the Rev. Thomas Wentworth Higginson, later to command the first Negro regiment in Civil War service.

Lucy, so the good pastor recalled, made a handsome bride, dressed in a beautiful silk of ashes-of-roses, who omitted the "obey" but promised to "love and honor." It amused and gave him secret satisfaction that after the ceremony the "heroic Lucy broke down and cried like any village bride!" Then both bride and groom read the soon-to-be-famous "Protest," which the Rev. Mr. Higginson thought so just and sensible that he sent it for publication in the *Worcester Spy,* urging other couples to follow its precept until such time as "the radical injustice of present laws be righted."

After declaring that the law refused to recognize the wife as an independent, rational being, while conferring on the husband an injurious and unnatural superiority, the document got down to cases, outlining in six clauses the "legal powers which no honorable man would exercise and which no man should possess." Summed up, the six items were a protest against the whole system by which the legal existence of the wife "is suspended during marriage."

There were few newspapers in the country that did not give generous space to the Protest. Mostly they ridiculed it. Some editors, who loathed Mr. Blackwell for his anti-slavery activities, were happy that by marrying a woman's-rights agitator "justice had at last overtaken him." Poets sang, wits performed, cartoonists had a wonderful time. It was perhaps only natural that many opponents of suffrage or any other female agitation and who recalled the free-and-easy morals allegedly advocated by Fanny Wright, pretended to believe that Miss Stone and Mr. Blackwell were not married at all; that their Protest was really in favor of living in sin. Francis J. Garrison, son of the *Liberator* editor, remarked that seldom had a husband and wife been subjected to more atrocious misrepresentation, calumny, and abuse than the couple "who had entered into that noble marriage covenant."

It is of interest in characterizing Lucy Stone to know that, not long before she wed, she discarded the bloomer costume she had been wearing four years, thus bringing down on her pretty head the accusation of the diehard bloomer girls that she was "deserting the Cause of hygienic dress reform." They should have known that so clear-eyed a rebel as Lucy did not mean to become a martyr to "bifurcated garments" so long as woman had no legal existence in the United States.

3.

THE BLOOMERS OF MRS. BLOOMER

THE bloomer costume which brought on a national uproar did not originate with woman's-rights pioneers. It was designed by Mrs. Elizabeth Smith Miller, daughter of Gerrit Smith, a prominent and wealthy abolitionist, and championed into notoriety, if not exactly fashion, by Mrs. Amelia Jenks Bloomer, a temperance reformer who edited an ultradry journal revoltingly named the *Lily*.

The garment quickly took the name of its champion, who described it as a bodice and full long trousers reaching to the ankle, over which was worn a short skirt reaching a little below the knee, much like the garb affected for many years by the Perfectionist women of Oneida Community. One might describe it in today's terms as a jacket, and slacks worn beneath a short skirt.

It seems doubtful that either the designer, Mrs. Miller, or the publicist, Mrs. Bloomer, thought of bloomers as a protest to men's domination. The costume was inspired by that worn by women taking the water cure, a then fashionable therapy for which scores of "retreats" had been established in all parts of the country. But Mrs. Smith designed it specifically as a costume for the long walks she liked to take about her country home. She found it so comfortable and convenient that she began wearing it constantly, and was so garbed when she came to Seneca Falls, New York, to visit her "adored first cousin," who was Mrs. Elizabeth Cady Stanton. Mrs. Stanton was a great friend of Mrs. Bloomer. Mrs. Bloomer was so charmed with the novel dress of Mrs. Miller, known as a glass of fashion and mold of form, that she made one for herself, promptly put it on, and just as promptly went walking on the streets of Seneca Falls, to the amusement or scandal of all right-thinking citizens. There were other and more lasting effects: A sudden and immense increase in circulation of the *Lily*, and eventually the entry of Amelia Bloomer's name into the dictionary, where it remains more than a century later.

Even before bloomers added luster to its history, Seneca Falls was the scene of what is generally recognized as the first woman's-rights convention in the United States, when, in 1848, a small group of men and women met in the Wesleyan Chapel there to discuss a "new declaration of independence," in which "all men" was substituted for "King

George," which had been drawn up by Lucretia Mott and Elizabeth Cady Stanton, the well-known anti-slavery speakers, and others, including Frederick Douglass, the noted "escaped slave." The new declaration listed a large number of alleged injustices, among which was the charge: "Man has made her, if married, civilly dead."

Mrs. Mott, devout Quaker and a most astute women, warned the group that their most dangerous enemy was the clergy. She mentioned missionaries being sent to convert East Indian women "who are immolating themselves on the funeral pile of their husbands," then asked, "how many women, in our very midst, are now immolated upon the shrine of superstition and priestcraft, in the assumption that man only has a right to the pulpit?" Mrs. Mott denounced by name the General Association of Massachusetts (Orthodox) to the Churches under their Care which had recently issued a pastoral letter describing by the fearful word "unchristian" those women who sought to enter public life.

Finding at the end of two days there was much more to discuss, and that—as Mrs. Stanton put it—the gift of tongues had been vouchsafed to them, the Seneca Falls group adjourned and moved to Rochester to hold another meeting. This was a one-day affair. Mrs. Stanton observed of it that, though few women responded to the demand for political rights, many at once saw the importance of equality in the world of work.

The press roused only slightly at this new note sounded by females, who, as editors were aware, had long since attended temperance meetings and recently were attempting to be heard at anti-slavery affairs. One Rochester paper saw only a group "composed of those holding to some of the various *isms* of the day" who stressed a "new, impracticable, absurd, and ridiculous proposition." The *Ledger* of Philadelphia dismissed the whole business as the work of "the women of Boston" who wanted "a George Sand for President of the United States, a Fanny Wright for Mayor, and a Mrs. Partington for postmaster." In his New York *Herald,* James Gordon Bennett remarked that, if the girls meant to wear the pants, they must be ready in case of war to buckle on the sword; yet "if we are not mistaken Lucretia Mott would make a better President than some of those who have lately tenanted the White House."

It is doubtful that many editors sensed any significant warning in the Seneca Falls and Rochester meetings. After all, abolition and state's rights held the center of the stage, with temperance a good side issue always handy to fill a column when needed, but woman's rights were still not even a recognizable subject. Yet within a year Elizabeth Blackwell, as mentioned, had been granted an M.D. degree by the Geneva Medical School in western New York; and within two years Antoinette Brown had been graduated in theology at Oberlin, though this ordinarily courageous school was so ill at ease in the dangerous matter as to omit

Miss Brown's name from the class list, a fact attesting to the strong feeling against the heresy of female preachers. Refused at first a ministerial license to hold a pulpit in (Orthodox) Congregational churches, the Rev. Miss Brown was ready to preach wherever churches of any creed would receive her. She was already active in the temperance and anti-slavery movements and now she was ripe also for the rights which her good friend and former classmate, Lucy Stone, was beginning to demand.

Little Lucy, as yet unmarried and still speaking for the Massachusetts Anti-Slavery Society, had been mixing too much talk of woman's rights with abolition to please her employers. She was admonished. "Well, Mr. May," she replied to the society's general agent, "I was a woman before I was an abolitionist. I must speak for the women." Hers was too eloquent a voice to lose, and Mr. May persuaded her to lecture for the society on Saturdays and Sundays, times which were looked upon as too sacred for any hall or church to be opened for a woman's-rights meeting, and talk as she would the rest of the week.

So Lucy Stone took to the road as a free-lance, booking her lectures ahead by mail, speaking in all sorts of halls and a variety of churches, the sole woman in Massachusetts or, for that matter, the United States talking about the rights of woman, bearing down hard on "their legal and political disabilities." It was for her efforts during this lonely period that she was later to be heralded, possibly first by the generous Elizabeth Cady Stanton, as "the Morning Star of the woman's rights movement."

The alert Miss Stone surely read about the little meetings at Seneca Falls and Rochester. She knew that in New England she herself had in two years roused thousands of Yankee women to contemplate their lowly status in a male world. She felt the time had come to organize a mass attack. In the spring of 1850, at the close of an anti-slavery convention in Boston, she and seven close friends met in an anteroom to talk over calling a national convention for the sole purpose of discussing woman's rights.

This historic convention met in Brinley Hall, Worcester, on October 23, 1850, at the official call headed by Miss Stone and signed also by eighty-nine men and women from six states. Each of the more than one thousand seats was filled. On the platform was a galaxy of well-known speakers, including William Lloyd Garrison, Charles C. Burleigh, Stephen Symonds Foster and wife, Abby Kelley; Frederick Douglass, and Wendell Phillips; then the women, Miss Stone, Lucretia Mott, Antoinette Brown, Sojourner Truth, and Ernestine L. Rose, born the daughter of a rabbi in Poland, who had been speaking in the United States against slavery since 1836, and was now ready to devote her great beauty and even greater eloquence to the rights of woman. Eleven states were represented in the large audience. The two-day meeting was so much a success that plans were made and committees appointed to make the National Convention an annual affair.

The women were getting the bit in their teeth. A year later Worcester welcomed the Second National Convention, larger even than the first, at which Wendell Phillips made "his great speech that was used by the women as a tract for the next seventy years, or until suffrage was won." At the third convention held in Syracuse, Susan B. Anthony, already noted for her work for temperance and abolition, made her appearance on the platform for woman's rights. Miss Anthony's conversion to woman's rights was a triumph to which Lucy Stone laid claim. Miss Anthony was garbed in bloomer costume, as were Lucy herself, Mrs. Stanton, and many of the delegates. But bloomers had about run their course. Mrs. Stanton was soon to be the first to shed them and return to conventional dress. Within a year or so Lucy decided to follow the older woman's lead. But Miss Anthony protested to Lucy, to ask, "If Lucy Stone cannot bear the martyrdom of the dress, who, I ask, can?" Antoinette Brown never adopted the garb, and advised others "not to become martyrs over a short dress." She thought it good riddance to be done with it. History is silent as to when Mrs. Bloomer went back to long skirts, but Mrs. Miller, who designed and first wore the emancipated costume, wore it much longer than the others. A clue to Mrs. Miller's persistence is indicated in a remark by Lucy Stone. "Mrs. Miller," said she, "has a fine figure and wears the dress to better advantage than any of the rest of us."

Looking back, and reading the uproar in current newspapers and periodicals, one wonders if the bloomer costume helped or hindered the woman's-rights agitations. Bloomers seemed to cause men to see red. And men of the press, who merely concentrated the opinions of other males, were angry enough without the sight of bloomers to villify everybody connected with the movement.

It appears to have been this third convention which roused the males of the United States to really savage attack. The other two meetings had been let off with mere ridicule. This one at Syracuse got the full treatment. *The Daily Star* (Syracuse) referred to "brawling women and Aunt Nancy men" who preached "such damnable doctrines and accursed heresies as would make demons of the pit shudder to hear." It was to be hoped these dangerous fanatics "would leave town as soon as possible. . . . Syracuse has become a byword . . . it is high time we should be looking after our good name."

The *Star's* abuse was mild compared to what James Gordon Bennett put into his New York *Herald*: Who were these women? What did they want? He thought most of them far from charming in appearance. Some were badly mated, hence hated the opposite sex. They were mannish, like hens that crow. (The male woman's-righters were henpecked husbands who should be wearing petticoats.) What did these aggressive female orators want? They not only wanted to vote, to hustle with rowdies at the polls. They also wanted to be members of Congress. They wanted to fill any and all other posts—those of lawyers, doctors, captains of vessels, generals in the field.

Mr. Bennett stood aghast at the indecencies of these women, and then turned loose some of his own obscenities. He thought how deliriously funny it would be if Lucy Stone, pleading a cause, took suddenly ill in the pains of parturition, and gave birth to a fine, bouncing boy in court. It would be even more comical if the Rev. Antoinette Brown were arrested in the middle of her sermon in the pulpit from the same cause. Funniest of all to contemplate, however, concerned Dr. Harriot K. Hunt, the female physician, who might, while attending a gentleman patient for *fistula in ano,* find it necessary herself to send for a doctor and to be delivered, there and then, of a man or a woman child, perhaps twins.

Having considered these delightfully humorous possibilities in regard to prominent women, none of whom was then married, editor Bennett cited an actual case, that of Mrs. Jane Grey Swisshelm, editor of the Pittsburgh *Saturday Visiter* [*sic*], an advocate of woman's rights, who "formerly ran about to such gatherings, but now stays at home because, after weary years of unfruitfulness, she has at length got her rights in the shape of a baby." This, Mr. Bennett believed, "was the best cure for the mania, and we would recommend it to all who are afflicted." As for the "Tom Foolery Convention at Syracuse," said the *Herald,* "the farce has run its course."

Mr. Bennett and all the rest of the editorial chorus were wrong. The national conventions continued to be held annually, moving to a different city each year, while state or regional conventions began to meet in Pennsylvania, Ohio, Indiana, New York, Massachusetts, and were gradually to spread. Woman's rights were fast becoming a religious campaign comparable to temperance and abolition. Horace Greeley supported them all in his powerful New York *Tribune,* but he also thought well of many other *isms.* Yet he early conceded that there was no adequate reason why women should not vote, and observed it was easy to be droll and facetious about these demands of female reformers. His paper reported their meetings truthfully even when much later Mr. Greeley ceased to speak editorially for suffrage.

Throughout the decade of the fifties, in the deepening shadows of war, the organized women's groups constantly exerted pressure on

Congress and legislatures, not yet demanding equal suffrage, though never losing sight of that objective, but seeking here and there to dent the legal walls long since erected by men. The walls did not crumble as did those of Jericho, yet here and there minor breaches were made. More liberal property rights were granted in one state, while in another women were given equal guardianship of their children. In Kansas, to which Mrs. Clarinda Nichols of Vermont had emigrated in 1853, a notable victory was achieved when, six years later, the constitutional convention adopted a number of suggestions by Mrs. Nichols providing new and radical civil rights for women, including the right to vote on all school questions.

Yet it turned out that the women of Kansas were "too apathetic to exercise their new legal rights." This fact was of course made much of by men to keep women in their place, but it was no surprise to the farsighted leaders of the agitation. The usually clearheaded Mrs. Stanton was not in the least discouraged. "The ignorance and indifference of the majority of women," she wrote, "is not remarkable. History shows that the masses of all oppressed classes in the most degrading conditions, have been stolid and apathetic until partial success has crowned the faith and enthusiasm of the few."

Even the enthusiasm of the few could not contend with the overpowering subject of the time. Like temperance, the rights of woman had to wait while the Union was fast falling apart. But when the shooting began, heroic females who wanted the vote and heroic females who never gave the vote a thought set out to prove that women were something other than the playthings, the brood mares, and the work horses of the lords of creation.

Within three hours after the 6th Massachusetts Regiment was fired upon in Baltimore, on its way to the front, Miss Dorothea Dix was on a train bound for Washington to offer her services. A bit later Surgeon General William Hammond appointed her Superintendent of Women Nurses in the Union Army, the first such in our history. Mary Livermore, a temperance reformer, dropped the white ribbon and became a dynamo of the United States Sanitary Commission. Though Clara Barton was later to organize the Red Cross, she got no official recognition during the war but managed to get to the battlefields, where she cared for the sick and wounded under fire, and her greatest contribution was in getting supplies for the relief of suffering where they were most needed, and promptly. Mathilda Joslyn Gage collected instances of females who, like Deborah Sampson Gannett of Revolutionary times, enlisted and fought as men until their sex was discovered. Private "Frank Fuller," née Frances Hook, of the 90th Illinois, carried a rifle and shot it until wounded and captured at the Battle of Chattanooga. A private of the 25th Michigan Cavalry turned out to be a Miss Elizabeth Compton. At least ten other females had similar experiences.

And there was the redoubtable Dr. Mary Walker. No bloomers for her. And no men, either. She went to war in the garb she had been wearing as a physician—pants, vest, and long flapping coat, to perform under fire as a surgeon to the end that Congress awarded her a special medal. At war's finish she continued to practice medicine, now garbed in striped trousers, frock coat, and silk hat, meanwhile conducting what she said was a campaign for female suffrage. It was most erratic. She hated men and loathed woman suffragists, whom she called sainted morons. She devised and talked a great deal about the Mary Walker Reform Dress, which started with an undergarment she described as a "complete undersuit in one piece . . . made with high neck and loose waist, and whole drawers, and long sleeves with wristbands." Occasionally she would get off the subject of whole drawers and such long enough to mention votes for women, only to remark that the greatest sorrows from which women suffered were caused by their unhygienic manner of dressing. "The want of the ballot," she liked to shout, "is but a toy in comparison!" When not otherwise engaged, Dr. Walker battled the nicotine evil. Even here her methods were unusual, for, to emphasize her point, she liked to step quickly up to a male—any smoking male— and knock the cigar or pipe from his mouth with a tightly rolled umbrella she carried for the purpose.

During the war years Mrs. Stanton, Miss Stone, and Susan B. Anthony engaged in various war activities, including the gathering of more than 400,000 signatures to an emancipation petition for presentation to Congress. This effort was carried on under style of the Women's National Loyal League, an effective cloak for the woman's-rights campaign, which in theory had been laid aside but not in fact, as witness a resolution adopted at the Loyal League's first meeting, to the effect that there should be equal rights for women as well as Negroes. Like most other "subversive" movements throughout history, woman suffrage went underground until the skies cleared.

4.

NEW HOPE IN THE WEST

EVEN before war came to halt virtually all efforts except those concerned with winning it, agitation for woman's rights had crossed the

Lake States to establish an outpost in Wisconsin, and another on the west bank of the Mississippi in Minnesota. Five years before the attack on Fort Sumter, Lucy Stone penetrated to farthest Wisconsin, carrying the banner. On the Fourth of July, 1856, she spoke about the slavery of Negroes and women in a grove at wild and picturesque Viroqua, though it was many years later before the people of Wisconsin developed an awareness of history and marked the site where Lucy spoke with a tablet calling attention to "the first anti-slavery and woman's rights speech ever made by a woman in the Great Northwest."

On her horse-and-buggy tour of the state Miss Stone saw signs causing her to believe Wisconsin would be hospitable to reformers of all kinds. On a beautiful lake named Surich she found a queer, half-crazy man who kept a school, a farm, a newspaper, and a store all going. This character had also fitted up a huge stable as a free habitation to the human race. He told her he had kept cattle long enough, and now dedicated the stable to Man under the style of Humanity's Barn. At Richland Center she called on an Ira Hazeltine, whom she described as a shrewd, money-making reformer, with long hair and beard, who, having resigned phrenological lectures for town lots, had become the village millionaire, with spiritualistic affinities and a general love of lucre and liberty. (Lucy was not easily fooled.) Yet Mr. Hazeltine showed his abilities as a promoter when he drummed up a large and attentive audience to hear her lecture on woman's rights.

Miss Stone spoke elsewhere in Wisconsin, too, and somewhere along the line, possibly at Kenosha, in the audience was a young printer and editor, Christopher L. Sholes, who, later that year as a state senator, wrote an eloquent report on sundry petitions praying that steps might be taken to confer upon woman the rights of suffrage in Wisconsin. Pointing out that "never, till woman stands beside man, his equal in the eye of the law as well as the Creator," State Senator Sholes went on to say that only then would the high destiny of the race be accomplished.

Whatever influence, if any, his friendly report may have had on woman's status in Wisconsin, it was infinitely less than his contribution twenty years later when, in 1875, manufacture of the first successful typewriter in the United States was begun by the Remington Arms Company. This machine was based on and perfected by patents granted to inventor Sholes. When the machine was considered along with the shorthand taught at Benn Pitman's Phonographic Institute at Cincinnati, only recently established, the way to an undreamed world was opened for women. By the turn of the century the then-daring and somewhat romantic figure of the stenographer had appeared.... Were not the wonder-working ways of providence beautiful to contemplate? Consider agitator Lucy Stone, inventor Christopher Sholes, innovator Benn (and Brother Isaac) Pitman combining, all unwittingly, to produce the incomparable female pioneer of the frontier of business.

During her effective campaign in "the Great Northwest" Lucy Stone did not cross the great river to penetrate the Territory of Minnesota. That honor was left to the controversial if downright remarkable Jane Grey Swisshelm, forty-two years old in 1857, when she left both her husband and her native Pittsburgh to settle in St. Cloud on the west bank of the Mississippi. The genial, hardy settlers naturally made her welcome to the new hamlet, unaware they were greeting a cyclone whose vortex raged with abolition, woman's rights, temperance, and many lesser reforms including, apparently, a few original ideas about orthography. She promptly bought a local weekly that was not doing well, turned it into what was less a newspaper than a journal of decided opinions, and came out under style of the *St. Cloud Visiter.*

To account even in some measure for Mrs. Swisshelm's subsequent career, one must turn to her biographer, Mr. L. B. Shippee, who saw his subject as one of those dreamers and seers who discover in their souls something which is out of tune with the particular portion of the universe in which their lot is cast. They must strive all their mortal days to bring to the exact degree of tautness the jangling string. . . . This is a happy analogy bringing as it does, at least to a non-reformer's mind, the thought of jangled nerves while the string is being tightened. But little matter; these stormy petrels of society had a function to perform which, to use biographer Shippee's handsome disregard of petrels, is "to sting their fellows into discontent."

The daughter of strict Scot-Irish Covenanters, Jane Grey Cannon became at fourteen a devout and active abolitionist. She taught school for six years, then married James Swisshelm, and went with him to Kentucky, where he vainly attempted to establish a business. He accomplished one failure after another, while Jane supported him by teaching. Meanwhile, too, the couple argued continuously over the doctrines of Covenanters and Methodists. Then, to this already-unhappy home, Mr. Swisshelm brought a panther and two bears for which he had bartered the remnants of his last business enterprise. Installing this menagerie in the woodshed, Mr. Swisshelm delighted in his domination over the panther, and though Jane narrowly escaped mangling by the monstrous cat, he refused for many months to get rid of it and his bears. By this time Jane's nerves were jangling.

With everything a failure the couple returned to Pittsburgh and now, though the panther was gone, Mother-in-Law Swisshelm came to live with them. She was a woman who lived without sin, who prayed in a loud voice, and shouted in meeting. She had always dominated her son, and now sought to dominate his wife. Jane went back to teaching school, and also began contributing to an abolition paper, *The Spirit of Liberty*. She could turn a neat phrase in print, and quickly developed a vitriolic glossary of adjectives to apply to the proponents of slavery. In 1847, with a legacy from her mother, Mrs. Cannon, Jane brought out the first issue of what one hesitates to call a newspaper and which she named the *Pittsburgh Saturday Visiter*.

Like the later *Visiter* in Minnesota, Jane's Pittsburgh weekly was drenched every issue with the venom she sprayed on slaveholders. Now and again she would devote a page to woman's rights. She seems not to have cared about suffrage, but demanded in no mealymouthed terms that women have equal standing with men in all matters of property rights. Her vehement pen soon caught the eye of Horace Greeley. Possibly encouraged by the great editor, Jane went to Washington and began contributing long articles to the *Tribune*, but also kept the *Visiter* filled with racy and even libelous comment on public figures. Her view "was poisoned in regard to Clay, Tyler, Taylor and other slave-holders," about whose private lives she wrote scandalously. Even Webster got the treatment, not because he was a slaveholder, which he wasn't, but Jane merely charged him with fathering children by Negro servants. The great Greeley was forced to apologize in the *Tribune* for some of Jane's unsupported statements.

This was the woman who, in 1857, asked her husband for a divorce, was refused, then fought a sharp successful battle to secure her personal property, and took off without him for St. Cloud, Minnesota.

One of the town proprietors of St. Cloud was "General" Sylvanus B. Lowry, a Tennessean, who lived in a semi-barbaric splendor in an imposing house overlooking the Mississippi, where he kept slaves, bringing them from and returning them to his Tennessee estate, and, though he was both genial and courteous, he was one of those born to command. The sway of his dominion was despotic and no man dared say him nay. But now had come a woman who dared to say him nay, and much else.

The early issues of the *St. Cloud Visiter* seem to have been calm enough, as befitted an editor new to the territory. Jane gave considerable space to an appeal for support of her venture. Among the replies was one from "General" Lowry, who said he was ready to advance all expenses incident to getting out the paper provided it would support the administration of President James Buchanan. In the eyes of editor Swisshelm, and of all other abolitionists, Buchanan was a creature of the slavocracy. To the astonishment of the few people in St. Cloud who happened to know anything of Jane's journalistic past she accepted Lowry's offer by agreeing to support the pro-slavery administration.

The next issue of the *Visiter* cleared up matters. In a leading article running to three columns Jane ladled out a dose of heavy-handed ironic support, praising the Buchanan regime because it stood for establishment of slavery in every state and territory including Minnesota, and bragging that within a short time slaveholders would be calling the roll of their slaves at the foot of Bunker Hill. Meanwhile, Jane suggested, the Northern mudsills who were wasting their time trying to vote themselves farms by the Homestead Act might do better instead to vote themselves kindly masters.

Deceived and betrayed by this vile daughter of Delilah, Sylvanus B. Lowry erupted with a violent denunciation of Mrs. Swisshelm and a threat to shut down the paper by court action. That night three men were seen to break into the *Visiter's* office. They smashed the little press, carried away the type forms, and tossed them into the river.

It was now the townsmen of St. Cloud who erupted. They called an indignation meeting to which, possibly for propaganda purposes, Mrs. Swisshelm came protected by an armed volunteer bodyguard. A company to re-establish the *Visiter* was formed, donations accepted, and new equipment ordered from Chicago. Lowry and his sympathizers laid low until the paper resumed. The first number of the revived *Visiter* was almost wholly devoted to Jane's own account of the vandalism committed by dastards she described so pungently that the least Lowry could do was to slap a suit for infamous libel on the paper. The suit was settled out of court when Jane agreed to shut down the *St. Cloud Visiter* for once and all. Two weeks later there appeared from the same premises a new weekly, the perversely named *St. Cloud Democrat*, as violently Republican a paper as the North could boast.

Ignoring Lowry by name, the *Democrat* took out after slaveholders and Democrats wherever found, heaping calumny upon them, and in another space attacking men of whatever party who could think of no reason why woman should not enjoy equal standing with her husband in courts of law. Jane kept drumming away on these subjects until the third year of the war, when her discontent at the way things were going became so great she dropped everything and went to Washington, to get a clerk's job in the War Department from Secretary Stanton himself.

It is more than possible that Stanton came to regret having anything to do with Mrs. Swisshelm. For a time she sent letters to Greeley for publication, some of which he considered too critical to print. Jane took an immediate dislike to Dorothea Dix, the chief of Woman Nurses, whom she considered cold and unsympathetic, too devoted to order and neatness. Above all she loathed Vice-President Johnson, and after Lincoln was assassinated, Jane started a new paper, the *Reconstructionist,* in which she termed the new president a common drunkard, and virtually charged him with having a hand in the assassination of his predecessor. Jane was terribly shocked when Johnson himself discharged her from her clerk's job in the War Department.

There was no money to keep the *Reconstructionist* going. Anyway the rocket that was Jane Swisshelm had burned itself out, though not before the scattered sparks had flickered out in newspaper comments all over the country. She never returned to St. Cloud, but went to Pittsburgh, where a long-drawn-out lawsuit brought her the old farm which she called Swissvale, and there she lived quietly for another two decades. As her biographer remarked, "She was done. No longer would she strive to remodel the world."

At this remove of seventy-odd years it is impossible to judge Jane Grey Swisshelm's contributions to the struggle for woman's rights. One had best bow to the opinions of her contemporaries, who, though far from uncritical and even occasionally feline, rated her as courageous, of firm convictions, and an all-around noble woman. Obviously she never worked happily in any reform group; she was the free-wheeling type. She liked to forge her own thunderbolts. The official *History* chides her for devoting one hundred and twenty-five pages in her autobiography to her own work in hospitals and three pages to the woman's-suffrage movement. It remarks that only once did she honor "our platform" at a convention. Yet one finds Jane Grey Swisshelm's name in virtually all of the major accounts of the agitations about woman's rights and abolition. It is interesting to observe that of all the millions of words Mrs. Swisshelm wrote, the quotation one usually sees is the surgically incisive reason she gave for leaving her husband.

"He had good abilities," wrote Mr. Swisshelm's former wife, "but no love for books. His spiritual guides derided human learning. My knowledge . . . made me that odious thing, a superior wife. . . . I must be the mate of the man I had chosen, and if he would not come to my level, I must go to his." That, with an assist from a catamount and a couple of black bears, sent Jane Grey Swisshelm across the distant Mississippi, to "bear the flaming torch of woman's rights into the great wilderness of the Northwest."

Though it is less than likely that Mrs. Swisshelm's activities in St. Cloud did anything to enhance interest in woman's status in Minnesota, there was good evidence that Miss Stone had been most effective in Wisconsin. But the end of the Civil War found attention centering once more on Kansas, where two constitutional amendments were to be submitted in 1867 to popular vote. One would grant the franchise to Negroes, the other to women. Out to the plains where Jayhawkers and Bushwhackers had killed each other that Kansas might be free-soil, or slavery, trouped the best talent of the woman's-rights movement. Lucy Stone, with husband Henry Blackwell, led the advance, and were followed by Miss Anthony, Mrs. Stanton, and by a new convert, the Rev. Olympia Brown, a fully ordained minister of the Universalist Church. Among them these speakers pretty much covered the state.

Both amendments were defeated. But because that for woman suffrage won nine thousand votes, only about one thousand less than for Negro suffrage, the women chose to view their defeat as a triumph. That nine thousand males of a single state should have cast nine thousand votes in favor of the women was not only a record but a milestone where no marker had before existed.

If suffrage had made a better showing in Kansas than the leaders expected, they were as startled as they were deliriously happy two years later when the Territory of Wyoming was formed and its legislature provided for equal suffrage. In 1869 the women of Wyoming actually went to the polls and voted. The whole affair had been accomplished so quietly that even such alert women as Mrs. Stanton, Miss Stone, and Miss Anthony were taken by surprise. Observing in a formal statement that a happy life is one without a history, the woman's-rights leaders remarked, rather helplessly, that because the vote had been obtained in Wyoming without agitation or strife, there was no struggle to record. Looking around, naturally enough for a heroine, they concluded she was Mrs. Esther Morris, a native of New York State who with her husband and three sons had moved to South Pass, Wyoming. She was even then a strong advocate of enfranchisement and succeeded in enlisting the support of Colonel William H. Bright, president of the first Legislative Council.

There was another, too—Mrs. Amelia Post, who, when Territorial Governor John A. Campbell hesitated to sign the bill, headed a body of women of Cheyenne who went to the governor's residence and announced their intention of staying until he did sign. Thus did the "magnificent territory of Wyoming lay the foundation for the first true republic."

At the very time this happy accident happened in Wyoming, what had been the solid ranks of the woman's rights movement were "torn asunder as though by a bolt of lightning." But the rift was no act of God.

5.

RANKS TORN ASUNDER

IT IS perhaps a simplification to explain the catastrophic split in the woman's-rights group as due chiefly to prima-donna trouble. True, there had been several clashes, notably between Miss Anthony and Mrs. Stone, but they were seemingly smoothed by the great good sense of Mrs. Stanton. These small fractures might even have been permanently healed had it not been for male politicians of boundless practicality who were alert to find uses for any organized body, even of women, and when the quite appalling news came out of "feminized" Wyoming, it was obviously high time to pay heed to females.

Woman suffrage in the new territory was not the only sign of things to come. Even the genteel noun "female" was being dropped by the more astute politicians, editors, and divines to describe the gentler sex, a triumph in large part due to Sarah Josepha Buell Hale, the matriarch of *Godey's Lady's Book*. Although the aged and formidable Mrs. Hale did not trouble herself about woman suffrage, she had begun, as early as 1850, to campaign against the word "female." "Females," she said over and over again, "could be mares or she-asses." She asked of men to know why they degraded the feminine sex to the level of animals? She also demanded that women be accorded the same educational privileges as men; and when Matthew Vassar endowed a college for that purpose, she asked him to lead in a great improvement in our language by calling it a college for *women*.

The philanthropist readily agreed. But habit is strong, and when the institution was ready to open, Mrs. Hale was horrified to find the main building bearing the awful legend VASSAR FEMALE COLLEGE. Promptly at the demand of Mr. Vassar, with Mrs. Hale possibly breathing down his neck, the New York legislative assembly acted to remove the offensive word. It was carefully deleted by a stonemason with a chisel, and for many decades to come young women attended VASSAR *******COLLEGE. Mrs. Hale viewed the improved legend with no little satisfaction, remarking that the long blank space was a symbol of the honor of womanhood.

Both Miss Anthony and Mrs. Stone were agreed that *female* should not be used to describe a woman; yet it is obvious that they both thought Mrs. Hale's triumph was a small thing. After all, these two women were out for blood; let the weaker sex be ladies, or women, or females; it did not matter much so long as they were granted equal rights with menfolk.

What occasioned the first serious rift between the strong-willed Mrs. Stone and the equally determined Miss Anthony and Mrs. Stanton was a male, George Francis Train, who called himself the Champion Crank and worked busily to earn the title. To describe Mr. Train in any adequate manner calls for a book, of which many have been written about him. For the present purpose one needs to know only that he was a spectacular promoter who often had a great deal of money. Having been much impressed by Susan Anthony, he sponsored one of her speaking tours and even appeared on the same platform, thus attracting by his national notoriety far-larger audiences than would otherwise have been the case. Both Miss Anthony and Mrs. Stanton found him charming; and when he offered to finance a weekly advocating equal rights, they did not hesitate. Train was ready to name it; it was to be *The Revolution*. Its editorial board was to be headed by Elizabeth Cady Stanton. Its business manager was to be Susan B. Anthony. Train conjured up its motto: "Men, their rights, and nothing more; Women, their rights, and nothing less. Price $2 a year."

Train's name did not appear on the masthead, but one column was reserved for his use, and in it he was soon talking up the "necessity" of greenback money, one of the several heresies he championed. This feature in *The Revolution* was considered by Miss Stanton and Mrs. Anthony a comparatively unimportant appendage. To a less innocent part of the public it was viewed as shocking evidence of the unhinged judgment of woman's-righters. Men of substance warned their women-folk that Greenbackism was a grave threat to the United States. When Train suddenly took off on a sensational trip to prove that the world could be girdled in eighty days, it did not add to *The Revolution's* influence; and though he proved it could be done in eighty days and thus inspired Jules Verne to write a famous book, Train lost interest in the paper to seek nomination to the presidency.

What Lucy Stone thought of Mrs. Stanton's and Miss Anthony's taking up with Francis Train was at first disbelief, a "monstrous hoax invented by the enemy." When the paper began to appear, she was aghast that her old friends should make woman suffrage absolutely ridiculous by associating it with Mr. Train, who was so erratic that for a time he was shut up in a lunatic asylum as actually insane. Mrs. Stone admitted the paper often contained brilliant editorials on woman's rights, but they came out side by side with the insane ravings of Mr. Train. William Lloyd Garrison wrote Miss Anthony in "astonishment that you and Mrs. Stanton should have taken such leave of good sense as to be travelling companions and associate lecturers of that crack-brained harlequin and semi-lunatic George Francis Train."

In a pointed editorial Mrs. Stanton stated that *The Revolution* could not be crushed even by the united efforts of "Republicans, Abolitionists, and certain women." Among these certain women surely was Lucy Stone. The lines were being drawn. Almost simultaneously two suffrage associations, the American and the National, were fighting each other to dominate woman's rights. It is of interest to know they were usually referred to, respectively, as the Boston group and the New York group. Prominent in the former was Mrs. Stone, who became associate editor with Mary A. Livermore in a new organ, the *Woman's Journal*; and Julia Ward Howe, said to have been converted to the cause by Lucy Stone herself. The prestige of the librettist of "The Battle Hymn of the Republic" was possibly unequaled in the United States, unless by that of Harriet Beecher Stowe.

The so-called New York group numbered the team of Stanton and Anthony, and many other prominent women including the aging Lucretia Mott. They hoped and tried to get Mrs. Stowe as a contributor to their organ, but the author of *Uncle Tom's Cabin* refused unless the name of *"The Revolution* be changed to The True Republic, or something equally satisfactory." The name was not changed. Mrs. Stowe remained firm.

The two groups went their own ways but did not dissipate their energies wholly in seeking domination. Snide remarks were passed in meetings. Reproachful editorials were published. There were heartaches, tears, accusations. Neither side, however, ever lost sight of the goal. Of the two papers the *Woman's Journal* was to have a long life. *The Revolution* lasted less than three years, which, according to Miss Anthony's biographer (Katharine Anthony), were the happiest years of her life. She was doing exactly what for long she had wanted to do, publishing a sincere reform journal. Every morning, when she arrived at her office on Park Row, New York, "she arrived on the wings of a dream." She may well have been in this condition when, near the end of *The Revolution's* days, she—and Mrs. Stanton, too—became enamored with the personalities of two sisters known as Victoria Woodhull and Tennessee Claflin. Whereupon, things began to move so swiftly that, before Miss Anthony and Mrs. Stanton hardly knew it, they and their allies of the New York group, or National Woman Suffrage Association, were involved in what with some reason was called the "Scandal of the Century." This was the Beecher-Tilton case.

In 1870, when the vivid sisters decided to take over what they no doubt considered to be the woman's-rights business, Victoria was thirty-two, Tennessee, twenty-four. For all practical purposes, however, they were as old as Eve, wiser by far, and from their lips dripped both honey-comb and blue vitriol. It was not of these two women St. Peter was think-ing when he observed that woman is the weaker vessel. A reporter of the Philadelphia *Press* looked at Victoria to see "a sphinx-like unflinching woman. No chance to send an arrow through the opening seams of her mail . . . She reminds one of the forces of nature behind the storm, or of a small splinter of the indestructible, and if her veins were opened they would be found to contain ice."

It is improbable that Mrs. Stanton and Miss Anthony knew much about the girls' background. Born Claflin in Homer, Ohio, of parents who even in that day were considered eccentric, the mother was not only a spiritualist but a disciple of Mesmer. Whatever may have been the oddities of Father Claflin, he was obliged to leave the small town just ahead of the sheriff on suspicion of arson. He also left wife and a sizable family to be cared for by the town. The citizens, counting no less than eleven Claflin mouths to feed, quickly staged a benefit, turned the receipts over to Mother Claflin, and bid her to take her progeny and go beyond the township of Homer, Ohio.

In no time at all the Claflin family were a wagon show moving across Ohio, with Victoria and Tennessee giving spiritualistic exhibitions and telling fortunes, while a brother, Hebern, became "Doctor" Claflin, the great authority on cancer; and all hands joined in selling Elixir of Life, on each bottle of which was a picture of Tennessee, the beauty of the family. Incidentally, both Tennie and Victoria married—for the first but not last time—while in their teens. They set up shop as clairvoyants in Cincinnati, moving as need be, and, in 1868, turned up in New York City.

One can scarcely question the necromancy of this pair of sisters. One of their first clients was none other than the aging Commodore Vander-bilt, the commonly hardheaded and prehensile mogul of railroads. Though it seems most unlikely that the Commodore was ever a thorough convert to spiritualism, he was getting on and he played with the idea, possibly on the theory that one can never be certain about such matters. It was soon after a conference at his home with Victoria and Tennessee that he had saltcellars placed under the legs of his bed. "Health con-ductors," he explained. The saltcellars and other therapy administered by the girls worked on the Commodore to such purpose that he prompted them to open a stock brokerage house in Broad Street where, within a short time, they reputedly made more than half a million dollars by trafficking in shares of the New York & Harlem Railway Company.

Then, in 1870, after a mere two years in the big city, the two country girls started *Woodhull & Claflin's Weekly*, which the record indicates to have been a sort of intellectual *Police Gazette*. On its logotype was a motto, "Upward and Onward," and a statement to the effect that the paper would be devoted to the interests of woman's rights, labor, spiritualism, and that it also favored birth control, and more liberal divorce laws. That might have seemed a large enough order even for a sixteen-page paper in whose healthy advertising columns were paid notices of every reputable brokerage house in New York City, but editor Woodhull was universal in her interests and she was to find room for other things as they occurred to her surging fancy.

It appears that Miss Anthony and Mrs. Stanton first met Mrs. Woodhull and Tennessee Claflin through the good offices of Elizabeth Tilton, who had worked for a time on *The Revolution*, and her husband, Theodore, also a journalist. The Tiltons were close friends of the Rev. Henry Ward Beecher, the more-than-eminent minister of Plymouth Congregational Church in Brooklyn; and friends also of his half-sister, Isabella Beecher Hooker, a devoted acolyte to woman's rights in the form they were presented by the National, or New York, group headed by Mrs. Stanton and Miss Anthony. The two sisters turned out to be as hot for suffrage as one could wish. Victoria dressed conventionally and in quiet elegance. Tennie was a cute little trick in what for that day was a mannish suit and a fetching alpine hat with a saucy feather. Both were very pretty. Both were expert conversationalists, with racy turns of speech that were refreshing if a bit odd compared to the gentility with which most discussions of woman's rights were carried on.

Mrs. Woodhull especially made a great impression on Theodore Tilton and almost as great on the others. Tilton was soon at work on an extravagantly eulogistic biographical sketch of her, whom he hailed as a modern Joan of Arc, for publication. She impressed Mrs. Stanton and Mrs. Hooker as just the speaker needed to put life into the National Woman Suffrage convention soon to be held in the national capital. As time neared for this event, Mrs. Hooker persuaded the hard-worked Miss Anthony to leave all arrangements for the meeting to her. Mrs. Stanton was to open the convention by presenting a memorial to a congressional committee.

Nothing of the kind happened. On the night before the National convention was to open, Mrs. Hooker, Mrs. Stanton, and Miss Anthony were astounded to pick up their evening papers to read that Victoria Woodhull was to present a memorial of her own to a special Judiciary Committee of the House of Representatives. None of the three suffrage leaders had had an inkling of it. "A lone eagle," wrote Miss Anthony's biographer, "had all unheralded swooped into the suffrage movement." The brash Mrs. Woodhull had gone alone to Washington, laid hands on several congressmen, among whom was Benjamin F. Butler, Massachusetts, and prevailed on them to let her appear before a House committee. Then she hastened to the press with the glad tidings.

It was obvious that Mrs. Woodhull planned to be the only woman present before the gentlemen of the House. But Miss Anthony worked fast, too. She got hold of Mrs. Hooker and Mrs. Stanton. They rounded up such delegates as they could find soon enough to attend the special meeting. If Mrs. Woodhull was embarrassed in the least, to see "a considerable number of women" come trooping in, she did not show it, but proceeded to give what one reporter said was by far the ablest argument that had been produced for woman suffrage. He also noted that the speaker was a beautiful woman, refined in appearance and plainly dressed, who read her memorial in a clear, musical voice with a modest and engaging manner. Mrs. Woodhull's argument was that she, as a woman, was already empowered by the terms of the Fourteenth Amendment to vote.

Having already stolen the show, the fascinating interloper was invited to repeat her address at the National Suffrage Convention, which had been postponed two hours on her account. She did so, though with what Miss Anthony thought was less fire and fervor than had attended her performance before her morning's congressional masculine audience. Yet Miss Anthony believed Mrs. Woodhull had introduced a new gleam of hope into the suffrage line of reasoning. Susan could even forgive the younger woman's double-dealing. But neither Susan nor Mrs. Stanton could do much about the rumors of Mrs. Woodhull's domestic arrangements; she was living in Great Jones Street, in Greenwich Village, with a Colonel Blood, who may or may not have been her current husband, and with them also at the same address abided a Mr. Woodhull, admittedly Victoria's divorced husband. The situation lent a certain piquancy to the editorials about "free association" in *Woodhull & Claflin's Weekly*.

Mrs. Lucy Stone had failed to be impressed by this new wonder discovered by the National Woman Suffrage leaders, and at the next meeting of the American Suffrage Association, that group passed resolutions deploring and denouncing what they called in so many words by the awful name of "free love." It was as if the Boston group had put the scarlet letter on all women of the New York, or National, group. In another realm this would have been described as vicious infighting. Miss Anthony was scornful of such tactics. Yet she, too, was growing uneasy about Mrs. Woodhull; despite her quick mind and unbounded energy there was something decidedly irregular about her, and her sister, too.

It was months later, while returning to New York after a tour of the Far West, that Miss Anthony learned what Mrs. Woodhull had been up to in her absence, of which more presently. With Mrs. Stanton, Susan had been touring Wyoming, Utah, and California. While the former remained in California, Susan went to Portland, Oregon, to see Mrs. Abigail Scott Duniway, a lone woman's-rights voice in the Pacific Northwest and where, as Susan quickly learned, women were a scarce commodity. It was Portland where Susan B. Anthony, aged fifty-one, received a formal proposal of marriage from "a prominent gentleman," and in Olympia, Washington Territory, she was "serenaded by a millionaire." Although Susan was not in the market, it is little wonder if she thought of this vast, lonely far corner of the United States as a land of opportunity.

Mrs. Stanton returned East ahead of Miss Anthony, who followed a few weeks later on a train that ran into a blizzard and required eight days to pass through Wyoming. Then, while changing cars in Chicago, Susan saw a copy of *Woodhull & Claflin's Weekly*, and learned that Mrs. Woodhull had not been vegetating. The paper announced that the National Woman Suffrage Association was organizing a new political group, the People's party, and in convention soon was to offer a candidate for President of the United States. Signed to this manifesto were the names of none other than Mrs. Stanton, Mrs. Hooker, Mrs. Matilda Gage, and Miss Susan B. Anthony. Susan did not need to be told who had thought up this shocking idea. She may even have guessed who might well turn out to be the People's party candidate for the office of chief executive.

As soon as her hand had steadied, Miss Anthony wrote and dispatched several telegrams. One demanded that her name be withdrawn from the preposterous announcement; the others canceled her lecture engagements in the Lake States. Then she caught the next train of cars for New York arriving three days ahead of the nominating convention, time enough perhaps to put a stop to the insane proposal of Victoria Woodhull.

Susan's conference with Mrs. Stanton, Mrs. Gage, and Mrs. Hooker was not, as rumor had it, a hair-pulling battle. These were not hair-pulling women. But the affair was certainly a sizzler. Susan spoke so harshly that the others huffed up. They refused to admit they had made a mistake in being cajoled by Mrs. Woodhull. They called Susan narrow-minded and domineering. They not only withdrew completely from running the convention, but Mrs. Stanton then and there wrote out her resignation as president of the National Woman Suffrage Association. It was a thorough and all-around "mad." The New York group of suffragists seemed to be falling apart.

Left alone to deal with the aggressive Mrs. Woodhull, Miss Anthony rose swift and sure to the occasion. She told Mrs. Woodhull and her adherents that they would not be permitted to meet jointly with the National association. Mrs. Woodhull was forced to find another hall. When next day the by now badly demoralized National meeting opened, Susan was obliged by Mrs. Stanton's absence to act as chairman. On a motion from the floor Susan was elected president of the association. Then Mrs. Woodhull suddenly stood up to move the meeting adjourn, to meet next day at *her* convention in Apollo hall. Susan refused to put the motion, whereupon Mrs. Woodhull, who seems to have taken care to do a good deal of efficient lobbying beforehand, leaped to her feet and put the motion herself. It was carried. Susan remained calm as she took aim and let go her next bolt. The proceeding, she declared, was out of order; neither Mrs. Woodhull nor many, if any, of those voting for the motion were members of the National Woman Suffrage Association. It was true, too, for the wily Woodhull had, in her haste, overlooked this important matter. Susan then declared the meeting adjourned, to resume next day in the same place. It was a stunning blow, but it did not quite silence Mrs. Woodhull, who took the floor without asking and started to talk at top speed, which was very great. The hoarse yet commanding voice of Miss Anthony broke through the tirade to order the janitor to turn off the gaslights. He did so. The meeting *was* adjourned.

The next day of the National's convention was a sad thing. Even Susan termed it a perfect fiasco. But there was action aplenty, and noise, too, in Apollo hall, where the People's-party outfit had a wonderful time adopting what they called a platform and nominating Victoria C. Woodhull as candidate for President of the United States.

In her diary Miss Anthony wrote that she had never been so hurt as by the folly of Mrs. Stanton, and observed that the woman's-rights movement had been demoralized by letting go the helm to Woodhull. The quarrel between the two old friends was to be healed quickly. As for Mrs. Woodhull, the rights of women interested her only for a moment as a way to exploit further her consuming egotism. She parted from the leaders of the movement apparently without regret and without recrimination, but with far-from-empty hands. All unwittingly Mrs. Stanton had provided her with explosive material which was soon to make *Woodhull & Claflin's Weekly* the most notorious newspaper in the country.

In that journal's celebrated issue of November 2, 1872, editor Woodhull ventilated, to use her own expression, a scandal whose main actor was the Rev. Henry Ward Beecher of Plymouth Church in Brooklyn. Mr. Beecher's correspondent was Elizabeth Tilton, wife of his close friend and protégé. The supporting cast included the injured husband, and a number of woman's-rights advocates, among whom were Mrs.

Stanton, Isabella Beecher Hooker, and even Susan B. Anthony. Here was no troupe of Broadway and demimondaine characters such as those who had recently staged the sensational affair in which a doxy named Josie Mansfield was involved with Jim Fisk, an old rounder, and Edward Stokes, the playboy, and which ended with the murder of Fisk in the Broadway Central hotel. What became the Beecher-Tilton case involved only people who until the moment Mrs. Woodhull cut loose were both "eminent and respectable."

It is impossible to recapture a sense of the respect and veneration in which Beecher was held in the early seventies. He had magnetism and eloquence, a commanding presence, and a comprehensive understanding of what was not yet known as public relations. If his sister, Harriet Beecher Stowe, was the best-known writer in the United States, Henry was not known simply as her brother; he was by far the best-known preacher in the United States.

To remove the hide of this national figure, editor Woodhull chose to operate on the premise of public service. The bawdy editors of *The National Police Gazette* had for many years been excusing their lewdest stories as "written in the public interest"; and similar editorial hyprocrisy was not unknown in papers remote from the gutter. So Mrs. Woodhull began her eleven-column piece by saying that what she was about to do she did with the utmost reluctance and only from a deep sense of duty. Her duty, it seemed, was to campaign against the outworn institution of holy wedlock. Then she let fly.

Citing her first authority as Theodore Tilton himself, the injured husband, Mrs. Woodhull said he had been convinced of the intimacy between his wife and her pastor, Mr. Beecher, by a story told him by his little daughter. This confirmed his own half-formed suspicions. His wife soon confessed all to her husband. In a transport of jealousy and rage Tilton tore the wedding ring from her finger, and stamped to pieces a photograph of Mr. Beecher. After elaborating a column or so on these facts, editor Woodhull paused briefly to say that Mrs. Tilton had confirmed them. Further, the Tiltons had discussed the matter with two eminent leaders of the woman's-rights movement. One of these was Paulina Wright Davis, the other Elizabeth Cady Stanton. It was from Mrs. Stanton, Mrs. Woodhull carefully recalled, from whom she had first heard of the affair. Thus did "the terrible siren" leave the indelible marks of her passing on the National Woman Suffrage Association.

Mrs. Woodhull went on to make it leeringly obvious that she did not in the least object to the conduct alleged against Mr. Beecher. Far from it. Mr. Beecher, she observed with the eye of an expert, was of immense physical potency and, quite naturally, of a demanding physical nature. Why, said she, the amative impulse was after all the physiological basis of all character; and the Rev. Mr. Beecher possessed it in such measure as to emanate zest and magnetic power to the whole audience of Plymouth Church. Indeed, this church had, for a quarter of a century, lived and fed—wrote Mrs. Woodhull with rising enthusiasm —and had been augmented and strengthened by the physical amativeness of Henry Ward Beecher. She was quite content with all this and content, too, with the alleged conduct of Mr. Beecher and Mrs. Tilton. It was only with the hypocrisy of the eminent divine that she pretended to quarrel.

The moral of the affair was of course that the shoddy institution of marriage should be reformed radically until it conformed to rational thought.

Eleven solid columns saying that adultery followed holy wedlock as closely as night followed day might seem enough meaty matter for one issue of any paper. But editor Woodhull loved her readers, and in this already outstanding number of her journal she found room for a short but possibly too frank piece dealing with a stockbroker named Challis, who, on one and the same busy evening, had successfully accomplished the seduction of two young women. What troubled the editor more than the seduction was that the dastard had boasted of it.

The November 2 issue of *Woodhull & Claflin's Weekly* had little more than reached the newsstands and got into the mails when two deputy United States marshals appeared at the paper's office with warrants for arrest of Victoria and Tennessee on a charge, preferred by Anthony Comstock, secretary of the recently organized Society for the Suppression of Vice, of having mailed an obscene publication. Though the allegedly objectionable matter cited in the warrant was not the Tilton-Beecher story but certain terms used in reporting the social activities of Mr. Challis, the lusty broker, an assistant district attorney before whom the sisters were arraigned, chose to refer to it as an atrocious and untrue libel on a gentleman whom the whole country revered. Meaning, of course, Mr. Beecher.

Victoria and Tennessee, who were dressed in plain dark suits of alpaca and wore hats described as most jaunty, were locked up in Ludlow Street jail with bond set at $8000 each. During the next eight months the girls were in, then out, of jail, and managed, with expert counsel, who was the diamond-studded and crafty W. F. Howe, to keep the daily press of the nation in sporadic uproar. The sisters, while out on bail, staged mass meetings in New York, Boston, and lesser cities. They collected funds to defend the freedom of the press. Now and then they came out with another issue of their own paper in which they reprinted the Tilton-Beecher story, thus bringing within reason the price of possessing this gamy document. (The November 2 issue, in which it originally appeared, had soared to forty dollars a copy.) And at last, in June of 1873, the case was dismissed, the judge ruling that the law under which the indictment was drawn did not apply to newspapers, but only to books, pamphlets, and pictures. On their acquittal the sisters were surrounded by a vast crowd of congratulating friends who virtually smothered them with flowers.

The Beecher-Tilton mess was only beginning when its instigators were freed. One is prepared to believe that the two sisters had enjoyed it immensely. They had carried off their parts successfully with a dash indicating the great talents they were prepared to devote to whatever course their future careers might take. And though their careers were not again to be connected with woman's rights, it would be churlish to dismiss them without mention that their names appeared in the will of Commodore Vanderbilt, who died in 1877, leaving a numerous family and an estate of $105,000,000. In a family squabble over the will, court hearings revealed that certain large sums had been set aside by the old Commodore to advance the noble work of spiritualism— under the trusteeship of Victoria Woodhull and Tennessee Claflin.

The far-from-backward sisters told the press they were greatly disappointed. The certain large sums, they said, were in no way adequate to promote spiritualism on the scale intended. They just happened to remember, too, that the Commodore owed them a little money—the residue, said they, of a deal in the stock market. They would however, in consideration of the great regard in which they held Mr. Vanderbilt's memory . . . Why, they would be glad to accept the certain large sums in lieu of the debt. The New York press said that these sums totaled to more than $100,000. No suit was brought. The matter seems to have been settled amicably out of court; and the sisters, who were known to to have been nearly penniless early in 1877, immediately hired a crew of servants and engaged six double first-class staterooms for a voyage to England. Somewhat later Mrs. Woodhull married John Biddulph Martin, member of a wealthy English banking family; and Miss Claflin married Francis Cook, soon made a baronet. At least Tennie became officially a "Lady."

The Beecher-Tilton affair was now public property, and the press was alert to keep the public informed. Plymouth Church held an investigation and a sort of trial during which police had to be called and found need to use their night sticks briskly in breaking up a riot within the sacred walls. The outcome was an "acquittal" of Beecher that satisfied almost nobody. Tilton then instituted a criminal suit against Beecher for the alienation of his wife's affections. This ended after one hundred and twelve days of court trial in a hung jury.

The whole disgraceful affair had been pretty much on public view for more than three years. Its influence on the woman's-rights movement was bad. The National group's leaders believed in Beecher's guilt, the American leaders in his innocence. Mrs. Stanton, who was reputed to hate preachers generally, championed Tilton "almost to folly." Lucy Stone supported Beecher staunchly, though with more circumspection and with less animosity toward opponents than displayed by either Mrs. Stanton or Mrs. Hooker. The over-all effect was to solidify the hostility of the two groups toward each other.

Poor Miss Anthony wept bitter tears. Was this dirty mess, which had absolutely nothing to do with the rights of woman, to wreck the entire movement? She tried to remain aloof to the dreadful uproar. She also showed an unfeminine lack of professional jealousy and private envy by adopting the Fourteenth Amendment to the United States Constitution as a base for her next propaganda effort, exactly as suggested by none other than the deplorable hussy, Victoria Woodhull.

6.

NO DOLL WAS ABIGAIL

THE Fourteenth Amendment provided that the rights of citizens were not to be abridged. It described citizens as all persons born or naturalized in the United States. Hence, said Mrs. Woodhull, women had the right to vote. What more were the girls waiting for?

There is reason to believe that this startling interpretation of the act had been supplied to Mrs. Woodhull by Congressman Ben Butler of Massachusetts, a man never short of ideas. She touched it off to burst over the woman's-rights horizon like a rocket shooting stars, and Susan Anthony, despite her suspicions in regard to the good faith of Mrs. Woodhull, decided to put the proposition to a test. In Rochester, N.Y., on registration day in November 1872, she led some fifty women to be registered as voters. Mostly they were refused, but Susan and fifteen others were good-naturedly, perhaps humorously, permitted to list their names. Four days later these sixteen women actually voted.

The press boiled up with excitement. Editorial pages demanded to know of the government why illegal voting had been done in Rochester. The sixteen bold women were arrested. Susan was elated. "We are in for a fine agitation in Rochester," she wrote Mrs. Stanton. The agitation went further than that. For almost a year, while Susan's case was moved from one court to another, and postponed numerous times, Susan and associates staged lecture campaigns that aired the question throughout New York and other states. Susan even voted again, this time in a municipal election in Rochester, and set off another hull-abaloo. When her case came at last for trial, the judge directed the jury to bring in a verdict of guilty. She was fined $100. Susan addressed the court. "May it please your honor," said she, "I shall never pay a dollar of your unjust penalty." Nor did she.

Letters of sympathy and encouragement poured in. So did donations amounting to a little more than a thousand dollars. Miss Anthony used much of this to pay for publishing a report of her trial, which in pamphlet form was mailed to libraries and newspapers all over the country. Her "martyrdom," however, did nothing to heal the breech between the National and American associations. The latter's organ, the *Woman's Journal*, Lucy Stone, editor, printed an honor roll of the women who had "worked wisely for woman suffrage during the year." The names of neither Miss Anthony nor Mrs. Stanton were on it. This was hardly surprising. The American group's leaders held that the National women, by their association with George Francis Train and the Woodhull and Claflin sisters, had been tainted with the easy divorce and even free-love tenets of those heretics. Indeed, Mrs. Stone and Mrs. Livermore and their associates had felt it necessary to organize, under Julia Ward Howe's leadership, a new subsidiary outfit, the Association for the Advancement of Women. This was a conservative, wholly genteel group suggested by Charlotte B. Wilbour, who had already founded Sorosis, and thought there should be a woman's-rights banner to which "discontented women could repair without losing their social status." Suffrage was not an item in the Association for the Advancement of Women's program. A few members of this new group thought it strange that Miss Anthony was not invited to join, and were told that "she could not be managed." It was obvious that the rift between the American and the National women was not healing.

Out in the Far West, however, one of Miss Anthony's converts had started to carry the banner to some purpose. She was Abigail Scott Duniway, already mentioned, born in Illinois, who at the age of eighteen had walked much of the way to the Oregon Country, accompanying her parents. She soon married. After nine years and six children support of the entire family was suddenly thrown upon her because of an accident to her husband. Though she was quite equal to the task, she was a clear-eyed woman who held a rather low opinion of her sex. "One half of American women are dolls," she remarked in a charmingly succinct sentence, "the rest are drudges, and we're all fools."

To turn dolls, drudges, and fools into sovereign citizens, equal on all counts to their lords and masters, was to be for Mrs. Duniway a task of forty years. Inspired by early copies of *The Revolution,* edited by Stanton and Anthony, she was then teaching school but soon quit, observing that her pay was only half so much as that paid a man for the same grade. With a capital of $30 she opened a millinery shop in small Albany, Oregon. More and more she brooded over the dismal condition of females in the republic. Her husband was sympathetic, remarking that women would never be any better off until they had the right to vote. "Then," said he, "women could help to make the laws, and the laws would soon come to treat women better."

Selling her store, Mrs. Duniway picked up and moved to Portland, a metropolis of 8000 population, where she set up living quarters on the ground floor of a large house and turned the upstairs into editorial and business rooms for *The New Northwest,* the first issue of which appeared on May 5, 1871. For the next fifteen years this paper was to startle, madden, and amuse a steadily increasing number of readers.

No doll was Abigail Scott Duniway. Her *New Northwest* was no pale and pious sheet, praying aloud to God and His males to grant women their rights. It was an ably written and ably edited weekly which, with no trace of self-consciousness, plunged headlong into Oregon-style journalism, a style as free-wheeling and personal as any in the West. Trenchant was the word for editor Duniway. "Brother Casey of the Dallas *Itemizer,*" she wrote, "has recently taken to himself a wife, got rid of his obscene editorial associate, and once more is getting out a respectable journal."

The newspaper brotherhood might sneer at or attack *The New Northwest,* but not with impunity:

We see that the *Itemizer* now comes out with eight pages, six of which are printed in Chicago [wrote Abigail]. If the remaining two were also printed in Chicago, the paper would be much more interesting to the general reader, and quite as useful to the citizens of Polk county.

As fast as they stuck out their necks, Abigail mowed them down. It was not only the way Oregon editors liked to perform, it was good also for circulation. Many a male who blanched at the mere thought of females voting took and read the *New Northwest* for its editor's ability to hold her own in a free-swinging male profession. Yet, editor Duniway never lost sight of her goal. Every issue contained an editorial, essay, or other matter concerned with the rights of women. Being gifted with shrewd understanding, however, Abigail offered readers more than propaganda. She advised in matters of cooking and household activities. She reviewed books. She encouraged poetry, and perhaps printed too much of it. One of her star contributors was Minnie Myrtle Miller, divorced wife of Cincinnatus Miller, who had taken to calling himself Joaquin and set up as a poet and genius, then ran off to London, leaving Minnie and several children to fare as they could. Abigail was not particularly set against divorce, but she believed that men should be responsible for their families, and she made it a part of editorial policy to remove a piece of the thick hide of Joaquin in almost every issue. ("Mrs. Miller is rearing the deserted children of this literary lion.")

Mrs. Duniway found time to do a good deal of lecturing, and when Miss Anthony came to tour the Northwest, that old trouper got some idea of pioneering. Seven days on a ship from San Francisco to Portland left Susan shaken; then the hardy Mrs. Duniway took charge and led her on an eight-week campaign such as the seasoned veteran of the road never forgot. By stagecoach, by river boat, by buckboard bouncing over corduroy roads, the two women made their way through misty valleys, over the Cascades into the region of appalling distances, often starting in the small morning hours to travel eighteen hours before the next meeting. The meeting place might be a barn; often it was a blacksmith shop. They got along well, and Susan, who had developed a rather grim attitude and exterior, noted that Abigail was always gracious and possessed of a wonderful sense of humor; while the Oregon woman was quick to appreciate the keen mind of the older and more experienced woman.

Within a few months after the Anthony-Duniway tour Abigail led in organizing a permanent Oregon Equal Suffrage group, and continued to lecture. Though she had small interest and even less faith in the so-called temperance movement, she joined the Portland chapter of it in order to infiltrate its meetings with her rights-for-woman propaganda. To stop her, the drys formed a choir which started to sing whenever Abigail rose to speak. Abigail countered effectively. At any lull whatever in the temperance proceedings, she stood up and, instead of going at once into her act, said "Let us pray." And pray she did for the next twenty minutes, during which she pleaded with the Lord that the mothers of the race might be freed from their servitude without wages.

Because she refused to recognize temperance as an important subject, many slanders were started against her. She was accused of drinking beer with men in hotel rooms. It was rumored she was a secret toper, virtually a sot. Once in Walla Walla, when she found every church closed to her projected meeting, she accepted the use of the back room of a saloon, which added considerably to the uproar against her.

In Jacksonville, Oregon, she was the target for eggs. She returned a week later and had to be protected from the chivalrous males of that mining town by the sheriff and half a dozen deputies. But she spoke. Nothing could stop her, even the fact that in time she came to the belief that the dolls did not want their rights, or the vote. Only a few women ever rallied to help her until the battle was all but won. Such aid as she got came from males. In 1884, after uncounted lectures and five hundred and seventy issues of *The New Northwest,* she was at last able to measure a little progress: the Oregon legislature passed a resolution to submit a constitutional amendment giving the vote to women. It was defeated. Mrs. Duniway knew how. "Masked batteries were opened in almost every precinct," she observed. "Multitudes of men who are rarely seen in daylight crowded forth from their hiding places to strike the manacled women down. Railroad gangs were driven to the polls like sheep and voted against us in battalions."

Stouthearted Abigail did not give up hope. She knew that Oregon was honeycombed with New England Yankees and Southerners who were pigheaded against woman's rights; and she turned her attention to neighboring Washington Territory, which soon passed a law, drafted by Mrs. Duniway, which gave women the franchise. She moved to Idaho and in 1896 won another victory. Oregon finally fell in 1912, and she who by then was seventy-eight and called Oregon's Grand Old Lady drew with her own steady hand the proclamation which Governor Oswald West signed. It was a magnificent triumph. Three years of life were still left to Abigail. She could contemplate the immense region of the Far Corner of the United States which she, more than any other, had won for suffrage. What made her unique among woman's-righters was that almost the last thing she wrote was a trenchant editorial against "the fallacy of Prohibition."*

When Mrs. Duniway began her lonely campaign in the Northwest, the woman's-rights movement was still operating through the two groups known as the National and the American associations. The first favored applying pressure to Congress for a federal amendment; the second thought that the best chance was by a state-by-state program. Though Mrs. Duniway entered the movement by way of the National, she had

* Fittingly a school and a park in Portland were named for her, and in 1944 there slid down the ways of Oregon Shipyards a Liberty-type vessel christened *Abigail Scott Duniway.* This was well enough, but a fighting ship would have been more appropriate for the female who tamed the he-men of the "Last Frontier."

a mind of her own, which had from childhood been influenced by the pragmatism of the pioneer. If there were no hall to speak in, not even a saloon's back room, then she would speak from the rostrum of a huge stump of Douglas fir. If Congress chose to sit twenty-eight hundred miles distant, then she would work through the legislatures of the claims she had staked out for herself. After all, Boise was not more than five hundred miles by river boat and stagecoach from Salem, while Olympia was a mere two hundred miles from the Oregon capital.

The split between the two suffrage groups was to last two decades. The leaders of both groups realized that they were making something of a public spectacle of themselves. Worse; solid male citizens told themselves and their women that it just wasn't in the nature of females to work with other females. It was a comforting thought to the men, who had enough to worry about anyway. Neither Mrs. Stanton (and Miss Anthony) nor Mrs. Stone seems to have been of a particularly feline nature, but they certainly held to their opinions with some of the determination of true fanatics, such as single-taxers and perpetual-motion inventors. Then in 1882 an unheralded event occurred that, given another eight years, was to heal the breach.

It had to do with money, a bequest of $56,000 jointly to Susan B. Anthony and Lucy Stone in the will of Mrs. Eliza Jackson Eddy of Boston. To appreciate what a stunner this was, one should know Mrs. Eddy was the first woman to bequeath so much as one dollar to the cause. But was it not the good Lord who in His sympathy, and by His mysterious ways, had merely chosen Eliza Jackson Eddy as His instrument to further "this momentous and far-reaching reform"?

Not at all, said Mrs. Stanton. It was even more wonderful. The intelligent Mrs. Eddy, who had long given her sympathy to woman's rights, had her own very good reasons for the bequest, which, as the rationalist Mrs. Stanton remarked with satisfaction, heralded a turn in the tide of benevolence. Instead of building churches and monuments to great men and endowing colleges for boys, women were henceforth to make education and enfranchisement of their own sex the chief objects of their lives.

Both Miss Anthony and Mrs. Stone knew about Mrs. Eddy's very good reasons. The daughter of Francis Jackson, of the wealthy textile family of Waltham and Lowell, she had married James Eddy, allegedly a common husband-tyrant type, who had carried off to Europe, without their mother's consent and to her great heartache, the Eddys' young daughters. He had done so quite legally by taking advantage of "the father's sole guardianship rights" under the one-sided Massachusetts law.

(Behold how myopic men, seeking to perpetuate their domination of women, defeat their purpose. May Mrs. Eddy's example not be lost on the coming generations of women. I rejoice in her wisdom as well as her generosity. Ever Yours, Elizabeth Cady Stanton.)

The will was of course contested, and nearly $10,000 was swallowed up in litigation, yet it would have been far worse if Mrs. Eddy had not been privy to the cunning of men's laws and knew that property could not be willed to a suffrage association but only to those societies designated as religious or charitable, and hence she made her bequest to persons, and jointly, to Miss Anthony and Mrs. Stone.

(Civilization would have been immeasurably farther advanced if our daughters had only learned the importance of having some knowledge of man-made law—Yours for Reform, Elizabeth Cady Stanton.)

Mrs. Stone and Miss Anthony were elated, separately, when the contested will was declared valid by the Massachusetts Supreme Court. Both women received a little more than $20,000. Mrs. Stone used her share to support the ever-hungry *Woman's Journal,* official organ of the American group. Susan's went toward completing the enormous *History of Woman Suffrage* that was begun in 1880 by the Nationals and was not to be finished until forty-two years later. But Mrs. Eddy's bequest was to accomplish an even more important thing: At the annual meeting of the American group, in 1887, the meeting unanimously adopted a resolution, namely, that Lucy Stone be appointed a committee of one from the American Woman Suffrage Association to confer with Miss Susan B. Anthony, of the National, and . . . that she be authorized . . . to appoint a committee of this association to meet a similar committee appointed by the National to consider a satisfactory basis of union.

Susan seems to have replied instantly, agreeing to meet Lucy either in Philadelphia, where the Americans had been in convention, or in Washington. Perhaps Lucy was playing hard to get. Neither place suited her. She had returned to Boston, allegedly in poor health, and requested Susan to come to her. Well, wasn't Lucy the elder? And what matter if only by two years? Miss Anthony went to Boston, and there, in the Park Street office of the *Woman's Journal,* the two leaders met. Almost two years were to pass before this armistice resulted in the National-American Woman Suffrage Association.

The slender olive branch was not frail. It withstood the bickerings, the outright spats, and the tears of twenty-odd months. Mrs. Stanton was elected president, Miss Anthony vice-president. Lucy Stone was chosen, unanimously, executive secretary. This was as it should be. These old leaders of the battered legions had survived the affrays of forty years. They had survived even the peace; and now they became the triumvirate to direct the talents that were being displayed in the younger generation.

At the close of this first meeting of the National-American association President Stanton was cheered to the echo. An immense bouquet of lilies was handed to Miss Anthony. Mrs. Stone could not be present, but daughter Alice Stone Blackwell was there to speak for her mother and was cheered. Miss Blackwell was already a prodigious young woman who had contributed greatly to the union of the two groups. Another coming champion for suffrage was Anna Howard Shaw, five feet tall, stout, jolly, with snapping black eyes, as eloquent as Lucy Stone in her prime. At the merger, too, though attracting little attention, was a young and recently widowed woman from Iowa, Mrs. Carrie Chapman, who before very long was to become a sort of Anthony-Stone-Stanton in one electrifying piece. Yet, there was still time for one more master stroke by the aging veterans, and it was Miss Anthony who delivered it.

For weeks the press had been telling of plans for a monster celebration to honor the four-hundredth anniversary of the discovery of America. It was to open in 1893 and continue throughout the year. From among the loud demands of many cities Congress had selected Chicago as the proper place to hold it. Susan Anthony didn't care a fig where it was held, but she was determined that woman's rights should receive more consideration than had been the case back in 1876 at the Philadelphia Centennial. She must work fast, however, for a World's Fair Bill was already being discussed in Congress.

From the experience of forty years Miss Anthony had learned how things were accomplished in Washington. She went there now, to call a meeting of prominent women, largely the wives of senators and congressmen. They agreed that women must have a hand in the plans and even the management of the fair. Susan drew up a Woman's Celebration Petition, which she gave to Senator Thomas Platt, a power in the upper house. She then went calling on the wives of cabinet members. When in March 1890 Congress passed the World's Fair Bill, she was happy though not astonished that the act contained provision for a Board of Lady Managers. At the age of seventy Miss Anthony had set in motion what turned out to be one of the most fruitful achievements of her career.

7.

MEN COME TO WATERLOO

IN THE enormous crowds attending the Columbian Exposition of 1893 in Chicago was a young and observant male who came away believing that "this World's Fair has positively set afire the suffragists." He had looked in wonder at the magnificent Woman's Building, fairly blinding with Mr. Edison's mazda lamps. He had gone inside to find an auditorium seating five thousand people, to find it filled with women who were abustle with "shuffling and cawing about their rights." He had noted the elegant décor, and the marble busts of Lucretia Mott, Mrs. Stanton, and Miss Anthony standing chaste, their blank marble eyes peering at nothing, yet their marble lips expressive of determination. Or, was it triumph?

The young man heard Miss Anthony and Miss Frances Willard congratulate officers of a brand-new organization called the Anti-Saloon League. He saw an astonishing parade of professional women including Jane Addams halting traffic in State Street. His copy of the "World's Fair Program" told him that each of the many state buildings of the exposition included generous space for what were described as "woman's exhibits." The same program indicated that all of these events and things were due to the fact that the exposition's officials included a Board of *Lady* Managers headed by the wealthy, capable, and charming Mrs. Potter Palmer.

It occurred to the young man that perhaps Mrs. Palmer was representative of what he thought of as the Titaness type and which was becoming feared or sneered at as the New Woman. A lot of new women were up to things. It seemed that almost any newspaper one picked up told of bills to enfranchise females being introduced in many states. A Rev. John Buckley had been imploring male voters to respect female moral superiority by making sure that it would not be soiled and degraded by putting a piece of paper in a ballot box. But a far more potent voice, that of the Honorable George Hoar, begged the men to let female moral superiority purify politics by giving the vote to them.

Both Susan Anthony and Lucy Stone found the fair a most gratifying experience. They spoke often. They drew large crowds. Their reception and everything else connected with the exposition were in great contrast to the Philadelphia Centennial of '76, which, as Miss Anthony bitterly recalled, had been arrogantly oblivious to woman's rights and their representatives. But now, in that Chicago summer of '93, the two aging work horses got more attention than they had ever known. It was well so. (This was to be Lucy Stone's last trip into the field.)

While the fair was still going full tilt a message came from the Denver women's group, reporting that a bill for woman suffrage was to be submitted to the legislature, and would headquarters please send a capable campaigner to stump Colorado. Susan and Lucy chose Carrie Chapman Catt to go. They could not have chosen better. She had remarried, after an understanding with her well-to-do husband, George W. Catt, that she should continue her work for suffrage. Now she took off for Colorado and a campaign which was to mark her for great things.

Calling on the Colorado W.C.T.U. for help, and even addressing meetings of the fearsome Populists, Mrs. Catt displayed both energy and excellent political judgment in a whirlwind tour that brought her to every city and mining camp in the state; and snatched, wrote an observer, a rousing victory "from the very jaws of terrible defeat." Lucy Stone lay desperately ill in Massachusetts, yet she still lived and a flash of joy came over her face when told that Colorado was going woman suffrage in a landslide. She called to her husband. "Send a check for one hundred dollars," she said, "to Carry Chapman Catt. She has a level head." Then Lucy died, and died as she had lived, a rebel. Hers was the first body of a woman to be cremated in New England.

On a wall at the National-American headquarters had long hung a great "Map of Woman Suffrage in the United States." All of it, save a single square patch of white marked "Wyoming 1869," had stood in deep shadow for fourteen years. The map looked a little less pitiful now, and Wyoming less lonely, with "Colorado 1893," in white beside it. Two years more and Utah, where the forceful Emmeline B. Wells, whose husband had served as president of the Latter-day Saints, had been working shrewdly, was added. Then came Idaho in 1896. Since early territorial days Abigail Scott Duniway's had been a lonely voice there, but now Mrs. Catt had come in time to help with the final campaign.

The suffrage map stood thus at the turn of the century, when Miss Anthony resigned as president of the National-American, and Mrs. Catt was elected to her place. The Old Guard was passing. Even Mrs. Stanton had grown unwieldly with age, though retaining still her commanding presence. Her obsessive animosity toward the clergy had not lessened. It congealed into an Ingersollish *Woman's Bible* that had little influence other than that of giving girls something to argue about. Mrs. Stanton died in 1902, Mary Livermore in 1905, Susan Anthony in 1906.

It had seemed to these old pioneers, long accustomed to abuse and ridicule and grimly ready to strike back in fury, that the younger leaders were introducing a policy of prudence. If prudence and indirection are the same thing, perhaps the veterans were right. The younger women wanted suffrage as much as the old war horses, but they believed that subtle indirection, including the flattery of politicians, might get them further and faster than head-on amazonian attack.

These younger leaders also comprehended that a growing number of their sisters considered that there were rights other than suffrage which were pretty important too. Among them was the "right" to control the number of children they should bear. When you came down to study it coldly, this might not be a right which an act of Congress could grant, but it was certainly a matter about which women should be informed—and informed without being called vile names because they wanted to escape the penalty of almost continuous pregnancy. Except for the wealthy or at least the well-to-do, American families were still sizable. The so-called upper classes seemed to have found some method of control.

Here was a subject that even the most emancipated felt could hardly be made a plank in their platform of woman's rights. Demands for less stringent divorce laws could be made, and in a few states the laws had been changed. But this other thing, this "going against the laws of God," why, it could not be discussed officially even in a closed meeting with the doors locked. Yet the young heirs of Mrs. Stone, Mrs. Stanton, and Miss Anthony recognized it as something that would have to be faced soon or late. One young woman of the period stated the problem clearly in a private letter. "It goes," wrote she, "back to the Garden, before Eve realized what would happen as a result of her cohabitation with Adam. We just *couldn't* go on forever bearing children like that. And if the domineering lummoxes in breeches would only leave us alone, we will work out birth control for ourselves."

Now the woman's-rights pioneers had been fearless in their attacks on the lummoxes in breeches; but except for Fanny Wright and Victoria Woodhull they had brought up short of the truly awful subject of limiting conception. One had to bear in mind it was these two women who were responsible for the taint of free love, which had split the movement for suffrage for twenty years. The taint was still there, though fainter, and care should be taken lest it turn virulent again.

So it was left to a few bold lummoxes in breeches to carry the word—and the onus—which John Humphrey Noyes and Dr. Charles Knowlton had published in mid-nineteenth century. In 1876 Ezra H. Heywood, an all-around reformer of boundless hope, had written and circulated *Cupid's Yokes*, which had to do with the "natural right and necessity of Sexual Self-Government." It was a work that went well beyond clarity. Heywood was arrested and sent away to prison.

Though reformer Heywood, of Princeton, Massachusetts, was the father of four fine and legitimate children—Angelo, Hermes, Psyche Ceres, and Vesta—and lived happily and in constancy with his wife; and though, as he said, he merely wanted to make of parenthood a choice rather than a penalty, the organized women did not dare to raise a finger, publicly, in his defense. The suffrage movement had already suffered enough from a misguided association with similar ideas. So far as the record shows, neither the American nor the National suffrage groups ever heard of Ezra H. Heywood or his *Cupid's Yokes.* Yet one of their members, Laura Cuppy Smith, took it upon herself as an individual to plead Heywood's imprisonment personally with President Rutherford B. Hayes and with such eloquence that the aged reformer was pardoned by executive order.

Things went even worse with a later sex emancipator, old Moses Harmon, editor of *Lucifer, the Light Bearer,* published in Valley Falls, Kansas. During a period of twenty-five years Harmon got into jail again and again, and finally into prison, for his efforts to change woman's slave status in regard to childbearing. His name nowhere appears in the official record of the woman's-rights movement.

It was left to the genius of a small, good-looking, and fearless woman to make of birth control a subject that, at last, could be discussed in open meeting, even in magazines and books, without going to jail for it. Yet even Margaret Sanger had to go to jail at first. Until she appeared there *was* nothing that could be called a birth control movement. She started from scratch.

As a visiting nurse in the slums of New York City's Lower East Side, she had come to close quarters with the horrible effects of continuous childbearing. Convinced that the poor would always be with us, and sickly as well as poor, so long as they continued to bring swarming families into the world of their poverty and degradation, young Mrs. Sanger brooded over the fact there was no way legally to give these mothers the information they wanted—and needed. Doctors put them off by saying it was a social problem. Social workers either spoke of God's will or threw up their hands. Then, after several years of reflection, Mrs. Sanger took the matter into her own hands. She began quietly to give advice on contraception. She also induced Emma Goldman, who called herself an anarchist, to add the subject to her lectures.

Mrs. Sanger well understood the dangers, but she was so encouraged by the obvious success of her secret campaign that in 1914 she published the first number of *The Woman Rebel.* Its stated objective was "to stimulate working women to think for themselves and to build up a conscious fighting character." It proposed to publicize not only woman's rights but the necessity of legally imparting advice on methods of limiting conception. The paper was soon barred from the mails, later admitted to the mails, and at last suppressed. Mrs. Sanger was arrested and jailed. In 1916 she was arrested again, this time for conducting a birth control clinic in Brooklyn. She appealed a conviction of the lower court.

While out on bail Mrs. Sanger developed a sort of grand plan to flood the United States with copies of her pamphlet entitled *Family Limitation,* a frank, practical, and simply written treatise. Thousands of copies were to be simultaneously distributed from many geographic points. Though the imposing plan fell through, the pamphlet was surreptitiously issued by a printer, whose name was never revealed, and seems to have enjoyed a wide circulation.

Mrs. Sanger's conviction in the birth control clinic case was sustained. The decision, however, was really a victory. In contesting her conviction Mrs. Sanger pointed out that to deny contraceptive advice to a woman with active tuberculosis, a bad heart, or other serious conditions was virtually to deny her right to life. The appeals court listened, and in a famous judgment it gave full effect to a statutory exception for physicians. It was made clear that they had every legal right to furnish contraceptive advice for the cure or prevention of disease.

With several small groups helping, Mrs. Sanger went ahead to organize the American Birth Control League. Clinics were established, soon or late, in forty-four states. And, after long meditation, the American Medical Association came out officially for birth control under, naturally, medical supervision. Long before then the subject had become a popular one for open discussion, both on the rostrum and in periodicals devoted to the things that interest women. But this is getting beyond the story. It is enough to say here that by the time woman suffrage achieved its goal Margaret Sanger almost singly had won another important "right" for her sisters.*

It is quite understandable that the suffrage workers refused to have anything to do officially with Mrs. Sanger's crusade. No matter that they privately wished her well, and admired her indomitable courage, they must keep their own crusade eminently "respectable." They must also exert a constant and increasing pressure on Congress and all the legislatures. Fifty years of agitation had so far won but four states to their side. But Mrs. Carrie Chapman Catt and a new generation of fresh young workers were, in less than two decades, to bring victory. That

* In an interview Mrs. Sanger told the author that any account of the birth control crusade, no matter how brief, should mention the names of Leonard Abbott, Dr. E. B. Foote, Dr. Robert L. Dickinson, and Dr. William J. Robinson, all of whom she said "did wonderful educational work."

they were able to accomplish so much and so quickly was in no manner due to magic. It was due in large part to the fact that changing economic conditions, bringing females into industry, in business, the professions, and even the arts, had begun to soften the American male, to gentle him.

The almost simultaneous appearance of the Sholes typewriter, of shorthand transcription, and the typist-stenographer has been mentioned. Other women who would have shrunk from factory work, or even from teaching, gladly went forth with a sense of adventure to become clerks, bookkeepers, telephone girls, trained nurses, librarians, newspaperwomen, social workers, doctors, lawyers, artists. The number of feminine breadwinners more than doubled between 1880 and 1900. Meanwhile the wives and daughters of the poor, both native and immigrant, were swelling the ranks of factory workers and virtually taking over the so-called needle trades.

Like it or not, females were becoming people. The very fact that some of them had "roused from their ages-old inertia" to the extent of organizing in opposition to what they termed "the danger of having the ballot thrust upon them" struck Ida Husted Harper as encouraging. They were at least alive, even if their anti-suffrage efforts were "childishly ineffective." Let them be. Suffrage was making steady progress. More than half the states had come to the point of letting women vote in school matters; four states gave them a vote on questions of taxation; one had granted municipal suffrage. And there was still the glory of all-out voting in Wyoming, Colorado, Utah, and Idaho.

The first decade of the new century was disappointing. No state came into the fold. Politicians remained civil toward the suffragists, but nothing more. Because of the ill-health of her husband Mrs. Catt resigned as president of the National association, and Miss Anna Howard Shaw took her place. Attempts were made to vote under the Fourteenth Amendment, as Susan Anthony had done long ago in Rochester, but they were futile. In Rochester, however, a modest victory was achieved when the aged Miss Anthony, with the help of her sister Mary and of Mary Lewis Gannett, at last persuaded Rochester university to admit women. But, good though this was, it was not suffrage.

In 1911 came the first bright new ray of sunshine since 1896: voters in the state of Washington declared women were fit to vote by a bill which was drawn up by the durable Abigail Scott Duniway, now seventy-seven. One year later and Mrs. Duniway's own state of Oregon came in. So did California and Arizona. These defections in the male front struck home in the halls of Congress and the legislative chambers of thirty-odd states. From this time on, as many women were to notice, the cool civility of politicians generally took on a new warmth. If there was no way to stem this revolt, it was well to be on speaking terms with its leaders.

The revolt was of course that of the new Progressives and old Democrats to unseat the ancient Republican regime that had endured almost two decades. Woman suffrage was incidental to it, though not to suffrage leaders who, on the day before President Woodrow Wilson was to be inaugurated, staged a huge parade in the national capital, a parade so impressive that it must have given him to reflect somewhat on the political status of women. It was known to suffrage leaders that Mr. Wilson had in the past shown no marked interest in their efforts. Hence the women timed the great demonstration with the idea that he should enter office "with a broader idea of the strength of the movement."

It was obvious that suffrage leaders had at last come to appreciate the veritable wonders that could be wrought by implied rather than open threat. Nor did they now let up for a moment. Within a month after inauguration day a joint session of Senate and House was presented with Resolution Number One for consideration. This called for a woman-suffrage amendment to the Constitution. And on May 3, in New York City, women staged another monster parade, much larger than the one which greeted President Wilson. Then, in July, there converged on Washington five hundred thirty-one Suffrage Pilgrims, armed with petitions they had been gathering in all parts of the country. Dressed in their best duds, they marched to call on the President, who seemed to close observers to present a façade just a little less austere than usual, as he accepted "the more than 200,000 signatures" asking that his administration do something *now* about suffrage.

If 1913 had been a heartening year, then 1914 was filled with marvels. To historians it was the year war broke out in Europe. To suffrage leaders in the United States it was the season of astounding events unconnected with the quarrels of foolish men. For instance, the badgered males of both Montana and Nevada broke down and agreed that their womenfolk should vote. Another event, which to say was almost beyond belief is merely an admission of the futility of language, was the death, or rather the last will and testament, of Miriam Florence Follin Peacock Squier Leslie Wilde, Baroness de Bazus, who bequeathed to Carrie Chapman Catt approximately two million dollars *for the furtherance of the cause of Woman Suffrage.*

This extraordinary woman was no more a baroness than was Carrie Chapman Catt. Her death in September 1914, when German armies were overrunning Europe, was minor news. Though the newspapers identified her correctly as Mrs. Frank Leslie, only the older suffrage women could remember her, and even the press disagreed as to her age, which was variously reported and ranged from sixty-five to eighty-one. But back in the purple seventies and eighties she was the daring and aggressive head of Frank Leslie's Publishing House, editor in chief of a whole raft of magazines and of *Frank Leslie's Illustrated Newspaper*, which was almost as sensational as Frank Leslie herself.

For she *was* Frank Leslie, not in the Lucy Stone manner, but by court action following the death of her best-known husband who had died bankrupt, in 1880, leaving debts of more than $100,000. The new Frank Leslie declared publicly that she would henceforth live as poorly as a church mouse until every cent was paid. This could have sounded like fairly wild talk to a public which for years had been treated to stories of the Babylonish lives of Mr. and Mrs. Leslie, of the sumptuous parties given at their estate near Saratoga, of the special and gaudy private railroad train in which the Leslies, together with their retinue of servants, had crossed the American Continent. But the new Frank Leslie meant what she said. For the next five years she lived in a tiny attic room "without a carpet, and the window so high that I could not get a glimpse of the sky unless I stood on a chair," and in that brief time she *did* pay all the debts bequeathed by her late husband. By then she was a national character, the Queen of Newspaper Row.

Despite the authentic aura of scandal which hovered around Frank Leslie, owing in part to several marriages and in part to rumors about her past and her antecedents, she was unquestionably the peer of all ladies of the press, and as such warranted attention by the equal-rights leaders, who were publicizing all outstanding women of their sex. Whatever man could do, woman could do and often better—that was the idea being promoted by Miss Anthony and Mrs. Stanton. In 1885 Miss Anthony took pains to meet Frank Leslie, and into the chaste pages of Volume III of the great and still-growing *History of Woman Suffrage* went a little story about this woman who "undertook to redeem the printing-house of her late husband, and did so in a very short time." The interview also quoted Frank Leslie: "When I had paid the debts and raised a monument to my husband," said she, "then I said to myself 'now for a great big pair of diamond earrings,' and away I went to Europe, and here are the diamonds." She seems to have shown the stones to Miss Anthony, and to have told her ... "they are perfect matches, of twenty-seven carats, or nearly as large as nickels."

And that fairly frivolous item was the only notice taken of Frank Leslie in the 3987 pages comprising the official record of the woman-suffrage movement from its beginnings to the turn of the century. Yet Mrs. Leslie became a dues-paying member of the National association, and much later attended at least one convention and was "spoken to kindly" by Mrs. Catt, who took pity on the little old lady bedizened with jewels, her face enameled in a desperate try to mask the years, simpering in her preposterous role of baroness.

And now, in 1914, it became evident that Mrs. Catt had never spoken to more purpose than to be courteous to Frank Leslie. Two million dollars! It is not to be supposed that any such sum would be turned over to Mrs. Catt without contest. Alleged descendants came forward singly, and in platoons, to say that their late relative was mentally incompetent. They were accompanied by regiments of plaintive lawyers, while regiments of indignant lawyers massed to prove Mrs. Leslie had died in possession of one of the clearest minds conceivable. What with legal fees and inheritance taxes Mrs. Catt finally received $977,875. The windfall came at a critical time, and the sagacious Mrs. Catt used it to increase pressure many times over on those lummoxes in breeches who still resisted.

It was evident that, despite the weakling males of Montana and Nevada, there were plenty of strong males holding fast to sectors of the barricades. On July 6, 1914, a mass meeting of men in Omaha issued a manifesto to "The Electors of the State of Nebraska." This remarkable document stated at some length that the greatest danger to the republic "is an excitable and emotional suffrage." Then it got down to cases, to ask American males to consider that terrible page of the French Revolution and the days of terror, when the thud of the guillotine and the rush of blood through the streets of Paris demonstrated to what extremities the ferocity of human nature can be driven by political passion. Who, the obviously frightened men of Nebraska wanted to know, led those bloodthirsty mobs? Who shrieked loudest in that hurricane of passion? *Woman.*

Having thus demonstrated they had at least read Dickens, if not Carlyle, the manifesto men went on to say that the United States had already extended suffrage beyond all reasonable bounds, and that it was time it was curtailed. In desperation it quoted an unnamed "woman of high standing" as saying that woman suffrage would "let loose the wheels of purgatory." And much, much more.

The astute Mrs. Catt welcomed such antique drivel. She reprinted the manifesto of Nebraska men, even to a complete list of the signators, together with their occupations, because "in language and in the business interests of the signers" it was thoroughly typical, she said, of the *open* opposition to woman suffrage, as well as of those who worked more secretly. To prevent any misunderstanding as to the identity of these secret enemies, she added a parenthetic line to the top signature of the manifesto, which was that of Joseph H. Millard, ex-U.S. senator and president of the Omaha National Bank: "(Largest creditor of Willow Springs Distillery.)"

Having put these last-ditch males in a proper perspective, the suffrage leaders continued exerting pressure as never before, and in 1915 staged a demonstration in New York City which put all other such affairs in shadow. Fifty thousand women marched in a superbly organized parade from Washington Arch to Central Park. Banners waving, bands playing, on they came, hour upon hour—battalions of stenographers, clerks, shopgirls; of professional nurses; of garment workers. A band of five thousand schoolteachers carried blackboards chalked with slogans. On they came, the massed might of awakened women, singing of the triumph sure to come, among them troops of college graduates with their colors, and delegations of "society leaders." Even Lillian Russell, for years the toast of Broadway, and who usually rode in hansom cabs, walked the long route for the glory of womanhood. On a reviewing stand in front of the Public Library, Mayor Mitchel and dignitaries, soon joined by Mrs. Catt, returned the salutes of the hundreds of divisions.

At the very head of the monstrous parade, on a magnificent white horse, rode Miss Inez Milholland, described ever after as the "beauty of the suffrage movement." A graduate of Vassar, who had won fame by championing girl strikers in the shirtwaist factories, Miss Milholland was a complete eyeful for any males holding the ridiculous idea that suffrage leaders looked anything like the hostile cartoons in the papers. On this great day for Woman, males lined Fifth Avenue by the hundreds of thousands, and a woman stood on the curb and observed their reactions.

Mrs. Doris Smith, a young widow from far Bellingham, Washington, had come to New York to study drama. Already indoctrinated with woman suffrage, she now watched while fifty thousand of her sisters marched to the scattered cheers, and to the volleys of boos, of what seemed to her to be a million or more males, mostly hostile. "Here would come," she recalled many years later, "here would come a vast phalanx of girl needle-workers, marching in perfect alignment, in their neat if unglamorous, even severe blouses and skirts, their flatheel shoes and black cotton stockings, their faces taut with the seriousness of great purpose. I was much moved by the spectacle, and tears came to my eyes. I cheered and applauded until my hands were blistered. But any noise I could make was drowned in the groans and booing of God's male creatures who surrounded me.

"But when they sighted the vision of the great white horse, astride which rode Miss Inez Milholland, dressed in snow-white and set off by vivid yellow-orange ribbons, the groans and boos died instantly, and waves of wild cheering seemed to rock the buildings." A man near Mrs. Smith ejaculated: "God a'mighty! Look at *that*!" Then he "yelled like a lunatic."

Boos or cheers, the girls came on. At six o'clock they were still coming up the avenue. It was an impressive demonstration, as even the hostile portion of the press was to admit next day. It wasn't long before the Nineteenth Amendment was actually introduced for the first time in the House of Representatives. The thing was fairly rolling now. Within two years Montana sent Miss Jeanette Rankin to Congress, the first woman to sit in that body.

By then Mrs. Catt had received nearly one million dollars of Frank Leslie's bequest. She began at once to spend it through the Leslie Woman Suffrage Commission organized for the purpose. During 1917-18 legislation to grant the all-out vote to women won approval in fourteen states. By then the end must have been in sight to almost everybody.

It came in 1920, when on August 26 the Secretary of State proclaimed that the Nineteenth Amendment had been ratified by the necessary number, or three quarters, of the states. On November 2, millions of women voted in their first general election. With a majority of their menfolk they made exceeding fine hash of the Omaha manifesto by electing Warren Gamaliel Harding president of the United States, and naming Calvin Coolidge vice-president.

Part Six

THY BROTHERS' KEEPERS

1.

THE CRIES OF BEDLAM HEARD

IT WAS proper that the typical rights-of-women woman was a single-minded person, often a fanatic, who kept her eye fair on the goal of suffrage. The vote was everything. With it women could usher in a civilization so perfect as to need no piecemeal reforms. The world would be free of poverty, of social vice, free even of the twin curse of alcohol and nicotine.

In the ranks of the early suffragists, true enough, were many also working for abolition and even more who wore the white ribbon of temperance. By and large, however, the dedicated feminist was content to leave most other reforms until woman should have the ballot.

The ballot was perhaps the last thing on earth of importance to Dorothea Lynde Dix, a tall, sickly, nervous, and excessively shy New England spinster who had no interest whatever in suffrage or any other woman's rights, but who when nigh the age of forty changed overnight from a genteel governess and schoolteacher into one of the most effective reformers the United States—or the world—has known. The transformation of Miss Dix occurred one cold March day in 1841 when she was asked to take a Sunday-school class in the House of Correction at East Cambridge, Massachusetts. She returned home that night so shocked and terrified at what she had seen that she did not sleep. What Miss Dix had seen was the condition of four insane persons held in confinement by the enlightened townsmen of East Cambridge.

These four unfortunates were not criminals. They were not even listed as "furiously mad." They were "harmless lunatics," to use a current phrase. Yet they were kept in one dark, airless room, the walls of which, so Miss Dix noticed, were shimmering white with frost. It was her first experience with the awful plight of the mentally ill of the time. From a wakeful night she arose with a compelling dream that was to drive her for forty-five years, to the end of her days. Thousands of her sisters were working to abolish slavery. Miss Dix wished them well. As for herself, she must abolish the almost universal superstition that insane persons were born depraved and that nothing could be done about it save to confine them as if they were wild and potentially dangerous animals.

To appreciate the task Miss Dix had taken as her own, one should recall that in 1841 the condition of the insane, like those she found slowly freezing in the East Cambridge jail, was not due to some hard-hearted keeper. She learned from inquiry that these conditions were about average and were generally considered to be good enough. What more could be done in the face of the common attitude? Though the medieval conception of insanity as a possession by devils had passed, it was supplanted by one just as cruel. This modification of the ancient theological idea was that insanity was "pure mental and moral, not physical, perversion," the violent outbreak of the murderous elements of "the fallen human soul." It was thus a fury of the mind, not a fury of an ill body acting on the mind. Because it was impossible to appeal to their reason they belonged outside the family of human beings.

In the United States of the period were six state or community hospitals which recognized the insane as people and provided for their care. Yet all six combined would not have been sufficient to care for those officially described in Rhode Island alone as lunatics. In all of the states both the violent and the mildly deranged were kept in close confinement, often with chains or manacles, in town jails and alms-houses, in state prisons; or "let out" for safe keeping to the lowest bidders, just as was the case with the indigent blind and deaf, idiot children, and mere paupers.

Though the insane were almost without exception housed in the worst quarters, they were treated in at least one respect the same as common criminals; many wardens and guards derived private incomes from charging visitors from ten to twenty-five cents to see them. The crazy house or ward in many a community was what today could be described as a tourist attraction. It was considered good sport to watch the odd creatures, to listen to the fantasies of their ravings, even to goad them to fury by questions, or by prodding them if sullen with sticks provided for that purpose.

It is not to be supposed that these barbarities were universally the custom, for here and there were a few reflective people who like Dorothea Dix thought that the "sight of Babylon in ruins was not so melancholy a spectacle as madness." But only she and they seemed able to hear the pitiable cries that came out of bedlam.

This Miss Dix, who at forty was about to discover her genius, was re-membered by pupils in her school as a tall, stooped woman, a strict disciplinarian, with burning blue eyes and a low sweet voice. She had been born in Hampden, Maine, on a bank of the Penobscot, of a non-descript mother and a weak vessel of a father who wandered over much of New England as a most ineffectual religious fanatic. Twelve years later, when the Dixes were pausing a while in Worcester, Massachusetts,

Dorothea had become so tired of stitching and distributing her father's religious pamphlets that she ran away to Boston to live with her paternal grandmother, the well-to-do widow of the late Dr. Elijah Dix.

A word about Dr. Dix. He appears to have been "the ancestral source" of the self-reliance and indomitable resolve which overleaped one generation to reappear in his granddaughter, or such was the opinion many years later of Miss Dix's biographer. Elijah Dix came to practice medicine by way of apprenticeship under Dr. John Green of Worcester and druggist William Greenleaf of Boston. He soon added to his medical practice by establishing a drug business "on the South side of Faneuil Hall," opened a chemical works for refining sulphur and purifying camphor in South Boston, and "sought vent for his vast energy" by speculating in Maine lands, and founded the towns of Dixmont and Dixfield. Success seems not to have brought popularity, possibly because he was "self-assertive and ambitious of power and position." He died when Dorothea was seven, leaving his widow with a Boston home so stately as to be commonly referred to as the Dix Mansion, and in the garden of which originated "the celebrated Dix pear."

If Dr. Dix contributed energy, resolve, and self-reliance to his granddaughter, the grandmother Dix also had some influence on Dorothea. The elder woman was the result of generations of Puritan training, a Spartan of unflinching nerves, ready to die at the stake, if need be, for her family, but whom "no threat of penal fires would have betrayed into the weakness of kissing them goodnight." Grandmother Dix was, in short, all chilled steel. Such a quality ensured a strict discipline of education and a general bringing-up that put iron into the blood. In the Dix Mansion Dorothea found a grim and joyless home, but nonetheless a home in which she was trained to habits of unremitting diligence.

The Widow Dix sent the youngster to school, where she proved to be a brilliant student, possibly precocious. At the age of fifteen she began teaching a private school in the Dix Mansion, and only a little later added a free school for poor children, which she conducted in the Dix carriage house. Her health had never been of the best, and the two schools, plus many household duties, worsened it.

Among her charges were the children of Dr. William Ellery Channing, who invited her to go with his family on a voyage to the West Indies. The trip did her much good. She became a close friend of the Channings, virtually living with them as governess, and she was thus exposed to the high intellect and humane beliefs of Dr. Channing, hailed generally as the father of the "New England Renaissance." Among Channing's disciples were Emerson himself, along with Bryant, Longfellow, Lowell, and Holmes. Much later Van Wyck Brooks was to say of Dr. Channing that he was responsible for half the great dreams which stirred nineteenth-century Boston. When one considers Miss Dix's long friendship with Dr. Channing and that she had listened to the "flaming eloquence" of his colleague, who was the Rev. Ezra Stiles Gannett, one is prepared to believe she already had the impulse which she accepted so fervently when she left the House of Correction in East Cambridge.

The first thing she did was to bring public attention to bear on the four lunatics confined in the frosty and filthy cell. After a brief but furious battle a stove was installed and some attempt at sanitation made. Then, so far as the public was concerned, Miss Dix dropped from sight. But she was busy enough. With encouragement from Dr. Samuel Gridley Howe, head of Perkins Institution for the Blind, and Charles Sumner, a rising young graduate from Harvard Law School, she visited the state prison at Charleston and some twoscore jails and almshouses in eastern Massachusetts. Going about as quietly as possible, notebook in hand, she conducted a two-year investigation of the various hellholes into which the Bay State's alleged lunatics had been stowed away for safe-keeping. Only when her dossier was filled and overflowing with as damning a mass of evidence as was ever collected did she sit down to write. Then she wrote, at white heat, her famous memorial to the Commonwealth of Massachusetts.

"I shall be obliged to speak with great plainness," began Miss Dix, with a bow to "woman's delicacy," and "to reveal many things revolting to the taste and from which woman's nature shrinks with peculiar sensitiveness." Having thus conceded the audacity of a female addressing, even by proxy or a written report, such an august body of males at all, she let them have it: "I proceed, gentlemen, briefly to call your attention to the present state of insane persons within this Commonwealth, in cages, closets, cellars, stalls, pens—chained naked. Beaten with rods. Lashed into obedience." With bitterly effective prose she went on to relate the dreadful practices current in what then was reputed to be and even may have been the most enlightened state of the Union.

Miss Dix did not dwell on generalities. "I tell," she cried, "only what I have seen." She named the places and the victims. At the Danvers almhouse she found a young woman confined alone in a tiny outbuilding. "There she stood, clinging to or beating the bars of her caged apartment, the contracted size of which afforded only space for increasing accumulation of filth—a foul spectacle, gentlemen—and there she stood with naked arms, disheveled hair, the unwashed frame invested with fragments of unclean garments, the air so offensive that it was not possible to remain beyond a few moments. . . ."

A vast silence, due neither to courtesy nor somnolence, blanketed the chamber. On went Miss Dix's indictment. At Newton she had talked to a woman chained to a wall, living in what amounted to being a toilet. At Groton she discovered a youth, a heavy iron collar around his neck, chained to a wall with six feet of great iron links. Miss Dix piled horror upon horror as her tour of hell in eastern Massachusetts continued. There was none of the period oratory in it. It was all simple, direct, burning with the cold fire of bitterness; a woman had produced in the State House a sensation greater than anything there since 1775.

Miss Dix's report was instantly attacked by the wardens of institutions, the town councils called selectmen, the low-bidders who boarded the indigent poor whether or not they were classed as insane or merely indigent. It was attacked by the frugal representatives of the rural districts who naturally must defend their frugal constituents. One and all they sought to show this female to be a typical example of why woman's place was still the home.

But Miss Dix had excellent backing. Dr. Howe was chairman of the legislative committee on institutions. Among her friends were Dr. Luther Bell, Horace Mann, and Charles Sumner. (Dr. Channing had died.) Then there was the great mass of nameless people who had read Miss Dix's report in their newspapers. Her dreadful charges etched their minds deeply. Massachusetts quickly developed a guilty conscience, and with a speed seldom given to legislative assemblies the Bay State solons provided for the addition of two hundred rooms for insane patients at the state hospital in Worcester. It was the forerunner of many measures taken in subsequent years.

Miss Dix hardly paused before she moved into Rhode Island, and the report she made public a year later was even more searing than that on Massachusetts. At Little Compton she found one Abram Simmons confined in a cell, all stone, even to the floor. It was double-walled, the keeper was eager to point out, so he would not be troubled with Simmons' "piercing screams." There was no light, no opening for air. The man was chained by one leg. The keeper's wife, a jovial sort, told Miss Dix laughingly that in winter she often had "to rake out as much as a bushel of frost at a time," yet Simmons "never showed the least sign of freezing." She said he had been confined in this den above three years.

Miss Dix prepared a special article on Abram Simmons. It was a sardonic piece, mordantly entitled "Astonishing Tenacity of Life," which the Providence *Journal* saw fit to publish. Beginning her indictment as though it were an article of scientific interest, she presently described the plight of Simmons in low-keyed prose studded with barbs, then closed seemingly in wonder that any human being could survive such treatment. Abram Simmons quickly took his place as a martyr to the thoughtless cruelty of the heirs and assigns of Roger Williams, who had thought he was founding a haven for the oppressed which he called Providence Plantations.

Before she left Providence, Miss Dix made a call on a local money-bags, a Mr. Cyrus Butler, who tried hard to divert this uninvited woman by conversing for some time upon the weather of Rhode Island, which he seemed to think was unusual. Preserving her temper, in spite of Mr. Butler's reputation as a no-milk-from-a-stone man, she heard him out, then gave him a brief yet effective account of the shame of Rhode Island, and touched ever so lightly on a God sure to avenge the injustice perpetrated on poor Abram Simmons. Mr. Butler listened to a commanding voice of eloquence and suppressed emotion. He was unequal to it. "Miss Dix," he asked helplessly, "what do you want me to do?" She told him: "Sir, I want you to give $40,000 to enlargement of the insane hospital in Providence." And Mr. Butler replied: "Madam, I'll do it." It hardly could have been as simple as that, yet Butler did give $40,000, and his name was put over the door of the new Butler Hospital.

The plight of Simmons was soon known throughout the states, though Dorothea Dix was known, then and later, to comparatively few people. She wanted it so. But the Philadelphia Society for Alleviating the Miseries of Public Prisons heard of her work. This was the foremost group in the country seeking penal reform. Inspired by her startlingly successful work in New England, it acted quickly to prepare a vigorous memorial to the Pennsylvania legislature demanding establishment of a hospital for the insane which would permit removal of those unfortunates from the penitentiary.

Miss Dix invaded New Jersey. Here in a dungeon she found a man, legs and arms chained, who the keeper said was extremely dangerous to approach. He would tear Miss Dix limb from limb were she to get within reach. She went directly up to the melancholy man, spoke to him, called him by his name. He stared a moment, then broke down and wept like a child. His chains were taken off. Miss Dix had him put into a clean bed in a decent room. After two months "he was so far recovered that he was performing useful tasks around the hospital." Time and again, during the next decade, Miss Dix was to enter filthy cells and cages, alone, to talk to the victims of man's ignorance. She demonstrated what care and medical attention—including what was not yet known as psychiatry—could do for the allegedly hopeless cases. The walls of their shadow world gradually fell away, to disappear like a mirage in the desert.

During the first four years after that shocking Sunday in East Cambridge Dorothea Dix visited eighteen prisons, three hundred jails, and more than five hundred almshouses and other institutions. In doing so she traveled something over ten thousand miles by stage, steamboat, and horseback, with occasionally a few dozen miles on primordial railroads.

One incident of this campaign survives: Once in Michigan the stage in which she was riding was held up by bandits. Miss Dix remonstrated with one of the robbers, telling him what a fool he was. He looked at the slim, graying woman. "My God!" said he. "I know that voice." He went on to say that he had heard her speak in the Walnut Street jail in Philadelphia. The robbers forthwith returned the passengers' watches, jewelry, and money.

With a drive that struck many as a compulsive thing this lone woman, beset by increasing trouble with her lungs, never once let up investigating, reporting to legislatures, making friends among the wealthy and influential, always getting their moral and often their financial support in the founding of hospitals and asylums. One after the other the states came into line—Indiana, Illinois, Kentucky, Tennessee, Missouri, Mississippi, Louisiana, Alabama, South Carolina, North Carolina, Maryland.

Meanwhile she memorialized Congress, to say she had seen more than nine thousand idiots, epileptics, and insane who were wholly "destitute of care and protection." This "vast and miserable company," said she, was "abandoned to the most loathsome necessities or subjected to the vilest and most outrageous violations." Her great hope, during several years, was for adequate aid from a bill before Congress for which she had agitated with her many friends in House and Senate. This was a land grant, proceeds from the sale of which were to be used specifically to care for the insane. Though the bill eventually passed both houses, it was vetoed by President Franklin Pierce.

In spite of which, hospitals arose in Miss Dix's wake. Because of her experience with only too many sadistic characters among keepers and other prison personnel she urged that these asylums be staffed by doctors and qualified nurses. She continued to keep in the background, permitting others the credit; all she cared was that hospitals were built—and conducted along the lines she thought best. Even here she seems not to have antagonized people overmuch. She commonly was both gentle and quietly assured. These qualities must have contributed to the remarkable success that was hers over forty years, but they hardly explain it. First and last she had to deal with legislatures, notoriously fickle, often corrupt, usually resentful of "outside" persons and influences. She had, too, to contend with community fears and jealousies; it wasn't just everybody who wanted to live near a lunatic asylum. Worse was the belief which faded ever so slowly that all this talk about "curing" insanity was dangerous poppycock. Taken all together, it is perhaps just as well to say that Dorothea Dix was touched with genius; that the sudden interest in the care of insane people was merely one of those trends—motherless, fatherless, the result of autogenesis—which so many historians find useful to explain anything which their trade union does not permit them to credit to the volition of an individual.

When her own native land seemed at last alive to the curative powers of humane treatment and medical attention in regard to its mental unfortunates, Miss Dix sailed for the British Isles and the Continent. Among the results of her four years abroad was the appointment by Queen Victoria of a Royal Commission to look into the condition of the insane in Scotland, and the subsequent establishment of several hospitals. And in Rome an asylum was founded.

Then, on the outbreak of war in 1861, as mentioned in a previous chapter, Miss Dix went to Washington to offer her services, and in June was appointed Superintendent of Women Nurses of the Union Army. It was a massive job. She found it useless to try to idealize war as she had idealized her work for the insane. Francis Tiffany, her biographer, remarks that nurse Dix "become overwrought and lost the requisite self-control." She saw "greedy physicians and attendants eat up and drink up the delicacies and wines for the sick." With her towering idealism she attempted "to stand over sick and wounded soldiers as the avenging angel of their wrongs." She became involved in arguments with medical officials and regimental surgeons. Her closest friends thought she pitched her demands too high; she failed to take into account the poor material of average human nature.

To the Secretary of War, Edwin M. Stanton, however, Miss Dix had performed prodigious wonders beyond telling. She had been the first on the ground and was the last to quit the post of duty. Her country owed her an infinite debt. Mr. Stanton ordered that "a Stand of Arms of the United States National Colors be presented to her."

With peace Miss Dix resumed her rounds of the now numerous mental hospitals, with the sound idea that they needed the watchful eye of one who considered with some reason that these havens were her children; and the officers of asylums learned something about a genuine perfectionist who was also a disciplinarian. Her visits were almost always unexpected. They happened at odd times of the day. Typical was an occasion when she called at an early hour to rouse all attendants and demand a trial of the fire-extinguishing apparatus. It proved to be either woefully out of order or innately useless. They heard about *that* one. More than once she observed that she had never found any suffering among "the officers of an institution." She was not a cynic. It was her way of saying that the patients, "these outcasts of the world," were entitled to the finest care it was possible to give them.

That this remarkable woman remained virtually anonymous all her long life is to be seen in a thumping big book entitled *Eminent Women of the Age,* published in 1868, in which were pictures and biographical sketches of Susan B. Anthony, Lucy Stone, Elizabeth Cady Stanton, and a whole crew of lesser suffragists, temperance workers, and such. In it there isn't a mention of Dorothea Dix. At the age of eighty she retired to a room set apart for her in the state asylum at Trenton, New Jersey, which she had always called her "first child." There she died in 1887, still largely unknown in the country to which she had given so much.

Dorothea Dix was one of the most distinguished, and surely remains to this day the most forgotten, outstanding woman America has produced in more than three hundred years. This is also the place to remark that although her great contribution was in the field of the mentally disturbed, her very career tended to influence penology. Her long agitation concerning how the insane were treated and housed quite naturally helped to speed prison reform, which had begun at least forty years before much if any thought was given to lunatics.

2.

POISON WEEDS GREW THERE

I

In only too many American cities there still stands at mid-century some hulking mass of brick and stone to recall our long struggle against crime. About its fortress walls and its turrets and towers there hovers a certain grim majesty which time bestows on monumental antiquities like castles and tombs. The long rows of tiny barred windows mark it as a prison. It is likely a hundred and more years old. It is obviously long since outdated. Most people who contemplate it at all do so in wonderment that in our own "progressive" age we should retain and still use this obsolete monument to the barbarous times of our forefathers.

People might rather look at it as a notable milestone of man's advancement. Before it was built there was little need of prisons, either in the American colonies or the early republic. In those purposeful times we hanged most of our criminals. As for the rest, we flogged them bloody, cropped their ears, then bade them go and sin no more. Such confinement as necessary before a quick trial and a speedy execution was provided for by the town jail. Most of our colonial statutes were based on English law and, at the time of the American Revolution, English law recognized two hundred and forty capital offenses. There was one exception—Pennsylvania, where in 1682 Governor William Penn and the Quakers of Philadelphia adopted a comparatively mild and humane code, and reduced the number of capital crimes by more than half. A house of correction was established in which imprisonment at hard labor was prescribed as punishment for a majority of non-capital crimes.

This radical departure from universal practice seems to have had little influence on the other colonies except Massachusetts, which soon established a house of correction in Boston, and the courts were instructed to sentence "sturdy beggars" and others guilty of minor offenses to hard labor. But in 1718, the very year William Penn died, the advanced Quaker penology began to be uprooted when the Pennsylvania Assembly adopted what for all practical purposes was the code of the Anglican and Puritan colonies. Larceny remained the only felony not declared a capital crime; it was made punishable by restitution, fine, whipping, and imprisonment.

Now that the ideals of humanitarians were to be ruthlessly destroyed, the "gloomy severity of the Middle Ages" returned to the American colonies. Mutilation and whipping were resumed in full measure. The hangman stood handy, rope in hand, to eliminate those who repeated their crimes. This sanguinary code was in force when the colonies revolted, and although Pennsylvania's new state constitution, adopted in 1776, directed a speedy return to the milder Quaker code, little could be done during the war.

The Quakers and their friends were as good as their word, and in 1786 set about revising the criminal code with the idea that "as freedom advances, so the severity of the penal law decreases." At the same time they also organized the Philadelphia Society for Alleviating the Miseries of Public Prisons. This was the first group in the modern world to assume responsibility for planning a humane penal system. Among its members were Dr. Benjamin Rush and Judge William Bradford, and its first efforts were to urge legislative action to add a cell house to the Walnut Street jail. Like all other jails of the day, this one was a "congregate" affair, which means that prisoners were herded together regardless of the crimes with which they were charged, and regardless of sex, age, and criminal experience. The society wanted the cell block for the solitary confinement of men convicted of felonies; the old jail would be used for detention of suspects, witnesses, and those officially described as misdemeanants.

The cell block was built. Combined with the old jail, it became a sort of state penitentiary, in that the warden, Caleb Lownes, was directed to receive convicts from other counties "until similar provisions could be made in their jails." Warden Lownes proved to be an excellent man. He set his prisoners to work, making shoes, weaving, beating hemp, picking oakum, carding wool, sawing wood, and even to "grinding plaister of Paris." Meanwhile, the Philadelphia Society for Alleviating the Miseries of Public Prisons began supplying Bibles to convicts, along with religious counsel; and aided in conducting training for crafts. Thus by 1800 the main ideas of American penal development for the next half century were to be seen in the Walnut Street institution in the center of Philadelphia. And so, regrettably, were the same troubles that were to mark our prisons of the present day.

These troubles stemmed from overcrowding, making Warden Lownes's industries impossible, fanned resentment of the prisoners, and presently resulted in a series of riots. Lownes resigned in disgust rather than try any longer to enforce discipline on 225 convicts held in cell room for seventy-two. Many a warden since will understand. So would a character who just then was busy earning a reputation as "the Notorious Stephen Burroughs of New Hampshire." Burroughs probably knew the interiors of more assorted jails and houses of correction than any of his contemporaries, not as a warden but as a prisoner.

The son of respectable parents of Hanover, New Hampshire, Stephen's father was a trustee of Dartmouth College and prominent in all reform matters, but was unable apparently to do much toward making Stephen an honest man. Like so many other perennial habitués of jails, Stephen liked to claim that he was innocent of the first crime he was charged with, that of larceny, which landed him in the town jail of Northampton, Massachusetts. The structure was not what could be termed a strong jail, and for the purposes of detaining him, Stephen was shackled to the floor of his cell for thirty-two days running. That was in December 1785, and the young man found it "most uncomfortable."

A little more than a year later he found himself in Boston's first attempt at a house of correction on Castle Island, in the harbor, dressed in what he described as a "parti-colored suit," which must have been an early form of the striped clothes of later years. Here he was so terribly whipped that his "shoes filled with blood." As soon as he had recovered, he engineered an escape, was recaptured on the mainland and returned to the island for further whipping and solitary confinement in a dungeon. After three years he was released, and set out on what in retrospect seems like a tour of New England and Long Island jails. In his memoirs he modestly admitted to having been "in many gloomy mansions," and that every last one of them was "a school for crime." Of inducement to reform he had met nothing; so the Notorious Stephen Burroughs "retired" to Canada, from whence he was pleased to flood New England banks with spurious bank notes.

Even though the Walnut Street prison experiment ended in failure, the startling success of its early years prompted other states to action. New state prisons were built by New York, Massachusetts, Maryland, and Vermont, but they did not all provide for cell blocks. The school of crime of the congregate rooms Burroughs had observed was continued. Virginia soon designed and built a penitentiary with cell blocks. But Connecticut, which only a little later was to lead all states in prison reform, decided to get along for the time being by "improving" an old copper mine used during the Revolution for the detention of Tories.

This den of horrors burrowed down deep into a hill in Simsbury. It was "improved" by erecting a main building and several shops on the surface above the mine. When not at work in the surface shops, prisoners were kept at the bottom of the shaft, where they sat and slept on platforms built of boards covered with straw; or, if they wished, they might roam at will a few rods down the old drifts that ran in every direction. A bell summoned the convicts to work, and up they came hand over hand on a ladder through a trap door, a few at a time, to be met by guards who first fettered their legs with irons, then conducted them—hopping and jumping—to the blacksmith shop. Shackled legs were not considered enough. In the smithy some took their places by the forge, where collars suspended by chains from the roof were fastened around their necks. Others were chained in pairs to wheelbarrows.

Meals were served in the shop. These were simple enough, if the one observed by a Mr. Phelps, a visitor, was typical. "A piece of pickled pork for each," he wrote, "was thrown on the floor and left to be washed and boiled in the water used for cooling the iron wrought at the forge. Meat was distributed in a similar manner for breakfast." But what struck Mr. Phelps most was "the horrid gloom of the dungeon quarters . . . and the thought of the impenetrable vastness supporting the awful mass above impending as if ready to crush one to atoms." He could hear the water dripping, dripping, trickling like tears from the walls. He heard the unearthly echoes of the human voice. He thought that all conspired to strike one aghast with amazement and horror.

This eerie hole of a prison, like another underground pen at Thomaston, Maine, was not constructed purposely for cruelty's sake, but to make prison an object of terror in the hope to deter men from crime. The burden and misery of such imprisonment was thought to be a not unjust retribution for the civic and moral damage of crime. Retribution doubtless came first, then determent. So at least was the belief of a Connecticut philosopher who wrote that "these ideas of public punishment had been imported with the Puritans who were accustomed to them by the religious conflicts of Europe." He thought that "the spread of rationalism with its attendant human sympathy" was the only hope for penal advancement.

The Quakers of Philadelphia may not have been technically rationalists, but they were humane above all other sects, and to them the failure of this Walnut Street prison only pointed to its shortcomings. Their prison society began at once planning for what they were confident would be the greatest penitentiary in the world. The first stone was laid at Cherry Hill in 1829. Six years more and there it stood, the Eastern Penitentiary, at a cost of $750,000, a staggering sum. Because even before it was finished this prison was one side of a controversy which lasted fifty years, it might be described here as built for the "solitary system."

Pennsylvania's vast new prison looked like a medieval fortress. It covered twelve acres on Cherry Hill, just outside Philadelphia. It centered in a rotunda from which branched like wheel spokes the seven stone corridors of cell blocks. There were four hundred large solitary cells which could be entered only from the corridors. Each cell had an individual exercise yard, securely walled to prevent any communication. Calling this prison representative of the solitary system was no misnomer. When a convict entered Cherry Hill, he was put in individual isolation from which he was never removed, unless dead or insane, until he had served his sentence.

The isolation went further than that. The convict had no contact with any other person except prison guards and officers, and an occasional visit from a clergyman. Relatives, even wives, were prohibited to visit him. Here on Cherry Hill the Quaker theory of imprisonment was to be seen to perfection. The convict was completely isolated, but not idle. In his lonely cell he was to work at small crafts with materials provided. He was expected to read the Bible. Above all he was to meditate upon his condition in the belief, or at least in the hope, that he would profit spiritually and be ready, when discharged, to enter society as a wholly reformed man.

All visitors to the Eastern Penitentiary at Philadelphia were impressed with its size, the generous space of its cells, and the fact that each cell had running water and toilet facilities. They were told how the few and simple disciplinary rules produced "subservience if not penitence" among the inmates. Most visitors, whether laymen or officials of other prisons, went away enthusiastic about what seemed at last the answer to the troublesome question of how to retrieve the lost men and women of society.

That this solitary-confinement, or Pennsylvania, system, as it was soon known, solved anything was of course a delusion of the good Quakers and non-Quakers, who, like many other Americans of the time, felt it their duty to erect a new society good enough to meet the brave hopes outlined so eloquently in the famous Declaration. It was, after all,

Philadelphia where the Declaration had been signed. Philadelphia was the most important city in the United States. It was the home of statesmen, philosophers, leading physicians, and scientific men. If the new nation was in need of a humane yet practical method of dealing with crime and criminals, then Philadelphia should lead the way; and the way was clearly, even massively, marked by the vast house of silent and solitary men on Cherry Hill.

II

The great Pennsylvania penitentiary was hardly more than in its preliminary drawing stage when an idealist named Louis Dwight was moving ahorseback throughout Eastern United States, visiting most of the jails and all of the few state prisons. Dwight was not only an idealist, he was a disappointed minister of the Gospel. Born of devout New England parents, he was preparing for the ministry at Yale College when (in 1813) an accident injured his speaking voice beyond mending. His chosen career went glimmering. Young Dwight himself went to work for the newly formed American Bible Society, becoming its first agent. If Providence had decreed that he could not speak the Word to those in need of it, then he should bring them the Word as the venerable prophets of old had set it down.

It was a time and a place of bursting energy searching for outlets. The outlets were no more likely to result in a cotton-mill empire or a raft of clipper ships than in a brand-new religious sect, an invention, or merely a thankless effort to ameliorate the miseries of unfortunates. Louis Dwight dreamed of mills and ships no more than he questioned the church of the Puritans. But the distribution of Bibles, so it turned out, was God's manner of revealing to this restless young man a dream fit for his prodigious energy and boundless idealism.

Louis Dwight's great dream was given to him in 1824, when he sought to cure a spell of ill-health and overwork by a horseback journey through southern New England. Being the indefatigable missionary he was, he filled his saddlebags with small Bibles, that there should be no lapse in the Lord's work while he gained new strength for the continuous war against evil. And what could give the Lord more satisfaction than to know that the devil's very own were reading the Bible?

Among the devil's own, in 1824, were the inmates of jails, workhouses, and prisons, none of which young Dwight had ever visited until now. The sight would have shaken far coarser-grained fellows than the sensitive young graduate in theology. The degradation so casually displayed was, he reported, beyond the imagination. Here was a bestial misery to belie the claim that New England was a Christian country. He had not yet come to Simsbury and the foul copper mine which Connecticut was pleased to call its state prison. But he soon came to it, and left it speechless with horror.

Devout though he was, Dwight realized that the distribution of Bibles alone would do nothing to change the vicious conditions he had seen in the jails of Massachusetts and Connecticut, and in the dreadful copper-mine prison. He did not believe many people knew that such evils existed. He thought if he could "bring before the Church of Christ a statement of what my eyes have seen," then there would be a united effort "to alleviate the miseries of prisons." To this end he organized the Boston Prison Discipline Society, which he was to make into the dominant influence of prison reform in the United States during the next thirty years.

Now that he had found his proper place in the Lord's work, Louis Dwight was transformed into a zealot. In a powerful and well-publicized report he told the good Christians of New England about the quarters they were providing for their strayed lambs and black sheep. His specific indictment of Connecticut's state prison was withering, and effective. At the next legislative meeting Connecticut voted to establish a new penitentiary at Wethersfield. It was to be built on "the Auburn pattern"; that is, convicts would be housed at night in separate cells, and during the day were to work together, though in complete silence, at industries or crafts which, it was planned, would reimburse the state for their keep.

The Auburn system was the result of New York State's experience with its new penitentiary in the up-state city. Solitary night cells cared for the prisoners when not at work. They worked in congregate shops under strict rules of silence. There was to be no communication whatever. Eyes were to be kept downcast. Lock-step marching to and from meals and shops was devised. The income from sale of products of the shops was to go toward paying the prison's expenses, an item of the Auburn system not to be ignored.

Meanwhile the Philadelphians, the very pioneers in prison reform, had found their Eastern Penitentiary so vast an improvement over the old Walnut Street prison that they could hardly doubt it to be what so many European experts had agreed was the ultimate perfection of a humane and efficient corrective penal system.

Louis Dwight, however, had grave doubts about it. He had become in a short time incomparably the most eloquent and militant force seeking prison reform, and as such he spoke in favor of the Auburn system. But that was not enough. Being a fanatic, he took pains to *speak* against the Pennsylvania system, starting a bitter controversy which continued into the 1870s, when, as Harry Elmer Barnes has pointed out, the advocates of both the Auburn and the Pennsylvania plans "came to see they had been supporting hopelessly crude and elementary penal systems." Yet either system was much superior to the unspeakable congregate type of prison they displaced.

That Auburn triumphed, as one after the other of the states chose to build their new penitentiaries for that system, does not mean it was superior to the Pennsylvania system in matters of correction or reformation, even though the aggressive Dwight, an honest man, was convinced that it was. Dwight was shrewd enough to bear down on the fact that the industrious convicts in Auburn paid for their keep, while income from the feeble crafts practiced in the solitary cells of Pennsylvania's touted prison was miserable in comparison.

The controversy rose and fell, with Dwight and his Boston Prison Discipline Society continously on the offensive. And jails and prisons grew continuously better, both physically and in their administration. Dwight's annual reports for his society were recognized at the start as classics in their field, and came to serve virtually as textbooks for governors, legislators, and prison officers throughout the country. Dwight did not forget the Word of God. He encouraged the Bible Society to increase its efforts at distribution in the prisons. He added to his own staff a number of preachers and sent them forth to act as prison chaplains in state institutions wherever a benighted legislature had failed to provide them. The implied shame was effective. States began to supply chaplains. Sabbath schools became a customary thing during winter months. In his study of American penal efforts Blake McKelvey observed that Dwight's program "was more aptly fitted to prepare the prisoner for a satisfactory adjustment to society after his discharge than the twentieth-century man might suspect." Dwight's idea was of course simply to save the prisoner's soul.

It is little to wonder that with a spokesman like Louis Dwight the Auburn system became virtually the American prison system. Through his eyes it was a beautiful example of what could be done with proper discipline in a "prison well constructed." From gate to sewer Auburn was a specimen of neatness. The unremitting industry, the entire subordination and subdued feeling of the convicts, he thought, had no parallel among an equal number of prisoners. In their solitary cells they spent the night, with no other book but the Bible. At sunrise they proceeded in military order, "in solid columns, with the lock march to the common hall where they partook of their wholesome and frugal meal in silence." Silence meant silence. Infractions of this cardinal rule of Auburn brought "corrective measures," usually the lash. When they were done eating and "at the ringing of a little bell, of the softest sound," said Dwight, the men marched to the workshops. Here, to the marvel of all visitors, was such industry as was not to be seen in the best (outside) factory. A convict never left his work, nor spoke, nor turned his head. It was all "the most perfect attention to business from morning till night." At the close of day, a little before sunset, the men returned, lock-step as before, to their solitary cells, where they ate the supper they had taken from the kitchen as they returned from the shops. After supper they could, if they chose, "read the Scripture undisturbed and then reflect in silence on the errors of their lives. They must not disturb their fellows by even a whisper."

All this must have sounded pretty fine to the public, which was constantly reminded that what Dwight termed "the unremitting industry of this noble institution" was paying its way without aid of taxpayers. And Dwight's ideal picture of Auburn's glories must have filled with envy the visiting wardens of comparatively abysmal and hectic prisons in Maine, Vermont, Indiana, Maryland, and other states still handicapped by the congregate system.

There was naturally another side to Auburn. In the effort to induce silence there had been far too much flogging. News of it got into the press. So did rumors and even investigations concerning the corruption of wardens and other personnel by the contractors of prison labor. Labor unions were still too weak to attack the general sale of prison-made products, but their grumbling indicated troubles ahead. No matter these faults, the Auburn system by mid-century had virtually taken over all American penitentiaries save in Pennsylvania. By then Louis Dwight had passed on, the Boston Prison Discipline Society with him.

Considered after more than a century, Dwight does not seem an especially appealing figure. Beside the philosophical and urbane civility of the Philadelphia prison reformers the Boston man appears a vigorous leader, surely, but also contentious, given to acrimony, maddening to all rational men in his righteous belief that an enemy of the Auburn system was an enemy of God. Possibly only a fanatic like Dwight could have performed the really prodigious task of abusing and shaming a good part of the United States into giving thought to its criminals, not only to their food and humane treatment, but to their souls. And he believed that God Almighty was the one great reformer of sinful men.

One feels assured that the Lord never had a more faithful servant than Louis Dwight. He may well have been most irritating to work with or under. Yet he was a veritable hero of dreamers. There was even something heroic to his end: Rising one day ill and shaking from what he must have known was his death bed, he demanded to be driven across Boston to the Lunatic Asylum, where he gave a comforting sermon to the inmates. Then he died.

III

It may be technically correct to put Louis Dwight among the so-called pulpit reformers, but the implied condescension that he didn't really know anything about what he was trying to reform is a gross injustice. He did use the pulpit, along with the press and the platform, to further his designs, yet he was, like Dorothea Dix after him, a fanatical eyewitness inspector of the very hellholes he wanted to abolish. He knew prisons from the moldiest bread to the things that crawled in the spoiled meat. He knew them from the frosty, filthy underground cells of Thomaston to the convicts working with iron collars around their necks in the smithy at Simsbury.

Pulpit reformer? This man had been down into the pit to see the hopeless creatures of the regions created for retribution and revenge.

Among Louis Dwight's bountiful legacies was Connecticut's new penitentiary at Wethersfield, a model on which were based nearly all of the American prisons built during forty-odd years after 1826. At Wethersfield, too, was founded a dynastic succession of remarkable wardens named Pilsbury. Still another product of this penitentiary was Zebulon Reed Brockway, who has been described by authoritative writers on the subject as an outstanding leader and even as the one vital genius in establishing a new type of institution significantly known as a reformatory.

The first of the Pilsburys was Moses, a stout veteran of the War of 1812, of education and means "acquired under difficulties," who made his home in Londonderry, New Hampshire, until 1818, when he was called to Concord to take charge of the new state prison. He was so engaged when Louis Dwight began looking for a man to "govern," as he called it, Connecticut's experiment in penology planned for Wethersfield. Dwight learned that Moses Pilsbury had done wonders for discipline at Concord; what was more, he "had caused the prisoners to earn their own support." On Dwight's recommendation Pilsbury was invited to help plan the arrangements and construction at Wethersfield. When it was ready, Warden Pilsbury took charge of moving into it the several-score manacled wretches from the Simsbury copper mine, who must have been dumfounded at the contrast, and startled, too, when Pilsbury assembled them to hear a reading of the Bible.

In the next three years Warden Pilsbury, together with "the influence of the Boston Prison Discipline Society"—which meant Louis Dwight—made Wethersfield into the generally acknowledged superior of all other prisons in the country. He retired in 1830, and was succeeded by his twenty-five-year-old son, Amos.

Young Amos Pilsbury was fit to deal with the hardest convict or the most officious politician. He was a ruggedly built man, and tipped the scales at two hundred and twenty pounds. Gray eyes peered reflectively from the strong, clean-shaven face of a Roman senator. He was lion-voiced, said an associate, and had "peremptory manners." In what was something of a rough-and-ready occupation Warden Amos Pilsbury was always perfectly groomed. He even wore "ruffled linen." There was no fear in him. The affair of convict Scott proved that.

A case-hardened character, sent to Wethersfield for fifteen years, Scott had been disciplined for an attempt to escape and had been heard to say he would kill the warden at the first opportunity. A barber by trade, Scott was assigned to the prison shop, and may have been astonished one day soon when Warden Pilsbury came in, sat down in the chair, and asked to be shaved. The speechless Scott, "though greatly agitated, performed the service well" and was afterward an obedient prisoner until the forced retirement of Pilsbury, when the barber killed a guard and was soon hanged.

The temporary retirement of Amos Pilsbury was occasioned by political appointees to the state board of prisons who preferred a warden more amenable to suggestions. There was not much "give" to the granitic Pilsbury. He resigned at once, then demanded an investigation by a legislative committee. His stand was wholly exonerated, and he returned as warden within a few months. For the next thirteen years his administration of Wethersfield was such as to bring prison boards and officials from almost every state to visit and witness "the Auburn System at its perfection."

The industries at Wethersfield showed a consistent gain every year, or what the Connecticut press was delighted to term "a handsome profit," a result that was "most gratifying to the good people of that state." Warden Pilsbury recommended that the handsome profits be used for the building of new jails with cells; and that, if anything were left over, to put it toward establishing a place to care for criminal and pauper lunatics. Discipline remained better than average, though Warden Pilsbury himself once suffered a deep knife wound "15 inches long" at the hands of a desperate convict. There was also a series of riots which came to an end when Pilsbury appeared with something new to Wethersfield in his hands. This was a cat-o'-nine-tails. Pilsbury "made good use of it on the leaders." The disorders ceased. The cat was used only rarely thereafter, for the "mere presence of the instrument seemed almost effective enough."

Warden Amos Pilsbury's fame was such that he was asked to come to Albany, New York, to aid with the plans and supervise the construction of the first, or one of the first, county penitentiaries in the United States. This was built to care for six hundred inmates, twice the number at Wethersfield; but the Albany institution was to house only short-termers, "men and women of low type, habitual drunkards, common prostitutes, local and migrant vagabonds, professional gamblers, petty thieves, bruisers, and others from the social scum." With Warden Pilsbury in charge it was believed that the Albany prison would display industrial efficiency and the inmates would thus earn their keep.

With the fine new structure ready the jails of Albany city and county began to transfer their misdemeanants, who found they were to earn their room and board by making rattan chair seats, by making shoes, and by braiding willow covers on demijohns, carboys, and jugs. The contract system was based partly on so much per day for each prisoner's time and partly by the piece. It was noted that Warden Pilsbury was a believer in early rising; prisoners here—as in most New England institutions—were roused to work an hour before breakfast. "Rising before dawn," as an observer wrote, "the establishment was astir at the earliest possible moment." It augured well for "a handsome profit" by the end of the year.

The Albany authorities were so pleased with things they asked Warden Pilsbury to recommend a suitable person to take charge of the county almshouse and hospital, which together commonly cared for more than one thousand inmates. Pilsbury knew just the man. He sent to Wethersfield for a deputy in that prison, Zebulon Brockway, on whom the elder man had long kept an eye. Brockway came. We shall meet him later.

Now it was New York City which came seeking the abilities of Amos Pilsbury. He went to the metropolis to take charge of the city's penal and charitable institutions on Ward's Island, which he handled most satisfactorily and was then virtually drafted to the office of chief of the metropolitan police force. But when Mayor Fernando Wood sought to instruct him in the methods expected of a political appointee, Chief Pilsbury promptly resigned and went back to Albany to resume wardenship of the county prison. He remained here until his death in 1873, leaving a flourishing institution that was to serve as an attractive model for at least six county prisons elsewhere; and leaving also a son, significantly named Lewis Dwight Pilsbury, who had been trained by his father and was soon to be appointed the first superintendent of all New York prisons.

The first effect of the Civil War on northern prisons was a marked falling off of commitments. As in other wars before and since the Army and Navy were not given to probing deeply into the past of men seeking to enlist, and they became a refuge for fugitives. Many jailbirds and convicts were turned loose on promise to enlist, and did so, often several times under as many names, after collecting the state bounty paid recruits. The services must also have absorbed a host of potential criminals. For the first time since they were built, the new prisons and jails had more cells than inmates. Yet the last shot of the war was almost as if it were a signal for criminals everywhere to resume business. Within a brief time northern prisons were crowded to capacity, and more; the press sought to find reasons for the sudden wave of crime, and demanded that legislatures drop all other matters to provide new prisons or to add cell blocks to old ones.

The war was also responsible for the sudden appearance of Enoch Cobb Wines, a man of truly enormous dreams. All Wines wanted was a world-wide organization of intelligent and kindly disposed men which, by the grace of God, would transform the prisons of the world into nothing less than universities of reformation. Dreamer that he was, Wines nevertheless recognized that such a universal transformation must have a source, a starting point. Providence provided it under name and style of the New York Prison Association. Inspired by the earlier and similar groups in Philadelphia and Boston, the New York association had accomplished little, quite possibly because it had been handicapped by what a historian of penology said was "an over-abundance of visionaries." And now, in 1862, to lead this ineffectual group of reformers, came a very prince of visionaries.

Enoch Wines had already passed fifty-six when he entered upon his major career with the New York Prison Association. Born in New Jersey and reared on his father's farm at Shoreham, Vermont, he was graduated from Middlebury College in 1827, spent two years aboard *U. S. S. Constellation* as a schoolmaster to midshipmen, and came ashore to operate a private school for boys at Princeton, New Jersey. It failed. So did another classical school he bought and operated at Burlington. He edited briefly a magazine in which he agitated for normal schools like that established at Concord, Vermont, in 1823 by Samuel Reed Hall. He wrote a book that weighed three and one-half pounds to prove that ideas about civil liberty and popular government originated in the Bible. Then, after more than two decades of failure in educational efforts, Professor Enoch Wines turned to theology with a license to preach granted by the Congregationalists. For six years he held pastorates in Vermont, New York, and Pennsylvania. Just before the Civil War broke out, he was invited to St. Louis to take charge of the newly founded City University. Almost at once it was forced to close, and the cruelly disappointed man of fifty-six was wondering which way to turn, when the God-given invitation came from the New York Prison Association.

Enoch Wines could have had but little knowledge of penology, but he displayed an organizing ability that put the New York association at the head of all prison societies. He doubled the group's contributions from the public. He induced the city of New York and the state to put the association down for cash in their budgets. And with Theodore Dwight, the genius of Columbia Law School, he made a survey of prisons in the United States and Canada which, among other things, indicated that a major trouble with penology was that "politics was boss," that not even the best of wardens was immune to removal at the whim of the boys in the back room.

The Wines-Dwight report made a noise in the papers just when prisons were starting to refill to overflowing, after the end of the war. For the next few years crime and prisons comprised a major subject of public interest. Wines was continually proclaiming the failure of the American prison system because it obviously did nothing "to cure criminals." He said the public had never accepted real responsibility for its criminals but was content only "to entomb them." Neither the Pennsylvania solitary nor the Auburn systems contributed anything toward cure of the disease. A revolutionary change was due. Old attitudes must disappear. There was only one hope, and it was reformation. Reformation would find its source in the "divine benevolence of education."

At the time Enoch Wines began expounding his message, the idea of reforming criminals was one of those things which most men agreed was a nice theory and had best be left in that category. The most "successful prisons" were those whose convicts *earned their keep,* as the phrase had it. The most noted wardens were those who knew how to meet and control the malingering of their wards in the prison shops, and the often corrupt agents of prison labor contractors. As for reformation, was that not wholly in the hands of the new chaplains?

There was at least one professional warden who welcomed Wines as a Moses. Zebulon Brockway, the former deputy of Wethersfield prison whom Amos Pilsbury had brought to Albany back in 1851, had gone on to take charge at the Rochester penitentiary, then to Detroit, to become first superintendent of what the Michigan city had built in the hope that it would be less a prison than a true house of correction. Though here as elsewhere the inmates were supposed to earn their keep, Brockway was given a fairly free hand to see what could be done for reformation. In little more than a decade he did a great deal.

From its first year the Detroit house of correction paid its way by the industries Brockway installed and ran with assured competence. Within four years he was granting small but actual wages to inmates who maintained good disciplinary records and exceeded the stint that

Brockway set for piecework production. With the co-operation of friends in Detroit he promised jobs to all discharged prisoners whose records, in Brockway's eyes, warranted such trust. He started agitation for laws to permit courts to prescribe what was soon to be known as the indeterminate sentence. He organized a Sunday school and asked his chaplain to provide morning chapel. In the woman's branch he added an evening class in education, and instituted a radical innovation, an experimental grading system said to be the first application of this theory to adults in the United States. With the inspired help of Miss Emma Hall, he prevailed on authorities to erect a house of shelter to which the better women could be removed and detained "under more liberal and homelike discipline" until expiration of their sentences. Under Miss Hall this department became the first genuine women's reformatory in the country. In both the men's and women's department Brockway began the policy of lectures in the popular lyceum manner. Here at Detroit was an institution Enoch Wines could point to as offering the divine benevolence of education.

IV

The quite remarkable achievements of Zebulon Brockway were doubtless accepted by Enoch Wines as proof that not only Michigan but the known world was ready for radical reform of the theories of penology. His soaring imagination was wholly impervious to doubt as he prepared to call an International Prison Congress at Cincinnati. Though his own New York association, and the Philadelphia society, politely refused to assume responsibility, Wines and a few friends went ahead with what must have been impressive invitations, and one day in 1870 Governor Rutherford B. Hayes of Ohio officially welcomed one hundred thirty-odd delegates who had come not quite from the entire known world but from twenty-four states, several provinces of Canada, and a few South American countries. Prominent prison reformers in France and Great Britain sent papers to be read along with some forty other commentaries presented to the congress.

The most able address of them all, says historian McKelvey, was that given by Zebulon Brockway of the Detroit house of correction. He entitled it "Ideal for a True Prison System for a State." In it he recommended that each state create a non-political commission with full power to build and control "reception" prisons for male adults in which each convict would be examined. The few incorrigibles were to be retained for life. The others would be transferred to intermediate reformatories, and there they should serve indeterminate sentences of a length to be suggested by a system of marks and grades. Education should be continuous regardless of prison industries. Each convict should be released as soon as he was reformed.

Brockway's over-all plan was based on the principle that convicts were to be deemed wards of the state and committed to the custody of a board of guardians until, in the board's judgment, they might be returned to society with ordinary safety and in accord with their own highest welfare. It was a noble address filled with revolutionary ideals. It naturally became the center of stormy discussion. In later years Brockway recalled of this address that he had felt himself at the time strengthened by "a mysterious, almighty and spiritual force," similar to that of the Disciples on the Mount of Transfiguration. Yet Brockway could not be dismissed as a pulpit reformer. The charge of gross idealism against him might be sustained, yet here was a warden aged forty-three who had been in active prison work for more than half his years, and the great beard that covered his chest was already gray and verging white. It told of continuous cares and dangers which stalked the life of any man engaged in protecting society from what some considered the properly caged wolves and jackals of society, and others declared to be merely its own victims.

And no matter Zebulon Brockway's idealism; it inspired this first prison congress in America to catch something of his vision. The assembled wardens, superintendents, chaplains, judges, and governors declared that society was indeed responsible for the reformation of criminals. Then they went away, many to cool their momentary enthusiasm in the hard, everyday monotony of herding convicts. Yet within five years after the congress at Cincinnati the state of New York erected at Elmira a reformatory so noted that the ancient controversy about the Pennsylvania and the Auburn systems was wholly forgotten in the revolutionary Elmira system, installed with the help of Zebulon Brockway, who was to head the institution for twenty-five years to the end of the century.

That the establishment of Elmira Reformatory cost the state a little more than one and one-half million dollars was to begin with an indication of New York's willingness to try a new method of dealing with criminals. Brockway was immensely pleased with its architecture, which he thought was "so little like the ordinary prison and so much like a college or hospital." He believed it would have a good effect on the inmates; and on the public, too, in that it would help change the common sentiment about offenders from the vindictiveness of punishment "to the amenities of rational educational correction." What turned out to be a handicap was the very name of the place. The public tended to think of it as a reform school for juveniles. It was nothing of the kind. Among the first inmates were one hundred experienced, but not hopelessly so, criminals transferred from Auburn and another batch from Sing Sing, these latter being for the most part vicious and untamed fellows.

Brockway had expected Elmira to be chiefly for first offenders, but the pressure of the state prison population was so great that he got all kinds. He managed, however, to segregate them to some extent, and instituted a careful system of grading by marks to divide the inmates into three classes, each of which was dressed in a distinctive garb. There was a library of several thousand books, many magazines, and "expurgated newspapers." A school with two evening classes a week was started. Brush making was the first industry and was later supplemented by work in various crafts.

Brockway was pleased that the mark system resulted in movement, in place of the usual inertia of prisoners; and happy that many prisoners proved anxious to consult with the superintendent, whom they came in time to consider their friend, interested in their welfare even to what they should do when discharged. An ethics class held by Charles A. Collin, a professor at Cornell, proved popular and came to number some five hundred inmates. Charles Dudley Warner, noted editor and writer, came occasionally to speak and to encourage conventional debates by the convicts. A reformatory magazine, *The Summary,* was founded.

Superintendent Brockway was periodically under fire by the press whenever a riot occurred, or when escapes were made or even attempted. These events happening in Sing Sing or even in Auburn would have been treated as the usual thing, but because of the aura of the juvenile reform school that persisted at Elmira they were sensationally reported in a manner to discredit Brockway's attempt to reform what for the most part were the case-hardened products of Sing Sing.

During the eighties the long agitation of organized labor against the employment of prison labor in gainful industry began to make progress, and in 1888 a New York law prohibited it in all state institutions. It was freely prophesied that the result would be a monstrous increase of insanity, imbecility, and other disorders. Brockway welcomed the change. He was ready for it, and as soon as the prison factory was closed he formed a military organization of several companies, as in a regiment, with a band. The pseudo-soldiers made their own dummy rifles. Chevrons and other insignia were prescribed. Officers appeared in a bright blue uniform with shoulder straps designating their rank. Brockway was soon convinced that the military drill, which came to include tactical evolutions on a battalion scale, was effective no less as exercise than as a morale builder. Brockway also increased the time devoted to education. He added instruction in twenty-two trades. He went so far as to engage a medical man to take charge of a "scientific diet."

The scientific consideration of the dietary needs of convicts was little short of astonishing. Zebulon Brockway was living up to his appearance of a tremendously bearded prophet of biblical type. Five years of the regime that followed the closing of prison industries convinced him that physical and mental education was of the first importance for all convicts; and for at least 10 per cent it was an indispensable basic procedure without which this minority would remain incorrigible.

Good Enoch Wines lived long enough to hear Elmira Reformatory hailed as "the greatest advance in penology the world has seen." Wines felt with good reason that he himself had sped the acceptance of the Elmira principle, namely that prisons were to "cure" criminals, not simply punish them. Surely this was an advance of infinite importance even though Wines, around whom this mid-century movement had gathered with all the intensity of a religious revival, immediately resumed efforts to make reality of his grandiose dream of the universal reform of penology. He promoted in Congress an office of "United States Commissioner," whose "duties" were to arrange another international congress of prison reformers, was appointed to the job, and went abroad to take a leading part in such meetings at London and Stockholm. Doubtless some good came from these conventions, but Wines lost contact with the comparatively petty triumphs and failures of prison reform at home.

The failures were many. The prohibition of prison industry which began in the eighties, when organized labor was feeling its strength, tended to make ruin of discipline. Not all wardens or commissioners were so farsighted as Brockway, and thousands of idle convicts presented a problem that even today has not been solved. One began to read of the rapidly increasing insanity in prisons, of numerous riots, and a general breakdown of morale in prisoners and wardens and guards. Yet the efforts of Wines and his friends in the New York Prison Association had served to enhance the public esteem of prisons and their officials, and had also done a great deal to change public thinking from punishment to reformation. New rivalries among states resulted in adequate construction, inspired by the example of Elmira, but mostly in those states where pressure of population growth had become insistent and tax money permitted.

In most of the newer states of the Far West, and in many of the old states of the South, the so-called penitentiaries were inadequate in size. They were also jerry-built structures which an observer wrote would "not hold a blind, one-legged, one-armed, and consumptive man who really wanted to get out." Because it was the particular pride of American pioneers to meet any and all emergencies head-on, it was a pioneer warden in a pioneer region who one day in 1866 emerged from the blacksmith shop of Oregon's well-filled yet well-ventilated state prison with a device he had just wrought on the anvil and which, he was heard to remark, would damn well keep prisoners where they belonged. Warden Gardner's terse and grim observation may have stemmed from the fact that during five months previous a total of one hundred and fifteen convicts had escaped from the rambling great board shack and its surrounding wooden stockade, to disappear without trace into the mighty forest that grew almost down to the walls.

With the natural pride of an inventor the warden called his new rig the Gardner Shackle. It went into prison terminology the world over as the Oregon boot. Sergeant J. R. Johnson, the penitentiary's historian, describes it as a stirrup fitted about the foot of the convict with an additional weight of from 15 to 25 pounds fixed in a locked position about the leg and supported by the stirrup. With weight on one foot and none on the other it was not possible to run at all or even to walk fast or long. "The early wardens," Johnson remarks, "were of the opinion it would be almost impossible to hold the prisoners without them."

Warden-inventor Gardner got a patent on the device, and found need to obtain a court order restraining use of the boot "without compensation to him." The Oregon prison's early reports often show items covering "rental of shackle," but how much income Gardner received from other prisons, if any, is not known. What is known is that use of the Oregon boot was widespread in Western United States throughout the rest of the century, and is still used today, both in this country and abroad, chiefly by officers transferring prisoners on trains or in automobiles.

As early as 1850 California was (and remained) the most populous of all Western states and the problem of its prison population grew just as fast. The old hulks of Spanish jails failed to retain even the least ambitious of prisoners, and by 1855 the state engaged a contractor to build a penitentiary and to work the convicts on a typical labor lease. The result was a makeshift structure of forty-eight cells near some clay pits on Point San Quentin. Within a brief time more than three hundred prisoners were somehow crowded into it, and there began a decade and more of escapes, of escapes prevented by the simple method of shooting, and of all-around brutality that became public scandal. The state voted to assume control. In an attempt to relieve the unspeakable conditions at San Quentin it was glad to accept a contract from a company which agreed to build a prison in return for a lease on convict labor to construct a company dam and canal at Folsom. It was no sooner done than it filled with prisoners. Even so, labor on the dam and canal lasted until 1892, by which time California had passed an act prohibiting leasing of its convicts. Meanwhile a California Prison Association was organized by the Rev. James Woodwurth, which memoralized the legislature to do something about the lax discipline and corruption of its prisons. California's response was to appoint what was officially described as "a moral instructor" to organize a reading school for the juveniles in San Quentin.

It seems probable, as historian McKelvey observed, that California from the first was faced with a convict population disproportionately large and that it was markedly troubled by the opium traffic. During the last year of the old century, when M. G. Aguirre was appointed chief warden, the state started to make notable progress under this able and enlightened official.

Throughout the latter half of the old century, the American jail lagged far behind penitentiaries in response to the reform movement. As late as the middle seventies an English visitor thought our best city jails overcrowded to demoralization. Single cells invariably held two prisoners, sometimes three, with nothing for them to do except "spend the whole day in idleness and injurious conversation." Even so, Miss Linda Gilbert of Chicago, soon widely known as "The Prisoners' Friend," had already started a forty-year campaign to ameliorate the lot of those held in what in large part were still vile pens compared to state prisons. What had started her career at the age of ten was the despairing faces staring out the barred windows of the Cook County jail, which she passed on her way to and from school.

Having learned that Cook County's charges were not supplied with any sort of reading matter, the young girl occasionally left a book or two at the jail. By the time she was grown she had determined on her career. With her own money she selected and purchased four thousand books to establish a prisoners' library in the Cook County jail. Jails in Buffalo and St. Louis came next, and in 1873 she went to New York. Here she saw the dismal quarters of the notorious Ludlow Street lockup and the substantial horrors of The Tombs. Still using only her own means, she supplied libraries to both of these institutions.

At about this time Miss Gilbert inherited a modest fortune. She moved East to make her home in Mount Vernon, New York, and in 1876 incorporated the Gilbert Library and the Prisoner's Aid Society to supply books to such American jails as would accept them. Meanwhile she contributed to newspapers and magazines advocating jail libraries and prison reform in general, and especially the need of ready employment of discharged prisoners. It may be doubted that her earnest work had any great influence on the very gradual improvement of jails, but Miss Linda Gilbert is an appealing figure in her effort to better the curriculum of what Louis Dwight had described as the seminaries of vice and crime.

At the end of the century only Zebulon Brockway remained of those early dreamers of the perfect, or rather the ideal, prison, that is, one established on the premise that at least ninety convicts of one hundred could be "cured." Younger wardens were taking charge of prisons that had been immeasurably improved by the efforts of, among others, the Quaker pioneers of Philadelphia, by Louis Dwight, by three generations of Pilsburys; by Enoch Wines, Miss Dorothea Dix, and the surviving Brockway, who, bearded like a patriarch of old, which indeed he was, lived on into the twentieth century.

V

Americans generally appear to have greeted the bright new century by looking back to 1800 for data upon which could be set up a glorious contrast. It was only natural that most of the contrasts stressed material achievements. Abstractions were, after all, more difficult to handle. They were less interesting to read or hear about. Better to compare facts about the advances in population, in area, industry, machinery, invention, finance.

As the bells and whistles and cannon announced the first moments of January 1, 1900, newspapers going to press carried statements attributed to eminent Americans. Elihu Root was certain that the greatest achievement of the past century had been discovery of the Bessemer process for making steel. But Chauncey Depew reached far back to Benjamin Franklin, with his kite and keys in the thunderstorm who, he said, led to Mr. Edison and his Mazda lamp. Many a lesser figure pointed to the marvelous expansion of the United States from the Appalachian range to the Pacific Ocean. And now the vast void which maps of 1800 had been content to label Great American Desert, or simply Unknown, was threaded with telegraph and telephone wires, with railroads, and dotted with towns and cities.

Yet a few well-known Americans spoke up to cite changes other than material. Henry George, Jr., thought the greatest thing of the nineteenth century had been the announcement by his father of the single tax, which was certain to destroy industrial slavery. The Rev. Newell Dwight Hillis, the brilliant clergyman of Plymouth Church,

Brooklyn, spoke of the past century as "one of the most fascinating chapters in the story of man's upward progress." He saw art, industry, invention, literature, learning as "captives marching in Christ's triumphant procession up the hill of fame." Even the laws, he thought, were "becoming more just, and rulers humane."

All in all, the voices had the sound of regarding the United States as having done marvelously well. Their authentic tone was that of almost complete satisfaction. Little else if anything seemed left to be done. This may well have been the attitude of professional penologists. The era of experimenting wardens virtually passed with the old century when old Zebulon Brockway retired on the last day of 1899. Though he continued active interest in prison matters to his death two decades later at ninety-three, no radical change of outlook or practice was to come from the leading figures of 1900.

The first effective dreamer in the prison world of the new century was Thomas Mott Osborne, a native of Auburn, New York, home of the famous prison. Born in 1859, he had grown up in the city, became one of its leading citizens, serving two terms as mayor and also on its board of education. More important, in the light of his later career, was that for several years he had been a trustee of the George Junior Republic in nearby Freeville, of which more later.

Osborne was a tall, handsome man, a born leader—said those who knew him—a staunch character, and of engaging personality. In 1913 he was appointed chairman of the New York State Commission for Prison Reform. Being the kind of man he was, Osborne thought he should have some sense of how it felt to be a convict. Donning a standard prison uniform, and taking the name Tom Brown, he entered Auburn, his real identity known only to the warden. For a week Tom Brown mingled without a slip among the convicts. No one seems to have suspected the masquerade. He asked questions tactfully. Working at making baskets in the prison weave shop, his partner was one Jack Murphy, a two-time loser doing twenty years to life.

"By good fortune," Osborne said later, "the officer in charge of the shop allowed his men to talk together, provided they did so quietly and without leaving their places, this though the Auburn rule of silence was supposed to be enforced rigidly throughout the prison." Convict Murphy was ready to talk of many things, including the possibilities of prison reform. He thought something could be done to while away the long and dreary prison Sundays. Perhaps a walk in the yard. Convict Tom Brown remarked that prisoners could hardly expect the guards to give up their day off; and "you don't expect the men could be trusted by themselves, do you?"

"Why not?" Murphy demanded. Tom Brown looked at him inquiringly. Murphy continued. "Why, look here, Tom," said he, and in his eagerness he came around to Brown's side of the worktable. "I know this place through and through. I know these men. I've studied them for years. And I tell you that the big majority of them in here will be square, if they get the chance. The trouble is, we ain't treated on the level. I could tell you of all sorts of frame-ups they give us." But Jack Murphy by no means thought all of them could be trusted. There were a "few dirty degenerates" that would make trouble, but "there ain't so very many of those."

Prisoner Tom Brown then wanted to know about the exceptions. "Wouldn't they quarrel and fight and try to escape?" Murphy had the answer to that one. "They couldn't do that without putting the whole thing on the bum," he said. "That would deprive all of us of our privileges. We wouldn't let that happen. We'd take care of those fellows." A moment later, warming to the idea, Murphy suggested that freedom of the yard on Sundays be given only to prisoners "with a good conduct bar." It would be a sort of Good Conduct League, he said.

The discussion was continued on other days. Murphy related that a while back the boys got up an Anti-Swearing League in the weave shop, with a penalty for "every bad or dirty word." The forfeits were paid in matches, and matches were rather scarce in Auburn. A Good Conduct League would of course "be a much bigger thing. It would be just great. It'll work, too."

In his cell that night Tom Brown meditated on Murphy's suggestion. Good or bad, it had come from an authentic convict. But was it a practical way to make prisoners feel responsibility? The talk continued next day in the weave shop. Murphy said the Good Conduct League he proposed could get discipline without officers appointed by the warden. "When a warden makes a trusty, he makes a stool pigeon," he declared with the dogmatic conviction of prison inmates beyond knowing.

Tom Brown countered by asking Murphy whether he thought that if the Good Conduct League officers were elected by the men themselves, the responsibility implied would do something to change their basic characters. The old convict replied that he did. Tom Brown thought so too, though he pointed out that they might turn out to be poor officers. They might be dictatorial, or weak, or just incompetent. But they would not be stool pigeons.

At the end of a week Tom Brown disappeared from the weave shop. Within a month prisoner Murphy was granted several interviews with the Auburn warden and the state superintendent of prisons. He got their consent to try the Good Conduct League plan. On a Sunday soon Tom Osborne, chairman of the New York State Commission for

Prison Reform, appeared in his proper identity at Auburn's morning chapel to explain to the assembled prisoners what he and Murphy had said and done. He called for a show of hands to indicate whether or not they wanted to undertake the experiment. The vote was unanimous. So began the first radical prison reform of the new century in the United States. It was to become famous not only at Auburn but elsewhere as the Mutual Welfare League.

Tom Osborne's plan of self-government grew out of his fifteen years' experience as an active trustee of the George Junior Republic, already mentioned. The founder of the Republic was William Reuben George, born near Freeville, New York, in 1866, who in New York City became interested in youthful delinquents of the Lower East Side. He tried to improve their chances of reform by organizing clubs, but soon concluded that surrounding conditions of poverty and vice were too great. Instead, he took youngsters to the country during summer vacation. This, too, was disappointing; George found the children did not seem "to appreciate benefits they did not work for," and he thought the summer had done them little good. In 1895 he tried a different idea. He moved more than a hundred boys and girls from the slums to an abandoned farm, where he set up a school. Many of the children remained throughout the winter. Next summer the George Junior Republic was officially started.

The Republic lived up to its name. The youngsters conducted their own government complete with president, vice-president, cabinet, judges, courts, even a jail. Elections were held and laws made at town meetings held regularly. Founder George lived with the young citizens but was careful in his guidance, never to offer advice unless it was asked for. Responsibility was what he was after, and he could see it gradually forming in the voting citizens, who were sixteen or over, and noted the influence of the example on the younger boys and girls.

Founder George's experiment attracted a good press. It also appealed to many substantial adults, such as Thomas Mott Osborne, who soon became one of the most active of the trustees. A number of well-to-do parents were so taken with the Republic they sent their children there rather than to the private summer camps they could well afford. When the Englishman Baden-Powell was founding the Boy Scouts he made a long visit to George's self-governing colony, which already had imitators in Europe and South America.

With certain changes and refinements the George Junior Republic was the basis for Osborne's Mutual Welfare League. The goal was self-responsibility. Osborne had long since come to the conclusion that any attempt at *direct* reform of prisoners was foredoomed to failure. Neither honest men nor criminals, he said, would tolerate "a bald proposition from anyone to alter their characters or habits, least of all if we try to gain such a change by coercion." They must be trained to be, not good prisoners, but good citizens.

If men in prison, Osborne reasoned, were to remain there all their lives, it would not be of great importance to society how they were treated there. But a majority of them would soon or late be released. This was the vital moment. What came after depended in large part on what the years in prison did to or for them. A hundred years of American experience proved, if it proved anything—Osborne believed—that most men left prison only to return. We had learned a great deal about governing men in prisons. We had not learned how to mend them. Perhaps they could learn to mend themselves if given the chance.

There is no need here to go into details in regard to the Mutual Welfare League. The rules of discipline of the prison were left chiefly to a body of fifty delegates elected by the inmates on a basis of representation of the several work or shop gangs. Infractions were dealt with by a board of five judges chosen by the delegates, though an appeal might be taken from their decisions to the warden. The decisions of the judges were carried out by the regular officers of the prison. No keepers or guards were allowed in the shops. Outdoor recreation, lectures, and entertainments were provided for.

Harry Elmer Barnes, one of the foremost penologists in the United States, says that the league at Auburn became "almost a sensation in penal circles." It was watched with unusual interest. Osborne was appointed warden of Sing Sing, a position he accepted against the advice of friends who warned him he would run afoul of crooked politics. Though he later admitted the advice was sound, he was influenced to take the job by a telegram from one of the Sing Sing inmates, sent out by the prison grapevine: "For God's sake, take the wardenship. All the boys anxious to have you." Doubtless they were, but not everybody else was.

At the notorious bastille on the Hudson, Osborne set up the same sort of self-government that was working so well at Auburn. "The atmosphere at Sing Sing," wrote an observer, "changed practically overnight." One of the first things accomplished by self-governing convicts was the cleaning up of the dope traffic, which, as in all prisons, involved not only the convicts but a number of guards. Discipline improved enormously. Penologists, newspaper reporters, and plain citizens came to see the magic wrought by the league. Possibly too much enthusiasm was displayed. In any case, the superintendent of state prisons, a political appointee, told Warden Osborne that he should stop "coddling the convicts." Osborne replied that as long as he was warden of Sing Sing the Mutual Welfare League would continue to have a say in its operation.

Then, early in August 1915, New York City papers carried a story to the effect that Osborne must resign or be ousted, then went on to quote the charges of the superintendent of prisons against the Sing Sing warden: he was quarrelsome, he had betrayed his trust, discipline had gone to pot, and "the whole course of prison reform is suffering from his mistakes." Osborne stood his ground. A lengthy investigation cleared him of all charges and he resumed his post. When a new superintendent of prisons was appointed and began to interfere with the league's functions, Osborne resigned in disgust.

Within a few months Osborne was appointed head of the naval prison at Portsmouth, New Hampshire, and here, said one who knew him well, he spent three of the happiest years of his life. When he took charge, the Portsmouth institution was a heavily barred prison having 170 prisoners and 180 guards. When he left, it was a large camp of 2500 inmates and no guards at all. He thought that Portsmouth had brilliantly vindicated the fundamental principles of the Mutual Welfare League.

Before his death in 1926, Thomas Mott Osborne wondered in print how far the league might go to protect society if it were given a trial under favorable conditions. It had never been tried under such conditions. At Auburn, he wrote, politics and official stupidity had almost completely smothered it. At Sing Sing politics of the foulest kind drove one warden from office, and the new warden inherited a seriously curtailed league. Yet, crippled as it was, it had won his confidence and support. And at Portsmouth, Osborne admitted, the league had disappeared. A new administration hastened to undo what the former administration had created.

Yet greathearted Tom Osborne did not for a moment believe that the league was dead. "It still lives," he cried, "in the hearts of the thousands of men who have felt its uplifting influence. Those who are going straight. Those who are not going straight because outside conditions have been too hard for them. Even those who have gone back to crime without regrets are somehow aware that they have had a fleeting glimpse of a better world from which they are shut out. No, the league can never die. The principle upon which it rests is eternal . . ."

Those are noble words. Osborne's was a noble effort. It is fitting that his name is honored by the Osborne Association, which under the leadership of a former associate, Austin H. MacCormick, continues to have no little influence on penology by "exposing poor standards, brutalities, and general apathy when found in American prisons."

People who were close to Osborne seem in agreement that his really great success was due almost exclusively to his dynamic leadership. Few could have accomplished what he did. Possibly he never realized the shortcomings of human nature. If he did, he coped with them as best he could with his appealing and compelling personality. The immense critical literature about Osborne indicates that the chief weakness of his Mutual Welfare League was his too optimistic reliance on the co-operation of *all* convicts. He could hardly have done otherwise, for there were then few facilities for classifying prisoners.

If as some bold penologists believe there may come a time when all penal institutions will have self-government, the experiment will have the advantage of what in post-World War I days was hailed as the great new hope. It was then called psychology. Students were at last coming to grip with what many held to be the real problem. He was the criminal *individual*. He could be analyzed. As historian Blake Mc-Kelvey saw it, penologists were exchanging the empirical approach of the reformers for that of "an analytical science." Even so, they were destined to meet repeated disillusionment. If one thing was certain in mid-twentieth century, it was that neither trial by error nor applied science had solved the bewildering problem. As these pages were written, riots in the penitentiaries of two states indicate that the poison weeds which bloomed so well in Reading Gaol of last century are far from extinct.

3.

THE WORLD OF MUTES

GOOD Louis Dwight never doubted that it was the intervention of God in the form of ill-health that set him on the gloomy path as light bearer in the world of prisons. For two hundred years Puritan divines had been quick to see the hand of Deity in such vagaries of chance as tended to the glory of Omnipotence and the spiritual improvement of man. Sermons were preached on these "Illustrious Providences." If the intervention appeared remarkably illustrious, then it was declared to be a "Wonder-Working Providence" and the sermon preached upon it was likely to be published.

Consider young Dwight, fresh from theological school, license in hand, forced by an accident to abandon the pulpit to seek health on the highways and to leave Bibles in dark places. And lo, a great vision was given to him. The Boston Prison Discipline Society, born of his dream, began at once to awaken, then to trouble the public conscience. It had been much the same with another young man, Thomas Hopkins Gallaudet, like Dwight a graduate of Yale who went on to finish theology at Andover only to find his health so impaired as to preclude preaching the Word. Then, during the winter of 1814–15, while recuperating in the Gallaudet home in Hartford, Connecticut, he became interested in Alice, the young deaf-mute daughter of Dr. Mason F. Cogswell. With infinite patience, but nothing to guide him save his own intelligence, he managed to "impart to her a knowledge of many simple words and sentences."

Dr. Cogswell was elated. He took the trouble to learn that there were at least eighty-four other deaf-mute children within the state, a fact he made known to "a number of gentlemen of the city" who met at his house to discuss the founding of a free school for these unfortunates. There was then no such school in the United States. An attempt had been made to start one, at the New York City Almshouse, by its chaplain, the Rev. John Stanford, who sought to teach the few mutes in residence to write the names of familiar objects on slates. It was far more difficult than he had anticipated. It was soon dropped. Another failure was reported from Baltimore, where a Colonel William Polling of Virginia had advanced funds for a small school to teach young deaf-mutes including his own three congenitally deaf children. Polling sent to England for a teacher, who was John Braidwood, a son of the founder of the first deaf school in the British Isles. But Braidwood, though experienced and personable, had little character. He squandered Colonel Polling's funds "in an irregular manner of life . . . and finally died a victim of intemperance."

Thus it was that the gentlemen meeting at Dr. Cogswell's voted to send young and ailing Thomas Gallaudet abroad to learn what was being done there to educate the deaf and dumb. England turned out to be a disappointing experience. Gallaudet's reception was invariably cool. The experts, if experts they were, seemed determined to keep their methods secret, both from one another and from foreigners. Gallaudet spent four months in learning little more than that the British schools were "barred with gold, and opened only to golden keys."

In Paris, however, he got a warm welcome from the Abbé Roche-Ambrose Cucurron Sicard, head of the Institut Royal des Sourds-Muets, where Gallaudet was made free to live and study for much of a year. The American was an inspired student who impressed Abbé Sicard so favorably that, when he was to leave for the United States, the warm-hearted priest permitted Laurent Clerc, one of his most brilliant instructors, to go with him. During the long voyage Clerc studied English with Gallaudet, who in turn continued to receive lessons in sign language from the Frenchman, himself a mute.

The intervention of Providence in the life of young Gallaudet, which had come in the form of bright little Alice Cogswell, was becoming evident: On April 15, 1817, the Hartford Asylum for the Deaf and Dumb opened its doors, with teachers Clerc and Gallaudet. There were twenty pupils, including Alice. Among the nineteen other deaf students were Sophia Fowler, who, shortly after graduation, became Mrs. Thomas Hopkins Gallaudet, and Eliza Crocker Boardman, who soon married Laurent Clerc.

Before the year was out, twenty-two more pupils presented themselves. It was apparent that the school must have more financial aid than the amount subscribed by the generous few "gentlemen of the city" who had established it. Taking their best pupils along, Clerc and Gallaudet gave demonstrations in churches and before New England legislatures to show that, contrary to general belief, the deaf could be educated. In his talks Gallaudet liked to cite earlier philosophers who had flashed their feeble rays of light down the ages, telling of John Bulwer, a contemporary of Milton and Bacon, who had made an attempt to interest people in starting a school to educate "those originally deafe & dumb." Nothing had come of it, Gallaudet related, and quoted old Bulwer, who had written: "I soon perceived by falling into discourse with some rationall men about such a designe that the attempt seemed so paradoxicall, prodigious, and Hyperbolicall, that it did rather amuse than satisfie their understandings."

Yet here and now were these deaf-mute children of Connecticut who could read with their eyes, even as you and I, and could communicate with each other and with hearing persons by writing or using the hand alphabet. The demonstrations staged by Clerc and Gallaudet and their pupils quickly brought legislative aid; while Congress hastened to grant 23,000 acres of wild land to the school. Massachusetts appropriated funds to send twenty pupils to Hartford. New Hampshire sent ten pupils. The Hartford Asylum became the American School for the Deaf, and the mother school for sixty-four similar institutions in the United States.

Gallaudet and Clerc were meanwhile preparing teachers for the deaf, and one of them, Harvey P. Peet, went to take charge of the New York school, which he ran with great success for three decades. Another Hartford alumnus, Lewis Weld, became principal for the Pennsylvania school. When Thomas Hopkins Gallaudet died, he left two sons, Thomas and Edward Miner, who devoted their lives to expanding and improving deaf-mute education in the United States and foreign parts, and formed a dynasty that endured a little more than one hundred years.

It should be said that until late in the nineteenth century the instruction of the deaf in America generally followed the methods devised by the elder Gallaudet and Laurent Clerc, which were the sign language, the manual alphabet, and writing. It was inevitable that other methods should be tried. Among these was one called the "oral system," which used signs sparingly and the manual alphabet not at all, but concentrated on lip reading and articulation together with writing. The oral system found champions in Massachusetts, among them the noted Samuel Gridley Howe, a most extraordinary man, possibly a genius, who had recently established the first blind school in the United States and had made one of his pupils, Laura Dewey Bridgman, an international celebrity. That the Bridgman prodigy was not only blind but a deaf-mute was sufficient reason to give heed to Dr. Howe when he declared that the oral system for instructing the deaf was far superior to the Gallaudet or manual system. The Gallaudets stood firm for the method they and their father had been using so successfully. The resulting controversy was much like that among prison reformers who even then were debating bitterly about the Auburn vs. the Philadelphia systems.

The state of Massachusetts was still sending its deaf-mutes for instruction to the Gallaudet school in Hartford. Dr. Howe said this was a mistake, and demanded that Massachusetts establish its own school and teach only the oral method. John Clarke, a well-to-do citizen of Northampton, was moved to build and endow such a school in his native town. It was named for him, and to take charge came Miss Harriet B. Rogers of Boston, a close friend and disciple of Dr. Howe. Miss Rogers announced officially that the Clarke School for the Deaf would teach by articulation and lip reading.

By this time, and owing in large part to the efforts of Amos Kendall, an act of Congress had established in Washington a national school for the deaf—later Gallaudet College—with Edward M. Gallaudet as superintendent, and his mother Sophia, the deaf-mute widow of Thomas as matron. The college's board of trustees suggested that the superintendent consider the oral method. Though convinced that the manual method was "best in most cases," Gallaudet admitted the practicality of "teaching a considerable number of the deaf to read from the lips." He even recommended that articulation be taught "as a *branch* of instruction in all deaf schools."

At about this time there came to Boston Professor Alexander Melville Bell, who, together with a brother and their father, had for two decades been "teaching the science of correct speech at the three capitals of Edinburgh, Dublin and London." Melville Bell had devised what he termed "visible speech," a system of symbols by which the position of the vocal organs in speaking was indicated. In Boston, Professor Bell lectured on his method and said that his son was finding it of greatest aid in instructing the deaf of London. The city of Boston had just opened a special day school for the deaf, the first of its kind anywhere Its principal, Miss Sarah Fuller, was so impressed with Bell's lecture she asked the Boston school board if they could not interest Professor Bell's son in coming to train her teachers in visible speech. The elder Bell had already decided to settle in Kingston, Ontario, to teach elocution in Queen's College there. He liked the New World. He wrote his son about the Boston offer, and on April 10, 1871, Alexander Graham Bell, twenty-four years old, arrived to teach the teachers of Miss Fuller's school the use of visible speech.

Miss Fuller, and many another Bostonian, were struck by the appearance of this tall, spare young Scot with piercing black eyes, hair of jet, and bushy coal-black whiskers that were imposing even in a period of notable beards. His countenance was as pale as it was grave. After three months at Miss Fuller's school he visited the Clarke Institution at Northampton, and the American Asylum at Hartford, then returned to Boston to open a sort of private normal school to which institutions could send teachers for training in the use of visible speech. He also rented a small room at the end of Exeter Place, off Chauncy Street, to use as a laboratory for experimenting with electricity in connection with a hearing device.

As early as 1865 young Bell had made a study of resonance pitches of the mouth cavities "during the utterance of vocal sounds." This led him to experiment with electricity as a means of transmission of speech to aid the teaching of visible speech to the deaf. Now, six years later in Boston, he devoted as much time as he could spare from teaching to his experiments. These presently took form along three related lines— a phonautograph with which he could show deaf pupils how to make their tone vibrations correctly, a multiple telegraph, and a speaking telegraph. One chooses to believe the romantic account that the telephone was a sort of by-product of the phonautograph which Bell was inspired to invent for one of his deaf pupils, who was Miss Mabel, daughter of Gardiner G. Hubbard.

In any case, on March 10, 1876, a weighty day in the history of communication, young Bell and his assistant, Thomas A. Watson, were working in the Exeter Place laboratory to perfect what Bell referred to as the harmonic telegraph. "Mr. Watson," Bell called into the instrument. "Come here. I want you." It was the first wholly intelligible sentence ever transmitted by wire. Less than a year later inventor Bell gave a lecture on the telephone at Salem during which, said the Boston *Globe*, "telephonic messages were transmitted between the hall in Salem and the Exeter Place laboratory with the most gratifying success." On

July 9, 1877, the Bell Telephone Company was incorporated in Boston, with Gardiner G. Hubbard as trustee. Two days later Miss Mabel Hubbard and Alexander G. Bell were married. Was there ever a more wonderful story? No novelist of the period, not even the Rev. Horatio Alger, Jr., could have conjured up so happy a combination of love and success which, in the idiom of the period, had been brought about by humanitarian efforts. It merely added lustre to know that the treasurer of the Bell Telephone Company was Thomas Sanders, father of a deaf-mute son who had responded as marvelously to the teaching of Bell as had Miss Hubbard. Both Sanders and Hubbard had given the young inventor generous financial help with his experiments. Both were to continue to aid him defend his patent rights against the many claimants in the approximately six hundred lawsuits which cluttered the courts for years. Bell was upheld in every case.

The commercial success of the telephone did nothing to end Bell's work for the deaf. When France awarded him the Volta Prize for invention of the "electric speaking telephone," he devoted the money to founding the Volta Laboratory in Washington, where he moved to continue experiments that resulted in the audiometer, in flat and cylindrical wax records, and an improved reproducer for use with Thomas Edison's new phonograph. When money started to roll in from these patents, Bell used it to endow the American Association for the Promotion of the Teaching of Speech to the Deaf. He wrote a treatise significantly entitled "The Formation of a Deaf Variety of the Human Race" in which he considered the phenomenon of the many deaf-mutes in Chilmark, Massachusetts, on Martha's Vineyard, who, in 1890, numbered one in every twenty-five of the population; and he cited the intermarriage of cousins and his belief that the isolation of the deaf tended toward intermarriage. The cure, he said, was that the deaf should learn lip reading and articulation, and thus "mix with the hearing world."

Meanwhile the early controversy about methods had resolved itself. Both Bell and the Gallaudets were as honest as they were devoted; and came in time to favor what was called the "combined method," which, though difficult to define, was first to teach pupils the manual alphabets and writing, then to proceed to lip reading and articulation, using the several electrical devices invented by Bell and others, including various hearing aids. Some schools used the single- and two-handed alphabets of the Gallaudets; others the Dalgarno glove alphabet as modified by Bell, which was the seventeenth-century invention of a Scot, James Dalgarno, author of *The Deaf-Mutes Preceptor*. On a white glove worn on the pupil's left hand the letters appeared on the joints of the fingers and palm. Bell favored this method because it could "be used

by the sense of touch while the eyes of the pupil are fixed on the
teacher's lips." He said it also permitted emphasis, and "thus the force
of accent and rhythm can be given."

Both accent and rhythm were sounded by one of Gallaudet's pupils
in the national school in Washington, when Master John O'Rourke,
seventeen, stepped to the platform and read three stanzas of Mr. Longfellow's *Psalm of Life,* in "a manner that elicited hearty applause." At
the Nebraska school in Omaha, Professor J. A. Gillespie, using the
audiophone, discovered that 15 per cent of his deaf-mutes had some
slight degree of hearing; and he could report that by use of the same
electrical apparatus the hearing power of several of these pupils had
"developed in a most gratifying manner." School periodicals were
being published at several of the institutions, and deaf-mute poets
appeared in their columns and even became something of a rage in
general magazines.

At the Illinois deaf school Miss Angie A. Fuller described what
being deaf was like:

> *No sound! No sound! an alien though at home,*
> *An exile even in my native land;*
> *A prisoner, too, for though I roam,*
> *Yet chained and manacled I oft must stand*
> *Unmoved, though sounds vibrate on every hand.*

Other periodicals of the deaf published verse by Howard Glyndon,
James Nack, Mrs. Mary Toles Peet, and of course the famous Laura
Bridgman, the blind mute of Hanover, New Hampshire. Then, there
was the outstanding alumnus of the Pennsylvania institute, the artist and
poet John Carlin, who had gone to Paris to study painting under Dela-
roche and returned home to set up as a successful illustrator and
miniature painter in New York. He had done the pictures for a *Paradise
Lost,* many portraits and landscapes, and illustrated his own book of
verse. Bearded now as Moses, and nearly seventy, he sang in good
meter *To the Fireflies:*

> *Awake, ye sparklers, bright and gay,*
> *Still nestling in your lair!*
> *The twilight glories fade away*
> *And gloom pervades the air.*
> *Come, then, ye merry elves of light,*
> *Illuminate the tranquil night,*
> *While low and high ye blithely fly,*
> *Flitting meteors 'neath the sky.*

The two sons of Thomas Hopkins Gallaudet, Thomas and Edward
Miner, lived into the new century, devoting their efforts to the deaf to
their last days, leaving as monuments Gallaudet College in Washington,

a church exclusively for the deaf in New York City, and the Gallaudet Home for aged and infirm deaf-mutes near Poughkeepsie. All of these markers together are perhaps inadequate reminders of a dynasty which for one hundred and one years had much to do with the "Wonder-Working Providences" which made the deaf "hear" and the mute speak.

Alexander Graham Bell lived on to die, in 1922, at seventy-five, long since a majestic presence, famous the world over for the telephone, honored by learned and scientific bodies of a score of nations. Success and fame sat well on his shaggy white head, out of which peered "the keen black eyes that dominated any situation." The gravity which had marked his early years, said one of his many biographers, had given way to a sympathy and joviality that won both old and young. On the August day of his funeral, held near his summer home on Cape Breton Island, Nova Scotia, "every telephone on the North American continent remained silent while he was buried."

On that day, too, Helen Adams Keller, almost as famous as the celebrated inventor, reflected that it had been Mr. Bell who had been responsible for the first step this blind deaf-mute had taken "up out of Egypt to stand before Sinai . . . so that I beheld many wonders."

4.

THE WORLD OF THE BLIND

THE blind waited. One can only wonder why efforts to educate them did not begin for almost two decades after Gallaudet's school for the deaf opened its doors in Hartford. Perhaps it was because the blind were so few. Possibly the blind were considered hopeless subjects anyway. Whatever the reason, there were institutions for teaching the deaf and dumb from Connecticut west to Ohio and south to Virginia before the first blind asylum in the United States got under way, with six pupils, in a private home on Beacon Hill in Boston.

At almost the same time three blind waifs in the New York City almshouse were given their first lesson in reading "raised type," and in Philadelphia two Quakers named Robert Walsh and Roberts Vaux were instrumental in starting a blind school.

That the efforts of three unrelated groups should have come to a head within a year was neither miraculous nor mysterious. They were unquestionably inspired by a recent article in the *North American Review* on the education of the blind, the work of William Hickling

Prescott, virtually blind since college days at Harvard, when an accident caused loss of one eye, and the other soon failed. Using a noctograph, which was a frame crossed by a number of brass wires, and writing with an ivory stylus on carbonated paper, he was already at work on his *Ferdinand and Isabella*, a three-volume history that was to put him in the very front rank of historians, both in Europe and at home.

The name of Prescott was long since illustrious in the United States, owing in some part to the young historian's grandfather, the late and gallant Colonel William Prescott, who on Breed's Hill in '75 had admonished his men to hold their fire until they could see the whites of British eyes.

But it was the sightless eyes of his contemporaries which had inspired young Prescott's magazine article, and now three schools for the blind were opened, one after the other, in 1832. That the Boston school seemed to take first place at once, and to hold it, was due chiefly to the most extraordinary man whom the founders prevailed upon to head the venture. He was Dr. Samuel Gridley Howe, a graduate in medicine from Harvard who, instead of settling down to practice, had, like his favorite author, Lord Byron, flown off to Greece to fight the invading Turks. For six years this knight-errant Bostonian fought guerrilla-style on land, served as a surgeon on a Greek warship, and at war's end hurried home to raise money and return to the devastated country with a shipload of clothing and food. In 1830, loaded with malaria, plus a chevalier's ribbon of the Greek Order of the Redeemer, and a helmet that had been worn by Lord Byron, he returned to Boston.

The New England Asylum for the Blind had already been incorporated following a meeting in the Exchange Coffee House called by Dr. John D. Fisher, a well-known physician, who on a visit to France had been much impressed by the work with the blind of Valentin Haüy. At the Boston meeting Dr. Fisher had exhibited the embossed books Haüy used for teaching, and samples of handcrafts done by the pupils. Dr. Fisher spoke enthusiastically of how instruction and training were removing the blind from beggary in the streets of Paris and making them self-supporting. The first blind school in America was incorporated on March 2, 1829. Nothing more happened just then. Dr. Fisher knew that he himself was not the man to organize what he thought of as a crusade.

Well, here now was the dashing young Howe, home again after six exciting years of crusading against the Turk. Tradition has it that Dr. Fisher hailed Howe one day on Boylston Street and suggested that he was just the man to organize the blind school. Howe had no interest in the blind or even how they might be educated, but he was a born crusader. If he fancied himself as the heir of Byron and all other knights who had gone before, then he was not far from right. He was out to change the world. (It was only a bit later when he married a Miss Julia Ward in order, said he, to reform her.) Dr. Fisher offered him a new crusade just when he needed something to occupy the place of the Greeks. Howe took fire instantly. It was to be The Blind.

A meeting of the blind-school incorporators, who included historian Prescott, was called. It was agreed that Dr. Howe should go to Europe to see what the leading schools were up to. He did so, and investigated systems thoroughly in the British Isles, France, and Germany. It was typical of him that he rejected several methods of teaching as "primitive" even by his own knowledge, which at the time could not have been very great, in favor of methods he thought up on the spot and was to try out later. It was also characteristic of Howe the crusader that, while on this trip for information in regard to teaching the blind, he should be arrested in Prussia on the charge of "bringing aid and comfort to Polish refugees" there, and held secretly in prison for six weeks. One is quite ready to believe he was guilty, too, for then and later Howe was the complete crusader, who operated by his own conscience and not according to law. Yet he returned to Boston in mid-1832 well versed, remarked Miss Ishbel Ross, in her excellent study of education of the blind, in "the prevailing techniques," and filled with great things to be done in this new crusade. With him to Boston he brought Emile Trenchéri of the Paris school to instruct in academic learning, and John Pringle from Edinburgh as master of crafts. It is perhaps unnecessary to mention that in the Boston school both learning and crafts were shortly to bear the mark of Howe the innovator.

Dr. Howe opened the school in his father's home at 144 Pleasant Street, with six pupils, varying in age from six to twenty years. It tells something of Howe's determination to understand the plight of his charges to know that he went about blindfolded much of the time. Each day began by repeating the motto Howe declared should govern the school: "Obstacles are things to be overcome." There were no books, so Howe spent evenings in the enormous labor of sticking gummed twine on cardboard to form letters, figures, even geographic maps and simple geometrical diagrams.

At the Philadelphia blind school Dr. Julius Friedlander was working on a type for embossing books from which a printer turned out a Gospel of St. Mark in 1833, the first book in America for the blind. Howe meanwhile was devising what became known as the Howe or Boston Line-type that was dominant in America until the point type of Louis Braille was much later adopted in an improved version worked out by Dr. John D. Russ and William Bell Wait in New York. The name of the obscure and blind Louis Braille, the French genius, however, rightly adhered to the point system, which a century later is still used by the blind the world over.

Young Dr. Howe soon recognized that his greatest obstacle was to be the general attitude of a public that thought nothing whatever could be done to make the blind economically and socially independent. So, when early in 1833 his trustees told him all funds for the school were exhausted, he knew the time had come to adopt a practice he had criticized the French blind schools for using, which was to stage public demonstrations.

Taking his two outstanding pupils, Abby and Sophia Carter, six and eight years old, he went before the legislature to show the blind *reading aloud with their fingers*. It was a startling thing. It was a moving thing, too, the bright, eager little faces, bands of green ribbon covering their eyes, their small fingers running over the homemade alphabet symbols, and lisping the letters—why, they made stuff and nonsense of the innately frugal ideas of the Massachusetts assembly. Another demonstration in a theater fetched the ladies of Boston, who organized a four-day fair in Faneuil Hall where bands played and thousands came to buy the donated needlework, pies, cakes, jellies, and such. More than eleven thousand dollars was raised for the school. Howe played a brilliant part in these affairs, with the dash that men envied and caused young women to sigh. He won both to his side, and within a short time the New England public seemed agreed that Dr. Howe and his charges were the most wonderful thing that had happened in a host of years.

The wonders continued, and now came the great merchant of the China trade, Thomas Handasyd Perkins, to offer Dr. Howe his elegant mansion on Pearl Street, together with its noble grounds, as a permanent home for the school, on condition that a fund of $50,000 be raised to endow it. Dr. Howe had only to sound the call. The fund was oversubscribed within a month. Additional property was bought for a playground. Howe and thirty-odd pupils moved in, and all Boston cheered and came to call. The school was renamed the Perkins Institution and Massachusetts School for the Blind. It was to go on to great triumphs, one of which was the wholly blind and deaf and dumb Laura Dewey Bridgman, already mentioned.

This remarkable child was the eight-year-old daughter of farming people of Hanover, New Hampshire, when Howe heard of her. He and Dr. Fisher drove to the little college town on the upper Connecticut and were captivated. Laura could knit, sew, set a table correctly. In her Howe sensed an immortal spirit. He thought that with aid this intelligent and attractive child could break through the wall of night and silence. Her parents consented to let her go to Boston, where she entered the Perkins Institution late in 1837. Here she was quickly a prodigy and for fifty-two years a legend of hope for the blind and the deaf, to the glory of Dr. Howe and the school. The simplest way to describe Laura Bridgman to present generations is to say she was the Helen Keller of her time.

To release what Howe rightly guessed was an unusual mind, he began by teaching Laura to recognize twenty-six signs representing letters of the alphabet. At the same time he selected articles in common use, like knives, forks, spoons, keys, and such, and on them pasted labels with their names printed in raised letters. These she was given to feel carefully. She soon distinguished that the crooked lines of *spoon* differed as much from the crooked lines of *key* as the spoon differed in form from the key. Next, small, detached labels, with the same words embossed on them, were put into her hands. She quickly observed they were similar to the ones pasted on the articles. She showed her perception of this similarity by laying the label *key* upon the key, and label *spoon* upon the spoon. Howe encouraged her by the natural sign of approbation, patting the head.

After a great deal of this work, the individual letters, instead of the complete words, were given to her on detached pieces of cardboard, and were arranged side by side to spell *key*, or *book*, or whatever. Then Howe scrambled them into a heap, like jackstraws, and made a sign to Laura to rearrange them herself, so as to spell out the same words. She did so. Howe was elated.

Hitherto, as he explained it, the process had been mechanical; and the success of it was no greater than teaching a very knowing dog a variety of tricks. The child had sat in mute amazement, patiently imitating everything her teacher did. But now her intellect began to function. She perceived that here was a way by which she could make up a sign of anything that was in her own mind, and show it to another mind. With what feelings we can only imagine, Howe watched while the mobile little face below the green eye bandage lighted up with human emotion, with expression. This was no longer the affair of a dog, a parrot. It was an immortal spirit, eagerly seizing upon a new link of union with other spirits. Howe remembered that he could "fix upon the very moment" this truth dawned upon the girl's mind and spread its light to her countenance. The terrible obstacle had been overcome.

Now that the "unsurmountable wall" had been breached, things went ahead fast for Laura. For the next couple of years she simply *had* to know the name of every object she could handle or feel. She had learned to question so rapidly with her fingers that Howe and the other teachers were hard put to keep up with her queries. It was soon observed with wonder that when her sleep was disturbed by dreams, she started to express her thoughts in an irregular and confused manner on her fingers, just as a normal child might mutter or even cry aloud. She learned easily to write and found joy in keeping a daily journal. Howe came to believe Laura was choosing her favorite companions from among the more intelligent blind children. She obviously rejected the others unless, Howe admitted, "she can make them serve her purposes, which she is evidently inclined to do." Laura might be blind and deaf, but she was human; if she felt she were not getting the lion's share of attention, she huffed and pouted.

On his first visit to America, in 1842, Charles Dickens began his tour in Boston and was taken to visit the Perkins Institution, where he met Laura Bridgman. Though this "most eminent author in the English language" found much to displease him on his tour, and was to say so snappishly in his *American Notes*, Boston came off brilliantly, owing chiefly, it is apparent, to Dr. Howe, the inspired teacher, and his pupil. There she was before him, Laura, this fair young creature with every human faculty, and hope, and power of goodness and affection, and but one outward sense—the sense of touch. Dr. Howe had found her encased in a marble cell, impervious to any ray of light or particle of sound, with her poor white hand peeping through a chink in the wall, "beckoning to some good man for help," to release her. And help had come. Here she was now, her face radiant with intelligence and happiness, her hair braided by her own hands, her dress, made by herself, a pattern of neatness and simplicity, her writing book on the desk she leaned upon.

Then the great Englishman noticed that, like all the blind at Perkins, Laura wore a green ribbon around her eyes, and a doll she had dressed lay near. "I picked it up," Dickens remembered, "and saw that she had made a green fillet such as she wore herself and fastened it about its mimic eyes." *That fetched him* in full measure, and of the thirty pages given in his book to Boston and Cambridge, no less than fourteen were devoted to the Perkins Institution and Massachusetts Asylum for the Blind.

Horace Mann, one of Howe's closest friends, had not waited to hear the opinion of others about Howe's work. "I should rather have built up the blind asylum," he cried, "than to have written *Hamlet*." And, he hoped, if "human vitality ever gets up into the coronal region" everybody would agree about Howe's achievement. When Howe and his bride, the handsome Julia Ward, visited England presently, they were royally entertained by Mr. and Mrs. Dickens and found themselves already famous in London because Dr. Howe was the man "who had freed a soul from prison."

On return to America, Howe found Mann under fire for his long fight for free common schools for all, and leaped joyfully into the hullabaloo in time to be denounced with Mann by a phalanx of Boston schoolmasters for educational heresy. Howe was also steamed up about teaching lip reading and articulation to the deaf, which he had investigated in Holland. Though he soon learned that the Gallaudets would have nothing to do with other than the manual system, Howe, as said earlier, had a hand in establishing the Clarke School for the Deaf at Northampton, which taught the oral system. But neither the blind nor the deaf nor general education was sufficient to keep such a universal reformer as Howe away from the question of slavery. He aided and abetted the madman John Brown in his Kansas activities and also with his raid on Harper's Ferry. Old Brown was soon hanged, the war was on, and Mrs. Samuel Gridley Howe heard Union troops singing a song about Brown as they marched. The sight and the melody haunted her all night, and before dawn she was up writing that her eyes had seen the Lord's coming and heard His trampling of the grapes . . . By war's end she was virtually a hallowed figure in the North and West, and lived on, a revered and majestic presence of a sort granted to no other woman. Dr. Howe died in 1876, "temporarily overshadowed," as a biographer remarked, by his gifted wife.

Though it turned out that Dr. Howe was permanently overshadowed by the woman he had married in order to reform her, his work for the blind endured, and at Perkins he left an able successor to carry it on. He was Michael Anagnos, born in Greece, who had been Dr. Howe's secretary and had married a Howe daughter, Julia Romano, who taught at Perkins. By then the blind school had been moved into larger quarters in what had been the Mount Washington House on Dorchester Heights, a once-fashionable hotel of gray and white marble with granite stairways of brassbound steps. It was here in 1887 where Anagnos opened the first kindergarten for the blind. The idea spread rapidly to the thirty-odd states which already had established schools for the blind. Yet Michael Anagnos is remembered because it was he who brought together Anne Sullivan and Helen Keller.

Anne Sullivan was the nearly blind valedictorian of the Class of 1886 of the Perkins Institution. Helen Keller was the blind deaf-mute child of intelligent and land-poor parents of small Tuscumbia, Alabama. What they wrought together is the incomparable story in the annals of the deaf and the blind.

Born in 1880, Helen was a normal child until nineteen months old, when she was stricken so suddenly that even her mother did not suspect what had occurred until she noticed the blue eyes did not close when she bathed her. Then, Mrs. Keller discovered that the child paid no heed to the loud ringing of a bell. By the age of three it was clear the child was not only blind and deaf, but mute.

At about this time Mrs. Keller first read about Laura Bridgman, the famous prodigy of the Perkins Institution. She took Helen to see an oculist in Baltimore. He could do nothing, he said, for her sight or hearing, and suggested that she talk to Alexander G. Bell, who had done so much for the deaf. Dr. Bell was taken by the little girl, and referred Mrs. Keller to Mr. Anagnos of the Perkins Institution, and in this manner Anne Sullivan and Helen Keller were brought together. Until Miss Sullivan's death, almost fifty years later, the two were companions.

If Miss Keller is, as many believe, a born genius, then Miss Sullivan was touched with genius too. As with the case of Laura Bridgman and Dr. Howe, Miss Sullivan broke down the fearful walls that held young Helen prisoner. She did more. With the technical help of Miss Sarah Fuller she taught Helen to speak. While returning by streetcar to Perkins after her seventh lesson Helen leaned forward and said in what Miss Sullivan recalled as hollow, breathy tones: "I am not dumb now." And much later, she taught her "to hear what others say" by placing her middle finger on the nose of the speaker, her forefinger on the mouth, and her thumb on the larynx.*

Most writers about the education of the blind tend to tell the story, during the past sixty years, in relation to the brilliant record of Helen Keller, and of course, Anne Sullivan. At ten Helen learned to speak. Fourteen years later she was graduated from Radcliffe. Her favorite companions have been great Americans, from the times of John Greenleaf Whittier and Mark Twain to the present. She recited Tennyson to Dr. Oliver Wendell Holmes. She contributed articles to the *Ladies' Home Journal.* Andrew Carnegie gave her an annuity. Caruso sang with her fingers on his lips.

From the first Miss Keller devoted much of her energy and talents in aid of the American Printing House for the Blind, founded at Louisville, Kentucky, in 1879, to carry on the work begun by Dr. Howe, who himself had compiled an encyclopedia, an atlas, a dictionary, and other educational books in raised letters. By 1950, according to Ishbel Ross, in her *Journey into Light,* more than 300,000 volumes printed in Braille circulated to 11,000 readers in the United States. By then the new Talking Books, which are recorded readings, had passed the half-million circulation mark. These and many another aid to the blind, such as trained guide dogs, special typewriters and accounting

* On her first appearance on television, January 6, 1957, Miss Keller was seen by millions using this method to hear what President Dwight D. Eisenhower was saying to her. It was a most dramatic thing. Miss Sullivan was by then long dead, her place filled by the just-as-devoted Polly Thomson, associated with Miss Keller since 1914.

machines, and a host of gadgets have been encouraged by the American Foundation for the Blind, whose great friend and early backer was Major M. C. Mogel, who gave it its present home in New York City.

No seeing and hearing person is fit to comment on what has been accomplished by dreamers like Dr. Howe and Dr. Gallaudet and the many who followed in their wake. But Helen Keller is fit. "In a thousand ways," she wrote, "they have turned my limitations into beautiful privileges, and enabled me to walk serene and happy in the shadow cast by my deprivation." Much later she touched again on the subject. "Family and friends may surround you with love," she observed of the handicapped, "but consolation cannot restore usefulness, or bring release from that hardest prison, a tomb of the mind and a dungeon of the body." Only what she called expert procedures could reclaim them to normal society. Although Dr. Howe and the first Dr. Gallaudet died before Miss Keller was born, they were the primitive instigators of efforts which became the expert procedures of today and which are available to the approximately six thousand blind deaf-mutes in the United States.

Part Seven

NOTHING TO LOSE BUT CHAINS

1.

WAR ON THE MONONGAHELA

I T IS easy to mark the time, even to the day and hour, when the
dreams of abolition came to the climax to dreadful nightmare. Set
it down as the twelfth day of April, 1861, when at 4 A.M. the guns
opened up on Fort Sumter at Charleston, South Carolina.

The one other resistant reform that called for gunfire had to do with
the vaguely stated rights of labor. The first formal and organized battle
in *this* struggle began at half-past four on the morning of July 6, 1892,
at Homestead, Pennsylvania. The opposing armies here were members
of the Iron & Steel Workers, the most powerful trade-union in the
United States; and a regiment of uniformed mercenaries of the Carnegie
Steel Company, Limited, biggest producer in the Pittsburgh district.

It is not to be said that the "Battle of Homestead" was the first violence in what years before Miss Fanny Wright had named the Class War.
There had been a number of spontaneous uprisings in which blood was
shed and property destroyed. Homestead was different in that it was a
planned battle. Tactics were displayed that would have done credit to
starred generals. Use was made of every military arm except cavalry.
If savagery counts, Homestead ranks high in that quality. In short,
capital and labor had recognized for the first time the fact that they
were formally at war.

One of the Iron & Steel Workers' outpost pickets that July morning
was a man on the Smithfield Bridge over the Monongahela River at
Pittsburgh. He had been there since twilight, walking his post, now in
smoky dark, now in the eye-rocking brilliance of a Bessemer in full
blow, a sudden burst of red fire that changed to violet, indescribably
beautiful, then to orange and finally to white, when it faded into the
gloom. But the drama of making steel was old stuff to the lone man on
the bridge. It had been a long and dull night for him.

But then, in the murky half-light before dawn, at a quarter-past three,
the watching man sighted a procession coming up the river. It was a
flotilla of two tugs, each towing a scow. The man recognized the tugs.
In the lead was the *Little Bill*, the other was the *Tide*, both of the
Carnegie Steel Company's fleet. The name boards of the scows were
familiar too. One said *Iron Mountain*, the other *Monongahela*. But if

these were the same ungainly tubs ordinarily used for moving the company's steel rails, then they had been worked over to some purpose. Instead of their being open vessels, their holds were now enclosed with rugged-looking woodwork.

The man on the bridge couldn't know what the scows contained, but he knew well enough it was not good. This man's name is lost to history. But what he did, as soon as the flotilla passed under the bridge, is well known: he hurried into drowsing downtown Pittsburgh to the Western Union Telegraph office to send an eight-word message addressed to Mr. Hugh O'Donnell, Homestead, Pennsylvania.

WATCH RIVER. TWO STEAMERS WITH SCOWS LEFT HERE.

Neither the watcher on the bridge nor Hugh O'Donnell knew that inside the two big scows were an even three hundred well-armed fellows who were soon to be famous or notorious as Pinkerton men. Songs and plays, and books were to be written about them. They had been recruited, armed, and garbed in blue uniforms by the Pinkerton National Detective Agency, on the order of Henry Clay Frick, the executive official of the Carnegie Company, in which he was a heavy stockholder. They had been assembled at Ashtabula, Ohio, then brought by rail to Davis Island Dam, some six miles below Pittsburgh, and there put aboard the two scows, one of which was fitted up as a bunkhouse, the other as cookhouse and dining room. Even as the scows passed under the Smithfield Bridge, the Pinkerton men were stowing away a good solid breakfast.

Their destination, of course, was Homestead, eight miles above Pittsburgh, where stood the biggest and most modern of the several Carnegie plants. It had been closed down five days before by Mr. Frick. Mr. Frick did not like labor unions. It was not long since he had fought his coke workers to a bloody finish at nearby Connellsville, and now he meant to smash the Amalgamated Association of Iron & Steel Workers, not only at Homestead but in the other Carnegie plants.

It is more than probable that Andrew Carnegie himself didn't like unions any better than Mr. Frick did; but Carnegie had long enjoyed posing as the "Workingman's Friend," and so he went away to hide in his native Scotland, leaving Frick to do the smashing.

There was one thing about Mr. Frick. He posed as nobody's friend. The steel they made at Homestead was no harder than Frick himself. When a few weeks earlier the union refused to accept a proffered scale of wage reductions, Mr. Frick said, "Very well," then set a crew of carpenters to building a high fence around the works—a substantial barrier containing small portholes just about the right size for the barrel of a Winchester. By this time the thirty-eight hundred employees were alarmed, as they had good reason to be. The plant was shut down. Warning notices against trespass were posted. So were armed guards. It was a lockout.

Approximately eight hundred employees, all skilled workers, made up the membership of the local union, and at an emergency meeting they elected Hugh O'Donnell as a captain general of affairs. He was described as a young man of high intelligence who was capable of swift decisions. With a small, selected staff he established headquarters, organized scout and picket details, posted men around the Carnegie plant, others to watch the river and the roads, still others to watch the saloons, the keepers of which were asked to "check drunkenness and loud talk" in their places.

Though Mr. Frick characteristically made no announcement after the lockout, it was taken for granted he meant to bring in strikebreakers. With this in mind captain general O'Donnell made certain preparations.

For the first five days of July, Homestead grew tense in the strange new silence that had fallen like a blanket over the teeming mill town. No smoke came from the stacks, no cinders fell on the wash lines outside the shacks that climbed the hill in tiers back from the river. Even the new clear air had something sinister about it. On the night of the fifth people went to bed with a feeling of unease.

The cargo of trouble was steaming slowly up the dirty waters of the Monongahela. At a lock just above Pittsburgh the tug *Tide* dropped out because of engine trouble. The *Little Bill* took both scows in tow. Just as the armada came abreast of Homestead, a long low moan roused the sleeping town. It came from the whistle on the Homestead Electric Light Works, blown by the alert Hugh O'Donnell himself. He had just received the message from his picket on the Smithfield Bridge at Pittsburgh. It was now 4:25 in the morning. It was going to be quite a day.

No man on horseback roused a countryside so quickly as the blast on the Homestead whistle. The horrible, stark town back of the steelworks leaped to sudden life. Shouts came from the rambling boardinghouses near the river, yells from the clapboard shacks on the hills. Doors banged, dogs barked, children cried.

Out from the city dock darted the small *Edna,* a launch chartered by Hugh O'Donnell just in case the enemy should approach by water. The *Edna* circled the *Little Bill* and its ominous tow, hailing her. There was no reply. The tug steamed straight for the landing dock inside the steel plant's fence. Again the *Edna* ran across the tug's bow, and a man shouted a demand to know who and what were these two arks. No answer. By now the shore was alive with the figures of running men. Many of them were carrying rifles, loading as they ran. All was ready now.

The tug steamed on to the water entrance of the big works, silent inside its hulking grime. A gangplank was put out from the leading scow, and somebody's nervous finger pulled the trigger of a rifle that was loaded and went off. Whose finger it was is not known, and though a congressional committee was later to argue this point for days on end, it doesn't matter in the least. Here was a naval force of three hundred armed men in blue uniforms who were being paid a total of $1500 a day to take charge of a steel plant and to guard it.

And here was a land force of thirty-eight hundred men, many of them armed, who believed their jobs were at stake. The one certain thing at such a moment is that somebody will shoot. Somebody had, and hell followed. Captain Hinde, in command of the Pinkerton men, went down in a welter of blood on the deck of the *Iron Mountain*, and the dry crackle of rifles ran all along the shore. The men of the invading navy were shooting too, and four strikers were seen to throw up their hands and go down.

The big whistle that had set the town astir now let go again, sending its hoarse bellow into every last nook of Homestead, and into Rankin and Braddock, across the river, too. It made a suitable bass to the staccato of Marlins and Remingtons and Winchesters. On the hill back of the steel plant women screamed, then grabbed their young and ran up higher, the better to see their men shoot and be shot.

The Pinkerton men were hopelessly outnumbered. They did the only thing they could. They stayed in their scows, taking pot shots through portholes at strikers who exposed themselves. During a lull in the shooting the *Little Bill* hurriedly took aboard a number of wounded bluecoats and backed out into the river, gunfire from the shore raking her fore and aft. She steamed away to the hospital at Braddock, where, once upon a time, British and French had fought a famous battle.

The whistle and shooting had aroused the workers at the Carrie furnace on the north side of the river. The second whistle blast may have been to indicate that it was time for the strikers' artillery to get into action. In any case, it was soon after when watchers on the Homestead side saw a puff of smoke rise up from near the Carrie furnaces. They heard the scream of a cannon ball. It was a poor cannon and a poor ball, both of them cast for a war thirty years gone, but the missile tore a ragged hole in the side of the *Monongahela*. The ordnance had been taken from its place in front of the G.A.R. Hall in Braddock. The Homestead army and their women on the hills cheered for the Braddock artillery, but not for long. A second shot from the aged cannon went too high to hit the scow and just right to strike and to shear off clean the head of young Silas Wain, one of the Homestead strikers who was crouching in the steel plant's yard.

It was a hideous death in full view of the greatest audience ever to watch a spectacle on the Monongahela. It did not matter that it was a strikers' cannon that had killed a striker. There in pieces lay the body of one who would have been alive save for the Pinkerton men. The Homestead fighters and watchers went into a frenzy.

From the Grand Army Hall in Homestead men and women pulled still another old fieldpiece, wheeled it into close range of the scows, and down the ancient's throat poured powder and an iron ball that may have been cast for Richmond. They primed and fused her, then touched her off to belch fire and smoke that made fine drama, but not practical war. The shot went wild, away over into the middle of the river. Try as they would the gunners could not depress the cannon's muzzle enough. The ordnance was abandoned.

Not the battle, though. Fresh ammunition and arms had arrived from Pittsburgh for the strikers, and they swarmed toward the scows shooting at the portholes. The portholes began to flash again with telling effect. Striker George Rutter went down as he was loading his own weapon. Striker John Morris grunted, grabbed at his stomach, and fell to the ground, to stay. Striker Pete Farris came forward on the run, a bright new Marlin in his hands, just in time to stop a Pinkerton bullet, and down he went in a heap. A moment later his friend, Harris Striegel kneeled to take aim at a porthole. The porthole flared briefly and the top of Striegel's head spattered a pile of pig iron behind him.

This sort of attack would never do. Captain general O'Donnell managed to call off his men, and set them to piling iron pigs and billets and Bessemer rails to make breastworks. Sharpshooters crouched low in the shadow of huge ingots. O'Donnell then moved a quarter of a mile upstream to direct a water-borne attack. Moored in the river was a raft of lumber. Orders were shouted. Willing hands rolled a barrel of oil onto the raft. An axe swung to break the head. The black-green ooze poured out over raft and water. A hunk of flaming waste was tossed. Men with long tapping irons from the mill gave the burning raft a push.

With flames leaping high the barge of fire moved slowly with the current downstream toward the hapless scows, while the immense crowd on the hills watched. A newspaperman estimated that the audience in this great natural amphitheater had grown to more than fifteen thousand persons, and now they cheered what for a few moments seemed to be the strikers' answer to the problem. Making a heat that could be felt on the streets of Homestead, the barge continued to move ruthlessly down toward the scows. Then it stuck on something and burned itself out, while the gallery above the town groaned and wept.

"Then," said Myron Stowell, who saw it, "then, many of the strikers could be seen dragging their bodies like snakes along the inside of the steel plant's yard." They were working their way to a single exposed flatcar that stood on a railroad spur inside the plant. The track, as all could plainly see, led directly down to the dock where the scows were moored. Pushing the flatcar a little, to get it behind a pile of pig iron, the strikers had to work in a hail of bullets. None was hit, and now they could work freely under cover and they worked fast, loading the car with barrels of oil and bales of waste, and touched her off. Up leaped the flames. The hand brakes were released. Fifty sweating men heaved hard. The car moved, it rolled, it was away down the slight incline to the dock. The gallery in the hills went fairly mad.

The car of fire gathered speed as it approached the end of track, but it never quite got there. A spread rail sent it reeling off the rails into the sand alongshore, to burn harmlessly. Yet the battle was far from over, and just then the deep-throated whistle of the Homestead Electric Light Works warned strikers that some new danger was coming. It was the *Little Bill* back from her trip with dead and wounded to Braddock. What the *Little Bill* meant to do neither striker nor Pinkerton men ever knew. Before she had more than gained midstream a long rattle of gunfire broke out from behind the iron and steel breastworks. In a moment there wasn't a pane of glass in her pilothouse, and bullets ripped long splinters in her side and decks.

Inside *Little Bill* her pilot, Captain Rodgers, lay on the floor of the wheelhouse and steered the best he could, which wasn't very good. The vessel steamed around in erratic arcs, first this way, then that way, while the boys on shore made her smokestack into a sieve and her sides and lifeboats were poxed with lead bullets. Captain Rodgers was steering for his life. He managed to keep her off the Homestead shore, and soon she was out of range and heading down-river for Pittsburgh.

It was now midafternoon. The morning had been hell on shore. It must have been no less inside the scows. Fifty-odd Pinkerton men had been hit by bullets. Two of them, J. W. Klein and T. J. Connors, lay dead and covered with canvas in a corner. The bottom decks were slippery with blood. It was obvious, after the *Little Bill* had fled, that no relief could be expected. At near three o'clock a long pike-pole with an undershirt waving from its end was poked up from the scow nearer shore. A burst of gunfire from the pig iron forts shattered the staff and shredded the flag of truce. If this refusal of armistice did not let the besieged Pinkertons know what to expect, they could hear the shouting from the breastworks. It indicated no quarter. "Kill them Pinks, every one!" That was the cry.

What happened next was recalled years later by an aging man, John

Mullen, who walked with a cane because his left leg had been amputated just below the knee. He was there in 1892 as a young private in the Homestead army, and a Pinkerton bullet got him in the leg just as he was running for the Carnegie pump house to help unpack several cases of dynamite that had been rustled somewhere by a detail of strikers. The boys bound his wound with torn shirting, then laid him down behind the pump house. He'd have to stay there a while, until more important business was attended to.

"In 1892," John Mullen told this writer, "many a steel worker had started life as I had, in the coal mines, and were more familiar with blasting powder than with guns. This was as simple as breathing. The Homestead boys got out their knives, made holes for the caps in the brown sticks, bit the caps with their teeth to hold them firmly to the fuses, then stuck them into the powder. Pretty soon I saw one of the lads run out of the pump house carrying a bundle of sticks, with a short fuse that was already smoking. He waited a moment, his eye on the fuse, then he ran a few more steps and heaved the bundle."

A spume of water shot up close to the near scow. When it fell, young Mullen could see a long jagged hole just above the scow's waterline. Another bundle fell smoking to the top deck. It lay there an instant, while Mullen prayed to God, he said, that it would explode. It did. It went up with a dull roar that sent planks flying. It made a hole so large that Mullen could see forms of the Pinkerton men inside the scow. They must have been desperate indeed by then. Three or four of them started shooting through the big hole. Men with a stretcher came to move Mullen, by then bleeding copiously, to the strikers' emergency hospital in a downtown boardinghouse.

The Battle of Homestead did not lag. While the dynamite attack was going on, a detail of strikers stormed uptown to raid the Homestead Fire Hall. In a moment they came tearing back down to the plant, dragging a hose cart. One of the big Carnegie water tanks was drained, and into it a hundred men poured oil, barrel upon barrel of it, rolling them upward on inclined planks. In another moment nozzle men were flushing oil onto the surface of the river, where it swirled sluggishly, then spread to make gaudy colors all around the besieged men-of-war. Bundles of flaming waste were tossed onto the spreading oil. It took fire, to burn bluishly in spots for a few moments, but really never got to going good. It soon went out. The scows were not even scorched.

While the hose-cart attack was going forward, President William Weihle of the Iron & Steel Workers Union tried to address a few hundred of the strikers back of the breastworks. Big Bill, seven feet tall and known as the Giant Puddler, was a commanding personality, but what he had to say was drowned in shouts and the explosions of dynamite. The dynamite attack was getting results. Again the frayed undershirt on the pike pole went up.

Telling the dynamite detail ot lay off, Captain General O'Donnell walked alone and unarmed down the embankment to the scows, and he and the Pinkertons parleyed. They asked only for safe conduct out of town. O'Donnell, an honest and earnest if unduly optimistic man, agreed. He called and appointed a guard to see that the Pinkertons came off the scows without arms. Then the doomed men were formed in double file and began the march uptown.

The plan was to escort the strangers to an old skating rink and to hold them there under guard until they could be safely moved out of town. It might have worked out that way had it not been for the wives of strikers. As the blue-clad men began to move up the terrible gantlet, screaming women set upon them. Using sticks, stones, tooth, and claw, they attacked with the singular abandon often noted in mobs of females. One harridan ran the sharp end of an umbrella into a Pinkerton's eye. It stuck there until he pulled it out himself. Others of the strangers were torn from the line of march by wild harpies who fell on them with awful fury and the design of sadistic obscenities.

Boys threw rocks and all manner of filth. Large, infuriated men yanked bluecoats from the ranks and beat them terribly. Forty-odd of the Pinkertons did not finish the march at all; they had to be dragged or carried to the skating-rink guardhouse.

Another mob was busy at the dock, pouring oil into the scows. The fire spread to the pump house and from it flames rose higher than the mill stacks. It all made a wonderfully fitting end to America's greatest industrial battle up to then, perhaps till now. Fourteen men were either dead or about to die. The seriously wounded numbered one hundred and sixty-three.

Newspapermen were pouring into Homestead from New York, Chicago, and elsewhere. For another five days the strikers ruled the town. State troops moved in on the twelfth and took over.

The Battle of Homestead shocked the nation. Until then few Americans suspected that the cleavage between workingmen and employers had reached the stage of organized warfare. In Congress, Senator John McCauley Palmer, Democrat of Illinois, arose to compare conditions to those of the Middle Ages, when barons rented their armies to kings, and remarked that the workers of Homestead or anywhere else had the right to resist attacks of mercenaries "in defense of their jobs and homes." Industrial corporations, said the senator, "must hereafter be regarded as holding their property subject to the correlative rights of those without whose services the property would be utterly valueless."

Public opinion may have not swung wholeheartedly to the Homestead strikers, but it turned wholeheartedly against Henry Clay Frick, Andrew Carnegie, and the steel company. Indicative of the revulsion toward "private mercenary armies" was a song that speedily appeared and became popular in beer gardens and variety houses in the Eastern states. It belongs with the earlier ballads against slavery, cal-o-mel, and rum in the category of rabble-rousers:

> *God help them tonight in their hour of affliction,*
> *Praying for him whom they'll ne'er see again.*
> *Hear the poor orphans tell their sad story;*
> *"Father was killed by the Pinkerton Men!"*

It is well not to dismiss maudlin doggerel. This tear-jerker was sung, both with and without colored slides, for another decade or more, and one can believe it had some effect in keeping fresh the horrors of Homestead. In the early weeks after the battle, however, the facts alone were sufficient to give the public grave thought which, in time, might have supported the stand taken by the Iron & Steel Workers Union. There wasn't time. This was the critical moment selected by a vain psychopath to commit a piece of idiotic violence that set public opinion swinging immediately against the rights of labor.

It was July 23. Seventeen days had passed since the battle. Henry Clay Frick sat in his office in downtown Pittsburgh. Suddenly a slight, dark young man entered, pulled a revolver from his pocket, and shot twice. Blood poured out of Frick's neck and ran down over his well-trimmed beard as he staggered to his feet. The second bullet took off part of his left ear. He grappled with the stranger as attendants came running to disarm the fellow, who tore away, a knife in his hand, stabbing Frick viciously. Frick was bloody, and game. He pointed to the assassin's mouth. "What is he chewing on?" he demanded. They choked the man and took a small capsule from his mouth.

The young man said his name was Alexander Berkman and that the melodramatic capsule contained "enough fulminate of mercury to blow us all to bits." He was a Polish-Russian immigrant of recent date who had come to America, he said, to help the downtrodden workers. His one idea of helping the slaves to lose their chains was to assassinate Mr. Frick the steel master. Berkman was no steelworker. He had no connection with Homestead, nor with the union workers. They had never heard of him. He had come alone from New York to perpetrate this piece of exhibitionism.

As a killer Berkman was as great a failure as he was a propagandist for labor. Toting a gun, a knife, and fulminate of mercury, he could manage only to wound his victim; and his victim displayed qualities which, if they did not quite make him a hero, brought him the admiration that goes of right to a man of iron nerve and determination. After the attack Frick remained in his office, bandaged head and neck, until the day's work was done, when doctors came to remove the bullet. He refused anesthetic. "I can help you probe better without it," he said. That night from his home Frick issued a statement, to the effect that no matter what happened to him, the policy of the Carnegie Steel Company would be henceforth to operate all of its plants with non-union crews. What had been a distinctly hostile press changed overnight. "Those who hate Mr. Frick most," observed the New York *World*, "admire the nerve and stamina of this man of steel whom nothing seems to be able to move." The *World* reporter had found Frick at his desk, looking slightly paler than usual and behind one ear "a hole stuffed with cotton."

The public quite naturally confused matters and put Berkman down as "one of the Homestead Rioters." Many a good union man, not only in steel but in other lines, cursed the name, not of Frick, but Berkman, an arrogant punk who fancied himself a liberator of chained and exploited labor. Not for forty-five years after Berkman's contribution did a steelworkers' union amount to much in the United States.

2.

THE NOBLE ORDER OF KNIGHTS

No ONE in the country could have been more appalled at the Battle of Homestead than idealistic Terence V. Powderly, Grand Master Workman of the Noble Order of the Knights of Labor, and for thirteen years the outstanding figure of organized labor in the United States. Homestead seemed final proof that workers would wait no longer for the peaceful, gradual establishment of a vague co-operative brotherhood of capital and labor which the fuzzy Knights promised would fix up everybody and everything, fine and dandy.

The Iron & Steel Workers union was no part of the Knights. It was affiliated with the new American Federation of Labor, which had no interest in co-operative brotherhoods but applied itself to the immediate problems of bread and butter and wages and hours. The day of the dreamy labor reformer was done, or so it seemed to Powderly, who soon resigned from the Knights to enter the law and politics. The new day belonged to the hard-boiled businessman type, ready to threaten, or fight, or to "make a deal" with employers of labor, according to which seemed most likely to result in higher wages and better working conditions. The difference between the old and the new kind of unions was to be seen even in the terminology used; the former had a "walking delegate," the latter called him a "*business* agent."

Terence Powderly was not the last of the idealistic leaders of labor. Debs and Haywood were to come later, but they were aggressive dreamers in such haste for Utopia, as we shall see, that they ran too fast and too far for their fellows. Powderly was in no hurry at all. He thought of his Knights as a great educational organization destined to usher in a Peaceable Kingdom of Labor and Capital. So had Uriah Stephens, who founded the Knights back in 1869; and before him William H. Sylvis had attempted something similar with the National Labor Union. None of these men put too much faith in economic action alone. Strikes might be necessary, and boycotts too, but along with these deplorable things must go arbitration of disputes, tenement house reform, workingmen's lyceums and reading rooms, free public lands, monetary reform like Greenbackism, votes for women, and even temperance.

These and other side issues were not a part of the original efforts of labor groups in colonial days and the early republic. In those times the virtually nonexistent rights of labor comprised little more than the right to eat sufficiently well to permit a man to work, though the Calkers' Club of Massachusetts Bay was astute politically, stating that one of its objects was "to lay plans for introducing certain persons into places of power and trust." Samuel Adams and other leaders of the period were quick to use the Calkers to advance their plans for revolution, and this may have been the origin of *caucus*, to describe political plotting. The Calkers Club was credited with considerable harassment of English troops, and after the war it was offering prizes "for the discovery of ways and means to cripple English trade." In 1817 one crew of Calkers broke out in a roaring strike because their employer, one Thatcher Magoun, had stopped their rum allowance. (They lost.)

As early as 1741 the bakers of New York City were arrested, tried, and convicted on the charge of conspiracy; they had refused to bake until their wages were increased, but there is no record that they were sentenced to any punishment. It was this anti-conspiracy law which kept labor fettered. It was held to be a conspiracy in restraint of trade for three or more workingmen to refuse to work at their usual jobs. It was used more or less effectively against the shoemakers of Philadelphia, the Typographical Society of New York, and the tailors and carpenters there also. William Cullen Bryant was one, if not the first, of the editors of daily newspapers to protest against the courts in the tailors' case. In his New York *Evening Post* the most famous American poet of the day wrote: "Strike the right of associating for the sale of labor from the privileges of freemen, and you may as well at once bind him to a master or ascribe him to the soil ..." But the author of *Thanatopsis* was, after all, a poet, hence a dreamer, who knew nothing about economic or business matters, and the conspiracy weapon continued to be used for another half-dozen years.

Yet, in 1842, Lemuel Shaw, the noted chief justice of the Massachusetts Supreme Court, handed down a decision which went far to provide a sound base for the legality of unions. It had to do with the Journeymen Bootmakers' Society of Boston, whose members had agreed not to work in any shop employing a person not a member of the society or union. Shaw found that common action to achieve a lawful object was not of necessity a criminal conspiracy. Though the decision left the sizable loophole of what was and what was not a lawful object, it gave support to the closed-shop idea.

Long before Justice Shaw's decision labor unions formed to raise wages and shorten hours sought to disguise their real nature with innocent-sounding names like the Columbian Charitable Society of Shipwrights and Caulkers. A little later, as idealism began to take hold of the leaders, if not of the rank and file, the romantic flavor of holy crusade appeared in the style of plain labor unions, such as the Knights of St. Crispin, the Sons of Vulcan, and the Sovereigns of Industry. The first labor paper in the United States, founded by the Evans brothers, started business by admitting it was the *Workingman's Advocate*, later became the *Daily Sentinel*, and still later was called *Young America*.

The first figure to achieve anything like a national status in the labor movement was William H. Sylvis, a native of Armagh, Pennsylvania, who learned his trade of iron-molding in the Forest Iron Works of Union County, from which he was "graduated" in about 1848, and took to the road in what he called his "freedom suit," a broadcloth coat, white shirt, woolen stockings, calfskin boots, and high silk hat. These marked his new status as a journeyman molder. After a few years of wandering from job to job, he took part in a strike staged by the Stove & Hollow-Ware Moulders in Philadelphia. This effort seems to have unleashed latent abilities which neither he nor his fellow unionists had suspected. Within a year he had issued a call for what became the Iron-Moulders International Union, and his eloquent address so stirred the delegates that it was made the preamble of the new union's constitution.

Two months before Sumter was fired upon, Sylvis called a convention of "Workingmen Opposed to War," but when the shooting started he helped to recruit a company for the Northern army. He declined the lieutenancy offered but enlisted as a teamster for nine months, then returned to civilian life and, singlehanded, reorganized the war-torn molders. The molders emerged from the war years by far the most powerful and best-disciplined union in the United States. A marvelous dream had taken hold of Sylvis, and now seemed a good time to bring it to reality. Though he never stated it clearly, for he was never a didactic man, his objective was some sort of a co-operative commonwealth. It was not to be a dictatorship of the proletariat, such as Marx was soon to announce, but rather an all-out society with room for all classes except "the monied aristocracy." The profit motive was to be replaced by co-operative groups, exchanging products and services.

Now, though still only in his thirties, Sylvis set out to organize the nucleus of the new society. This was the National Labor Union. He had something of the personal appeal that commands loyalty and affection, the same appeal men were to find later in Henry George and Eugene Debs. He was of medium height, with a light beard and mustache, and "a face and eyes beaming with intelligence." He had little money of his own, and though the molders voted him small sums from time to time, he ranged the East and the Middle West mostly by riding in freight cars, or often in the cabs of friendly locomotive engineers. His clothes became worn and shabby. His enthusiasm did not. One after the other trade-unions signed up for the National, and in 1868 delegates representing more than 600,000 workingmen elected Sylvis president of the National Labor Union. Nothing like it had happened before. One of President Sylvis's first acts was to appoint a lobbying committee to remain in Washington during sessions of Congress. Their duties were to promote legislation for an eight-hour day, and a host of other things including the enforced arbitration of labor conflicts. (Sylvis had been from the first against the strike as a weapon.) Though he did not bring temperance into the activities of the National Labor Union, he himself was an active temperance worker, and was also devoted to money reform and the rights of woman. In fact, his many interests alone would doubtless have prevented the National Labor Union from achieving anything like the success he had hoped for, and when he died in 1869, it began to disintegrate almost at once. No matter the failure, Sylvis had at least accomplished one thing, which was to spread the idea of organized labor as nothing before had done.

In the very year Sylvis died nine tailors of Philadelphia met in the firehouse of the American Hose Company to organize a society dreamed up by one of their number, Uriah Stephens, an incurable romantic forty-eight years old who had been educated for the Baptist ministry, taught school, learned the trade of garment cutter, then went awandering to the West Indies, Mexico, and California before settling down in Philadelphia to help organize the local tailors into a union which proved ineffective. Because it had failed in large part through pressure by the employing tailors, this new group was to be not an "open union" but a secret one.

Possibly because he was already a member of the Masonic order, the Ancient Order of Odd Fellows, and the Knights of Pythias, Uriah Stephens composed an elaborate ritual and the imposing style of the Noble Order of the Knights of Labor for the new group. But its name was to be kept secret. To all outsiders the society was to be known, and of course puzzled over, as the Five Stars, though in print it would be simply asterisks *****, thus.

The goal of the Five Stars did not concern current wages and working conditions. When the time came the Noble Order of the Knights of Labor was to come into the open, to reveal its majesty as a single unified fraternity founded, so founder Stephens described it, "upon the immutable basis of the Fatherhood of God, and the logical principle of the Brotherhood of Man." Though membership was generally open to all wage earners and even former wage earners, there were certain exceptions. These were specified by name as lawyers, doctors, bankers, stockbrokers, professional gamblers, and dealers in or makers of liquor. "Thus," pointedly remarked a provision in the constitution of the Noble Order of the Knights of Labor, "thus we gather into one fold all branches of honorable toil." What was to happen to the untouchables was left unclear. Possibly they were cited because of personal prejudices of Baptist Stephens, who, in any case, was hardly consistent, for the constitution stated elsewhere that the Knights had "no quarrel with legitimate enterprise, no antagonism to necessary capital."

Progress of the Five Stars was slow. More than two years passed before a second lodge—or assembly—was organized. This was made up of Philadelphia ship carpenters. By 1878 the Five Stars had assemblies in New York, New Jersey, West Virginia, Ohio, Indiana, Illinois. Members included railway workers, miners, iron- and steelworkers, both skilled and unskilled, and numbered almost ten thousand. Then, in convention at Reading, delegates set up a general assembly as supreme authority and elected Terence Powderly to be Grand Master Workman, a title straight out of the realm of social fraternities. The most important act of the general assembly was to remove its secrecy. The Five Stars euphemism was dropped. The Noble Order of the Knights of Labor appeared in shining armor. No longer would meetings be called "by five stars and a circle enclosing a triangle marked on sidewalks, and walls," or by an anonymously signed notice in a newspaper. Secrecy may well have induced many to join the order and unquestionably acted as a protection against attacks by employers, but the Knights thought it best to free themselves of any ambiguity because still fresh in public memory was the hanging of ten members of the secret terrorist society of the Molly Maguires by the state of Pennsylvania.

Though the Molly Maguires were a very special group and were no part of the mainstream of American labor movements, they muddied the water not a little. The name was that used by a secret ring of members of the Ancient Order of Hibernians, which had been organized in Ireland to oppose the encroachments of landlords but in the United States was maintained to seek control of relations between miners and mine operators. Membership was composed wholly of Irish Roman Catholics, but the order never had sanction of the Church. Its operations were largely confined to the hard-coal or anthracite mining region of Pennsylvania, in which state it had been incorporated as a "humane, charitable, and benevolent order." The activities of the Mollies made the avowed benign purpose of the Hibernians appear like a euphemism blown up out of hell itself.

The first murder of a mine boss laid to the Mollies occurred on June 14, 1862, in Carbon County. More than fifty other bosses or company men died from violence in the region during the next two years; and uncounted beatings of men and acts of sabotage were reported. Arrest of suspects got nowhere. Perjury was a pleasure to commit. After a brief lull violence resumed in 1871 and steadily increased until late in 1875, when wholesale arrests brought scores of alleged Mollies to jail. Twenty-four were convicted by the evidence collected by James Mc-Parlan, a spy-detective employed by the Pinkerton National Detective Agency. As Jim McKenna, the Pinkerton agent had lived among the miners with whom he worked, drank, sang, and danced, posing as a fugitive from justice and part-time counterfeiter. He was accepted at face value and was soon a member, then an officer of the Ancient Order of Hibernians. Fourteen men were sent to prison. Ten were executed.

The trials were still progressing in the courts when the Mollies and most other news were pushed off the front pages by a spontaneous upheaval of railroad workers that for three weeks during the summer of 1877 seemed destined to bring all the lines to ruin. A wage cut was the spark. Tinder was ready from four years of general economic depression. Except for the Brotherhood of the Footboard, which had only recently changed its style to Locomotive Engineers, the strikers were mostly unorganized. The strike spread with startling speed. Troops were called out here and there. Public sympathy was largely with the strikers because, wrote an observer, the railroads for years had engaged "in a saturnalia of plunder through excessive rates and fares, stock manipulation, bribery and other forms of fraud." When the smoke cleared, more than one hundred men had been killed, several hundred hospitalized, and property valued at millions of dollars destroyed.

The Knights of Labor took no part in the disturbances, yet the over-all effect was invigorating by making it clear to the working class that disorganized mobs could win nothing from employers who closed ranks to present a more or less united front. Before the year was out, thousands joined the new Socialist Labor party, and more thousands joined the Knights. Economic conditions improved for about five years, then worsened and were accompanied by the usual wage cuts and lay-offs, and walkouts and strikes. Grand Master Workman Powderly remained firm against strikes as ever—and against liquor, too—but he could not control the local assemblies of the Knights, which struck and struck again in the textile industry; in support of the shoemakers, carpet weavers, molders, telegraphers; and finally to support shopmen employed by the Wabash and the Union Pacific railroad systems. These two affairs were important strikes and the Knights won them. Despite Powderly, who continued to press the idea of co-operatives as the way to Utopia, the rank-and-file Knights, and often its board of directors, demanded action.

Then, as times grew better, the Knights went into a spectacular boom during which organizers could hardly cope with the demand for organizing new locals. In a single year total membership of the Knights rose from 100,000 to more than 700,000. The labor movement in the United States had seen nothing like it. Here was the one big union to bring in the co-operative commonwealth of labor. Or such was Powderly's idea. He soon discovered he had completely lost control of his host. They were not interested in their Grand Master Workman's vision. They wanted simple things and wanted them now—better wages and a shorter workday.

The press looked at this phenomenal labor union with the suspicion or fear that is often directed toward anything new or strange. Was it not a monster that could stay the nimble touch of the telegrapher or the heavy stroke of the tracklayer? That by edict could compel its subjects to buy this product, to refrain from buying that one? Would it not array labor against capital, both for stubborn self-protection, or for violent organized assault?

Unquestionably the Knights began to feel the sudden power that had come to them. Poor Powderly complained to his directors that the Knights had turned arrogant, that arrogance went always before a fall, that the co-operative commonwealth was in danger. He complained again that, though he was against strikes, his Knights were doing little else but strike and "making enemies." He sat morosely in his sanctum, while the press called him the Czar of All Workingmen, and stroked the "most magnificent moustaches in the country"; complaining that, far from being a czar of labor, he could not even control the activities of the smallest and most remote local union of the Noble Order.

While the Knights were climbing to their new eminence, there had come to the United States a German anarchist, Johann Most, a man of striking looks and personality possessed of a violent temperament, who in New York began publication of a German-language paper, *Freiheit*. With a picturesque background of prisons in Berlin and Vienna he had also served a term in London for extolling the assassination of Czar Alexander II by Russian nihilists in 1881. He was hailed as a hero in New York by the small group who called themselves anarchists. In addition to editing his paper, Most wrote a sort of handbook with the alluring title of *Science of Revolutionary Warfare; or, a Manual of Instruction in the Use and Preparation of Nitroglycerine, Dynamite, Gun-Cotton, Fulminating Mercury, Bombs, Fuses, Poisons, etc., etc.*

In Chicago at this time was Albert Parsons, who had been the Socialist Labor candidate for mayor and was now editing *The Alarm*, a propaganda paper for something called the International Working People's Party. Parsons found Herr Most's handbook of interest, and began publishing extracts from it, such as the essay on dynamite, which wasted no words:

Dynamite! Of all the good stuff, that is the stuff! Stuff several pounds of this sublime stuff into an inch pipe (gas or water pipe), plug up both ends, insert the cap with fuse attached, place this in the immediate vicinity of a lot of rich loafers who live by the sweat of other people's brows, and light the fuse. A most cheerful and gratifying result will follow.

This was the kind of material Parsons was printing in 1885, when Powderly was preaching the peaceful idealism of the co-operative commonwealth of toil. Between these two extremes was the precursor of the American Federation of Labor, then known as the Federation of Organized Trades and Labor Unions and which, at its annual convention, adopted a mild resolution calling for an eight-hour day in all industries. The federation leaders knew well enough that their less-than-50,000-member group would get nowhere without help from the Noble Order of the Knights. The Knights ignored an invitation to join in an eight-hour demonstration planned for May 1, 1886. Grand Master Workman Powderly did not consider the eight-hour day as a panacea for anything; he said so in many words, publicly, and six weeks before the date set he issued a private circular to the officers of local assemblies to the same effect.

Not much of anything happened on May 1. On the third, however, riots broke out at the plant of the McCormick Reaper Works in Chicago, where a lockout had been in progress. Scab labor was now brought in and the strangers attacked by the discharged union employes of the works. Police were called. Shooting started, and left six men dead and many wounded. Only a couple of hours later thousands of circulars were distributed on the streets. They were printed in both English and German, and in big black type said: REVENGE! WORKINGMEN TO ARMS! The smaller text related that "six of your brothers" had been killed by police that afternoon because "the poor wretches had the temerity to disobey the supreme will of your bosses," and demanded that the hideous monster of capital be destroyed. *"To arms! We call you to arms!"*

Next morning the streets were snowed with small leaflets calling all workingmen to a mass meeting of protest in the Haymarket, Randolph Street, between Desplaines and Halstead. The time was announced for half-past seven. It was May 4.

Mayor Carter H. Harrison read one of the leaflets. He told the police to keep hands off the meeting. Let them talk. Though the mayor had grown rich in real estate, and loved fine cigars and silk underwear, he championed the proletariat. He had declared publicly that nine out of every ten citizens were with the workers who wanted the eight-hour day. Let them talk. He himself would attend this street meeting in the Haymarket.

He was there, too, among the three thousand or more men, women, and children, when the speaking began. The weather, which had been bleak and windy, turned to rain. The crowd started thinning rapidly. The mayor stayed on, lighting match after match to relight his cigar. When a friend suggested he stop it, lest he draw violence to himself, he replied that he wanted the people to know their mayor was there. He was their friend. After a while he went back to the Desplaines Street police station to tell the chief it was a tame meeting, that nothing was likely to occur, and that the reserves who were standing by in case of emergency should be sent home. The orders were given. The mayor and the chief went home. This left Inspector Bonfield in charge.

The rain continued to fall, the crowd continued to thin, leaving less than five hundred men to hear the last speaker, who was Samuel Fielden, an Englishman and ex-Methodist minister. A police detective in the audience listened briefly to Fielden, then ran to the station to inform Inspector Bonfield that the orator had said that "the law must be throttled, killed, and stabbed." Bonfield was both brave and excitable. He had been on the carpet before for his rashness, and now his temperament betrayed him. Ordering one hundred and seventy-six of his men to fall in, he marched them to the Haymarket.

Samuel Fielden had just reached his concluding remarks when the police came into the square, and Captain Ward stepped out of the front rank and shouted for the crowd to disperse "in a peaceable manner." There was a moment of silence.

"Why, Captain," said Fielden, "we *are* peaceable."

Again silence, then a blinding flash, and the Haymarket filled with noise and smoke. It was a bomb tossed by an unknown hand, and it must have contained a mighty charge, for sixty-seven police went down on the cobblestones, seven to die, the others to go to hospitals.

Inspector Bonfield ordered his men to fire, and they did, wounding each other and also hitting many of the crowd who were trying to get out of there as soon as possible. How many of the crowd were killed was never known, though police thought the number was large but that the victims had been spirited away during the excitement.

Chicago was first stunned, less perhaps by the carnage in the Haymarket than by the incredible fact that a bomb, the notoriously classic weapon of Old World anarchism, had exploded in the heart of the great busy city by the lake. Stark horror seemed to have Chicago in its grip—speechless, motionless, helpless. Only briefly. Then came hysteria. Anarchists with bombs were reported moving in the alleys, or plotting in the rooming houses of the spreading slums. The police staged raid after raid, and appeared to have found the most incriminating evidence in places where it would result in the most harm to the alleged anarchist "leaders," who, save for Parsons, the American, and Fielding, the Englishman, were "foreigners" with names like Spies, Schwab, Fischer, Engel, Lingg, Neebe, Seliger, and Schnaubelt.

Arrested also in wholesale lots were several hundred workingmen suspected—said the police—of maintaining "dynamiter's lairs." Revenge may well have prompted the police to unusual ferocity, and they beat and otherwise abused scores of innocent men who were not even members of a labor union. The public was demanding a good dose of hanging, and the hysteria moved swiftly to its ordained goal. Indictments were made, and in June seven alleged anarchist leaders went on trial. The proceedings had begun, when into the courtroom walked Albert Parsons, editor of *The Alarm,* who had escaped from the Haymarket while smoke still hung in the air, to flee into Wisconsin. He had returned of his own volition to stand for the cause, he said, with his brave comrades.

Justice, or at least the law, was swift and sure. All were found guilty of conspiring to commit murder, even though nothing approaching evidence as to who threw the bomb was uncovered. Four men,

Parsons among them, were hanged. One, Lingg, committed suicide in his cell by exploding a dynamite cartridge between his teeth. The death sentences of the other three were commuted to imprisonment for life by Governor Richard Oglesby.

There remained one other who was to become a victim of the Haymarket affair. In 1893 John P. Altgeld, governor of Illinois, pardoned Fielden, Neebe, and Schwab, and stated his reasons clearly. These men, said he, had been convicted in a trial that had been both unfair and illegal. It was an act of mercy as courageous as any ever performed by a man in public life. And it brought the ordained reward—personal abuse, the wrecking of Altgeld's political career, and unquestionably had a great deal to do with bringing about his financial ruin.

It was also ordained that the hanged anarchists should become suitable martyrs to what left-wing orators for many years never referred to other than the Cause of Labor, though, no matter who tossed the bomb, the Haymarket affair was really a disaster to the cause of labor. It set radical and conservative elements bitterly at odds with each other. It prejudiced the public against labor, organized or otherwise. It presented employers with the best kind of excuse for almost any sort of action they cared to employ against unions. It stopped the rising eight-hour movement dead in its tracks. Above all else, the Haymarket introduced a new and dangerous force into industrial strife.

Not long before he was hanged, Albert Parsons explained it. Dynamite, he said, was a symbol of power which made one poor man equal to a king's army. Gunpowder had freed the common man from the tyranny of the robber barons in feudal times. "Dynamite," he went on, "is democratic; it makes everybody equal. The Pinkertons, the police, the militia, are absolutely worthless in the presence of dynamite. They can do nothing with the people at all. Dynamite is the equilibrium. It is the annihilator. It is the disseminator of authority; it is the dawn of peace; it is the end of war. It is man's best and last friend; it emancipates the world from the domineering of the few over the many, because all government in the last resort, is violence; all law, in the last resort, is force. Force is the law of nature, and this dynamite— this newly discovered force, makes all men equal and therefore free."

This prescription for equality and freedom was going to be given a thorough tryout during the next two decades before it was seen to be a delusion as fatuous as that of the grandiose co-operative commonwealth of labor dreamed up by old Powderly for his antique if Noble Order of the Knights of Labor.

3.

COXEY'S ARMY OF THE COMMONWEAL

The Haymarket bomb served to separate the sheep from the goats, the boys from the men. Which was which depended on where one stood. More accurately, the Haymarket affair divided labor into two camps, one led by dreamers, the other by hard-boiled opportunists.

The idealistic Knights of Labor started to fall apart even before the anarchists had been hanged or sent to prison; while the far-from-idealistic American Federation of Labor was even then being organized with the simple plan of getting everything it could, not only at the expense of employers but also at the expense of the unorganized proletariat, of organized labor outside the new federation, and of the country as a whole. Get all you can, let the devil have the rest—that seemed to be the motto. To head this pragmatic outfit, Samuel Gompers was elected, a man as practical as Andrew Carnegie or John D. Rockefeller.

The American Federation was just the sort of group able to survive the troubled last decade of the nineteenth century. Cautious, hard-headed, and conservative Sam Gompers took office planning to profit by the blunders of the fuzzy Knights, and to let any ultraradical groups as wanted to fight most of labor's battles in the open field, while the federation would be ready to take advantage of their victories and defeats.

The first great formal battle in the industrial wars of the nineties was, as related, the affair at Homestead, Pennsylvania. At almost the same time trouble that had long been brewing came to a head in the remote Coeur d'Alene region of Idaho, when the hard-rock miners protested the importation of eighty non-union men by the Helena & Frisco company. Shooting started. Five union men were killed by mine guards, while other protesters were climbing the sheer wall of a mountain above the mill, toting cases of dynamite. There they shut off the water in the flume that led to the mill, then let case after case of the explosive go sliding down the dry flume, the last case smoking from a fuse. The Frisco mill went up like an umbrella. Federal troops arrived. Martial law was declared, and hundreds of miners were rounded up and placed in stockades. A grand jury returned almost five hundred indictments. No miner was convicted of a crime. The most important result of this isolated battle was the organization in Butte, Montana, of the Western Federation of Miners, which only in name was to resemble the American Federation.

The mercurial elements of life in the United States were perhaps never made so clear as in 1893. The greatest world's fair ever seen on this side of the Atlantic opened in Chicago with thunders of music and flurries of rockets and Roman candles. The year closed in a black and bitter winter with factories closed, three million men vainly seeking work, and long bread lines in Boston, New York, Chicago, and all other centers. One read in the papers that it was a financial panic brought about because the government of British India had suspended the free coinage of silver. Although the causes were many, it did not matter too much to workingmen who were suddenly turned into mendicants. All they knew was that something was damnably wrong in the United States of America.

The time was ripe for the legendary Man on Horseback, and he appeared in a sudden flash of light that illuminated small Massillon, Ohio, then spread to the far corners of the republic. He was Jacob S. Coxey, a man who, for all his successful stone quarry and heretofore blameless and conventional life, was as filled with assorted dreams as any young poet mooning over Dawn or Love or Niagara Falls. Long a devoted Greenbacker inflationist, he had joined the Populists in 1892, and was also a convert to theosophy, the doctrines of which included a belief in reincarnation. Drawing possibly upon all three sources, he had arrived at the one sure remedy for poverty. This was the Coxey Plan: The United States Treasury would issue five hundred million dollars in legal-tender notes to be expended on good roads throughout the country. All idle men who applied were to be given work at not less than $1.50 for a day of eight hours. By putting the government into competition with private industry all employers who paid less or demanded longer hours would automatically find themselves in hard case. It would settle the rising eight-hour agitation without difficulty.

To publicize this simple prescription for prosperity, its well-heeled propounder organized the J. S. Coxey Good Roads Association of the United States. He wrote a bill embodying the idea and got a friendly congressman to introduce it in the House. And now, in 1893, when Chicago was crowded with the hundreds of thousands come to see the great world's fair, Coxey engaged a man of many talents to go forth and tell the good tidings to the people. This was Carl Browne, a native of Iowa, a tall, heavy type with long unkempt hair streaked with gray, who wore a combination goatee and mustache arrangement like that of Buffalo Bill Cody. His buckskin getup also was inspired by Cody, though it was a shoddy imitation of the superbly turned out Prince of the Plains.

Among several other qualities Browne had a voice like that of a locomotive. He had developed it while agitating for Denis Kearney's anti-Chinese party on the sand lots of San Francisco. He had edited radical labor organs for which he also drew cartoons. He also was a religious fanatic devoted to the teachings of the late Helena Petrovna Blavatsky, a hypnotic charlatan, editor of *Lucifer*, author of *The Key to Theosophy*.

To convert the Philistines to the J. S. Coxey Good Roads idea, Browne prepared a "financial panorama" illustrating the evils of the existing economic system, plus the happy times to follow just as soon as the proposed legislation became law. He rigged the panorama on a frame, nailed it to a farm wagon, hitched on a pair of horses, and set out overland like any high-pitch medicine man, to sell the elixir of prosperity. In Chicago he staged a series of open-air meetings on the lake front that were so successful the city authorities ordered him to leave town.

It is more than possible Browne had had run-ins with the police in the past. He knew how to handle things. Removing his sombrero, high boots, and fringed jacket, he got a haircut and returned to Chicago, where a kindly man of medicine, old Doc Bozarro, permitted him to act as his assistant with a platform show dispensing Kickapoo Indian Sagwa. It was understood that during the show Browne should dispense the good word about Coxey's plan, about Populism in general, and also speak well for theosophy. It all turned out wonderfully fine, leaving "untold thousands" converted to the Coxey Plan. At season's end Browne returned to Massillon to commune with his employer.

As a heartbreaking winter approached, discontent prompted more than a million Americans to cast their presidential votes for General James B. Weaver, candidate of the new People's party, whose members called themselves Populists. The bread lines grew longer. More factories were shut down. Foreclosed mortgages piled up. Farmers burned their ten-cent corn for fuel. In small Massillon, Ohio, Coxey and Browne burned midnight oil to think up some way to dramatize the desperate plight of the country and force the administration to act; and one pregnant evening an idea came to Coxey with all the force of true prophecy. "Browne," he cried, "we will send a petition to Washington with boots on!"

In 1894, when Coxey was ready to announce it in late January, the idea of a march on the national capital was a mind shaker, a revolutionary thing such as could have been conceived only by a genius of evil or a patriotic savior to deliver the republic from impending destruction. Working like the madmen they were, Coxey and Browne wrote pamphlets and circulars which by mid-February were being distributed by the ton. The purpose of the march was naturally to urge Congress to pass Coxey's Good Roads Bill. The marchers were to come not only from Massillion, which was merely headquarters to organize and lead the event, but from all parts of the United States. The vast army was to arrive in Washington in time to stage a monster demonstration before the steps of the Capitol at noon on May 1.

The press may well have been cynical of the plan, but certainly it was a good story and fit to be deplored or ridiculed editorially, and Jacob Coxey was quickly made into a national character. Browne got a good deal of mention too, and rightly, for he was not short of ideas, one of which was that the marchers were an Army of Peace carrying the standard of Jesus Christ before which neither hell nor the minions of the devil of Wall Street could long stand. Indeed, the hosts rising like magic from the grass roots and the city pavements would march as the Commonweal Army of Christ. Hardly pausing, artist-cartoonist Browne got out his oils and forthwith painted the banner of the Commonweal. This turned out to be a striking portrait of Christ which reporters thought bore more than a casual resemblance to Browne himself, who had refashioned his neo-Cody whiskers in the manner of conventional portraits of the Saviour. Beneath the picture was an unforgettable legend: "Peace on Earth Good Will to Men, He Hath Risen but Death to Interest on Bonds."

The "Bonds" referred to a second or supplementary idea of Coxey, who proposed that municipal improvements be financed by federal loans covered by non-interest-bearing bonds.

The press was enchanted. From this time on Coxey had to spend his money no longer to get publicity. The newspapers of the United States, from metropolitan dailies to the smallest country weeklies, were delighted to have something to print other than dismal accounts of the deepening panic. By early March the hotels of Massillon were inadequate to house the men of the press services and special correspondents of the larger papers. They found much to write about.

He who was now called General Coxey asserted he would leave Massillon on March 25 with a large body of marchers and reach Washington with at least one hundred thousand men. Presently a small circus tent was set up. A small number who were described as tramps appeared and were housed and fed in the tent; and then came a large number of the sort of fringe characters who apparently live, unknown, faceless, and unheard of, to emerge from the mists only when something out of the ordinary is in the works. One thinks of them as hiding in some remote and secret clubroom, yet attuned by unseen wires to what is going on in the rest of the world, ready to leap into the limelight when and wherever it is brought to focus.

Converging on Massillon, during the last weeks of March 1894 were the dim nobodies of this brotherhood soon to shine brightly if briefly in the blinding glory of Coxey's Commonweal. There was Cyclone Kirtland, a professional astrologer, who read the stars and told the reporters that Coxey's army would be invisible in war and invincible in peace. Decked in a gaudy blanket and feathers was Honore Jaxon, a half-breed Indian reputed to have been active in the Riel Rebellion in Saskatchewan and still "wanted" by Canadian authorities who meant to hang him. There was Douglas McCallum, wearing a silk hat and fur-lined overcoat, who planned to march but instead of camping with the army would stop at hotels and sell copies of his latest work, a book entitled *Dogs and Fleas, by One of the Dogs.* There was Oklahoma Sam Pfrimmer, a cowboy, who agreed to act as horseback courier for General Coxey. There was to be another silk hat in the army, this one on the gray head of Christopher Columbus Jones, not quite five feet tall, sixty years old, who announced he had recruited two professors and one hundred students of Lehigh University, who would join the ranks in eastern Pennsylvania. He too was a theosophist, and turned a neat phrase for the boys of the press. "I believe," said Christopher Columbus Jones, removing his silk tile, "I believe in the reincarnation of Coxey's bills in Congress."

There were many others noted by the press, among them almost of necessity, a "Mysterious Stranger," who identified himself only as Smith but obviously was a military man who set up drill squads and displayed such qualities of leadership he was quickly promoted to assistant marshal. As the announced day of departure approached, every freight into Massillon brought recruits for Marshal Smith to work on. On Easter Sunday the little city was crowded to see the Commonweal Army begin its march on Washington.

Observers likened it to a circus parade. A color-bearer marched at its head, followed by Marshal Browne, now in full regalia and mounted on a magnificent stallion. Then came General Coxey himself, patently no foot soldier. He rode in a handsome phaeton which was followed by a carriage containing Mrs. Coxey and their infant son, whose baptismal name was nothing less than Legal Tender Coxey. At the head of the main column of two hundred or so tramps, hoboes, bums, and otherwise unemployed walked a color-bearer carrying the official banner of the Commonweal, with its portrait of Christ or Carl Browne and the reference to bonds. Behind the column lumbered several horse-drawn wagons piled high with provisions, stoves, cooking utensils, and tents.

Riding, or walking, front, center, and rear, were forty-three special correspondents, four telegraph operators, and two linemen. The correspondents who ridiculed the meager size of Coxey's army as it marched out of Massillon were soon to change their tune. In Pittsburgh and Homestead alone it picked up more provisions and some seven hundred more men, while all over the Far West the proletariat was beginning to move eastward, not on foot but by rail. As General Coxey progressed across Pennsylvania, telegrams from beyond the Mississippi told how his division generals and their armies were doing.

In California, General Charlie Kelly had raised one thousand five hundred men, who congregated in San Francisco. Alarmed at such a congress of tramps, the bay-city police did what they could to herd them over to Oakland. At Oakland the authorities took one look and readily gave them leave to board outbound freights. Just to make sure, two hundred and fifty armed deputies escorted them to a train for Sacramento. In the California capital they were permitted to solicit food and clothing from business houses, then took off for Utah. Territorial Governor West called out the National Guard to meet the army at Ogden with Gatling guns set up handy to the railroad station, and two thousand loaves of bread.

On went Kelly's command in twenty-six boxcars of the Union Pacific to Cheyenne, which refused to let the train stop within the city limits but supplied generous provision of bread, coffee, and other eatables. Council Bluffs met them with two companies of Iowa militia and more food and they went into camp for purposes of rest and to "boil up" their clothes. At Des Moines they were greeted by General Weaver, the Populist who had recently received a million votes for president, and a band and entertainment in the Trades Assembly Hall, and General Kelly also addressed the students of Drake University. Kelly's division was still in Des Moines when Coxey and his outfit arrived in Washington. Kelly was much put out that the commander in chief had been in such haste. "Coxey's whole fate," he told the Des Moines newspapers, "depends on my army."

Well, they would go on to Washington anyhow. But not by rail. The railroads had soured on the Commonweal. They refused transportation at less than regular passenger rates. Their trains entered and left Des Moines guarded by details of armed men. Organized labor came to the rescue, with a hundred local carpenters directing construction of one hundred and thirty scows. Kelly's command was holding up well, and into the scows clambored 1245 men to start the voyage down the Des Moines River. The heretofore-excellent discipline was slipping. Many of the boys accused Kelly of spending too much time with two young women who had got aboard the navy. Several scows were damaged in shallow rapids. Food grew scarce. George Speed, a sort of ranking colonel, and in any case a commander who meant that his own detail should eat well, managed to get his ship ahead of the main navy to pick up provisions that were meant for the whole outfit. Another colonel, William Baker, was soon seen to be deep in liquor, thus violating a cardinal regulation.

At Ottumwa, Kelly's navy came into town between ten thousand curious watchers along the banks of the river. Here, too, several of his men tangled with deputies of the Rock Island railroad and were seriously injured. Eleven days out of Des Moines the Commonweal reached the Mississippi, in bad weather. In chill wind and driving rain the boys lashed their scows together to form a gigantic raft and were taken in tow by a chartered steamboat, to be met at St. Louis by an excursion steamer bearing a brass band and representatives of local labor unions. Then on to the mouth of the Ohio and up that stream, still in tow. It was now July, and men were tiring of being heroes of the Commonweal. They deserted in droves into Indiana and Kentucky, while at Wheeling, West Virginia, a wholesale lot was arrested, tried, and sentenced to fifteen days in the workhouse.

Meanwhile other divisions of the Commonweal were organizing and moving eastward from Chicago, Colorado, and Los Angeles. What Donald L. McMurry, historian of the Commonweal movement, holds to have been "the most intractable and troublesome of all the armies" were those formed in the Rocky Mountains and the Pacific Northwest. For most of three months these hardy men of the tall timber and the hard-rock mines "kept United States marshals, militia, and even the Regular army busy protecting railroad property." They stole trains at gun's point, terrorized small towns, and put fear in the hearts of Portland, Tacoma, Seattle, and Spokane. Hundreds of them were arrested and jailed. There was some shooting, one death, and many wounded.

The Commonweal's "Petition in Boots" reached its height in May when General Coxey's original division reached Washington, five hundred strong, and paraded up Pennsylvania Avenue in good order, at its head a brass band, at its rear a detail of kilted bagpipers. Coxey had announced he would deliver an address from the Capitol steps. Some thirty thousand people were waiting to see what would happen, and so were most of the Washington police force. Coxey, Browne, and Christopher Columbus Jones, his silk topper still shining, walked alone toward the Capitol. Before Coxey could mount the steps, mounted police were upon him. All three Commonweal men leaped over a low stone paling that surrounded the grounds and disappeared into the shrubbery. Police jumped their horses and followed. Browne, complete with sombrero, high boots, and fringed shirt, was quickly collared and treated roughly. Coxey and Jones were arrested in a more genteel manner. The immense crowd booed and cheered, and the police lost their heads, to charge swinging their clubs wildly. Fifty or more people were beaten or trampled. One newspaper account reported the police to have been senselessly vicious and brutal.

The affair was not quite done, though the rest was anticlimax. The

three Commonwealers were found guilty of carrying banners and walking on the grass, and sentenced to jail for twenty days plus a five-dollar
fine. Coxey appeared before the House Committee on Labor to ask
for a hearing for himself and comrades, but they would not consider
the matter. Poor Coxey's troubles did not come singly; as he prepared
to enter the Washington jail, he was served with notice that his first wife
was suing him for abduction of their child. This was not little Legal
Tender Coxey, the fruit of his second marriage.

Browne, who had been considerably roughed up by the police, was
bailed out and returned to the Commonweal camp, where he made
a speech about how liberty lies weltering in her own blood in the nation's
capital city tonight, then pointed to the damp, dark dungeon in which
he had spent nearly five hours, and referred to Belshazzar of old, the
curse of interest on money, and a number of favorite topics of Populist
orators.

But it was little old Christopher Columbus Jones who suffered the
most hideous punishment of all. A month or so later, while acting as
commander of the Commonweal camp at nearby Bladensburg, he was
arrested, along with two hundred Commonwealers, and had to undergo
the process of enforced barbering by the state of Maryland. Anyone
familiar with the contemporary portraits of Populists will appreciate
Jones's fate. A smooth-shaven Populist was wholly unfit to be a leader
in the People's party.

The public excitement over Coxey's Army had faded long before the
last of the slowly starving members of it finally left the capital for home,
or wherever it was they went to. A new excitement had begun in May
as a strike of employees of the Pullman Company, builders of Palace
Cars at Pullman, Illinois, but had quickly exploded into what the press,
which had been more amused than frightened by the Commonweal Army,
called by the forthright name of rebellion and charged it to the sinister
genius of Eugene V. Debs.

4.

THE DEBS REBELLION

THE only thing in common about the march of Coxey's Army
and the Debs rebellion is that both were events of 1894. For all the
irritations they caused, and their run-ins with authorities, the Coxeyites
were treated with more kindness than cruelty. Theirs was considered

generally a merely fantastic adventure, a comedy staged by tattered clowns directed by poor imitations of Phineas T. Barnum and Buffalo Bill Cody.

About the Debs affair there was nothing even slightly humorous. Debs's boys were playing for keeps. They had "nothing to lose but their chains." Their opponents comprised "the massed might of the ferocious, adamant and all-conquering moguls of American railroads." The hyperbole is perhaps excusable, as of 1894.

In that year Eugene Victor Debs was thirty-nine years old, a tall, lean, gangling man, already balding, whose intensity of nature seemed largely concentrated in the light from his eyes, in the quality of his voice, and his eloquent hands. Born in Terre Haute, Indiana, of immigrant parents from Alsace, he worked as a youth in the local railroad shops, then became a locomotive fireman on the Terre Haute & Indianapolis line. He helped to organize a lodge of the Brotherhood of Locomotive Firemen, was made secretary, and was soon appointed editor of the brotherhood's magazine. In 1880 he was elected national secretary and treasurer of the firemen's union.

After a dozen years of devoted efforts to improving the status of locomotive firemen Debs had come to the conclusion that craft unionism, like that of the four railroad brotherhoods, was a mistake; that the vertical or industrial type of union, such as the Knights of Labor, was the way to meet the various combinations of employers. Debs naturally knew that the Knights in 1894 were well on the downgrade, yet this did not mean the industrial union was wrong; it simply proved that leadership of the Knights was incompetent.

So, inspired by Debs, a few like-minded railroad workers formed the American Railway Union. No crafts here. All railroad employees of all railroads in the country in one great union, that was the goal. For reasons that seemed good to him Debs began organizing with special attention to the Great Northern, the pride of James Jerome Hill, a shaggy-headed bull of a man, quick of temper, vindictive, fit to deal with anything that walked or that ran on wheels. Debs was elated to find Hill's employees fairly tumbling over each other to sign up for the one big union of railroaders.

In April, 1894, Debs was ready. The A.R.U. asked the Great Northern for an increase in wages. It was refused. The union struck so effectively that the entire line was paralyzed. In eighteen days the company gave in, and the men returned to work with most of their demands satisfied. So spectacular a success was electrifying. Employees of most of the many roads fanning out from Chicago started joining the A.R.U. By early June, Debs found he could muster 150,000 members, of whom some 4000 were, strictly speaking, not railroad workers at all but employees of the Pullman Company, makers and operators of sleeping, dining, and chair cars. When engineers or train-men protested to Debs that Pullman employees should not be admitted to A.R.U. membership, he replied that such thinking was what had kept the four brotherhoods from getting anywhere, that all workers who depended even indirectly on railroads should be in one big union that was capable of backing the demands of any portion of its membership.

Though the workers of the Pullman Company shops had recently taken a wage cut that brought income down to a little less than sub-sistence level, there were other things giving them discontent too. They disliked the manner in which the so-called "model" town of Pullman was run. Pullman town had long been the pride of George Mortimer Pullman, who had founded it in 1880 with the idea it should be the finest industrial community in the country. It did look pretty elegant to visitors, impressive, too, located on the south shore of Lake Michigan, with macadamized walks and streets decorated with shrubs and flowers, and several fine structures with marble fronts.

Pullman employees, however, had discovered marble fronts to be inedible; and that the air of elegance remarked by visitors did nothing to clothe their families. Like it or not, they had to live in Pullman if they worked for the company; they had to live in and pay rents for a company house, trade at a company store, buy their water and gas from the company, pay the company for sweeping the streets, for washing the streets, for collecting the garbage; and, in order that they might achieve culture, they must subscribe to the company rental library.

The rents for the company tenements, which in most instances had no bathtubs and only one water faucet for every five families, were much higher than charged in nearby communities. Now, in May 1894, the rents and other charges remained where they had been, but wages had gone down, and many employees discovered they could no longer keep up with the rent.

It seems probable that the Pullman management must have known that organizers for the American Railway Union had approached Pull-man employees, but it is doubtful they knew a majority had actually joined it. George M. Pullman had long since made it known that members of labor unions would not be recognized in his plant. So, without reference to any union, Pullman employees sent a committee of three of their number to call on Mr. Pullman, to ask that wages be restored to the levels of 1893. It was quite unthinkable, replied this highly successful industrialist who seemed bound also to prove himself the most fatuous of his kind. Why, he went on, the reason the company continued to operate at all, in these times, was solely to give employees work. No consideration to a wage increase would be given. Company rents would remain where they were.

The committee reflected that in 1893 the Pullman Company had paid 8 per cent dividends to its stockholders. Neither they nor the employees were impressed by Mr. Pullman's humanitarianism in keeping the plant open. Yet work continued as usual on the day following the committee's futile efforts. That is, until about noon, when news raced through the works that the company had discharged the grievance committee. Hundreds of men dropped their tools then and there and went home. That night, for the first time in its history, a mass meeting of employees was held in the streets of Pullman. Next morning more than 2500 men did not show up for work. By night virtually all the force was out.

A central strike committee was elected to notify the company of three demands: reinstatement without prejudice of the discharged committeemen, lowering of rents, restoration of wage cuts. The company would not discuss matters, and posted notices to the effect that the Pullman works were closed for an indefinite period. Mr. Pullman was unworried. But he was indignant that his employees showed so little appreciation and loyalty. A little fasting would bring them around.

Debs was worried enough. He had a strike on his hands but no funds in the new union to feed the families of four thousand strikers. Meeting in Chicago, delegates of the American Railway Union voted to assess their members three cents a day each to support the Pullman strikers. A day or so later the convention discussed a boycott of all Pullman-made cars. Debs counseled patience, and the A.R.U. sent a committee to the company to suggest that the strike be arbitrated. Mr. Pullman replied briefly. There was nothing, he said, to arbitrate. Fellow industrialists pleaded with him to arbitrate. Mr. Pullman remained unmoved. The matter came to a head on June 26, when the A.R.U. ordered its members to operate no trains of which Pullman cars were a part. The battle was on. It was to develop new techniques in class warfare, both in the field and in the courts.

Though many railroad officials told each other privately that Mr. Pullman was worse than stupid, they felt that they must close ranks to defeat the A.R.U.'s boycott. Representatives of twenty-four lines formed the General Managers Association for the purpose, set up headquarters in Chicago, and went into action. Among this group were several men of great force that was matched by their ruthlessness. They simply had to be ruthless or they would not have been representing railroads in 1894. They were products not of the mellow "Concord philosophy" of Mr. Emerson, but of the newer jungle-survival philosophy of Mr. Herbert Spencer. The General Managers' first move was to issue a public statement: the boycott against Pullman was unfair and not in the public interest; the General Managers had decided to act unitedly to defeat the American Railway Union.

The A.R.U. did not then issue a statement, but its more than 150,000 members were acting unitedly. Two days after the boycott began, Pullman-car traffic out of Chicago was virtually nonexistent. Within a week Pullman cars clogged sidetracks and even whole yards at the Far Western end of the Northern Pacific, and all along the routes of the Northwestern, the Union Pacific, and the Southern Pacific railroads. Everything seemed to be going fine for the union. The A.R.U. men were jubilant. Debs publicly praised the excellent discipline of the boycotters, and warned them to take care that no property was damaged.

The General Managers issued orders, and twenty-four railroads began promptly to discharge any worker who cut out a Pullman car from any train. Just as soon as a man was fired, the entire train crew quit. By late June almost every road in the Middle and the Far West was partially or wholly demoralized.

The General Managers sent an appeal to President Cleveland, stating that members of the A.R.U. had delayed and otherwise interfered with the United States mails when they refused to move trains made up of Pullman cars with a mail car at the rear end, until the Pullmans had been cut out. Remarking that if every soldier in the United States Army was needed to deliver a postal card in Chicago, then that card should be delivered; the forthright Mr. Cleveland ordered the 15th Infantry and several troops of cavalry to the scene. Governor John P. Altgeld of Illinois was angered. "The railroads are paralyzed," he wired the President, "not by reason of obstruction but because they cannot get men to operate their trains. I ask for immediate withdrawal of Federal troops from active duty in this state." The President did not reply. Two thousand regulars moved into Chicago under command of General Nelson A. Miles, and set up camp on the lake front.

Simultaneously with the request for federal troops the high command of the railroads asked the United States Marshal at Chicago for special deputies, and within a few days 3600 men had been deputized and armed. These men served, possibly uniquely, both as United States officers of the law and as employees of the railroads, being paid by one or another of the twenty-four lines. Violence entered the affair almost as soon as the deputies went to work. Freight cars in the yards started to burn. The A.R.U. claimed the arson was due to *agents provacateurs* paid by the railroads. The General Managers charged it to "anarchistic members" of the union. Anarchists had been a favorite public menace in Chicago since the Haymarket affair.

Things started to warm up on July 5, when federal troops helped to move the first meat train of Swift & Company out of the Union Stockyards, and a vast crowd gathered and was dispersed by cavalry charges and infantry with bayonets. The mayor of Chicago demanded that Governor Altgeld send soldiers. Five regiments of militia were mustered and ordered into service.

The shooting started on July 6 when two men were killed in a street riot. Next day, as a company of militia was moving a train at Loomis and Forty-eighth streets, it came into conflict with a mob estimated at more than three thousand persons. The soldiers were set upon. Gunfire rattled. Twenty civilians were killed on the spot or died later of wounds. All hands were playing for keeps. The boycott was holding. On the day of the bloody riot thirteen of the twenty-four railroads operating out of the Chicago area ceased to run any trains at all. The others were operating only mail and a meager passenger service.

By this time the strikers at Pullman started to picket the big plant on bicycles. Soup lines and commissaries had been set up outside Pullman's city limits to feed strikers and their families. Discipline remained good.

Working around the clock, commander-in-chief Debs of the A.R.U. was displaying brilliant leadership in what obviously was growing into the bitterest formal class-war struggle since Shay's Rebellion of 1786, only on an infinitely larger scale. News was coming in almost by the hour: state or federal troops, or even both, had been ordered into service in Michigan, Iowa, and California. The situation grew so grave that President Cleveland on July 9 issued an extraordinary proclamation, warning all persons of Illinois against assembling in crowds. Next day he extended the warning to North Dakota, Montana, Idaho, Oregon, Washington, Wyoming, Colorado, and California.

Sympathetic walkouts of locomotive engineers, telegraph operators, switchmen, and car cleaners took place here and there. Although the railroad brotherhoods were officially against the boycott, many brotherhood men really favored the A.R.U., and Lodge 233 of the Firemen turned in its brotherhood charter and joined the A.R.U. in a body.

But the next move of the General Managers was a stunner. They prevailed on the Attorney General of the United States, Richard Olney, to obtain a series of injunctions which, when divested of their legal verbiage, prevented any form of picketing or even of boycott. Debs and three other officers of the A.R.U. were indicted on charges of having interrupted interstate commerce, obstructed the mails, and intimidated citizens in the free enjoyment of their rights and privileges. All of which, doubtless, they were guilty of. Debs and the others were arrested, then freed on bail.

Debs now faced a desperate situation. He tried to stage a general strike in Chicago. Samuel Gompers of the American Federation of Labor spoke strongly against such a move, and recommended that Federation unions pay it no heed. Only the cigar makers and the bakers struck. Debs, seeing that the end was near, proposed to the General Managers to call off the strike and boycott if the Managers would agree that all members of the A.R.U., save those convicted of crimes, would be reinstated in their former jobs without discrimination. The Managers did not trouble to reply. They knew they had hit the A.R.U. a fatal blow.

Debs was arrested again, this time for contempt of court. Nearly seven hundred A.R.U. members were arrested and charged with offenses ranging from murder to intimidation. The strike, the boycott, and the American Railway Union were broken. The movement of trains, complete with Pullman cars, began. The troops were withdrawn in Chicago and elsewhere. Debs remained in jail until February 1895, when he was put on trial. The trial was halted when a juryman was taken ill, was postponed a number of times, and finally dropped. Debs's counsel, Clarence Darrow, explained matters. "Both sides," he said, "recognized that Debs had led a great fight to benefit the toilers and the poor. It was purely a part of the world class-struggle for which no individual can be blamed."

The strike and boycott changed nothing for the moment, though they must have convinced Mr. Pullman that his employees were not the happy and contented family he had believed. The struggle caused the railroad brotherhoods to feel more certain than ever that their own form of unionism was superior to any other, and went on to success and what left-wingers termed, with a sneer, respectability. The Debs rebellion, more importantly, showed how court injunctions could be used most effectively against labor groups.

There was one more thing about the uprising, and it cannot be measured but only guessed at. This was the lasting influence on Eugene Debs of his six-month stay in jail. He spent the time reading and brooding. Before the strike he had been merely one of many in the ranks who thought that labor as a whole could not benefit from craft unionism. He may have stood a little left of center, though only a little; he accepted capitalism with all its flaws as the proper form of society. He emerged from jail transformed into the perfect white knight of the working class, the champion of socialism at its extreme left. From that moment, until his death thirty-one years later, he was the incomparable symbol of discontent.

He must have sensed something of his new stature on release from custody at Woodstock, near Chicago, where a special train was waiting to take him to the city and where, at the station, more than one hundred thousand people were waiting to give him a tremendous ovation. Men and women wept and tried to touch him. Strong men bore him aloft on their shoulders. When he spoke those near heard him say that the time had come to regenerate society: "We are on the eve of a universal change."

Other men have been given ovations—statesmen, soldiers, even reformers have been cheered, saluted, fêted—only to know quickly enough the fickleness of the crowd. If Eugene Debs had been merely the fortuitous hero of a dramatic struggle, he, too, would have seen how soon the public temper can change. But Debs had *character*. Even men who feared, hated, or loathed him admitted as much. He could be neither bought nor frightened, either by the agents of capital or the pay-off men of ambitious union officials. For another three decades he was to go his own often erratic and independent way, wearing whatever label capital or labor chose to pin on him, but following the flickering lights and the burning bushes he believed would lead him and his host of the discontented to the land of the Big Rock Candy Mountains.

5.

DYNAMITE

EUGENE DEBS may never have spoken by name of the Big Rock Candy Mountains, yet that was the very place he had in mind when he finished his six-month semester in Woodstock jail. Victor L. Berger, the Milwaukee socialist, had called to leave him Karl Marx's *Capital,* which he found stimulating though it did not shake his belief that Americans could by the ballot alone usher in the new society for Utopia; and other books and pamphlets arrived almost daily for the modest, gentle, and naïve man who had so suddenly found himself a national figure, a hero to millions.

There was the enchanting *Looking Backward* of Edward Bellamy, a Utopian romance of high literary quality, which told how the Brotherhood of Humanity had at last, in the year 2000, defeated "the brutal law of the survival of the fittest and most cunning." There was Ignatius Donnelly's gloomy *Caesar's Column,* which pictured the inescapable horrors that would happen if the United States did *not* accept Populism. Fresh from the press, too, was the little yellow-backed work entitled *Coin's Financial School* and dedicated "To Those Trying to Locate the

Seat of the Disease That Threatens the Life of the Nation." Its author, William Hope Harvey, knew the answers in 1894. (He knew them still almost forty years later when the Liberty party nominated him for President in 1932, an office he failed to win, whereupon he started to build, near Rogers, Arkansas, but never finished, the Pyramid, a concrete monument "60 feet square at its base and 130 feet tall," in which he planned to bury "a history of our civilization and the Cause of its Downfall.")

On his return to public life Debs announced that he was a socialist and took to the lecture platform. It was characteristic of the man that he used most of the lecture fees to pay off debts accumulated by the American Railway Union. His next effort was also wholly in character. He took the stump for William Jennings Bryan, technically a politician, in reality a galvanic revivalist for the old-time-religion, who had just hypnotized Populists and Democrats by declaring, with the classic periods of a Roman orator, that the Republicans were NOT "to press down upon the brow of Labor this crown of thorns," and thus "crucify mankind upon a cross of gold." It was a noble empty line, and it fetched thousands of people far less naïve than Debs. Only four years later Debs himself became a Socialist-party candidate for President of the United States, and he was to run again and again for that office, the last time when he was Convict Number 9653 in a federal penitentiary yet still attracted more than 900,000 votes at a period when most Americans, labor and anti-labor, had come to dismiss Utopia and the Big Rock Candy Mountains as a chimera.

The collapse of Debs's American Railway Union dream, and the rapid decline of the Noble Order of the Knights of Labor, left the labor movement pretty much to the four railroad brotherhoods and the American Federation of Labor. The brotherhoods considered themselves the aristocracy of labor. They had no interest in workers in other industries. Certain unions in the Federation also displayed no little pride in their particular trades, and felt quite superior to common or unskilled workers.

The American Federation, as mentioned, had been put together by Samuel Gompers, born in the ghetto of London and reared in the Lower East Side of New York City, where he became a cigar maker. Though forced to quit school at ten, he spent his spare time in Cooper Union, reading books and attending lectures; and in the cigar shop, because of his durable voice, became the favorite reader among his fellow workers. Work in cigar shops was paid by the piece, the rolling of cigars was not noisy, and most shops purchased newspapers, magazines, and books from a fund to which all contributed. While the others worked, one man would read aloud for an hour or so at a stretch, his fellows turning over to him a specific number of cigars to make up for his lost time. Gompers read particularly well, his audience was interested in almost anything touching on labor or economics, and thus the young man early made an acquaintance with numerous prophets in these fields, including Karl Marx.

In later life Gompers recalled that, though Marx inspired him with "some wild plans for human betterment," he calmed down before he became associated with any radical group and seems never to have felt the least urge to bring Utopia, no matter what name it went by. What he did do, however, was to reorganize the Cigarmakers' Union after a disastrous strike and build it into a sound, businesslike outfit that was to become a model for all other craft unions in the United States. To make it so, Gompers insisted on increasing membership dues to unheard-of amounts in order to build up a fund; and he also urged the adoption of sickness, accident, and unemployment insurance. He bore down heavily on the importance of the union label.

With the Cigarmakers' as a prosperous example of craft unionism, Gompers, using diplomacy and pressure, began to attract the few other independent craft unions to his idea of a federation; and to raid the Knights of Labor as chance offered. Though he was no orator, he had a driving force and used it persistently to hammer away at the foolish idealism of the Knights and the Socialists and their silly talk about a co-operative commonwealth. Let us be practical men, he said, and stand together to get the best wages, hours, and working conditions possible under the existing industrial system. Short, stocky, almost gnomelike in appearance, yet he knew how to meet the boys in the saloons and beer gardens, in contrast to the puritanical Powderly, who was forever boring his Knights about temperance. When necessary, Gompers put on a silk hat and Prince Albert to meet the moguls of industry, even presidents of the United States, and could match them in elegant manners and talk, either small or ponderous.

In the same year of the Haymarket bomb the slow, steady work of Gompers paid off with forming of the American Federation of Labor, of which he was elected president. From that time to his death thirty-eight years later, Gompers and the AFL meant the same thing to most Americans. And for almost as long the name of Eugene Debs was identical with the left-wing movement in labor and politics. The struggle for dominance of which these two figures are handy and accurate symbols began in earnest when Debs was released from jail after the American Railway Union fiasco. The two men presented a striking contrast—Debs, the mercurial dreamer of a socialist paradise; Gompers, the strictly non-visionary businessman determined to get all he could in wages and benefits for the comparatively few so-called aristocrats of labor.

After stumping the country for the Populists, only to see them disappear into the ranks of the silver Democrats, Debs helped to organize the remnants of the American Railway Union as the Social Democratic Party, which, together with a splinter group of the old Socialist Labor party, ran him for President of the United States. But Socialists, for all their harping about a co-operative commonwealth, were never able to get along with each other; and in 1901 Debs and others seceded from the older groups to organize the Socialist party of America, the stated goal of which was to transform "the present system of private ownership of the means of production and distribution into collective ownership of the entire people." It is well to state that the happy condition sought was to be obtained by orderly means, namely the ballot. Hence success must depend "upon education and organization of the masses." As the Socialist presidential candidate in 1904, Debs polled an astonishing 402,321 votes.

He had already joined the staff of the *Appeal to Reason,* a weekly paper which as a stirrer-up of the masses has probably never been equaled; and because henceforth it was accepted as being Debs's chief propaganda medium, it might be well to look briefly into the *Appeal's* wild and bloodshot eyes. It was founded by Julius A. Wayland, a dreamy tramp printer fit to consort with Eugene Debs or almost any other apostle of discontent, who, unlikely enough in such a man, made a little money from a real estate speculation in Colorado, then lost it all in financing a vague experiment which he called the Ruskin Commonwealth and referred to with capitals as The Coming Nation. His comrade co-operators drifted away, still uncured, some to join the Fairhope Single-Tax Colony, others to the anarchistic Home Colony on Puget Sound.

Even Wayland himself had a good deal of steam left over from the Ruskin-Coming Nation failure. He went at once to small Girard, Kansas, and on April 3, 1897, broke out again, this time with his *Appeal to Reason,* announcing that the paper would kill you or cure you inside of three months. The dimes came rolling in, many of them from hard-shell Populists, others from the ark of socialism, which, like Noah's held a variety of species. Though Wayland called it a socialist sheet, just for the sake of a handle, the paper was ready to support almost anything that conventional people termed radical.

The citizens of stictly conventional Girard were shocked to find their village harboring such a snake in the grass. Wayland and his printers often had to work behind closed strong shutters, and at times, as Wayland and Debs let go some particularly evil blast, they worked with loaded Winchesters at the type cases. One of the printers was Fred Warren, who noted that Wayland was prone to feed his subscribers solid doses of doctrinaire socialism, pretty dull to all save hairsplitters. Warren suggested leavening the columns with lighter stuff, possibly even lurid, though always to connect the item with a sound curse against capitalism, or to point a moral leading toward socialism. It wasn't long before the *Appeal* brightened considerably with articles about the white-slave traffic, which was shown to be a direct outgrowth of "The System" and was also described in some detail and with more than a little imagination. Thus did Joseph Pulitzer and William Randolph Hearst influence what quickly became and remained the most successful socialist organ in the country.

The *Appeal* laid in a stock of vermilion ink, which Warren used like an artist. Great black Second Coming headlines, interspersed with hot red titles and borders, soon made the paper inflaming even to illiterates. It financed the young and unknown Upton Sinclair while he wrote *The Jungle,* and was first to publish this book which shook the country to its stomach, turned meat eaters into vegetarians, and had something to do with national legislation called the Pure Food and Drug laws. Every week the *Appeal* tied into capital with venomous joy. It attacked the rich on every score including a number of sneers Thorstein Veblen hadn't thought of.

While associate-editor Debs devoted his columns largely to support of the rising new Western Federation of Miners, Warren continued to raise some new menace every few weeks, such as the immorality of somebody or other taken in adultery who, for the *Appeal's* purpose, was labeled capitalist, though he was more likely a deacon or a prole-tarian. The *Appeal* would term the story an exclusive exposé, and pause briefly in its recital to remark: "We do not relish digging into this muck of filth and degeneracy, but we owe it to victims of a corrupt System to tell this story in all its hideousness." The victims loved it.

Both Warren and Debs thought a martyr story necessary at least once a month, and more often than not the martyr was one of the *Appeal's* thousands of volunteer subscription agents who had been insulted or at-tacked as a nuisance; and he was pictured as a Christian at the stake, with the unholy Romans, dirty capitalists to a man, lighting the fires around him. This always called for a "Martyr Defense Fund." Hundreds of thousands of dollars were raised by this method, and no doubt some of the cash was actually spent in attorney fees, though much more of it went into new subscriptions to promote the Red Dawn. And when, a little later, editor-emeritus Wayland grew morose and sat down to read a few passages in his favorite *Looking Backward*, and then blew out his brains with an automatic pistol, the *Appeal* enthusiastically charged that the Grand Old Man of Socialism had been hounded to his death by the slavering agents of plutocracy. By this time the paper was printing more than two million copies a week. One week before long it was to reach 4,100,000 copies. They were read, too. In Puget Sound logging camps, in the mining towns of Idaho, Montana, Colorado, and Utah, in farm homes and hobo jungles, the *Little Old Appeal,* as it was affectionately known, was read to pulp—and *believed,* every word.

It was little wonder with champions like Eugene Debs and the *Appeal,* that industrial unionism, as contrasted with Sam Gompers and his amalgamation of trades and crafts, was making great strides all over the American West. Not, however, without resistance and punitive action by employers. Indeed, the first few years of the new century witnessed a struggle that has been called with no great exaggeration the Rocky Mountain Revolution. The opposing forces were the new Western Federation of Miners, and the various associations of mineowners and operators. Into this vast battlefield went Debs, a man fearless, eloquent, and wonderfully naïve, to rouse the slaves and damn their masters.

This was the primitive industrial frontier of America, in a period of expanding enterprise explosive in its haste and its power. Out here men seemed not to have time to think overmuch. They merely threatened one another briefly. Then they took action. Because it was still a period of trial and error, the action stood an even chance of being the wrong thing. The bolder empiricists tried shooting, and dynamite.

Striking miners were shot down by mine guards, militia, and federal troops in Montana, Idaho, and Colorado. They underwent mass arrests and deportations. Mines and smelters were blown up. So were mine captains, mine operators, strikebreakers, and innocent bystanders. Neither Debs nor anybody else in the United States had known a reign of terror such as prevailed in Western mining districts during the five years after 1900.

In his organizing work for the miners Debs became close friends with the Western Federation's secretary-treasurer, William D. Haywood, a hulking figure of a man, big-shouldered, big-necked, big-handed, every line of his body proclaiming enormous strength. His one good eye, as coldly blue as ice, was shaded by a mop of brownish hair. His jaw looked neolithic. His character had long since been moulded. He was hard, tough, immensely resistant, and warped by the life he had led in the mines, the things he had seen. There was no little of the dreamer about him. He was immediately attracted to Debs. Both men liked the bottle. Both men believed that working-stiffs needed a lot of education to prepare them for the coming "Cooperative Commonwealth."

After many discussions about this proposal for a sort of bureau of education for the workers, Debs, Haywood, and a few others gathered in Chicago, in the same hall where the anarchists used to meet before the Haymarket bomb, to make plans. It was still a day for manifestoes, and the group drew up a characteristic manifesto to formulate the "One Big Union of the Industrial Workers of the World": Class divisions had grown more fixed ... class antagonisms had grown sharper ... used-up laborers were thrown on the scrap heap to starve ... wages grew less ... working hours grew longer ... capitalist success rested on the blindness and ignorance of the working class ... the class struggle must go on until the workers were ready to take over the tools of production.

Two hundred thousand copies of the manifesto were printed and distributed. A call was issued to hold a convention in Chicago on June 27, 1905. On that day the convention opened with Haywood in the chair. "Fellow workers," he roared, "the aims and objects of this organization shall be to put the working class in possession of the economic power, the means of life, and control of the machinery or production and distribution, without regard to capitalist masters." He paused a moment for effect, and then with happy analogy let his audience know who they were. "We are," said he, "the Continental Congress of the Working Class."

One of those present, George Speed, made an observation remindful of that of Emerson on the Chardon Street Convention of universal reformers held half a century before in Boston. Speed looked around him to see "the greatest conglomeration of freaks that ever met in convention." There was Lucy Parsons, widow of the hanged Haymarket anarchist; Mother Jones, the vitriolic old agitator dating back to the Knights of Labor's early days; Robert Rives La Monte, a young intellectual who was later to debate socialism, in print, with Henry L. Mencken; "Father" Thomas J. Hagerty, the former Catholic priest, big, black-bearded, and now editor of a labor paper; William E. Troutmann of the radical United Brewery Workers; Charles Sherman of the United Metal Workers; Daniel De Leon of the Socialist Labor party; Eugene Debs, president of the new Socialist party of America; and several score more members of left-wing unions.

All present were doubtless devoted to the idea of the "One Big Union"; yet what brought them together in the first place was not their idealism but the binding influence of their common antipathies, which was the American Federation of Labor with its divisions of crafts. Debs was the only person of national standing present. In his enthusiastic address he told the gathering that the Industrial Workers of the World was the first and only organization fit to meet capital on its own ground and defeat it. Following Debs to the platform was Daniel De Leon, a professorial type with badger-gray whiskers, editor of *The People,* a man who had no peer as a doctrinaire. No theologian made finer distinction in matters of dogma than De Leon could muster in socialism. Big Bill Haywood disliked words like "dogma" and "indoctrinate."

Haywood refused nomination for election as first president of the

I.W.W., which came to be known simply as the Wobblies, and returned to the headquarters in Denver of the Western Federation of Miners. The strength of the new I.W.W. lay in the miners' affiliation with it; yet De Leon was already referring to the Western Federation as "proletarian rabble." He had set out to capture control of the Wobblies, and he did capture it a little later and split the One Big Union into two schisms that probably would have wrecked it beyond mending, had it not been for a chain of events set off by the still-unheard-of Harry Orchard, a man who had not the least interest in the Wobblies.

The first of the momentous chain of events took place on the last day but one of the year 1905, in small Caldwell, Idaho, when at snowy evening, Frank Steunenberg, ex-governor of the state, opened the gate to his modest home and was blown apart by a waiting bomb. On January 1, 1906, Harry Orchard, who described himself as a dealer in sheep, was arrested.

The second event to become public was delayed until February 17, when in Denver Bill Haywood was arrested, along with Charles Moyer, president of the Western Federation of Miners, and George A. Pettibone, identified merely as a friend of Haywood and Pettibone. The three men were hustled aboard a Union Pacific special train. The tracks were cleared and what Debs was soon to call "The Kidnappers' Special" sped out of Denver for a fast overnight run to Boise, capital of Idaho, where the three prisoners were jailed. Only then was the confession of Harry Orchard given to the press.

Orchard's confession cleared up a host of matters that had been veiled in mystery. The operators of the Vindicator Mine high in the Rockies learned who set the infernal machine that killed two of their superintendents during a strike of the Western Federation of Miners. The people of Independence, Colorado, learned who blew their railroad station and thirteen non-union miners to kingdom come, and maimed twenty-four others, several of whom suffered amputation. In Denver the list of unsolved crimes was reduced by two, for Orchard told how he had shot Lyte Gregory, a mine detective, and blew up Merritt W. Walley, by mistake, when that classically innocent bystander was so unfortunate as to trip a bomb that had been set for William H. Gabbert, chief justice of the Colorado Supreme Court. In San Francisco police were interested to learn identity of the arch-fiend who had dynamited a whole apartment house there and critically injured Frederic W. Bradley, president of the Mine Operators Association.

I, said Harry Orchard, committed all these crimes. I was paid in cash for my efforts by the Western Federation of Miners in the persons of Charlie Moyer and Bill Haywood; and sometimes by George Pettibone, who though not a Federation official often acted for them.

There were other crimes which, said Orchard, he had committed on his own. These included several successful arson jobs; the abandonment of a wife and children; bigamy; and an affair of burglary that did not pay off. He recalled also that during a strike at the Bunker Hill & Sullivan Mining & Concentrating Company, in the Coeur d'Alene mine district, it was he who had laid and touched off the "lifter charge" of dynamite to blow up the company's great concentrator building. This had helped to prepare him for the professional work he was to begin only a couple of years later for the Western Federation as "The Man with the Black Valise."

For none of these crimes, either professional or amateur, had Orchard been suspected, much less arrested, until he set the bomb that killed Frank Steunenberg, the ex-governor of Idaho. Now that he had been caught, he had thought it best to confess all his evil deeds. "I was afraid to die," he said, "unless I unburdened my conscience." He even remembered that his real name was Albert E. Horsely, a native of Ontario, Canada, but having fled that province ahead of the sheriff, he operated variously as John Little, John Dempsey, T. S. Hogan, and Harry Orchard.

In *The Appeal to Reason* Debs leaped to the defense of Haywood, Moyer, and Pettibone: "Arouse, ye Slaves!" he cried, "Their only crime is loyalty to the working class!" This Orchard is an agent of the mine operators, paid to discredit unionism by criminal acts that could be laid to strikers. Consider to whom Orchard made his confession. It was not an officer of government but James McParlan, a private detective in the employ of the same Pinkerton who sent the three hundred armed guards to Homestead; who had broken up the Molly Maguires of the coal mines. Indeed, this McParlan was the same labor spy the Pinkertons had employed to hang the Mollies. He was vile beyond words.

Debs tore over the circuit in Western Federation territory, speaking to local unions in all the Western states and British Columbia, demanding money to defend the three martyrs to class hatred. Telluride, Silverton, Cripple Creek; Bingham Canyon and Cottonwood; Goldfield and Grass Valley; Butte and Anaconda; the Coeur d'Alenes; Oregon's Sumpter Valley; British Columbia's Trail; even Homestake, South Dakota—all the unions rallied to Debs's cry and raised more than $50,-000 immediately. And Debs's old friend, Clarence Darrow, his defender during the American Railway Union strike, came to Boise to act with counsel for the Western Federation defense, which was headed by E. F. Richardson. It was announced that William E. Borah, Boise lawyer, about to take his seat as a United States senator, would aid in the prosecution. Eighteen months were to elapse before the trials got under way.

Part of the long delay was occasioned by the defense, which had asked for habeas-corpus writs for the accused. These were refused, lastly by the United States Supreme Court, which denied it eight to one, Justice McKenna dissenting in a sharp note in which he referred to removal of the three men from Colorado to Idaho as kidnaping. Debs issued a blast that was technically close to contempt. If kidnaping were thus a legitimate practice, he said in the *Appeal*, then let us all take advantage of it. "For every workingman kidnapped, a capitalist must be seized and held for ransom . . . The kidnapping of the first Capitalist will convulse the nation and reverse the Supreme Court."

Even before the trials began, the case had created more bitter feeling than anything since the Haymarket affair. The President of the United States, even, was not immune to the prevailing hysteria. In a private letter that was made public, Theodore Roosevelt wrote that whether or not these three men were guilty they were "undesirable citizens." This made a noise, and Debs made a vitriolic attack on the President, meanwhile ordering a million lapel buttons on which was inscribed "I Am an Undesirable Citizen" and which began to appear all over the country.

Clarence Darrow grew worried because of Debs's continued attacks on "The System." The lawyer did not want "the added burden of having to acquit Socialism as well as the defendants," and wrote to Debs asking him not to come to Boise to report the trial for the *Appeal*. Debs stayed away from Boise, but he could not be quiet and now he called not only for a national general strike "until our comrades are freed," but for "the workers to form an army and march to Idaho to set free these martyrs to the cause of Labor."

William Dudley Haywood was selected to be tried first. As the jury was being chosen, men of the press to the number of fifty-four papers arrived in Boise. So did a large number of labor representatives, of free-wheeling reformers of all sorts, and men of the mine operators' associations. Protest parades were held simultaneously in Chicago and other cities. The eyes of the nation were on the small capital city of remote and sparsely populated Idaho.

Harry Orchard had turned state's evidence. To convict Haywood, the prosecution must rely chiefly on Orchard's confession. To free Haywood, the defense sought to show Orchard was a monumental liar and an *agent provocateur* employed by the mine operators to discredit the Western Federation of Miners.

The specific charge against Haywood was that he conspired to bring about the murder of ex-Governor of Idaho Frank Steunenberg, who in 1899 had ordered troops into the Coeur d'Alene mining district to quell the violence incident to a strike. Hence Steunenberg was an enemy of labor and should be done away with, according to Haywood as reported by Orchard. For the defense Darrow attempted to show Orchard had a personal reason for killing the man. When this failed, Darrow returned to what was his main theme, anyway—that Orchard was the paid agent of mine operators. Defense also put Orchard on the stand to show what an inhuman monster he was. Orchard did not mind:

Q. Why did you shoot Lyte Gregory *three* times with a sawed-off shotgun?
A. He didn't go down until the third shot.
Q. You kept pumping until he did go down?
A. Yes, sir, I kept pumping until he went down dead.

Orchard did not mind when counsel sought to show his all-around dishonesty:

Q. It was your habit to lie about everything, wasn't it?
A. Yes, sir, whenever it suited my purpose.

Orchard remained unruffled when counsel, seeking to show his utter depravity, questioned him about the time he had toted a bomb into a Boise hotel, with the idea of planting it in Governor Steunenberg's room there:

Q. This bomb would have blown the hotel to pieces, wouldn't it?
A. Yes, sir.
Q. And you were willing to do this?
A. Yes, sir.
Q. Did you expect to stay in the hotel that night?
A. No, sir.
Q. You were willing to kill everyone but yourself?
A. Yes, sir.

Here was a notable Goth. By neither euphemism nor explanation did Orchard seek to mitigate the long series of horrors he had perpetrated. He was merely a professional killer. Day after day he underwent as fierce a cross-examination as veteran reporters could remember, and remained cheerful and courteous. At no point was he tripped. Even if he was telling the truth, his replies to repeated questions did not vary in the least detail; and if he was lying, then his was a performance to astound even a Barrymore, one of whom, Ethel, was in Boise with *Captain Jinks of the Horse Marines*, and was fascinated with Orchard on the stand. "Why," said Miss Barrymore, "he looks like a respectable grocer."

After seventy-eight days of grueling action, the reservoirs of witnesses for both the state and the defense were exhausted. Mr. Darrow made his final plea for Haywood, and Mr. Borah gave the closing argument for the state. Darrow of course stressed the case as a battle between capital and labor, and with eloquence possibly not heard in a court since the days of Webster. In a slouchy gray suit hanging draped on his hulking figure, a wisp of hair falling across his forehead, he walked up and down before the jury, his left hand in a coat pocket, right hand holding his glasses and making gestures of attack, of appeal, astonishment, contempt. His mobile, furrowed face synchronized perfectly with the gestures. So did the organ that was his voice, emitting snarls where needed, a shout or bellow on occasion, then a purposeful and purple phrase cloaked with an emotional hush, and a whisper of accusation, or pity.

Mr. Darrow was addressing the jury. He was also telling the United States through the assembled men of the press that the trial of Big Bill Haywood was an inquisition as damnable as that of long ago which had burned religious heretics at the stake. The modern inquisition was composed of "the mine owners of Idaho and Colorado," who with their vast resources had subverted the state. The tool of this hellborn combination was Harry Orchard.

Mr. Borah was not asleep. "This is merely a murder trial," he said. "We are not fighting organized labor."

Mr. Darrow paid him no heed. He went on to conjure up the horrible vision of Wall Street and what, in this Granger country, was even worse—the railroads. It all was a masterly summation for the defense. He knew he had touched the jury in tender spots, and he closed by reminding them that thousands of men who labor and suffer, and women and children weary with care and toil, "will kneel tonight and ask their God to guide your hearts."

Though there was less poetry in Borah than Darrow, the prosecuting counsel marshaled his evidence with consummate skill and considerable dramatic power. He reminded the jury just what this trial was about: It had to do with murder, and behind murder was the red menace of anarchy. The man from the New York *Times* wrote that the evidence as summed up by Mr. Borah was "terrific, crushing, destroying."

But Judge Fremont Wood was still to be heard. Radicals everywhere, including Debs, had for weeks been denouncing Wood as a mere puppet, a tool of the plutocracy. What they did not take into account was the possibility that Judge Wood was not only a just man but a most courageous man. Now that the lawyers were done, he instructed the jury, and he was as clear as crystal. "Gentlemen," he told the twelve men, "under the statutes of this state, a person cannot be convicted of a crime upon testimony of an accomplice, unless such accomplice is corroborated by other evidence."

The jury did not believe that Orchard had been corroborated by the many witnesses who had been put on the stand to prove that he was telling the truth. Early next morning they returned a verdict of not guilty. Eugene Debs was jubilant. Truth had not been crushed to earth. Two more "victims" remained to be tried, but now that Haywood had been freed, there was hope for the others. Debs said so in a bubbling, buoyant couple of columns in the *Appeal*, which went to press with a run of approximately four million copies, red ink and all.

George Pettibone was to be tried next. Even before selection of a jury began, something like a thunderbolt took the headlines away from Boise. On the last day of September—it was 1907—at about half-past ten at night Harvey K. Brown was blown up and fatally mangled when he opened the gate to his home in Baker City on the upper reaches of Powder River in the mining district of Oregon's Blue Mountains. Baker City was one hundred and fifty miles west of Boise.

Who was Brown? He was the sheriff of Baker County, Oregon, who just happened to be in Caldwell on the night Governor Steunenberg was killed, and was the first to identify "Thomas Hogan" as Harry Orchard. He also arrested Steve Adams as an accomplice of Orchard in another murder. Now Brown had died in the night at his own gate, just as Steunenberg had died. It is a long and complicated story. It is not even mentioned in the several biographies of Clarence Darrow, or in his autobiography. All that needs be said here is that the affair of Harvey K. Brown is as deep a mystery today as it was fifty years ago.

George Pettibone's trial in Boise was an anticlimax. He was acquitted with little noise. The case against Charles Moyer was dropped. Harry Orchard pleaded guilty, was sentenced to be hanged, then the penalty was commuted to life imprisonment. Judge Wood made it clear he believed Orchard had spoken nothing but the truth and that he, the judge, considered Haywood and Pettibone guilty as charged.

Orchard was returned to the Idaho penitentiary where he had already spent more than two years, awaiting disposition of his case. Now he was in for life, and life for Orchard turned out to be quite a span. He died in the penitentiary hospital on April 13, 1954. He was eighty-one years old. One may bear in mind that he was no dedicated partisan either of labor or capital. He was strictly a professional, a "most wicked man for hire to the highest bidder." As such he was truly a Gothic figure of some stature in an era when the enemy camps of capital and labor both harbored barbarians beyond number.

It was with some reason that radicals considered the outcome of the Idaho trials a triumph for the left-wing labor movement. They had stopped their bickerings and closed ranks long enough to defeat the minions of capital in the attempt to railroad Bill Haywood to prison. Now was the time for a supreme effort.

Socialists in convention again selected Debs to run in the presidential campaign of 1908. *The Appeal to Reason* laid in a stock of fatter, blacker type than usual, and helped to raise an astounding $20,000 in nickels and dimes to give good old Gene a chance to stump the whole United States in a manner never before dreamed of by radicals. Into a splendid three-car railroad train chartered for the occasion, and christened the Red Special, went candidate Debs and his political entourage to plead the cause of socialism against the plutocracy represented by William Howard Taft and William Jennings Bryan.

Here was notice that the Socialist party of America had come of age. The press had lots of fun ridiculing what it described as a "luxurious attempt" to ape the old conventional parties, though there were editors who feared the Red Special was less a comedy piece than a herald of revolution. The baggage car was packed with bundles of socialist literature including the *Appeal*, in charge of young Tom Mooney, soon to gain prominence in San Francisco. The Special was to run up and down and across the country for three months, while Debs spoke in cities large and small, at way stations and whistle stops. He was in fine form. "Ye Gods! but these are pregnant days!" he told interviewers. "The hosts pour in from all directions—men, women, babies. Even the babies are up in arms against the Capitalist system. The farmers, too, are revolutionary to the core. They are ripe and ready for action."

Yet in spite of large enthusiastic crowds that surrounded the Red Special when it stopped with the message of hope, and for all the personal appeal of Debs for most people, socialism in November mustered only 421,000 votes, a slight increase over 1904. Debs was not cast down. Employers, he said, had intimidated their employees by posting notices that, unless Taft were elected, the plants would be closed.

The radicals began bickering again. The Western Federation of Miners pulled out of the Industrial Workers of the World. Bill Haywood left the Miners to lead the Wobblies into the most sanguinary and spectacular battles of the next few years, a sort of bloodstained trail to international glory, or infamy. The Socialists were too tame for him, even though he and Debs remained friends. Meanwhile Sam Gompers had been making steady progress with the American Federation of Labor, quietly for the most part, until 1910.

THE WONDERFUL WOBBLIES

EARLY in the century Samuel Gompers, head of the American Federation of Labor, testified before a congressional committee to the effect that violence was "no recognized part of Labor's plan." The use here of "recognized," a qualification, may have been a calculated ambiguity. Presidents of unions, no less than presidents of nations, have occasion to be studiously vague. Yet Mr. Gompers went on to say that labor needed only be strong in numbers, in effective organization, in the justice of its cause, and the reasonableness of its methods.

These were fine, ringing words, and one does not doubt that Mr. Gompers devoutly hoped that they were true, for he himself was a man who preferred to win by opportune strategy and intrigue rather than battle. Yet three years later, in an interview, he admitted that certain AFL unions were using strong-arm tactics. He deplored them righteously, but pointed out, airily, that such tactics were unlawful acts and were thus the concern of the police. It was most difficult, he intimated, to keep an organization of a million and a half workingmen wholly free from criminals.

Indeed it was, and at about one o'clock in the morning of October 1, 1910, an explosion in the labor-hating Los Angeles *Times* killed twenty men and made a shambles of the building. Joe Harriman, the Socialist attorney, was prompt to tell the Associated Press that the explosion had been due to leaky gas pipes. But most people who read the papers were reminded of the terrible technique of Harry Orchard. The job in the *Times* building could not be Orchard's work; he was safely in prison. But the public was quite prepared to accept the statement of the Los Angeles paper that it had been the victim of a "unionist bomb."

Seven months later William J. Burns, a private detective, arrested the brothers McNamara, James B. and John L., and one Ortie McManigal. It was to be a long affair. Two years later Ortie McManigal had turned state's evidence, was freed, and "disappeared"; and the two McNamara boys, personal friends of Sam Gompers and high in the councils of the American Federation of Labor, had confessed to setting the bomb in the *Times* building, and were in prison. That was not all; a whole raft of gorillas, or hatchet men, of the International Association of Bridge & Structural Iron Workers, an AFL affiliate, had been tried on various charges, in a dynamite conspiracy, and most of them convicted of having used explosives on buildings being erected with non-union labor.

The prosecution offered six hundred and twenty exhibits in evidence —pieces of exploded bombs, fuses, cans of nitroglycerine, and other ordnance. To a newer generation the name of McNamara came to mean terrorism much as Harry Orchard had meant in the past. Clarence Darrow came as counsel for defense of the two McNamaras. This time things went badly for him. Without notice to Darrow, they changed their not-guilty pleas to guilty. The case ended in fiasco, but the McNamaras went to prison; and Darrow was tried twice for jury bribing, resulting in a hung jury and an acquittal.

Perhaps never was the difference more marked between a fanatical idealist and a wholly pragmatic man than the attitudes during this period of Eugene Debs and Samuel Gompers. In the presidential campaign Gompers had done everything possible to belittle and harass the Socialist candidate, just as he had also deplored and attacked the Western Federation of Miners as "a pack of anarchists." But when Gompers' Boys, the McNamara brothers, were arrested, Debs immediately warned his now-great reading public that this case against the AFL unions was "a repetition of the Haywood outrage." Beware the slimy capitalist press. Be not deceived, but "Arouse, ye hosts of Labor, and swear that the villainous plot shall not be consummated!" And though the AFL was far better heeled than the Socialists, Debs used *The Appeal* to raise funds for the McNamara defense.

William Dudley Haywood had a vision all his own. He thought the Socialists were a bunch of doctrinaires. He considered the American Federation of Labor to be a congress of "labor fakers," a term which, despite his stock of remarkably abusive language, he reserved for especial depravity. Both the doctrinaires and the fakers would have to be plowed under or converted to the One Big Union, the Industrial Workers of the World, the Wobblies.

Exactly what sort of a day Bill Haywood's Red Dawn was to usher in cannot be described with any clarity. It varied. It changed from year to year, from season to season. Haywood was a mercurial, a moody character. There was nothing orderly about his plans to get to the Big Rock Candy Mountains. He played strictly by ear. He was supposed to have an office in Wobbly headquarters, yet seemed to carry what he called his "important papers" in the band of his Stetson hat. He was careless, fearless, the perfect leader of what he termed working-stiffs which were not to be confused with skilled workmen. Nor should the Wobblies be confused with communists. It is true Haywood fled to Russia and there he lived until diabetes got him. He died in Moscow, as alien a figure as any preacher of the Gospel. He and his Wobs were as radical as any commissar; yet they were as foreign to the Pan-Slavic police state as could be imagined. Many who knew him believed that Big Bill died less from diabetes than from bitter disappointment with what Russia had done to the revolution.

Most Americans past middle age will readily recall the vision conjured up by the name "Wobbly." He was a dangerous fellow, a saboteur, a setter of fires in forests and wheat fields, intent on fanning the flames of discontent into the great purifying holocaust of the Red Dawn; a nihilist devoted to the extermination of all open and disguised tools of the capitalists, who were ogres wearing sixteen-ounce watch chains of solid gold across their obese stomachs and silk hats on their simian heads. And smoking the biggest cigars ever made.

Haywood had much to do with making this wonderland of the Wobblies. True or false, the scenes rise up out of the mists of forty and more years ago, vivid with fire and smoke and blood, for all old enough to remember. So do the very letters I.W.W., which came to seem less the initials of a labor union than a symbol. Chalked on the wall of a bunkhouse, or scratched in the privy of a railroad depot, I.W.W. was a challenge and a warning; it leaped at the eye from the middle of a column of type; on the frosted window of a Skid Road hall it stopped men in their tracks.

Wherever the Wobblies were *there* was turmoil. Another characteristic was the amazing rapidity with which they got around the country. When the iron miners of the Mesabi Range went on strike, Wobbly loggers from Oregon flooded into Minnesota on freights to help picket the mines. Dirt-movers of Montana construction camps appeared overnight as if by magic around California hop fields, ready to riot or picket and sing the cynical or sentimental lyrics written by Joe Hill (strom) and other Wobs for the *Little Red Song Book*. And when extraordinary emergencies demanded immediate attention, the boys rose to the occasion by abjuring the freights to ride the blinds of passenger trains and thus make express time to the scene of action. Miners from Butte had to move fast to McKees Rocks, Pennsylvania, in time to get into the shooting. They made it. So did Columbia River loggers to Lawrence, Massachusetts, when Big Bill sounded the call for help in the textile strike there.

Many of the Wobs were young, foot-loose fellows who followed the harvest north from Texas to Saskatchewan. In winter they worked in the sawmills of Louisiana or Wisconsin or Washington; or the logging camps. Thousands of them were hard-rock miners who had dropped their Western Federation papers to carry the red card of the Wobs. There was also a criminal element of gamblers, thieves, and stick-up men, who carried red cards only to stand in well with railroad brakemen who were often in sympathy with Wobblies and would let one ride a freight for a dollar or fifty cents, or even free.

The Wobbly press was as colorful and as noisy as its membership. Editors never troubled themselves about facts, but they had to know how to manufacture propaganda. If no Wobbly hall had been wrecked for a fortnight, or no Wobbly organizer beaten up by police, ye ed would hitch up his galluses and come out with a rousing exposé banner-headed "TIMBER BARONS HIRE JESUS-BILLY TO QUIET SLAVES," the Jesus-Billy being the Rev. Billy Sunday, considered by many employers a good sedative for employees who had begun to grumble about wages. Off and on the I.W.W. papers had a columnist, one of whom signed himself "T-Bone Slim" and knew his Paine, his Veblen, Marx, Kropotkin, and John Stuart Mill. Slim also liked to lay into his great colleague in the pay of Hearst whose stuff he referred to as *brisbanalities.*

Wobbly martyrs appeared regularly, and one of them, the same Joe Hill who wrote doggerel verse for the *Little Red Song Book,* was made into an imposing legend as soon as he was executed in front of a firing squad of the state of Utah. While organizing copper miners Joe or somebody killed a man in a holdup, and Joe went into I.W.W. hagiography and his portrait was hung in Wobbly halls, an ikon draped in black.

The Wobblies also developed Rebel Girls, the first and foremost being Elizabeth Gurley Flynn, who rolled into Spokane in a boxcar to mount a soapbox on Trent Avenue and breathe hell-fire at the cops in a "Free Speech" battle. The Flynn was young and strikingly handsome, wore a Western hat turned up in front, a flaming red tie around her pretty throat, and could abuse capital and its tools in a splendid voice of low register and high inflammability. In an unreflective moment the idiotic police arrested this beauteous firebrand of the Skid Road and threw her into jail. The Wobbly press shouted: "TOOLS OF TIMBER BARONS JAIL REBEL GIRL," and unhappy Spokane swarmed with an invasion of itinerants from all over the West, come to protect this inhuman treatment of womanhood. They marched and spoke and rang rude songs. They were arrested by platoons to crowd the jail, where their nightly howls frightened little children and all capitalists. It was too much. The prisoners were released. Forthwith Spokane was safe for I.W.W. speakers. The Flynn took off to help start the revolution in Lawrence, Massachusetts, then to keep Paterson, New Jersey, awake nights; and so to the Mesabi Range in Minnesota, where hell had broken loose and the fires needed only a little stirring.

Big Bill Haywood was alert. From Duluth he sounded the alarm to call his flying squadron of agitators, and challenged United States Steel's mining division, and assorted Rockefellers, Morgans, Olivers to Armageddon. The Wobbly hosts came, among them Frank Little, later lynched at Butte; Carlo Tresca, whose murder at Fifth Avenue and Fifteenth Street, in 1943, still mystifies Manhattan police; the Flynn, and Sam Scarlett, who reminded Jack Reed of "a Yeoman at Crécy." The shooting started promptly, and Arthur (Old Warhorse) Boose was jailed, bailed, and lammed to Oklahoma, where he became "Arthur Fritz," and began to organize the oil-field workers.

Almost simultaneously the I.W.W. stirred in Everett, Washington, where they took over a strike of shingle weavers but were denied the exercise of free speech. In Seattle they chartered a steamer, the *Verona,* packed her with four hundred Wobblies, and headed for the Sawmill City. Two hours later they were met at the dock by the Everett sheriff and posse, and when the smoke had cleared seven men were dead, sixty-eight wounded, and two hundred in jail. Haywood's talented editors made it into "The Everett Massacre." The courts failed to convict anyone.

A few months later the I.W.W. staged the greatest strike the lumber industry had known. Eighty-five per cent of logging camps and sawmills were shut down in the face of wartime demand for lumber for the United States Army. "This is a Capitalist war," Haywood announced. "If the Capitalists want lumber, then let them give us bigger pay and the eight-hour day." Spikes allegedly appeared in logs at those mills which continued to operate. Logging trains were derailed. Mysterious fires broke out in timber and mill. Wobbly stickers showing horribly grinning black cats—symbol of sabotage—were found glued to the windows of camp and sawmill offices. There were riots of the log drives of Montana, Idaho, and eastern Washington, where river crews fought Wob pickets. Tough mill foremen threw I.W.W. organizers into log ponds. Even tougher camp foremen beat them up. Real Wobblies were gluttons for punishment. It took courage to be one in 1917.

Haywood & Company had not only taken on the massed hordes of capitalism; through dual unions they were trying to wreck the American Federation of Labor and also the Western Federation of Miners. Matters came to a showdown one night in Butte, where President Charles Moyer of the Western Federation was attempting to speak when the hall was attacked by many of the three thousand hostile miners gathered in the street. When Moyer and audience fled out a rear door, a delegation from the street crowd, described by the press as Wobblies, staged a gun-point raid of an Anaconda company powder magazine, toted explosives into the union hall and set off the first of the twenty-five blasts that were required to reduce the structure to rubble.

Samuel Gompers cried havoc. Haywood kept a fairly straight face, to observe with indignation that dynamiting of the Butte union hall reminded him of the American Federation technique so brilliantly displayed by the McNamara brothers. "Gompers' Boys," as Big Bill called them in derision.

Staunch old Debs refused to concede, at least in public, that the dynamiters at Butte had been other than "paid agents of the Waddell-Mahon Detective Agency."

It was getting terribly late for Socialists, Wobblies, or anybody else in the United States who was not ready—to cite a potent phrase of the time—to save the world for democracy. The so-called Palmer Raids of the federal government began. Dangerous radicals in the ranks of labor, parlor Socialists, the religious fanatics of Pastor Russell, soon to be known as Jehovah's Witnesses, and persons belonging to no group but suspected of harboring independent thought were arrested and jailed. Into the same ancient cells that had confined the Haymarket anarchists in Chicago went Haywood, Ralph Chaplin, editor of *Solidarity,* and other Wobblies found at general headquarters. A reporter from the Chicago *Daily News* came to interview Haywood. He was Carl Sandburg, who wrote that Big Bill "spoke the defiance of the Industrial Workers of the World to its enemies and captors . . . He didn't pound the floor, shake the iron clamps nor ask for pity nor make any kind of play as a hero." Sandburg said Haywood talked "in the even voice of a poker player who may or may not hold the winning hand," and was impressed "with the massive leisure" with which Haywood "discussed the 10,000 crimes with which he was charged." Editor Chaplin was absorbed with reflection on the dead anarchists who had been confined here, and soon he was at work on his first prison poem, a moving thing called *Mourn Not the Dead.*

Debs was still at large, though his time, too, was running out, and within a few months more he was arrested in Canton, Ohio, after a speech to the Socialists in convention there, and charged with violation of the Espionage Act, of which he was found guilty and sentenced to ten years in a federal penitentiary. One hundred and sixty-six Wobblies were charged with similar or worse acts, and ninety-three of them sent to prison, among them Haywood, Chaplin, and Arthur (Old Warhorse) Boose, who much later told a reporter that a good deal of the incriminating matter used to convict the Wobblies came from Haywood's correspondence, all of which tactically should have been destroyed as soon as read. "Bill was always careless of his mail," the Old War-horse said sadly but without recrimination.

The World War ended November 11, 1918. Haywood and the other Wobblies were in Leavenworth prison, while efforts were being made for a new trial. Haywood, Chaplin, and several more of the prisoners were admitted to enormous bail. They were at liberty, working up an amnesty campaign for all "political prisoners," when the I.W.W. became involved in a most melancholy affair at Centralia, Washington, in the heart of the big-timber country. On Armistice Day, 1919, the new American Legion held an observance and parade. When directly in front of the local I.W.W hall, the local contingent of the marching Legionnaires halted. It has never been proved whether what happened was by design or because of a gap between the several units and an effort to close ranks. In any case, the Centralia Legion halted near the Wobbly hall. What occurred in the next few seconds has been hopelessly in dispute ever since.

What is horribly known is that shouts and cries and the crackle of gunfire broke out simultaneously. Parade watchers saw three Legion-naires fall in the street. There was a rush on the Wobbly hall, and Wesley Everest went out the rear door firing as he ran. Chased to the brink of a nearby river, the Wobbly and ex-army veteran turned and shot his nearest pursuer dead. Everest was taken and put in the Centralia jail, and early that grim evening every light in town flicked out without warning. A group of men moved into the jail, took Everest, and went away. Next morning Everest's bullet-ridden body was hanging from a bridge.

Whether the Legionnaires halted in mid-parade to raid the I.W.W. hall, as I.W.W. defense counsel claimed, or whether, as the prosecution held, the Wobblies deliberately committed murder, has been discussed in print thousands of times. Four Legionnaires were dead, anyhow, and so was one Wobbly. Eight I.W.W. members were sent to prison for varying sentences. The affair was the beginning of the end of the Wobblies as a power, and often a terror, in the timber regions of the Northwest. There were, however, other and more potent reasons for the rapid fading of Bill Haywood's dream of a happy commonwealth of labor. Bill Haywood himself was being prepared for what, in another profession, has long been known as the "Big Con." In Haywood's case the Big Con had to do with Russian communism.

In September of 1919 the American Communist party was organized in an old church building on Throop Street, Chicago, which was then serving as an I.W.W. hall. Jack Reed, he of the *Ten Days That Shook the World*, was chairman of the meeting. Haywood seemed impressed that "Moscow will stand behind the IWW." He showed some communist literature to Chaplin. "Ralph," he said, "here is what we have been dreaming about. Here is the IWW all feathered out." He seemed to think that Moscow was going to make the I.W.W. the industrial wing of the communist world revolution. Chaplin and other members of the Wobbly general executive board were skeptical.

Haywood seemed to be breaking down, anyhow. His notable reserve of physical strength had lessened. A diabetic condition had worsened. His eyes were failing. He showed a tendency to sit and stare out of the window. When the comrades from Russia and their American friends invited the I.W.W. to send an emissary to Moscow, Wobbly George Williams went, on a forged passport, and returned to make an unfavorable report. Haywood was incensed. "The world revolution," he said, "is bigger than the IWW. It is our only choice." Some thought so, others didn't. From that time on there was dissension in the Wobbly ranks.

One day soon Haywood and Chaplin were approached by American communists with an offer of fake passports and a voyage to Russia. Haywood would be placed in charge of a big construction project, and also be Lenin's adviser in organizing the labor front in Russia and the Red International of Labor Unions; Chaplin would be "poet laureate of the world Revolution." That's what the comrades said. The comrades solemnly pledged that Haywood's and Chaplin's bondsmen would be fully reimbursed from Moscow. Chaplin refused to skip. Haywood's trunk was already packed. He disappeared, leaving Chaplin in an embarrassing spot.

Many Wobblies held Chaplin responsible for Big Bill's decision to run out on his bondsmen, who were Mary Marcy and William Bross Lloyd, who had put up property valued at $150,000 to meet the $30,000 bond. Chaplin was desperately chasing the elusive comrades about getting the promised money. The American Communist party had gone underground; but one day Chaplin was told that Jack Reed himself was coming to the United States, bringing "crown jewels" of the Russian nobility to be sold here and the cash used to reimburse the bondsmen. "I was to meet Reed," Chaplin recalled, "at one of the party's hideouts in the Catskill Mountains, where arrangements would be made to turn the funds over to the IWW."

Chaplin was elated. He did not know it yet but he was now getting a piece of the Big Con himself. He and an old-time Wobbly who had joined the Communist party, Charles Ashleigh, were given railroad tickets, liberal expense money, and instructions. At the train they were met by "a Comrade of foreign appearance" who had little to say but stayed close. In New York City they were taken to a top-class hotel where rooms had been reserved under phony names. Chaplin was told he was "John Fox." The plot was thickening. Chaplin felt a creeping unease; never before had someone, an unknown, at that, chosen a name for him.

Still another comrade took charge of Chaplin and Ashleigh for a night train trip up the Hudson, followed by a long ride in a closed automobile to a big old farmhouse on a lonely road somewhere in the hills. This place was guarded by a couple of Great Danes of Baskerville size and apparent ferocity. Chaplin thought it was all needlessly mysterious. The feeling of entanglement in a web he could not see took hold. The place turned out to be crowded with some twenty-odd men, several of whom he knew to be present or past members of the I.W.W. or of one or another of the Socialist groups. The big shots of the occasion were the "confidential agents from the Workers Fatherland." The agenda of this meeting, so Chaplin noticed, had been prepared in advance. Such efficiency chilled him.

Off and on for another five days and nights Chaplin sought to get information on the matter he had specially come for, the funds from the "crown jewels." He was put off by several excuses, and told to occupy himself composing a suitable resolution to protest the continued incarceration of Tom Mooney, an AFL local official who had been sent to prison on the charge of setting off a bomb during a Preparedness Day parade of 1916 in San Francisco. Then, on the last night of the farmhouse meeting, Chaplin heard the dogs barking. This surely would be Jack Reed straight from Moscow with the jewels. Instead Chaplin was called from bed and taken to a small room and told that a courier had just come from abroad with the information that Reed had been arrested in Finland and relieved of the jewels he was bringing to make good the bond on Bill Haywood.

Well, this was it, the Big Con in international labor relations, Bolshevik style.

"John Fox" returned to Chicago in time to read in the papers that the Supreme Court had refused to review the cases against Haywood, Chaplin, *et al.* Chaplin returned to Leavenworth, to spend another three years in prison, or until one day in 1923, when, as he was trimming the roses in the hospital yard, a commutation of his sentence, signed by President Warren G. Harding, arrived.

Harding had already pardoned Eugene Debs, who, while in prison at Atlanta, had polled 919,799 votes for president. The figure exceeded Debs's vote of 1912, but it was hardly a mandate for socialism.

Bill Haywood wasn't going to make it either. He never came back, but died, as said, in Moscow, where he had been sugar-teated briefly by the comrades, then put aside as a sort of stuffed relic of mild historical interest.

The Wobblies continued to decline, then split. They first resorted to slugging each other with blackjacks over possession of I.W.W. headquarters, then took the matter to the bourgeois courts. The result was two distinct groups, each claiming to be the original blown-in-the-bottle Industrial Workers of the World. Two papers appeared with I.W.W. on their mastheads. Not only Chicago but many other cities had two Wobbly halls, each carrying the old trade-mark and complete Wobbly iconography including portraits of Joe Hill, Frank Little, and the Centralia boys. It was most shameful. It was also terribly hard on the cause. Organizers were embarrassed when they approached workers, for the purpose of collecting dues, to find that a delegate of the "other" I.W.W. had been there first. The effect on Wobbly finances can be imagined. Peace was made only after a struggle from which the group never recovered. From a top membership of perhaps 100,000 they had dropped so far that headquarters ceased to report membership publicly at all.

As for the Socialists, Debs urged them in 1924 to support the insurgents headed by Robert La Follette. Since then they have kept an organization in the field, but have never threatened the republic with overthrow by vote or insurrection. Debs himself never recovered from the shock of the complete ruthlessness of the revolution in Russia. He could not really stomach the incongruities of orthodox Marxism. Though doubts must have assailed him, and though age and illness had taken its toll, he still spoke up for the "Second American Revolution," which was to complete the work begun in 1775. . . .

When in 1926, they laid Old Gene away for keeps, Norman Thomas, the magnetic ex-Presbyterian minister and Debs's successor as head of the Socialist party, paid a moving tribute to him who was the most beloved figure to appear in the ranks of labor in the United States. People who were anarchists, people who were rock-bound conservatives, people who stood between the poles, all loved Debs the man. They would neither actively work for his happy commonwealth nor even vote for him as president of their country. Yet they loved him. Debs's friend, Ralph Chaplin, thought he knew why: It was because and in spite of the fact that Debs shared the wrath of Jeremiah with many of the prophets of an earlier America, only he of them all was touched with the gentleness of Jesus.

7.

LABOR JOINS THE TRUSTS

THE decline of the Wobblies and the Socialists, plus the failure of Russian communism to attract any potent numbers, must indicate a reluctance to follow inspired dreamers by an overwhelming majority of American workers. It was so from the beginning; what was true of William Sylvis and Terrence Powderly was also true of Eugene Debs and Bill Haywood—and even more so of William Z. Foster and Earl Browder, the American communist "leaders." First and last, labor in the United States has been concerned almost wholly with improving its economic and social position within the existing system of capitalism.

All of which seems to show that the hard, pragmatic vision of Samuel Gompers made him the first true prophet of American labor. A labor union was merely a business and it was to be operated as such. If crooks and racketeers now and then got control of labor unions, it was no worse than the general run of business. And anyway, it was the job of government to police breakers of the laws.

On these premises Sam Gompers ran the American Federation of Labor. At his death in 1924 he was the acknowledged leader of labor in the country. Indeed, other than for the railroad brotherhoods, which always stood apart, the American Federation *was* organized labor in the United States. Gompers had set the mold. He had been quick and sure to ride herd on maverick unions, to get them into the corral and brand them with the union label of the Federation. The mold hardened. Gompers aged but did not change. While new technology was reducing the use of hand labor by 10 per cent, meanwhile increasing production twice over, Gompers continued to demand enactment of medieval apprenticeship laws.

To his heirs Gompers bequeathed a sort of die-hard association of specialist craftsmen, for which industry had less and less use. The advancing machine steadily decreased their number. Nor did the Federation make any notable effort to organize the millions of the unskilled who had no unions. It seemed content to take on the genteel garb of conservative respectability as it steadily declined into senile decay. At the end of the prosperous 1920s the Federation was as complacent as Wall Street in accepting the promise of assured economic advance.

The crash of 1929 was felt first in Wall Street, but it was not long before everybody knew things had changed. Quite soon some fifteen million men and women were unemployed. Still there was no move on the part of labor, organized or otherwise. There was nothing even faintly like the upheavals that occurred during the hard times of the seventies, the eighties, the nineties, and even later. Labor was going hungry, yet it remained apathetic. George Soule wrote that although there was a distinct drift of intellectuals into the radical camp, with a rising interest in communism, he could find no such trend in the ranks of labor. The workers "just sit at home and blame Prohibition," he said.

As conditions steadily worsened, however, people simply had to find a scapegoat. Blaming Prohibition for the Depression was blaming their mothers and grandmothers who gave it to them more or less in fair exchange for the ballot. What was needed was an individual, not a whole temperance movement, to serve as whipping boy, and on whose head to lay the blame and the damnation for the universal predicament such as the oldest living citizen could not remember. They looked around and chose the most "logical" candidate. He was Herbert Hoover. They had already elected him President of the United States, and now they elected him father of the Depression. They might just as well have given the distinction to Nicholas Murray Butler or Al Capone.

The new president, Franklin D. Roosevelt, acted swiftly to meet a task greater than any that had faced the nation since 1860. His administration formulated what it called the New Deal, much of it taken bodily from the almost forgotten Populists of the nineties, along with Jacob Coxey's public-works program. It set about reforming the stock market. It set prices for farm produce. It made loans to industrial enterprises. It devalued the currency. It passed laws designed to speed the organization of labor into unions. The response was immediate and enormous. In spite of itself the American Federation was swamped with demands for admittance.

The old-line craft leaders did their best to block campaigns to organize industrial unions; and presently the labor movement, at the very time of its greatest opportunity, split in two. The insurgents organized new unions, or even dual unions, in the mass-production industries. They struck for higher wages and for recognition by employers; jurisdictional disputes grew into slugging matches and occasionally broke out with gunfire. It seemed to innocent bystanders that labor, in the forms of the American Federation and the new Congress of Industrial Organizations, was devoting more time to fighting each other than to fighting employers.

William Green, head of the American Federation, took occasion to describe the man who quickly became and remained the symbol of the new insurgents. He was John L. Lewis. This was the man, Mr. Green declared, who sought ends other than the welfare of the workers; he had given the lie to the democratic process. He had raised the voice of dualism and disunity; it was a voice which, while pretending to unite, sought to disrupt. It was, in short, a voice seeking dictatorship.

Whatever Mr. Lewis may have sought, his was a voice that could be heard, and he retorted that Mr. Green's American Federation represented twenty-five years of unbroken failure to organize the workers. And because Mr. Lewis fancied himself an elegant orator, he added a handsome flavor of antique erudition to his stricture. "Alas, poor Green," observed Mr. Lewis to the press, "I knew him well. He wishes me to join him in fluttering procrastination, while intoning *O tempora, O mores!*" The boys were delighted to put the remark into their stories.

John Llewellyn Lewis reminded nobody of Debs or Haywood. About him was the melodramatic pose of a tragedian of the old school. He looked and spoke like a ham actor. In and out of the ranks of labor there were men who called him a windbag; others said he was an elemental force. Born in Lucas County, Iowa, of Welsh parents, at twelve he was a pit boy in the coal mines who went steadily upward and onward in the United Mine Workers of the American Federation of labor, and by 1919 he was ruling the coal miners with a heavy hand and fighting the coal operators. A little more and he had also to stem a revolt in the union ranks against his leadership. Then came the Depression and federal legislation encouraging labor unions. Nobody else in organized labor acted so promptly and to such purpose as Lewis.

Still fresh in mind is the struggle he waged that resulted in the Congress of Industrial Organizations and more bitterness than labor had known since the nineties. By 1938 the CIO group claimed more than 3,700,000 members as against 3,400,000 members for the American Federation. By then, too, the split was complete. The Federation started to set up industrial unions. The CIO began to charter craft unions. A bewildered public, beset by strikes, violence, and racketeering, was inclined to consign both sides to the devil.

There was still time for one more chance to usher in an almost custom-made and virtually patented Utopia for the working class, indeed for everybody. It was presented by Howard Scott, an impressively tall and voluble man who had long been a familiar figure in the radical-bohemian circles of New York City, the poets, painters, and various dabblers in the arts typified by Greenwich Village. Based on Thorstein Veblen's *The Engineers and the Price System*, Scott dreamed up a more-or-less peaceful revolution that could be had without a bomb being set off or a shot fired. Or almost. He had it all done up in one package called Technocracy, an over-all plan so simple, said he, that even a trade-union official could comprehend it: With his blueprint of Technocracy twelve engineers in strategic spots could bring capitalism to its knees in three days.

The Engineer with a capital letter, the planner, had been slowly emerging as the new hero and magician of modern industry. He was not to supplant the scientist-god of the late nineteenth century, but as a scientific engineer he *was* a man of science. This engineer-planner was above politics, above the petty wars of capital and labor. He was so scientific he disdained to measure toil by the hour, or by the dollar, or by the sweat of the brow. Everything was *energy,* and energy was a matter of ergs and joules. It was pretty impressive.

The Depression did nothing to discredit this new hero. He has been ready all the time to point the way, but the prehensile captains of industry, while urging the engineer to eliminate waste and increase production, were sharp enough to keep him fettered lest he foster a revolution by revamping his magic for the benefit of all classes. Bear in mind, ye slaves—only *twelve* of these magicians could in *three* days bring capital to its knees. . . .

It was probably only natural that Technocracy should attract the discontented. Even before the crash Howard Scott had been employed by the I.W.W. to engineer—that is, to plan scientifically—a Bureau of Industrial Research for the coming Wobbly Commonwealth. In his captivating memoirs, *Wobbly,* Ralph Chaplin described graphically his first meeting with the technocratic prophet. He was impressed with the plan, for after all, the engineer was included in the "One Big Union's" own chart for the new society. But though Chaplin was a poet and artist, as well as the I.W.W.'s editor, he was not attracted to the bohemian atmosphere in which Scott seemed to thrive. All the time Scott was so plausibly discoursing about "tear drop automobiles, flying wing airplanes, and technological unemployment," Chaplin was "looking at the other side of the studio, where an appalling phallic watercolor painting was displayed among blueprints and graphs on a big easel."

Scott's official connection with the I.W.W. was very brief, yet many a Wobbly was to embrace Technocracy with all the fervor they had previously devoted to the Industrial Workers of the World. So did a few surviving single-taxers, and a whole horde of college professors, many of whom also turned out to be plastic material for the Big Con of the American Communist party. From Maine to Oregon, and in many places in the South, one could see old halls freshly labeled "TECHNOCRACY," while along the highways, contending for attention with Dr. Pierce's Golden Medical Discovery, were neat Technocracy signs in modest pastel shades displaying the mystic symbol of the "Great Monad" of eternal life, which, oddly enough, had been adopted half a century earlier, as its trade-mark, by the Northern Pacific Railroad Company. An array of imposing academic sponsors pronounced engineer Scott to be the man of the hour, and said that the hour was already striking.

The masses, however, did not rise. They might be jobless, and underfed, but they just did not want Technocracy. One is hard put to name another prophet who rose overnight to such eminence only to disappear so quickly and manifestly, leaving no trace, as Howard Scott. Even good Dr. Francis E. Townsend, inventor of the Townsend Revolving Pension Plan, made a more lasting impression than Scott's Technocrats. Scott's twelve engineers who in three days were to make pulp of capitalism had gone down the drain to join the Noble Order of the Knights of Labor in the limbo where *Progress and Poverty* and *Looking Backward* were on the required reading list and the house phonograph played a cracked record of *The Big Rock Candy Mountains*. Technocracy was to be the last train for Utopia in the first half of the twentieth century.

Both the American Federation and the CIO surged ahead out of the Depression and into the years of a new World War, to emerge as giants fit to live in the land of New Gath. Their internecine warfare had become an uneasy peace. Then, in 1956, the two groups merged to form a union of more than fifteen million members. Here was a trust in the accepted popular meaning of the word, equal to meet with and not only to talk business to the colossi of steel, of oil, of motors and whatnot, but often to dictate the terms.

Of the socialist dreams of co-operative commonwealths and all such trumpery nothing remained. If there was any longer even a euphemism for Utopia, it was security. Security seemed to have come to govern all, in and out of unions. For better or worse, the great majority of Americans demanded security in place of what, in former times, was called opportunity. There remained, to be sure, no few adventuresome spirits in the ranks of unionism who, protected by the cloak of honest labor, operated some of the most vicious, cruel, and efficient rackets ever devised.

Obviously the great danger of this new One Big Union was the very danger that labor in the past had deplored in the one big union of employers called the trusts, or simply "The System." It was the danger of power concentrated in a great corporation. The simplest workingman knew that a corporation is a legal fiction which assumes the financial liability that otherwise would rest on the individual stockholders; nor are the individual stockholders to be held morally responsible for the acts of the corporation. It is here that the corporate fiction enters the realm of metaphysics. It has been observed that a corporation, whether engaged in selling oil or selling labor, almost automatically takes over the consciences of the individual stockholders.

Labor had become the biggest kind of big business. Only a handful of aged veterans could remember the days when capital was warned, in purple strophes, that no longer was the crown of thorns to be pressed down upon the brow of labor. Nor was labor to hang crucified upon a cross of gold. Now labor had even lost its chains, of which for generations it had been said to have nothing else to lose. These war cries that once made men see red and sent them roaring into the streets now seemed amusing antiquities as quaintly naïve as the name and style of the Sons of Vulcan and the Noble Order of the Knights of Labor.

EPILOGUE

ONE fine day in the summer of 1840 Ralph Waldo Emerson sat down in the quiet of his study, in lovely rustic Concord, to confide to his journal an astonishment at what he called the enormous fertility of projects for salvation of the world. Concord was only eighteen miles from Boston. It was Boston to which most of the salvationists hurried to get their prescriptions filled. The air above the Charles was fast filling with their outcries and demands.

No man alive was more intellectually curious than Mr. Emerson, who seemed so hospitable to all new ideas that many people believed him to be a reformer, and a radical reformer, at that. He was not a reformer. He merely enjoyed discussing ideas, and it mattered little to him whether they had to do with reforms, or the oversoul, or the nature of poetry. For all the buoyancy of his transcendental philosophy he was at rock bottom a skeptic.

It is true that once he went so far as to try Sylvester Graham's diet, but only briefly and doubtless halfheartedly. He was never to take part in Brook Farm or any other so-called experiment in living. He did come to speak up for abolition, yet even here it was obvious he was no zealot; and it was held against him that there was no fire in his talks. First and last, he was to be a critic rather than a crusader. He was still under forty when he observed of men that only in spring and summer were they reformers, that in winter they stood fast by the old ways and customs. He was hardly a day older when he wrote it down that "reform has no gratitude, no prudence, no husbandry."

On this particular day in 1840, as he approached his daily and welcome task of recording random reflections in his journal, he may have been freshly reminded of some singularly inane proposal for salvation. He had already seen the congress of the Friends of Universal Reform in action, and had come away amused at the sight and the noise they made. He is still amused, but there is now, as he writes in his journal, a flavor of asperity to his observations. He is irritated.

The country is full of rebellion, he writes. It is full of kings. Hands off! let there be neither control of nor interference with the administration of things. Even the insect world is to be defended and cared for. It has already been too long neglected, and a society for the protection of ground worms, slugs, and mosquitoes is to be incorporated without delay. He notes, too, that the adepts of homeopathy and hydropathy are on the loose, and also phrenologists, all of them crying miracles. Others are attacking the institution of marriage as the fountainhead of social evil. There is an awful din of opinion and debate. There is a disposition of scrutiny and dissent in civil, festive, neighborly, and domestic society. He notes a restless, prying, conscientious criticism everywhere. "I confess," he writes, "that the motto of the *Globe* newspaper is so attractive to me that I seldom find much appetite to read what is below in its columns: *The world is governed too much.*"

Mr. Emerson is patently fed up with salvation by crusade. Observe that he seems not to doubt the honesty of reformers. He remarks that they are restless and prying, but they are also conscientious. These are qualities that must have tended to add to their unpopularity. They were, to begin with, visionaries. They were also restless—that is, they never let up, they were forever harping away on one string. The monotony was maddening. They were always prying, which was to say they were curious to impertinence—peering, peeping, inquisitive. Worst of all was that only too many of these men and women bringing salvation wore their righteousness thick and heavy.

No, dreamers and visionaries and prophets were not often, if ever, easy people to have around one. Tyrants, a philosopher wrote, have no consciences, while reformers have no feeling. He thought that the world suffered as much from the one as from the other.

When Emerson's friend Henry Thoreau sought to bring the government to its knees by refusing to pay the town poll tax, and was put in Concord jail, it was Emerson who came to pay the tax and free him. "Henry," said the Sage of Concord, looking in the iron door, "I am surprised to find you in *there*." And Thoreau thereupon unloaded a heavy cargo of self-righteousness upon the kindly Emerson. "Ralph," he retorted bitterly, "I am surprised to see you *out there*." Having thus indicated that all decent men *should* be in jail, Thoreau was content to rejoin society, doubtless believing he had struck a fatal blow against the republic, and incidentally given Emerson his comeuppance.

On another occasion, as related, it was Emerson who came to the rescue of Bronson Alcott and his numerous family after that philosopher's disastrous idiotic experiment at Fruitlands. The experience seems not to have humbled old Alcott in the least; with something besides barley and apples to eat, and with warm clothes on his back, he set up at once as the Orphic Oracle of all New England.

No, visionaries were not always easy-wearing friends. If they were bringing salvation they might, when they first started the job, be modest and humble, but in time righteousness was thrust upon them by their disciples, and they quickly came to wear it as proper and of right. There is good evidence that, when Miss Frances Willard began her career, she was an extremely modest woman, one of the kind spoken of as "retiring." After twenty-five years of adulation by her host of followers, who declared her to be a saint, the pretty old maid was still gentle but she had developed the practice of carefully counting and comparing the bouquets given her at public meetings, and a saying went the rounds that Miss Willard's affair with Miss Willard should be stopped by the police.

When John Bartholomew Gough crawled out of the gutter, he was a man most subdued and humble; after four decades of denouncing the Viper in the Glass to immense audiences, who *paid* to hear him, he might still be revered to millions, yet there were honest reporters for honest newspapers who detected in Gough more than a modicum of pose, along with an air of too much saintly condescension.

There was, of course, nothing of pose in the deadly Carry Nation. Still, one is appalled to contemplate a life in *her* company.

To the world Samuel Gridley Howe was the plumed knight of humanitarian striving. Only a few knew that he married Julia Ward Howe in order, to quote Howe himself, to reform her. Even fewer knew that he tried to run his own household along the lines of an institution. Fewer still knew that he asked his wife for a divorce so he might marry a younger woman. It was to be the most bitter irony of his fate that, far from "reforming" his wife, she wrote the lyrics for a song that turned *him* into "Mrs. Howe's husband."

Long years after his death John Humphrey Noyes was remembered by his son Pierrepont as seeming more like an abstract power than a father.

Josiah Warren, America's first anarchist, may have been a notable exception among reformers. He merely laid out a blueprint for Utopia, and when his fellow Americans displayed not the least interest—well, it was *their* loss, and no hard feelings. So, Warren got out his beloved old French horn from its case and resumed blowing the resonant and melancholy notes that gave him such pleasure. One fancies him in the salvationist Valhalla, blowing away, oblivious to the uproar of his self-righteously indignant companions.

There was, of course, Henry George, a man personally beloved by millions who nevertheless thought his single tax belonged with Mother Goose, and loved him in spite of it. After all, a man is entitled to at least one heresy, so long as it is wholly rational and hence has no chance of being adopted.

Millions loved Eugene Debs, too, though more millions feared him as they would the devil. His was possibly the most engaging personality of all the major dreamers of his time. But few of those who loved him would give him their vote, while the others, among them all capitalists and the upper-class proletarians who were manacled, not to the pick and shovel, but to a splendid craft, would have nothing to do with him. Time has blotted out memory of the juvenile fury of his worst emotional outbursts. And his successor, the less emotional but more intellectual and just as genial Norman Thomas, has had the effect of making socialism something that can be talked about without raising voices to the pitch of crusade. Debs is dead only thirty years. Could he return, he might be dumfounded at much he saw, yet he would see also that a great deal of what he fought for had been won. The steadily advancing welfare state might entrance him.

Bill Haywood refused the martyrdom of prison, to flee abroad and to die a faded minor subcommissar among the Bolsheviki, the most hated of all their virtually countless enemies by members of the Industrial Workers of the World. The Wobblies were alone in wanting to canonize Big Bill. When he turned communist, he lost his chance at sainthood.

Although it came to pass that Sam Gompers, rather than Debs or Haywood, seems to have been nearest the role of the true prophet of labor, Sam became neither a martyr nor a first-class saint. He believed that the workingman considered himself an incipient capitalist temporarily with no money other than his wages, but as filled with hope as any Alger hero. On that plan Gompers proposed to operate, and he never wavered. Sam could be pompous. He emitted clichés as ponderous and empty as those of the presidents, senators, and industrialists he liked to mix with. For the press he delivered homely little truths that sounded like *Bartlett's Quotations,* as well they may have been. But Little Sam kept his eye on the goal, which was businesslike and not idealistic unionism, and kept also his iron grip on the American Federation. He was good for labor. He was even dramatic, if you compared him with his successors. But Gompers was simply not the kind of material of which lesser men make gods. He was more comparable to Andrew Carnegie than to Eugene Debs.

As for Terence Powderly, Grand Master Workman of the Noble Order of the Knights of Labor, he stands in the shadows as a chromatic and faceless mustache, still telling his downtrodden masses to give up the drinking of beer and whiskey and wait patiently for the co-operative commonwealth of labor. General Jacob Coxey, father of Legal Tender Coxey, fares no better than Powderly. When Coxey died in 1951 at an immense old age, he could be recalled, if at all, as the comical leader of a mass of clowns made up to look like the late Nat Wills, tramp comedian, all of whom were arrested by a posse of Keystone Cops and charged with trespassing on the Capitol lawn in Washington. Comedians may be loved. They cannot be made into gods or martyrs or even leaders of minor causes.

Of all the good and forgotten men who once achieved real distinction for their efforts to improve life in the United States, the prison reformers seem the most totally forgotten. One thinks of Louis Dwight, Zebulon Brockway, and others, including the several Pilsburys, as having done prodigious work in the face of determined opposition. The public just did not want prisons to be bettered. It resented all amelioration of the lot of prisoners. Convicts were enemies. Keeping them locked up was what counted. Never mind trying to make them over into useful members of society. At least half the time Dwight and the others, right down to Tom Osborne, were considered dangerous visionaries, seeking only to coddle felons, to turn them loose to resume their nefarious and often murderous occupations.

Such are the opinions held in large part to the present day. The average American seldom thinks of prisons except when he periodically notes a staggering sum in his state or city budget for their support, or reads of another prison riot, or sees a crime story in which it is mentioned that the criminal is a parolee. Whereupon he cries *"Coddling!"* which is practically the only form of criticism the layman can think of. No, let the reformer of prisons and criminals rest content, if he can, in the knowledge that he did the best he could, but let him not look for fame, or even commendation from anybody except others in his field—if there.

There is of course a female ward in the dreamers' Valhalla, and there can be no doubt as to its queen. She is neither an angel of mercy, as nurses used to be known, nor a schoolteacher, nor one of the courageous amazons who demanded of the dominant and domineering males that women be given the vote along with a number of other rights. She is Frances Willard, the white-ribboned, all-conquering enemy of alcohol. As a woman she stands alone of her sex amid the seventy-nine Great Men of America, as selected by the various states, in Statuary Hall of the national Capitol.

Here is an illustrious eminence almost beyond the imagination. It could have happened nowhere else on earth except in the United States. And Miss Willard's being there *is* beyond the imagination of visitors from abroad. Many a Latin and many a Briton have started at the chaste marble statue of this lone woman, standing there on equal terms with Washington and Jefferson, with Webster and Calhoun, with Grant and Lee, and inquired to know how came she to this unique honor. They are told, correctly enough, that Miss Willard is there because she was president of something named the Woman's Christian Temperance Union; and that the Union was the foe of strong drink, including the lightest of light wines and of all beers. If the Briton coughs and the Latin chokes, it is because they are gentlemen trying to cover a ribald astonishment.

There is another graphic measure by which we Americans gauge the distinction of our great men and women. This is the Hall of Fame on the University Heights campus of the University of New York City, and within it are the eighty-three national heroes and heroines selected by a group of electors appointed by the University. Washington and Jefferson are there, so is Webster but not Calhoun, and Lee but not Grant; and so, too, is Miss Willard, the sole woman to stand in both Statuary Hall and the Hall of Fame.

The Hall of Fame is more hospitable to woman than the other. In it are the statues of Miss Willard and five other women. Among them, though she had to wait till 1950, is Miss Susan B. Anthony, the only genuine rights-of-woman woman in the Hall. No doubt Miss Anthony deserves the honor, even if it must have been a heart-rending experience to choose at all with such contenders as Elizabeth Cady Stanton and Lucy Stone. So far as Mrs. Stone is concerned, she achieved the distinction of getting into the lexicons by way of *Lucy Stoner,* to designate a married woman who retains her maiden name. Even Amelia Jenks Bloomer made it too, if only as the popularizer of an ugly garment.

The vagaries of posthumous fame are neither to be explained, nor excused. One can only accept them, and still wonder why this man or this woman was tossed to some peak of eminence, high or low, to remain as a symbol, reasonably secure and shining in the beautiful mellow light of history; while others are almost as forgotten as if they never lived. History is not so divisible as to permit of neat partitions clearly marked, with their importances accurately assessed. The assessors discover that they must do a lot of hemming and hawing, that they must argue this, and concede that, to the end that they wind up their efforts in a mass of qualifications. Fame, however, does not pay strict attention to history, with its dull facts and qualified ambiguities. It alights where it chooses, and often remains there. Carlyle, who wrote much of heroes, thought that fame was no sure test of merit. It was an accident.

On the whole those dreamers Emerson called salvationists have been treated as well by posterity as, and possibly more tenderly than, they were by their contemporaries. One should bear in mind that many of them were not easy to get along with, not what is known as good company. One should remember that they met suspicion and even resentment when they were alive and crying, "This is the way" through the wilderness. They were often mistaken guides in a wilderness which seemed pathless and impenetrable to their fellows, who after all may have been right.

One may muse on what they would say, could they return from the shadows to look upon the United States today. As they were born prophets, one may be sure that they would not be speechless, no matter the impact upon them of a country that has moved, either ahead, or sideways, or even backward, according to who is speaking, during the past fifty years and at a speed which makes us of later generations wonder if we have not been in too great a hurry.

I choose to think, or perhaps I only *feel,* that the United States today is infinitely a "more perfect union" than that conceived by the Founding Fathers. By "union" I do not mean only our political arrangements. I mean a more perfect society. For all its many faults, it is a society in which life, liberty, and the pursuit of happiness are recognized as never before to be the rights of all. These rights were not ours simply because of a bold statement in the Declaration. We got them in large part, during the past one hundred and eighty years, by the efforts of assorted dreamers and visionaries who were basically seeking perfection.

Only a few of their names can be found in our schoolbooks. Fewer still stand in marble or bronze in our halls and parks. The mass of Americans knows little or nothing of them. Never mind. They dreamed nobly, and they acted. Taken all together, they were enormously effective in making the United States a better place to live than it otherwise would have been and is. They were a daft, earnest, honest, and all-but-incredible lot of men and women. I think of them as a sort of national conscience.

BIBLIOGRAPHY

PART ONE—THE PERFECT SOCIETY

Edmonds, Walter D., *The First Hundred Years*, Oneida, 1948.
Hinds, William A., *American Communities*, Oneida, 1878.
Nordoff, Charles, *The Communist Societies of the United States*, New York, 1875.
Noyes, George Wallingford, *John Humphrey Noyes, the Putney Community*, Oneida, 1931.
Noyes, John Humphrey, *Male Continence*, Oneida, 1873.
Noyes, Pierrepont, *My Father's House*, New York, 1937.
Parker, Robert A., *A Yankee Saint*, New York, 1935.
Wells, H. G., *The Future of America*, New York, 1906.

PART TWO—THE SHAKERS OF TREES

Brink, Carol, *Harps in the Wind*, New York, 1947.
Carmer, Carl, *The Hudson*, New York, 1939.
Colt, Miriam Davis, *Went to Kansas*, Watertown, New York, 1862.
Dictionary of American Biography, New York, 1928-1944.
Ditzion, Sidney, *Marriage, Morals and Sex in America*, New York, 1953.
Emerson, Ralph Waldo, *Essays*, Boston, 1883.
Horton, H. P., "The Story of Modern Times," in *Long Island Forum*, Bay Shore, Long Island, New York, February 1944.
Macdonald, George E., *Fifty Years of Freethought*, 2 vols., New York, 1931.
Sears, Clara Endicott, *Bronson Alcott's Fruitlands*, Boston, 1915.
Shephard, Odell, *Pedlar's Progress*, Boston, 1937.
Swift, Lindsay, *Brook Farm*, New York, 1900.
Trowbridge, John T., "A Reminisence of the Pantarch," in *The Independent*, February 26, 1903.

PART THREE—THE VIPER IN THE GLASS

Adams, Charles Francis, *Three Episodes of Massachusetts History*, Vol. 2, Boston, 1892.
Asbury, Herbert, *Carry Nation*, New York, 1950.
———, *The Great Illusion*, New York, 1950.
Brink, Carol, *Harps in the Wind*, New York, 1947.
Dwyer, James L., "The Lady with the Hatchet," in *The American Mercury*, March 1926.
Gough, John B., *Sunlight and Shadow*, Hartford, 1881.
———, *Platform Echoes, or Leaves from my Note-Book of Forty Years*, Hartford, 1886.

Gunning, Robert, "The Hypocrite's Cocktail," in *The American Mercury*, December 1942.

Jordan, Philip D., *Singin' Yankees*, Minneapolis, 1946.

Krout, John Allen, *The Origins of Prohibition*, New York, 1925.

Maguire, John F., *Father Mathew*, London, 1863.

Merz, Charles, *The Dry Decade*, New York, 1931.

Poling, Daniel A., *John Barleycorn*, Philadelphia, 1933.

Walker, Joseph, *Vinegar Bitters Almanac*, New York, 1874.

Werner, M. R., *Barnum*, New York, 1923.

Willard, Frances E., *Glimpses of Fifty Years*, Chicago, 1889.

PART FOUR—GOD MADE THE LAND FOR USE

Allen, Ethan, *A Brief Narrative of the Proceedings of the Government of New-York*, Hartford, 1774.

Beales, Carleton, *American Earth*, Philadelphia, 1939.

Beard, Charles A. and Mary R., *The Rise of American Civilization*, New York, 1927.

Beer, Thomas, *The Mauve Decade*, New York; 1926.

Billington, Ray A., *Westward Expansion*, New York, 1949.

Bizell, W. B., *The Green Rising*, New York, 1926.

Brainard, Dudley S., "Nininger, a Boom Town," in *Minnesota History*, June, 1932.

Buck, Solon J., *The Agrarian Crusade*, New Haven, 1920.

Christman, Henry, *Tin Horns and Calico*, New York, 1945.

Connecticut Courant, files of, Hartford.

Ford, Miriam Allen de, "The Amazing Ignatius Donnelly," in *American Parade*, Vol. II, No. 2, Girard, Kansas.

George, Henry, *Progress and Poverty*, New York, 1879.

George Jr., *The Life of Henry George*, New York, 1900.

Greene, Evarts B., *The Revolutionary Generation*, New York, 1943.

Hall, Benjamin H., *History of Eastern Vermont*, New York, 1858.

Hicks, John D., *The Populist Revolt*, Minneapolis, 1931.

———, "The Political Career of Ignatius Donnelly," in *Mississippi Historical Review*, VII, 1921.

History of Delaware County, New York, New York, 1880.

Hofstadter, Richard, *The Age of Reform*, New York, 1955.

Holbrook, Stewart H., *The Yankee Exodus*, New York, 1950.

———, *Ethan Allan*, New York, 1940.

Jones, Matt B., *Vermont in the Making*, Cambridge, Mass., 1939.

Kelley, Oliver H., *Origin and Progress of the Order of the Patrons of Husbandry*, n.p., 1875.

Leopold, Richard W., *Robert Dale Owen*, Cambridge, Mass., 1940.

Lillard, Richard G., *The Great Forest*, New York, 1947.

Maxey, Edwin, "The Father of the Homestead Bill," in *Overland Monthly*, July, 1908.

Morrison, Samuel Eliot, and Commager, Henry Steele, *The Growth of the American Republic*, 2 vols., New York, 1940.

Myers, Gustavus, *History of the Great American Fortunes*, 1936.

Nock, Albert J, *Henry George*, New York, 1939.

O'Callaghan, E. B., Ed., *Documentary History of New York*, Albany, 1850.

Parrington, Vernon Louis, *Main Currents of American Thought*, New York, 1930.

Pell, John, *Ethan Allen*, Boston, 1929.

Pringle, Henry F., *Theodore Roosevelt*, New York, 1930.

Puter, S. A. D., *Looters of the Public Domain*, Portland, Ore., 1908.

Thompson, Zadock, *History of Vermont*, Burlington, 1842.

Turner, F. J., *The Frontier in American History*, New York, 1920.

PART FIVE—THE RIGHTS OF WOMAN

Anthony, Katharine, *Susan B. Anthony*, New York, 1954.

Beebe, Lucius, *Comstock Commotion*, Stanford, Cal., 1954.

Blackwell, Alice Stone, *Lucy Stone*, Boston, 1930.

Brooks, Van Wyck, *The Flowering of New England*, New York, 1936.

Broun, Heywood, and Leech, Margaret, *Anthony Comstock*, New York, 1927.

Ditzion, Sidney, *Marriage, Morals and Sex in America*, New York, 1953.

Hibben, Paxton, *Henry Ward Beecher*, New York, 1942.

Leech, Margaret, and Broun, Heywood, *Anthony Comstock*, New York, 1927.

Pattee, Fred Lewis, *The Feminine Fifties*, New York, 1940.

Shippee, L. B., "Jane Grey Swisshelm; Agitator," in *Mississippi Valley Historical Review*, December 1920.

Stanton, Elizabeth Cady, *et al*, *The History of Woman Suffrage*, 6 vols., 1881–1922.

Stern, Madeline B., *Purple Passage, the Life of Mrs. Frank Leslie*, Norman, Okla., 1953.

Thornton, Willis, *The Nine Lives of Citizen Train*, New York, 1948.

Walker, Sibyl, "No Doll Was Abigail," in *The American Mercury*, August 1948.

Woodward, Helen Beal, *The Bold Woman*, New York, 1953.

Wright, Richardson, *Forgotten Ladies*, Philadelphia, 1928.

PART SIX—THY BROTHERS' KEEPERS

Bacon, Edwin M., Ed., *King's Dictionary of Boston*, 1883.

Barnes, Harry Elmer, *New Horizons in Criminology*, New York, 1947.

———, *The Story of Punishment*, Boston, 1930.

———, *The Repression of Crime*, New York, 1926.

Brockway, Zebulon R., *Fifty Years of Prison Service*, New York, 1912.

Burroughs, Stephen, *Memoirs of the Notorious Stephen Burroughs* (a reprint), New York, 1924.

Chaplin, Ralph, *Bars and Shadows, the Prison Poems of Ralph Chaplin*, Ridgewood, New Jersey, 1922.

De Land, Fred, *Dumb No Longer*, New York, 1908.

Dickens, Charles, *American Notes*, London, 1893.

Gallaudet, E. M., *The Life of Thos. Hopkins Gallaudet*, 1888.

Gallaudet, Edward Miner, and Bell, Alexander G., *Education of Deaf Children*, Washington, D.C., 1892.

Johnson, Sgt. J. R., "The Penitentiary," in *Marion County History*, Vol. 2, June 1956, Salem, Ore.

Keller, Helen, *The Story of My Life*, New York, 1909.

Kelley, Joseph, *Thirteen Years in the Oregon Penitentiary*, Portland, Oregon, 1908.

Lewis, O. F., *The Development of American Prisons and Prison Customs*, New York, 1922.

McKelvey, Blake, *American Prisons*, Chicago, 1936.

Marshall, Helen E., *Dorothea Dix*, Chapel Hill, N.C., 1937.

Osborne, Thomas Mott, *Prisons and Common Sense*, Philadelphia, 1924.

Richards, Laura E., *Samuel Gridley Howe*, New York, 1935.

Ross, Ishbel, *Journey into Light*, New York, 1951.

Sanborn, F. B., *Dr. S. G. Howe, the Philanthropist*, Boston, 1891.

Teeters, Negley K., and Barnes, Harry Elmer, *New Horizons in Criminology*, New York, 1947.

Tharp, Louise Hall, *Three Saints and a Sinner*, Boston, 1956.

Tiffany, Francis, *Life of Dorothea Lynde Dix*, Boston, 1891.

PART SEVEN—NOTHING TO LOSE BUT CHAINS

Adamic, Louis, *Dynamite*, New York, 1931.

Chaplin, Ralph, *Wobbly*, Chicago, 1948.

Coleman, J. Walter, *The Molly Maguire Riots*, Richmond, Va., 1936.

Coleman, McAllister, *Eugene V. Debs*, New York, 1931.

Commons, John R., and others, *History of Labor in the United States*, 4 vols., New York, 1918–35.

David, Henry, *The History of the Haymarket Affair*, New York, 1936.

Dulles, Foster Rhea, *Labor in America*, New York, 1940.

Holbrook, Stewart H., *Iron Brew*, New York, 1939.

———, *The Rocky Mountain Revolution*, New York, 1956.

———, "Coxey's Army and Populism," in *The Oregonian*, Portland, March 7, 1937.

Lewis, Lloyd, and Smith, Henry Justin, *Chicago, the History of Its Reputation*, New York, 1929.

McMurry, Donald L., *Coxey's Army*, Boston, 1929.

Morais, Herbert M., and Cahn, William, *Gene Debs*, New York, 1948.

Steffens, Lincoln, *Autobiography*, New York, 1931.

Stowell, Myron B., *Fort Frick, or the Siege of Homestead*, Pittsburgh, 1893.

Thompson, Fred, *The I.W.W. Its First Fifty Years*, Chicago, 1955.

Yellen, Samuel, *American Labor Struggles*, New York, 1936.

INDEX

Abbott, Lyman, 55-56, 63, 70, 73
Abolition, agitation for, 35, 75, 78, 83, 149, 178, 190
Adams, John, 58
Adams, Samuel, 289
Adams, Steve, 325
Addams, Jane, 213
Address on the Effects of Ardent Spirits, 66
Adventist faith, 7, 177
Advocate, The, 146-47
Age of Reason, The, 146
Agrarianism, 139
Aguirre, M. G., 254
Alabama, 107, 153, 233, 274
Alarm, The, 295, 297
Albany (N.Y.), 75, 85, 122-24, 129-30, 134, 136-37, 140, 248; Burgesses Corps of, 141; prisons of, 245-46
Albany (Ore.), 207
Alcohol, abuse of, 55 ff.
Alcott, Amos Bronson, 36, 40-41, 174, 344
Alcott, Louisa May, 36, 41-42
Allen, Ethan, 119, 121-33, 139, 159
Allen, Heman, 130-31
Allen, Henry, 19
Allen, Ira, 128-29
Altgeld, John P., 298, 310-11
Alwato language, 43
American Anti-Slavery Society, 178
American Association for the Promotion of the Teaching of Speech to the Deaf, 266
American Bible Society, 240, 242
American Birth Control League, 217
American Congressional Temperance Society, 64
American Federation of Labor, 288, 295, 299, 312, 314-15, 319, 326-28, 331, 337-39, 341, 346
American Foundation for the Blind, 276
American Legion, 333
American Lyceum movement, 87

American Printing House for the Blind, 275
American Railway Union, 307-12, 314-16, 321
American Revolution, 135-36, 143, 150, 235
American School for the Deaf, 263 f.
American Temperance Society, 64
American Temperance Union, 64-68, 72-74, 76, 85, 90
American Woman Suffrage Association, 196, 199, 205-6, 209, 211, 216
Amherst College, 45, 96, 147
Anagnos, Michael, 274-75
Anarchism (anarchists), 42-44, 165, 216, 295, 297-99, 310, 316, 318, 332, 336, 345
Ancient Order of Hibernians, 293
Anderson, David, 69
Andover (Mass.), 64
Andover Theological Seminary, 4, 59, 262
Andrew, John A., 83
Andrews, Stephen Pearl, 43-44
Anthony, Katharine, 85, 196
Anthony, Susan Brownell, 85-86, 187, 193-94, 206-7, 213-15, 218, 220, 235; converted to woman's rights, 179, 184; and Eddy bequest, 210-11; marble bust of, 213; Northwest toured by, 208; and reconciliation with Lucy Stone, 211; statue of, in Hall of Fame, 348; Train associated with, 195-96; as vice-president of National-American Woman Suffrage Association, 211; Woman's Celebration Petition drawn up by, 212; and Woodhull, Victoria, 197-202, 205
Anti-Monopolist, The, 156
Anti-Rent association, 137, 139, 143
Anti-Renter, The, 143
Anti-Saloon League of America, 96-97, 104-10, 213
Appeal to Reason, 316-18, 321-22, 325-26, 328

Perkins, Thomas Handasyd, 271

Perkins Institution for the Blind, 230, 271-75

Perry, Gates, 6

Peruna, 90-91

Pettibone, George A., 320-21, 325

Pfrimmer, Sam, 303

Phelps, Timothy, 133

Philadelphia, 57-58, 61, 70, 72, 75, 80, 131, 162, 182, 211, 233; blind school in, 270; Eastern Penitentiary at, 239-41; Knights of Labor organized in, 291-92; as most important city in U.S., 240; prison system at, 239-41, 247; Quakers of, 236, 239, 255, 268; shoemakers of, 289

Philadelphia Centennial, 212-13

Philadelphia Society for Alleviating the Miseries of Public Prisons, 232, 236-37, 249

Phillips, Coles, 29

Phillips, Wendell, 183-84

Phoenix, Brattleboro, 6

Phonautograph, 265

Phrenology, 45-46, 48, 73, 177, 344

Pierce, Franklin, 233

Pilgrims, Bullard's, 7

Pilsbury, Amos, 244-46, 248

Pilsbury, Lewis Dwight, 246

Pilsbury, Moses, 244

Pinkerton men, in "Battle of Homestead," 280, 282-86

Pinkerton National Detective Agency, 280, 293, 321

Pitman, Benn, 188-89

Pittsburgh, 95, 189-90, 192, 279-81, 283-84, 287, 303

Plan of Division, for Oneida Community, 27

Platt, Thomas, 212

Plymouth Church, 198, 201, 203-4, 255

Police Gazette, National, 25, 202

Polk, James K., 148

Polling, William, 262

Populism (populists), 157-59, 214, 300-1, 304, 306, 313-14, 316, 338

Populist Revolt, The, 159

Portland (Me.), 68, 77-79

Portland (Ore.), 152, 200, 207-8, 305

Portsmouth (N.H.), 122, 260

Post, Amelia, 193

Poultney (Vt.), 7, 122

Powderly, Terence V., 288-89, 292, 294-95, 298, 315, 337, 346

Prendergast, William, 118, 136

Prescott, William, 269

Prescott, William Hickling, 268-70

Press, Philadelphia, 197

Price, Hiram, 97

Pringle, Henry, 165

Pringle, John, 270

Prison reform, 241, 244, 247-52, 254-61, 347

Prisoner's Aid Society, 254

Prisons, in United States, 230, 236-57, 259-60

Progress and Poverty, 163-64, 341

Prohibition, 36, 60, 76-79, 97, 105-8, 209, 338; repeal of, 109-10

Prohibition party, 83, 96

Providence (R.I.), 75, 232

Puck magazine, 25

Pulitzer, Joseph, 317

Pullman, George Mortimer, 308-9, 312

Pullman Company, *1894* strike against, 306, 309-12

Puter, Stephen A. Douglas, 151-52, 160

Putney, 3, 5-13, 20, 55

Putney Corporation of Perfectionists, 4, 6, 9, 12

Quakers, blind school of, 268; penology of, 236, 239, 255

Radical, The, 146

Rankin, Jeanette, 223

Rappite-Harmonists, 42

Rebel Girls, of I.W.W., 330

Reconstructionist, 192

Red Special, 326

Reed, Jack, 333-35

Reese, David M., 65

Reformed Drunkards, 68-69, 71, 79, 86

Reid, John, 125-29

Rensselaer County (N.Y.), 136

Rensselaers, 134, 137-39, 144

Republican National Convention of *1884,* 96

Revised Statutes of Vermont, 3

Revolution, American, 135-36, 143, 150, 235

Revolution, The, 195-96, 198, 207

Rhode Island, 57, 68, 79, 228, 231-32

Richards, Mark, 8, 12

Richardson, E. F., 321

Richland Center (Wis.), 188

Rifenburg, Bill, 140

Rights of Man, 171

Ripley, George, 39

Robe, Wirt, 90

Robinson, Samuel, 120

Rochester (N.Y.), 85, 182-83, 205-6, 218, 248

Rocky Mountain Revolution, 318

Rodgers, Captain, 284

Rogers, Harriet B., 264

WITHDRAWN

MAINSTREAM of AMERICA